BUCHANAN'S
Dictionary of
Quotations

by mike buchanan, for lps publishing:

in the name of god, go!
(2010)

the fraud of the rings
(paperback version of *the marriage delusion*)
(2010)

the marriage delusion: the fraud of the rings?
(2009)

two men in a car (a businessman, a chauffeur, and their holidays in france)
(2008)

guitar gods in beds. (bedfordshire: a heavenly county)
(2008)

by mike buchanan, for kogan page:

profitable buying strategies: how to cut procurement costs and buy your way to higher profits
(2008)

BUCHANAN'S
Dictionary of
Quotations
for right-minded people

edited by
mike buchanan

lps publishing

publisher's note
every possible effort has been made to ensure that the information contained in this book is accurate, and the publisher and author cannot accept responsibility for any errors or omissions, however caused. no responsibility for loss or damage occasioned to any person acting, or refraining from action, as a result of the material in this publication, can be accepted by the publisher or the author

first published in great britain in 2010 by lps publishing

apart from any fair dealing for the purposes of research or private study, or criticism or review, as permitted under the copyright, designs and patents act 1988, this publication may only be reproduced, stored or transmitted, in any form or by any means, with the prior permission in writing of the publisher, or in the case of reprographic reproduction in accordance with the terms and licences issued by the cla. enquiries concerning reproduction outside these terms should be sent to the publisher at the following address

lps publishing
1 goodrich avenue
bedford mk41 0de
united kingdom

www.lpspublishing.co.uk

copyright © mike buchanan 2010

the right of mike buchanan to be identified as the author of this work has been asserted by him in accordance with the copyright, designs and patents act 2008

isbn 9780955878480

british library cataloguing-in-publication data
a cip record for this book is available from the british library

printed in great britain by the mpg books group, bodmin and king's lynn, england

© getty images, cover image of gordon brown at kandahar airport, afghanistan, december 2009

to margaret thatcher, baroness thatcher of kesteven

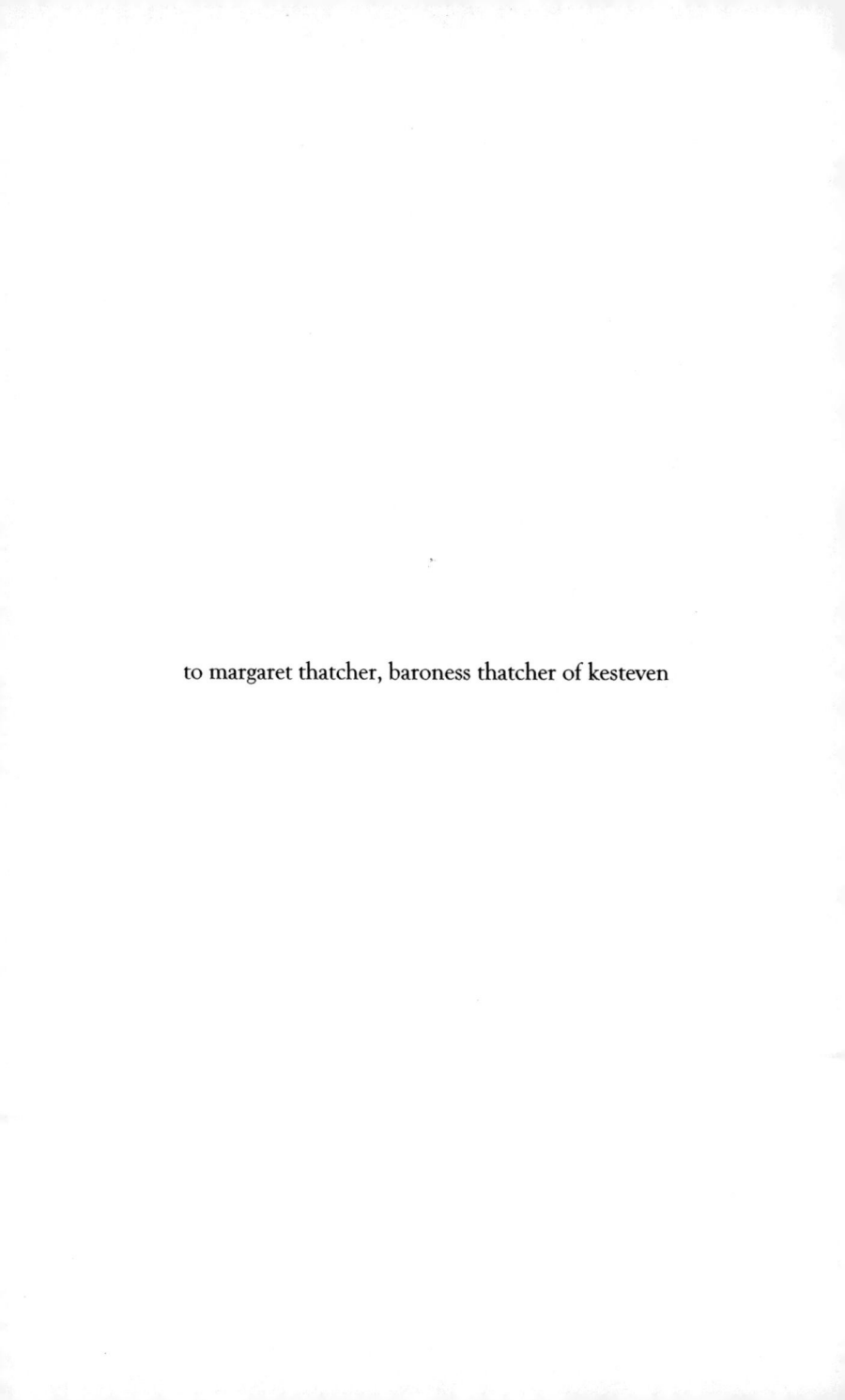

contents

	acknowledgements	ix
	introduction	xi
	how to use the dictionary	xv
	dictionary	1
apx. 1	political correctness	408
apx. 2	the different natures of men and women	414
apx. 3	the letter to the rt. hon. david miliband m.p.	428
apx. 4	if the battle of trafalgar had been fought in a politically correct age . . .	429
	books referenced in the appendices	431
	quotations: index of writers, speakers, shows	432

acknowledgements

My first thanks must go to the writers and other people whose material I have reproduced in this book. My acknowledgements to the creators of the internet websites I've drawn upon heavily, and to the editors of dictionaries of quotations I've drawn upon lightly, including the excellent Oxford series. Not forgetting *The Wit and Wisdom of Mark Twain* (1999) and Simon Hoggart's *Punchlines: A Crash Course in English with John Prescott* (2003).

My thanks to the talented cover designer Lewis Dellar, of John Chandler Book Design.

My thanks to the ever-patient Nigel Mitchell at MPG Biddles, the book's printer, both he and his company being a pleasure to work with as always.

My thanks to my hard-working cheerful and glamorous assistant Sharon Smith, for working long hours to meet a tight deadline.

My thanks to Wikipedia for many of the mini-biographies of the speakers or writers of the material in the book.

In my last book *The Marriage Delusion: the fraud of the rings?* – recently published in paperback format with the title *The Fraud of the Rings* – I thanked The Rt. Hon. Harriet Harman Q.C. M.P. for the material she had unwittingly provided for that book. I thank her again for motivating me once more to make my little contribution to driving out of our public life her dour brand of politically-correct feminist socialism.

My thanks to a former business associate and now a friend, Andrew Heslop. I hope 2010 is the year in which he stops working so hard in business and starts to pursue his writing ambitions.

My final thanks to you, dear reader, a right-minded person at a time when all that we hold dear about the United Kingdom has been attacked by left-wing politicians for too long. Let us hope the outcome of the coming general election will result in the end of their incompetent administration.

introduction

A warm welcome to *Buchanan's Dictionary of Quotations for right-minded people*. The inspiration for the book was an unlikely one. I was working on another book when it occurred to me that I might include a section of quotations for 'right-minded' people. Those with right-of-centre political persuasions, those frustrated with life in an ever more politically correct, risk averse, feminist and socialist country. People who are, like myself, appalled at the damage done to Great Britain and its people by Labour governments since 1997, damage which continues under the watchful eye of a Prime Minister unelected as leader even by his own party, Gordon Brown. And let's not forget the damage done by his dismal deputy, Harriet Harman.

My original idea was to find enough quotations with right-of-centre insights, including some of a humorous nature, to fill a few pages of the book. I started to look on the internet for such quotations, and something became obvious very quickly: there were *thousands* of them. And so the idea of this dictionary emerged.

What struck me time and again, working through quotation collections, was that the right-of-centre quotations were grounded in a realistic view of human nature, drawing on the lessons of history. While the left-of-centre quotations were based upon a wildly optimistic and naïve view of human nature, ignoring the lessons of history. This bore out my lifelong experience of people with the different political persuasions. We may challenge left-wing thinking on many grounds, but the experience of socialist administrations around the world over many decades tells us all we need to know. Socialism is going to be successful in the future, we are promised. Although it never has been in the past, nor is it ever so in the present.

I had a number of criteria for including quotations in this book. The majority of the quotations reflect right-of-centre political perspectives, are insightful or inspiring, or are likely to amuse people who hold them. Some have little overt political content. There are lengthy sections from Woody Allen, *The Devil's Dictionary*, Winston Churchill, Bertrand Russell, John Prescott, George Bernard Shaw, Oscar Wilde, P.G. Wodehouse, Mark Twain and others. Politically incorrect quotations were almost guaranteed inclusion.

Very occasionally our left-wing opponents manage to raise their game and say or write something amusing or insightful, and those quotations are included.

Dan Quayle had to be in the book. When on form, he could almost rival our own national treasure, John Prescott. A sample Quaylism:

> A mind is a terrible thing to waste . . . You take the UNCF model that what a waste it is to lose one's mind or not to have a mind is being very wasteful. How true that is.
> Addressing the United Negro College Fund

Three successive socialist administrations since 1997 have turned the United Kingdom into a predictably unpleasant and depressing place to live. It's hardly surprising that the British people have been drinking even more that their customary intake of alcohol in recent years. They badly need the solace it brings.

My daily newspaper, the unbiased printer of truth *The Daily Telegraph*, includes at least one story every day guaranteed to make its readers cry, 'This country is going to the dogs!' A fine example from the 27 January 2010 edition:

> A jobcentre refused to accept an advertisement for a 'reliable' worker because it discriminated against unreliable people. Nicole Mamo, who runs a recruitment company, posted a request for a domestic cleaner on her local Jobcentre Plus website. It asked little of applicants other than that they had a good command of English and 'must be very reliable and hard-working'. However, when she contacted Jobcentre Plus in Thetford, Norfolk, a member of staff told her the advert would not be displayed, in case unreliable workers sued for discrimination.

The British people have been denied - firstly by Tony Blair, then by Gordon Brown - the referendum on the new European Constitutional Treaty which the Labour Party promised in its 2005 general election manifesto. Such was Blair's and Brown's contempt for the electorate that they did not even bother to explain to the British people, by way of recognising their legitimate interest in the matter, why they believed the treaty was good for Britain. The denial of the referendum was one of the most appalling blows against democracy in Britain in our lifetimes. I have little doubt that if such a commitment were made and cynically broken by a political party in a country whose citizens bore arms - the United States, say - the citizens would march on the seat of government. But being British, and therefore armless enough, all we do is moan.

Why are so many people in Great Britain so unhappy in the modern era? People with right-wing political persuasions tend to be both hard-working and optimistic by nature, and it has taken 13 years of left-wing government to wear us down. But why are people with left-wing persuasions also unhappy in The U.S.F.R., The Union of Socialist Feminist Republics (1997 -), formerly the United Kingdom? Envy, an emotion guaranteed to induce misery, is deep in the soul of left-wing people. It is their most defining characteristic.

The first two appendices in this book contain extracts from my fourth book *The Marriage Delusion: the fraud of the rings?* Their relevance to this book is that they explore feminism (*gender* Marxism) and political correctness (*cultural* Marxism). Feminism and political correctness are socialist in origin - their adherents seek equality, but always upwards. They are responsible for much of the unhappiness we see around us in the country.

Very few people in the modern era would argue that women should not have equal opportunities of advancement as men. But it's become perfectly clear that the ultimate goal of leading feminists, such as Harriet Harman, never was equality of opportunity. That was simply a sellable and necessary stage on the journey to what they really wanted, the ultimate validation of their dire philosophy: *superiority of outcome* for women. If the happiness of the majority of men and women and the economic wellbeing of the country have to be sacrificed to deliver that goal, so be it. Again, being British, we do little but moan, and let these manipulative women pursue their damaging and undemocratic agendas at the expense of the majority of the electorate.

In common with others holding right-of-centre political persuasions, I hope Harriet Harman will be elected Labour Party leader after the 2010 general election. Unintelligent women will vote for her simply because she's a woman and is only interested in promoting 'women's interests', while intelligent women will see her for the opportunistic, manipulative, unrepresentative and undemocratic women she is. I can scarcely believe that any man, intelligent or otherwise, would vote for the Labour Party if she were its leader.

Before long we shall have the 2010 general election, and with it the opportunity to eject the current execrable administration. Let's not waste that opportunity.

Finally, I have included a few quotations from a friend, Paul Carrington, who is also my occasional chauffeur, and a lifetime socialist. He featured at length in my bestselling travelogue *Two Men in a Car (a businessman, a chauffeur, and their holidays on France)*. Readers of a nervous disposition should perhaps avoid the section of his quotations. But it has to be said that his use of colourful language can be almost poetic at times.

mike buchanan

bedford, february 2010

how to use the dictionary

Quotations are sequenced in alphabetical order of the writer's or speaker's surname, or a show's name, with a few exceptions, including royalty (so Queen Elizabeth II is in the 'E' section) and pseudonyms (so François-Marie Arouet is under 'V' for Voltaire).

Where an individual is mentioned elsewhere in the book, whether as the speaker or writer of a quotation or as, for example, the recipient of a communication, or the editor deemed the person worthy of indexing for any reason, the person's surname is shown in bold (John **Adams**) and is indexed. The index covers speakers, writers and shows. In line with common practice, where a term starts with the word 'The', the entry is indexed in line with the following word: so *The Office* is indexed under 'O' rather than 'T'.

a

Edward Abbey 1927-89
American author

What's the difference between a whore and a congressman? A congressman makes more money.

No tyranny is so irksome as petty tyranny: the officious demands of policemen, government clerks, and electromechanical gadgets.

One man alone can be pretty dumb sometimes, but for real bona fide stupidity, there ain't nothin' can beat teamwork.

Diane Abbott 1953-
British Labour Party politician

Some weeks ago, before Hazel Blears resigned, a number of us went to a minister very close to Gordon Brown and told him Hazel just had to be fired. The minister responded with, 'But who could we replace her with?' I laughed and told him, 'Just about anyone with a pulse, to be honest!'
*BBC Radio 4 interview, on the resignation of fellow Labour MP Hazel **Blears***

Being an MP is the sort of job all working-class parents want for their children – clean, indoors, and no heavy lifting.

Tony Abbott 1966-
Canadian Conservative Politician

What it is to me is a little rich girl who is basically whoring herself out to the Liberals.
*of Belinda **Stronach's** crossing the floor to join the Liberal Party*
   in *GlobeandMail.com* (online edition) 18 May 2005

Absolutely Fabulous British sitcom, 1992-2004

Edina Monsoon (Jennifer Saunders)

Why, oh why, do we have taxes, huh? Just so we can have bloody parking restrictions, and bloody ugly traffic wardens, and bollocky pedestrian bloody crossings! Why not just have a Stupidity Tax? Just tax stupid people!

Bella Abzug 1920-98
American politician

Richard **Nixon** impeached himself. He gave us Gerald **Ford** as his revenge.
   Rolling Stone Linda Botts 'Loose Talk' (1980)

Dean Acheson 1893-1971
American politician

I will undoubtedly have to seek what is happily know as gainful employment, which I am glad to say does not describe holding public office.
Time 22 December 1952

Great Britain has lost an empire and has not yet found a role.
speech at the Military Academy, West Point, 5 December 1962

Lord Acton 1834-1902
English historian

Liberty is not a means to a higher political end. It is itself the highest political end.

It is bad to be oppressed by a minority, but it is worse to be oppressed by a majority. For there is a reserve of latent power in the masses which, if it is called into play, the minority can seldom resist. But from the absolute will of an entire people there is no appeal, no redemption, no refuge but treason.

The man who prefers his country before any other duty shows the same spirit as the man who surrenders every right to the state. They both deny that right is superior to authority.

Power tends to corrupt, and absolute power corrupts absolutely.
letter to Bishop Mandell Creighton 1887
lecture, 26 February 1877

Abigail Adams 1744-1818
Wife of John Adams, the second President of the United States, and mother of John Quincy Adams, the sixth

I begin to think, that a calm is not desirable in any situation in life . . . Man was made for action and for bustle too, I believe.
letter to John Adams 1774

These are times in which a genius would wish to live. It is not in the still calm of life, or the repose of a pacific station, that great characters are formed . . . Great necessities call out great virtues.
letter to John Adams 19 January 1780

We have too many high sounding words, and too few actions that correspond with them.

Ansel Adams 1902- 84
American photographer and environmentalist

No man has the right to dictate what other men should perceive, create or produce, but all should be encouraged to reveal themselves, their perceptions and emotions, and to build confidence in the creative spirit.

Douglas Adams 1952-2001
English writer, dramatist and musician

Human beings, who are almost unique in having the ability to learn from the experience of others, are also remarkable for their apparent disinclination to do so.
Last Chance to See (1990)

Franklin P. Adams 1881-1960
American journalist and humorist

The following quotations are from *Nods and Becks* (1944):

When the political columnists say 'Every thinking man' they mean themselves and when candidates appeal to 'Every intelligent voter' they mean everybody who is going to vote for them.

The trouble with this country is that there are too many politicians who believe, with a conviction based on experience, that you can fool all of the people all of the time.

Elections are won by men and women chiefly because most people vote against somebody rather than for somebody.

Henry Adams 1850-1906
American farmer, public official and politician

The following quotations are from *The Education of Henry Adams* (1907):

Politics, as a practice, has always been the systematic organization of hatreds.

Practical politics consists in ignoring facts.

The progress of evolution from President Washington to President Grant was alone evidence to upset Darwin.

John Adams 1735-1826
second President of the United States, 1797-1801

Fear is the foundation of most governments.
Thoughts on Government (1776)

The jaws of power are always opened to devour, and her arm is always stretched out, if possible to destroy the freedom of thinking, speaking, and writing.
A Dissertation on the Canon and Feudal Law (1765)

Democracy never lasts long. It soon wastes, exhausts and murders itself. There was never a democracy that did not commit suicide.
letter to John Taylor 15 April 1814

I agree with you that in politics the middle way is none at all.
letter to Horatio Gates 23 March 1776

The law, in all vicissitudes of government . . . will preserve a steady undeviating course; it will not bend to the uncertain wishes, imaginations, and wanton tempers of men . . . On the one hand it is inexorable to the cries of the prisoners; on the other it is deaf, deaf as an adder to the clamours of the populace.
argument in defence of the British soldiers in the Boston Massacre Trials, 4 December 1770

I always consider the settlement of America with reverence and wonder, as the opening of a grand scene and design in providence, for the illumination of the ignorant and the emancipation of the slavish part of mankind all over the earth.

We have no government armed with power capable of contending with human passions unbridled by morality and religion. Avarice, ambition, revenge or gallantry would break the strongest cords of our Constitution as a whale goes through a net. Our Constitution is designed only for a moral and religious people. It is wholly inadequate for any other.

The proposition that the people are the best keepers of their own liberties is not true. They are the worst conceivable, they are no keepers at all; they can neither judge, act, think, or will, as a political body.

John Quincy Adams 1767-1848
American statesman, 6th President of the US; son of Abigail Adams and John Adams

Fiat justitia, pereat voelum [Let justice be done, though heaven perish.] My toast would be, may our country be always successful, but whether successful or otherwise, always right.
    letter to John Adams 1 August 1816

Wherever the standard of freedom and Independence has been or shall be unfurled, there will her heart, her benedictions and her prayers be. But she [America] goes not abroad in search of monsters to destroy.
    speech to House of Representatives, 4 July 1821

Courage and perseverance have a magical talisman, before which difficulties disappear and obstacles vanish into air.

Samuel Adams 1722-1803
Statesman, political philosopher, one of the Founding Fathers of the United States

We cannot make events. Our business is wisely to improve them . . . Mankind are governed more by their feelings than by reason. Events which excite those feelings will produce wonderful effects.
    J. N. Rakove *The Beginnings of National Politics* (1979)

Let us contemplate our forefathers, and posterity, and resolve to maintain the rights bequeathed to us by the former, for the sake of the latter.
    speech, 1771

The Constitution shall never be construed . . . to prevent the people of the United States who are peaceable citizens from keeping their own arms.

Scott Adams 1957-
American author

Nothing defines humans better than their willingness to do irrational things in the pursuit of phenomenally unlikely payoffs. This is the principle behind lotteries, dating, and religion.

Mortimer J. Adler 1902-2001
American philosopher, educator and author

The basic natural right that a just society or government should try to secure – and aid or abet – for every individual is not, and cannot be, the right to happiness, but it is rather the right to its pursuit.
    The Time of Our Lives (1970)

Herbert Agar 1897-1980
American poet and writer

The truth which makes men free is for the most part the truth which men prefer not to hear.
Time for Greatness (1942)

James Agate 1877-1947
British diarist and theatre critic

The English instinctively admire any man who has no talent and is modest about it.

Spiro T. Agnew 1918-96
American Republican politician

A spirit of national masochism prevails, encouraged by an effete corps of impudent snobs who characterize themselves as intellectuals.
speech in New Orleans, 19 October 1969

In the United States today, we have more than our share of the nattering nabobs of negativism.
speech in San Diego, 11 September 1970

Jonathan Aitken 1942-
British Conservative politician

I realise I am about as welcome in the Tory party as Banquo's ghost.
in *Sunday Times* 15 February 2004

I wouldn't say she's open-minded on the Middle East so much as empty-headed. She probably thinks Sinai is the plural of sinus.
on Margaret Thatcher

If it falls to me to start a fight to cut out the cancer of bent and twisted journalism in our country with the simple sword of truth and the trusty shield of fair play, so be it.
statement, London, 10 April 1995, after press reports that as Minister of State for Defence he had violated the ministerial code of conduct; a libel action started by him collapsed in 1997, and he was later convicted of perjury

Kehlog Albran

A priest asked, 'What is Fate, Master?'
And he answered, 'It is that which gives a beast of burden its reason for existence. It is that which men in former times had to bear upon their backs. It is that which has caused nations to build byways from city to city upon which carts and coaches pass, and alongside which inns have come to be built to stave off hunger, thirst and weariness.'
'And that is Fate?' said the priest.
'Fate? I thought you said Freight,' said the Master.
'That's all right,' said the priest. 'I wanted to know what Freight was too.'
The Profit

Alcuin c.735-804
English scholar and theologian

And those people should not be listened to who keep saying the voice of the people is the voice of God [*Vox populi, vox Dei*], since the riotousness of the crowd is always very close to madness.

Works (1863)

Richard Aldington 1892-1962
English poet, novelist and biographer

Patriotism is a lively sense of collective responsibility. Nationalism is a silly cock crowing on its own dunghill.
The Colonel's Daughter (1931)

Henry Aldrich 1647-1710
English academic

If all be true that I do think,
There are five reasons we should drink;
Good wine – a friend – or being dry –
Or lest we should be by and by
Or any other reason why.

Buzz Aldrin 1930-
American mechanical engineer, retired United States Air Force pilot and astronaut

I believe that every human has a finite number of heart-beats. I don't intend to waste any of mine running around doing exercises.

John Alejandro King

Whenever I read Jean-Paul Sartre's famous quote, 'Hell is other people,' it's like he's right there in the room with me.
My War On Terror!

If you're not scared or angry at the thought of a human brain being controlled remotely, then it could be this prototype of mine is finally starting to work.

Cecil Frances Alexander 1818-95
Irish poet and hymn-writer

The rich man in his castle,
The poor man at his gate,
God made them, highly or lowly,
And ordered their estate.
'All Things Bright and Beautiful' (1848)

Nelson Algren 1909-81
American novelist

Never play cards with a man called Doc. Never eat at a place called Mom's. Never sleep with a woman whose troubles are worse than your own.
in *Newsweek* 2 July 1956

Fred Allen 1894-1956
American comedian

English coffee tastes like water that has been squeezed out of a wet sleeve.
Treadmill to Oblivion (1956)

Tim Allen 1953-
American comedian and actor

Women now have choices. They can be married, not married, have a job, not have a job, be married with children, unmarried with children. Men have the same choice we always had: work or prison.

Woody Allen 1935-
American screenwriter, film director, actor, comedian, writer, musician and playwright

More than any other time in history, mankind faces a crossroads. One path leads to despair and utter hopelessness. The other, to total extinction. Let us pray we have the wisdom to choose correctly.
'My Speech to the Graduates'

Bisexuality immediately doubles your chances for a date on Saturday night.
The New York Times 1 December 1975

She wore a short skirt and a tight sweater and her figure described parabolas that could cause cardiac arrest in a yak.
Getting Even (1971) 'Mr Big'

Don't knock masturbation – it's sex with someone I love.

For the first year of marriage I had basically a bad attitude. I tended to place my wife underneath a pedestal.

His lack of education is more than compensated for by his keenly developed moral bankruptcy.

How can I believe in God when just last week I got my tongue caught in the roller of an electric typewriter?

How to make God laugh: tell him your future plans.

I am at two with nature.

I don't want to achieve immortality through my work . . . I want to achieve it through not dying.

I was thrown out of college for cheating in the metaphysics exam; I looked into the soul of the boy sitting next to me.

I want to tell you a terrific story about oral contraception. I asked this girl to sleep with me and she said 'no'.

I will not eat oysters. I want my food dead – not sick, not wounded – dead.

I recently turned sixty. Practically a third of my life is over.

I took a speed reading course and read *War and Peace* in twenty minutes. It involves Russia.

I hate reality but it's still the best place to get a good steak.

I can't listen to that much Wagner. I start getting the urge to conquer Poland.

I'm astounded by people who want to know the universe when it's hard enough to find your way around Chinatown.

If only God would give me some clear sign! Like making a large deposit in my name in a Swiss bank.

If it turns out that there is a God, I don't think that he's evil. But the worst that you can say about him is that basically he's an underachiever.

In real life, Diane **Keaton** believes in God. But she also believes that the radio works because there are tiny people inside it.

It seemed the world was divided into good and bad people. The good ones slept better . . . while the bad ones seemed to enjoy the waking hours much more.

Life is divided up into the horrible and the miserable. The horrible would be terminal cases, blind people, cripples. The miserable is everyone else. When you go through life you should be thankful that you're miserable.

Life is full of misery, loneliness, and suffering – and it's all over much too soon.

Money is better than poverty, if only for financial reasons.

My one regret in life is that I am not someone else.

My Lord, my Lord! What Hast Thou done, lately?

My wife was an immature woman . . . I would be home in the bathroom, taking a bath, and she would walk in whenever she felt like it and sink my boats.

Most of the time I don't have much fun. The rest of the time I don't have any fun at all.

My education was dismal. I went to a series of schools for mentally disturbed teachers.

Not only is there no God, but try getting a plumber on weekends.

On the plus side, death is one of the few things that can be done just as easily lying down.

The lion and the calf may lie down together, but the calf won't get much sleep.

There are worse things in life than death. Have you ever spent an evening with an insurance salesman?

There are three rings involved with marriage. The engagement ring, the wedding ring, and the suffering.

Those who can, do. Those who can't, teach. Those who can't teach, teach gym.

To you I'm an atheist; to God, I'm the Loyal Opposition.

Unbearably lovely music is heard as the curtain rises, and we see the woods on a summer afternoon. A fawn dances on and nibbles slowly at some leaves. He drifts lazily through the soft foliage. Soon he starts coughing and drops dead.

We were married by a reformed rabbi in Long Island. A very reformed rabbi. A Nazi.

What if everything is an illusion and nothing exists? In that case, I definitely overpaid for my carpet.

What if nothing exists and we're all in somebody's dream? Or what's worse, what if only that fat guy in the third row exists?

When I was kidnapped, my parents snapped into action. They rented out my room.

Whosoever loveth wisdom is righteous, but he that keepeth company with fowl is weird.

Whosoever shall not fall by the sword or by famine, shall fall by pestilence, so why bother shaving?

You can live to be a hundred if you give up all the things that make you want to live to be a hundred.

Ally McBeal American television series, 1997-2002

Ally McBeal (Calista Flockhart)

We're women. We have a double standard to live up to.

Luis Walter Alvarez 1911-88
American physicist

There is no democracy in physics. We can't say that some second-rate guy has as much right to opinion as **Fermi** .
   D. S. Greenberg *The Politics of Pure Science* (1969)

The American Declaration of Independence 4 July 1776

We hold these truths to be self-evident, that all men are created equal, that they are endowed by their Creator with certain unalienable rights, that among these are life, liberty and the pursuit of happiness.

Oscar Ameringer 1870-1943
American socialist organiser, humorist and editor

Politics – the gentle art of getting votes from the poor and campaign funds from the rich, by promising to protect each from the other.

Leo Amery 1873-1955
British Conservative politician, father of Julian Amery

For twenty years he has held a season-ticket on the line of least resistance and has gone wherever the train of events has carried him, lucidly justifying his position at whatever point he has happened to find himself.
of H. H. Asquith
   Quarterly Review (July 1914)

I will quote certain other words. I do it with great reluctance, because I am speaking of those who are old friends and colleagues of mine, but they are words which, I think, are applicable to the present situation. This is what Cromwell said to the Long Parliament when he thought it was no longer fit to conduct the affairs of the nation: 'You have sat too long here for any good you have been doing. Depart, I say, and let us have done with you. In the name of God, go.'
   in the House of Commons, 7 May 1940

Henri-Frédéric Amiel 1821-81
Swiss philosopher, poet and critic

Liberty, equality – bad principles! The only true principle for humanity is justice; and justice to the feeble is protection and kindness.

Hardy Amies 1909-2003
English couturier, who from the 1950s was royal dressmaker to The Queen

A man should look as if he bought his clothes with intelligence, put them on with care, and then forgot about them.
   Mail on Sunday 27 May 2001

Sir Kingsley Amis 1922-95
English novelist, poet and critic

His mouth had been used as a latrine by some small creature of the night, and then as its mausoleum.
   Lucky Jim (1954)

He was of the faith chiefly in the sense that the church he currently did not attend was Catholic.
   One Fat Englishman (1963)

A man's sexual aim, as he had often said to himself, is to convert a creature who is cool, dry, calm, articulate, independent, purposeful into a creature that is the opposite of these; to demonstrate to an animal which is pretending not to be an animal that it is an animal.
   One Fat Englishman (1963)

If you can't annoy somebody with what you write, I think there's little point in writing.
   Radio Times 1 May 1971

The delusion that there are thousands of young people about who are capable of benefitting from university training, but have somehow failed to find their way there, is . . . a necessary component of the expansionist case . . . More will mean worse.
   Encounter July 1960

It was no wonder that people were so horrible when they started life as children.

Martin Amis 1949-
English novelist, son of Kingsley Amis

His divorce had been so vicious even his lawyers had panicked.
Yellow Dog (2003)

Cleveland Amory 1907-98
American writer

'Do you mean to say,' he joshed, 'that the Union Club has come to a day when a man can bring his mistress to the club?' Along with the great club revolution, the doorman remembered the great club tradition. 'You may, Sir,' he replied stiffly, 'if the lady is the wife of one of the members.'
Who Killed Society (1960)

Morey Amsterdam 1908-96
American actor and comedian

Thirty days hath September, and my Uncle Fred for speeding.

Anarcharsis
Scythian Prince of the 6th century BC

Written laws are like spiders' webs: they will catch, it is true, the weak and poor, but would be torn in pieces by the rich and powerful.
Plutarch *Parallel Lives* 'Solon'

Clive Anderson 1952-
English radio and television presenter

Is there no beginning to your talents?
to Jeffrey Archer, English author, actor, playwright, convicted criminal and former politician

Pamela Anderson 1967-
Canadian/American actress, glamour model, producer, author, activist and former showgirl

I always liked the Kennedys as politicians. They had such great hair.

When you have nothing to live up to, you can't disappoint anybody . . . When you form a full sentence, you're a genius.
looking on the bright side of being universally considered a 'dumb blonde'
quoted in *Entertainment Briefs* (online edition) 2 October 2005

Count Julius Andrássy 1823-90
Hungarian statesman

A fight between a shark and a wolf. They may show any amount of natural animosity but after snapping at each other they could no nothing more than pass on.
quoted by Lord Salisbury in 'Hatfield Papers', Andrew Roberts *Salisbury: Victorian Titan* (1999)

Maya Angelou 1928-
American novelist and poet

The sadness of the women's movement is that they don't allow the necessity of love. See, I don't personally trust any revolution where love is not allowed.
in *California Living* 14 May 1975

Robin Angus
Personal Assets Trust plc

He (Gordon **Brown**) has proved himself to be unintelligent and obtuse, a natural big government man and a slave to complexity and obfuscation.

Kofi Annan 1938-
Ghanaian diplomat, Secretary-General of the United Nations

You can do a lot with diplomacy, but of course you can do a lot more with diplomacy backed up by fairness and force.
*of the agreement reached with Saddam **Hussein** over weapons inspections, February 1998,*
  Mail on Sunday 1 March 1998

Anne, British Princess Royal 1950-

When I appear in public, people expect me to neigh, grind my teeth, paw the ground and swish my tail – none of which is easy.
The Observer 22 May 1977

Anonymous

Ambition is putting a ladder against the sky.
  American proverb

Every man likes the smell of his own farts.
  Icelandic proverb

The advice of a wife is worthless, but woe to the man who does not take it.
  Welsh proverb

If you ever need a helping hand, you will find one at the end of your arm.
  Yiddish proverb

All the 'isms' are 'wasms.'
  said to have been the comment of a Foreign Office spokesman on the signing of the Molotov-Ribbentrop Pact in August 1939
  Peter Hennessey *Whitehall* (1990)

Beneath that extraordinary exterior there is a little pink quivering Ted trying to get out.
  comment of a former Cabinet colleague on Edward **Heath** in 1993
  Peter Hennessy *The Prime Minister: the Office and its Holders since 1945* (2000)

Harold wanted to be a combination of the Head of MI5 and News Editor of the *Daily Mirror*.
  Downing Street official shortly after **Wilson**'s resignation
  Peter Hennessey *The Prime Minister: the Office and its Holders since 1945* (2000)

The best defence against the atom bomb is not to be there when it goes off.
   contributor to *British Army Journal* in *Observe* 20 February 1949

Dalton **McGuinty**: He's an evil reptilian kitten-eater from another planet.
   Canadian Conservative press release attacking the Liberal leader (premier at the time of writing, February 2010)
   during September 2003 Ontario election campaign
   in *London Free Press News* 13 September 2003

For the sake of brevity we have followed the common practice of using the phrase 'Communists' throughout to include Fascists.
   Radcliffe Report *Security Procedures in the Public Service* (April 1962)

Hark the herald angels sing
Mrs Simpson's pinched our king.
   contemporary children's rhyme on the abdication of **Edward VIII**
   Clement **Attlee** letter 26 December 1938, Kenneth Harris *Attlee* (1982)

Have I said something foolish?
   Athenian statesman, on being cheered by the populace

Hear ye! Hear ye! All persons are commanded to keep silent, on pain of imprisonment, while the House of Representatives is exhibiting to the Senate of the United States articles of impeachment against William Jefferson **Clinton**, President of the United States
   formal announcement read by the serjeant-at-arms
   Guardian 8 January 1999

I like my Prime Ministers to be a bit inhumane. The PM has insufficient inhumanity . . . He wants to be liked.
   a senior civil servant, shortly after John **Major** had become Prime Minister
   Peter Hennessey *The Prime Minister: the Office and its Holders since 1945* (2000)

I never vote. It only encourages them.
   elderly American lady quoted by comedian Jack **Parr**

Liberty is always unfinished business.
   title of 36th Annual Report of the American Civil Liberties Union (1 July 1955 – 30 June 1956)

Lost is our old simplicity of times,
The world abounds with laws, and teems with crimes.
   On The Proceedings Against America (1775)

My name is George Nathaniel Curzon,
I am a most superior person,
My face is pink, my hair is sleek,
I dine at Blenheim once a week.
of Lord Curzon
   The Masque of Balliol (c.1870)

The nearest thing to death in life
Is David Patrick Maxwell Fyfe,
Though underneath that gloomy shell
He does himself extremely well.
*of David Maxwell Fyfe, later Lord **Kilmuir***

Now that the Cabinet's gone to its dinner,
The Secretary stays and gets thinner and thinner,
Racking his brains to record and report
What he thinks they think they ought to have thought.
   anonymous verse, undated, S. S. Wilson *The Cabinet Office* (1975)

Prudence is the other woman in Gordon's life.
of Gordon **Brown**
   unidentified aide, quoted in BBC News online 'Budget Briefing' 20 March 1998

Psychological flaws.
of which, according to an unnamed source, Gordon **Brown** *needed to 'get a grip'*
   Observer 18 January 1998; attributed to Alastair **Campbell**, but denied by him

Reorganising the Civil Service is like drawing a knife through a bowl of marbles.

There is one thing stronger than all the armies in the world; and that is an idea whose time has come.
   in flyer for *Nation* (15 April 1943)

Those on the opposite side are your opponents; your enemies are on your own side.
   traditional advice to a new MP

Under capitalism man exploits man. And under Communism it is just the reverse.
   joke told to J. K. **Galbraith** at a dinner given for him during his lecture tour of Poland by the Polish Economic Society, May 1958
   J. K. Galbraith *A Life in Our Times* (1981)

We trained hard ... but it seemed that every time we were beginning to form up into teams we would be reorganised. I was to learn later in life that we tend to meet any new situation by reorganising; and a wonderful method it can be for creating the illusion of progress while producing confusion, inefficiency, and demoralisation.

We value excellence as well as fairness, independence as dearly as mateship.
   draft preamble to the Australian constitution, made public, 23 March 1999

We wouldn't trust Labour to deliver a pizza – let alone a Parliament.
   view of the Scottish Nationalist Party
   unattributed; Brian Taylor *Scottish Parliament* (1999)

Why is there only one Monopolies Commission?
   British graffito; incorporated in the Official Monster Raving Loony Party Manifesto (1987)

To be is to be – **Rousseau**
To be is to do – **Sartre**.
Dobedobedo – **Sinatra**.

If you can't plug it in the mains or fuck it, the editor's not interested.
of Andrew **Neil***, Scottish journalist, when editor of* The Sunday Times

Accountancy is a profession whose idea of excitement is sharpening a bundle of No.2 pencils.
   Time 19 April 1993

When in danger, or in doubt,
Run in circles, scream and shout.
>*The Norton Book of Light Verse* (1986) ed. Russell Baker

A great man! Why, I doubt if there are six his equal in the whole of Boston.
of **Shakespeare**
>said to W. E. **Gladstone** by an unnamed Bostonian

The Church of England is the Tory Party at prayer.
>often attributed to Benjamin **Disraeli**

This is a rotten argument but it should be enough for their Lordships on a hot summer afternoon.
>a minister making a speech in the House of Lords inadvertently read out this annotation, which a civil servant had scrawled on his brief
>Lord Home *The Way the Wind Blows* (1976)

Many are cold, but few are frozen. F. Muir.
>inscription on the service sheet at Frank **Muir**'s funeral on a wintry day in January 1998

Conservatism is hardly more than an instinctive belief that today's society is built on several thousand years and that in those years men have found things they should fasten to.
>*Wall Street Journal* 29 April 1955 'Editorial'

Alimony is the screwing you get for the screwing you got.

Cleanliness is next to Godliness – but only in an Irish dictionary.

Everyone is entitled to be stupid, but some abuse the privilege.

I like a girlish girl, a womanly woman and a manly man, but I cannot abide a boily boy.

Politicians are like nappies (U.S.: diapers). They both need changing regularly, and for the same reason.

Yasser Arafat 1929-2004
Palestinian statesman, President 1996-2004

Palestine is the cement that holds the Arab world together, or it is the explosive that blows it apart.
>*Time* 11 November 1974

Geoff Arbuthnot

Arrogant and right is surely better than humble and wrong.

Jeffrey Archer 1940-
English author, actor, playwright, convicted criminal and politician

An entire family of divorcees and they're head of the Church of England. It's going to make the person out there wonder if it's all worth it.
on the **Royal Family** *in 1992*

If the angel Gabriel had stood with the name of Winston **Churchill**, Ken would still have won.
*on Ken **Livingstone** becoming mayor of London in 2000*

Go down the corridor, you'll find the nearest one on the left, just after the Picasso.
   instruction to dinner guests seeking a bathroom

I'm down to my last hundred million.
   explaining why he sold his **Andy Warhol** painting

And I did wonder – because it's now three years ago since I left prison – whether there would come a time when I would forget it, or it would be in the past as anything else might be – no, it's there every day of my life.

But I certainly made mistakes, for which I regret, I think most human beings in their lifetime make mistakes, mine ended up in two years prison – two very remarkable years from which I learnt a lot.

But the thing I felt most strongly about, and put at the end of one of the prison diaries, was education.

I feel I have had a very interesting life, but I am rather hoping there is still more to come. I still haven't captained the England cricket team, or sung at Carnegie Hall!

I spent my first three weeks there on a wing with 21 murderers. I met some very evil people there but also some men who'd had no upbringing, no chance in life.

I'm not involved in politics any more and they're quite right.

When I was three, I wanted to be four. When I was four, I wanted to be prime minister.

We all make mistakes but one has to move on.

Mary Archer 1944-
British scientist and wife of Jeffrey **Archer**

I am a little surprised, not at Mrs Currie's indiscretion, but at a temporary lapse in John **Major**'s taste.
*on the revelation by Edwina **Currie** of an affair with the former Prime Minister*

Robert Ardrey 1908-80
American dramatist and evolutionist

We are born of risen apes, not fallen angels, and the apes were armed killers beside.
   African Genesis (1961)

Hannah Arendt 1906-75
German Jewish political theorist

The most radical revolutionary will become a conservative on the day after the revolution.
   New Yorker 12 September 1970

Equality . . . is the result of human organisation. We are not born equal.

Aristophanes c.450- c.385BC
Greek comic dramatist

You have all the characteristics of a popular politician: a horrible voice, bad breeding and a vulgar manner.
   The Knights (424BC)

Under every stone lurks a politician.
   Thesmophoriazusae (411BC)

Aristotle 384-322 BC
Greek philosopher

Therefore the good of man must be the objective of the science of politics.
   Nicomachean Ethics

We make war that we may live in peace.
   Nicomachean Ethics

Man is by nature a political animal.
   Politics

That some should rule, and others be ruled, is a thing not only necessary but expedient, for from the hour of their birth some are marked for subjection, others for rule.
   Politics

Where some people are very wealthy and others have nothing, the result will be either extreme democracy or absolute oligarchy, or despotism will come from either of those excesses.
   Politics

The most perfect political community is one in which the middle class is in control, and outnumbers both of the other classes.
   Politics

They should rule who are able to rule best.

If liberty and equality, as is thought by some are chiefly to be found in democracy, they will be best attained when all persons alike share in the government to the utmost.

Excellence is an art won by training and habituation. We do not act rightly because we have virtue or excellence, but we rather have those because we have acted rightly. We are what we repeatedly do. Excellence, then, is not an act but a habit.

Both oligarch and tyrant mistrust the people, and therefore deprive them of their arms.

Dick Armey 1940-
American Republican politician

Three groups spend other people's money: children, thieves and politicians. All three need parental supervision.
   The Freedom Revolution (1995)

Louis Armstrong 1901-71
American singer and jazz musician

All music is folk music, I ain't never heard no horse sing a song.

Robert Armstrong 1927-
British civil servant; Head of the Civil Service, 1981-87

It contains a misleading impression, not a lie. It was being economical with the truth.
  referring to a letter during the 'Spycatcher' trial, Supreme Court, New South Wales, November 1986
  Daily Telegraph 19 November 1986

William Armstrong 1915-80
British civil servant, Head of the Civil Service, 1968-74

The business of the Civil Service is the orderly management of decline.

Matthew Arnold 1822-88
British poet and critic

That sweet city with her dreaming spires.
of Oxford – where Arnold was Professor of Poetry at the university 1857-67
  'Thyrsis' (1865)

Thomas Arnold 1795-1842
English historian and educator, father of Matthew Arnold

As for rioting, the old Roman way of dealing with that is always the right one; flog the rank and file, and fling the ringleaders from the Tarpeian rock.
  from an unpublished letter written before 1828

Raymond Aron 1905-83
French sociologist and political journalist

Political thought, in France, is retrospective or utopian.
  L'opium des intellectuels (1955)

Arthur 1981 film

Arthur Bach (Dudley Moore) and Hobson (John Gielgud)

ARTHUR: I'm going to take a bath.
HOBSON (Butler): I'll alert the media.

George Asaf 1880-1951
British songwriter

What's the use of worrying?
It never was worth while,
So, pack up your troubles in your old kit-bag,
And smile, smile, smile.
  Pack up your Troubles (1915 song)

John Ashcroft 1942-
American Republican politician, Attorney General of the US, 2001-04

We may never know why he turned his back on our country and our values, but we cannot ignore that he did. Youth is not absolution for treachery.
on John Walter Lindh, an American who fought for the Taliban
  Newsweek 28 January 2002

Paddy Ashdown 1941-
British Liberal Democrat politician

There can be no place in a 21st century parliament for people with 15th century titles upholding 19th century prejudices.
  Independent 24 November 1998

Herbert Henry Asquith 1852-1928
British Liberal statesman; Prime Minister, 1908-16

The office of the Prime Minister is what its holder chooses and is able to make of it.
  Fifty Years of Parliament (1926)

He is a Chimborazo or Everest among the sandhills of the Baldwin Cabinet.
of Winston **Churchill**
  Roy Jenkins *Asquith*

It is fitting that we should have buried the Unknown Prime Minister [**Bonar Law**] by the side of the Unknown Soldier.
  Robert Blake *The Unknown Prime Minister* (1955)

Happily there seems to be no reason why we should be anything more than spectators.
of the approaching war
  letter to Venetia Stanley, 24 July 1914

Lady (Margot) Asquith 1864-1945
British political hostess, wife of Herbert Asquith

Kitchener is a great poster.
  More Memories (1933)

There is nothing more popular in the House of Commons than to blame yourself. 'I have killed my mother. I will never do it again,' is certain to raise a cheer.
  Off the Record (1943)

No amount of education will make women first-rate politicians. Can you see a woman becoming a Prime Minister? I cannot imagine a greater calamity for these islands to be put under the guidance of a woman in 10 Downing Street.
  Off The Record (1943)

Lord **Birkenhead** is very clever but sometimes his brains go to his head.
  Listener 11 June 1953

He can't see a belt without hitting below it.
of Lloyd George
  Listener 11 June 1953

He has a brilliant mind until it is made up.
   on Sir Stafford Cripps, Labour Party politician

'Margo' – the 't' is silent – as in 'Harlow'
   the film actress Jean Harlow inquired whether the name Margot was pronounced 'Margo' or 'Margot'

Raymond Asquith 1952-
English diplomat

The only two general maxims in which I have much belief are '*Carpe Diem*' and 'never have your hair cut outside Bond St.'

Kemel Atatürk 1881-1938
Turkish general and statesman, commander of Turkish forces at Gallipoli, President of the Turkish Republic 1923-38

Gentlemen, it was necessary to abolish the fez, which stands on the head of our nation as an emblem of ignorance, negligence, fanaticism and hatred of progress and civilisation, to accept in its place the hat, the headgear worn by the whole civilised world.
   speech to the Turkish Assembly, October 1927

Brooks Atkinson 1894-1984
American theatre critic with *The New York Times*

The following quotations are from *Once Around the sun* (1951):

The perfect bureaucrat everywhere is the man who manages to make no decisions and escape all responsibility.

In every age 'the good old days' were a myth. No one ever thought they were good at the time. For every age had consisted of crises that seemed intolerable to the people who had lived through them.

'There is a good deal of solemn cant about the common interests of capital and labour. As matters stand, their only common interest is that of cutting each other's throat.'

At Last The 1948 Show satirical British television show 1967

JOSIAH: When we were kids we had to live in a small shoe box in the middle of the road.
JOSHUA: A cardboard box?
JOSIAH: Yes
JOSHUA: You were lucky. We lived for three months in a rolled-up newspaper in a septic tank. We used to get up at six, clean the newspaper, eat a crust of stale bread, work fourteen hours at the mill, day-in, day-out, for sixpence a week, come home, and dad would thrash us to sleep with his belt.
OBADIAH: Luxury!
   Lines from 'The Good Old Days Skit'

Eli Attie
Writer and political operative

We can aspire to anything, but we don't get it just 'cause we want it. I would rather spend my life close to the birds than waste it wishing I had wings.
   House M. D., *Dying Changes Everything* (2008)

Clement Attlee 1883-1967
British politician, leader of the Labour Party, 1935-55, Prime Minister, 1945-51

Why does Mosley always speak to us as though he were a feudal landlord abusing tenants who are in arrears with their rent?
   at a meeting of the Parliamentary Labour Party, 20 November 1930, a few months before Oswald **Mosley** was expelled from the Party

A period of silence on your part would be welcome.
   in reply to a letter from the Chairman of the Labour Party, Harold **Laski**, asking that Attlee should not form a new government

A monologue is not a decision.
   to Winston **Churchill**
   Francis Williams A *Prime Minister Remembers* (1961)

A lot of clever people have got everything except judgment.
   Francis Williams A *Prime Minister Remembers* (1961)

I should be a sad subject for any publicity expert. I have none of the qualities which create publicity.
   Harold Nicolson diary, 14 January 1949

The Cabinet does not propose, it decides.
   response to a memorandum from the Ministry of Works saying, 'We have read the Cabinet's proposals.'
   Tony Benn diary, 20 May 1974

Few thought he was even a starter
There were many who thought themselves smarter
But he ended PM
CH and OM
An earl and a knight of the garter.
   describing himself in a letter to Tom **Attlee**, 8 April 1956
   Kenneth Harris *Attlee* (1982)

Russian Communism is the illegitimate child of Karl **Marx** and **Catherine the Great**.
   speech at Aarhus University, 11 April 1956

Often the 'experts' make the worst possible Ministers in their own fields. In this country we prefer rule by amateurs.
   speech at Oxford, 14 June 1957

Democracy means government by discussion, but it is only effective if you can stop people talking.

I believe that conscience is a still small voice and not a loudspeaker.
   attributed (1955)

It's a good maxim that if you have a good dog you don't bark yourself. I had a very good dog in Mr Ernest **Bevin**.
   attributed (1960)

Judgment is needed to make important decisions on imperfect knowledge in a limited time.
definition of the art of politics
   attributed

W. H. Auden 1907-73
English poet

To save your world you asked this man to die:
Would this man, could he see you now, ask why?
   'Epitaph for the Unknown Soldier' (1955)

He knew human folly like the back of his hand,
And was greatly interested in armies and fleets;
When he laughed, respectable senators burst with laughter,
And when he cried the little children died in the streets.
   'Epitaph on a Tyrant' (1940)

Our researchers into Public Opinion are content
That he held the proper opinions for the time of year;
When there was peace, he was for peace; when there was war, he went.
   'The Unknown Citizen' (1940)

Private faces in public places
Are wiser and nicer
Than public faces in private places.
   'Orators' (1932) dedication

At Dirty Dick's and Sloppy Joe's
We drank our liquor straight,
Some went upstairs with Margery,
And some, alas, with Kate.
   'For The Time Being' (1944)

Norman Augustine 1935-
American aerospace businessman

If stock market experts were so expert, they would be buying stock, not selling advice.

Aung San Suu Kyi 1945-
Burmese political leader

It's very different from living in academia in Oxford. We called someone vicious in the *Times Literary Supplement*. We didn't know what vicious was.
on returning to Burma (Myanmar)
   Observer 25 September 1988

Marcus Aurelius 121-180
Roman emperor 161-180, Stoic philosopher

Virtue they will but abuse, and taunt her with bitter reviling.
   Meditations (180)

Never let the future disturb you. You will meet it, if you have to, with the same weapons of reason which today arm you against the present.
   Meditations (180)

Jane Austen 1775-1817
English novelist

It is a truth universally acknowledged, that a single man in possession of a good fortune, must be in want of a wife. However little known the feelings or views of such a man on his first entering a neighbourhood, this truth is so well fixed in the minds of the surrounding families, that he is considered as the rightful property of some one or other of their daughters.
Pride and Prejudice (1813), opening lines

You have delighted us long enough.
said by Mr Bennet to his daughter Mary, who had been singing
Pride and Prejudice (1813)

There is not one in a hundred of either sex who is not taken in when they marry. Look where I will, I see that it is so; and I feel that it *must* be so, when I consider that it is, of all transactions, the one in which people expect most from others, and are least honest themselves.
Mansfield Park (1814)

It is indolence . . . indolence and love of ease; a want of all laudable ambition, of taste for good company, or of inclination to take the trouble of being agreeable, which make men clergymen. A clergyman has nothing to do but be slovenly and selfish; read the newspaper, watch the weather, and quarrel with his wife. His curate does all the work and the business of his own life is to dine.
Mansfield Park (1814)

They came from Birmingham, which is not a place to promise much, you know . . . One has not great hopes from Birmingham. I always say there is something direful in the sound.
Emma (1815)

From politics, it was an easy step to silence.
Northanger Abbey (1818)

A woman especially, if she have the misfortune of knowing any thing, should conceal it as well as she can.
Northanger Abbey (1818)

Where so many hours have been spent in convincing myself that I am right, is there not some reason to fear I may be wrong?

Alan Ayckbourn 1939-
English dramatist

I mean, damn it all, one minute you're having a perfectly good time and the next, you suddenly see them there like – some old sports jacket or something – literally beginning to come apart at the seams
of women
Ronald in *Absurd Person Singular* (1971) Act 3

My mother used to say, 'Delia, if S-E-X ever rears its ugly head, close your eyes before you see the rest of it.
Bedroom Farce (1977)

Whatever you do, keep clear of thin women. They're trouble.
A Small Family Business (1987)

Sir Alfred J. Ayer 1910-89
English philosopher

It seems that I have spent my entire time trying to make life more rational and that it was all wasted effort.
Observer 17 August 1986

My god, my god, I shall die a happy man if I can make one person disbelieve in God.
Observer 1 July 1989

Ayesha
Moorish princess, mother of the last Sultan of Granada

You do well to weep as a woman over what you could not defend as a man.
reproach to her son Boabdil (Muhammad XI), who had surrendered Granada to Ferdinand and Isabella

b

Isaac Babel 1894-1940
Russian short story writer. He died in a concentration camp in Siberia as a result of one of Stalin's purges

No iron can stab the heart with such force as a full stop put just as the right place.
  Guy de Maupassant (1932)

They didn't let me finish.
  to his wife, on the day of his arrest by the NKVD, 16 May 1939

Johann Sebastian Bach 1685-1750
German composer and organist

There is nothing remarkable about it, all one has to do is hit the right keys at the right time and the instrument plays itself.

Sir Francis Bacon 1561-1626
English philosopher, statesman, scientist, lawyer, jurist and author.

For also knowledge itself is power.
  Meditationes Sacrae (1597)

It is well to observe the force and virtue and consequence of discoveries, and these are to be seen nowhere more conspicuously than in those three which were unknown to the ancients, and of which the origins, though recent, are obscure and inglorious; namely, printing, gunpowder, and the magnet [Mariner's Needle]. For these three have changed the whole face and state of things throughout the world.
  Novum Organum (1620)

If a man will begin with certainties, he shall end in doubts; but if he will be content to begin with doubts he shall end in certainties.

There be three things which make a nation great and prosperous: a fertile soil, busy workshops, easy conveyance for men and goods from place to place.
  attributed S Platt ed. *Respectfully Quoted* (1989)

The following quotations are from *Essays* (1625):

In civil business, what first? boldness: what second and third? boldness: and yet boldness is a child of ignorance and baseness.

There be [some] that can pack the cards and yet cannot play well; so there are some that are good in canvasses and factions, that are otherwise weak men.

Nothing doth hurt more in a state than that cunning men pass for wise.

Fame is like a river that beareth up things light and swollen, and drowns things weighty and solid.

So when any of the four pillars of government are mainly shakened or weakened (which are religion, justice, counsel, and treasure) men had need to pray for fair weather.

Neither will it be, that a people overlaid with taxes should ever become valiant and martial.

'What is truth?' said jesting Pilate; and would not stay for an answer.

In the youth of a state arms do flourish; in the middle age of a state, learning; and then both of them together for a time; in the declining age of a state, mechanical arts and merchandise.

Arthur ('Bugs') Baer 1897-1969
American columnist and writer

Alimony is like buying oats for a dead horse.

Joan Baez 1941-
American folk singer, songwriter and activist

His songs were brilliant; people have never been able to copy them. He always had a rainbow pen.
on Bob Dylan
  Independent 19 January 2004

Action is the antidote to despair.

Walter Bagehot 1826-77
English economist and essayist

In happy states, the Conservative Party must rule upon the whole a much longer time than their adversaries. In well-framed politics, innovation – great innovation that is – can only be occasional. If you are always altering your house, it is a sign either that you have a bad house, or that you have an excessively restless disposition – there is something wrong somewhere.
  'The Chances for a Long Conservative Regime in England' (1874)

Capital must be propelled by self-interest; it cannot be enticed by benevolence.
  Economic Studies (1880)

No real English gentleman, in his secret soul, was ever sorry for the death of a political economist.
  Estimates of some Englishmen and Scotchmen (1858)

Dullness in matters of government is a good sign, and not a bad one – in particular, dullness in Parliamentary government is a test of its excellence, an indication of its success.
  Saturday Review (16 February 1856)

Public opinion is a permeating influence, and it exacts obedience to itself; it requires us to think other men's thoughts, to speak other men's words, to follow other men's habits.
  National Review (July 1856)

Years of acquiescing in proposals as to which he has not been consulted, of voting for measures which he did not frame, and in the wisdom of which he often did not believe, or arguing for proposals from half of which he dissents – usually de-intellectualise a parliamentary statesman before he comes to half his power.
  National Review (1861) 'William Pitt'

He believes, with all his heart and soul and strength, that there is such a thing as truth; he has the soul of a martyr with the intellect of an advocate.
of **Gladstone**
National Review (July 1860)

In every country the extreme party is most irritated against the party which comes nearest to itself, but does not go so far.
The Economist 22 April 1876

Good government depends at least as much on an impartial respect for the rights of all as it does on energy in enforcing respect for the authority which protects those rights.
The Economist 27 May 1876

If . . . the country should ever look on the proceedings of Parliament as an intellectual and theatrical exhibition, no merit in our laws, no excellence in our national character, could save our institutions from very serious danger.
The Economist (1861)

There is no method by which men can be both free and equal.
The Economist 5 September 1863

Persecute a sect and it holds together, legalise it and it splits and resplits, till its unity is either null or a non-oppressive bond.'
The Economist 27 April 1867

The highest and most important capacity in the Leader of the Opposition is to be able on special occasions to resist the mistaken wishes of the party which he leads.
The Economist (1874)

A great Premier must add the vivacity of an idle man to the assiduity of a very laborious one.
The Economist 2 January 1875

The being without an opinion is so painful to human nature that most people will leap to a hasty opinion rather than undergo it.
The Economist 4 December 1875

The characteristic danger of great nations, like the Romans or the English, which have a long history of continuous creation, is that they may at last fail from not comprehending the great institutions which they have created.
Fortnightly Review 1 November 1876

The following quotations are from *The English Constitution* (1867):

It is fair to say that men are ruled by their imaginations; but it would be truer to say they are governed by the weakness of their imaginations.

The natural impulse of the English people is to resist authority.

It has been said, not truly, but with a possible approximation to truth, that in 1802 every hereditary monarch was insane.

In such constitutions [as England's] there are two parts . . . first, those which excite and preserve the reverence of the population – the *dignified* parts . . . and next, the *efficient* parts – those by which it, in fact, works and rules.

The eager qualities, the imperious will, the rapid energy, the eager nature fit for a great crisis are not required – are impediments – in common times.

The mystic reverence, the religious allegiance, which are essential to a true monarchy, are imaginative sentiments that no legislature can manufacture in any people.

No orator ever made an impression by appealing to men as to their plainest physical wants, except when he could allege that those wants were caused by some one's tyranny.

By the structure of the world we often want, at the sudden occurrence of a grave tempest, to change the helmsman – to replace the pilot of the calm by the pilot of the storm.

It has been said that England invented the phrase, 'Her Majesty's Opposition'; that it was the first government which made a criticism of administration as much a part of the polity as administration itself. This critical opposition is the consequence of cabinet government.

An Opposition, on coming into power, is often like a speculative merchant whose bills become due. Ministers have to make good their promises, and they find a difficulty in so doing.

The House of Commons lives in a state of perpetual potential choice: at any moment it can choose a rule and dismiss a rule. And therefore party is inherent in it, is bone of its bone, and breath of its breath.

A severe though not unfriendly critic of our institutions said that 'the cure for admiring the House of Lords was to go and look at it.'

If you want to raise a certain cheer in the House of Commons, make a general panegyric on economy; if you want to invite a sure defeat, propose a particular saving.

The order of nobility is of great use, too, not only in what it creates, but in what it prevents. It prevents the rule of wealth – the religion of gold. This is the obvious and natural idol of the Anglo-Saxon.

It is nice to trace how the actions of a retired widow and an unemployed youth become of such importance.
of Queen **Victoria** and the future **Edward VII**

Women – one half of the human race at least – care fifty times more for a marriage than a ministry.

Royalty is a government in which the attention of the nation is concentrated on one person doing interesting actions. A Republic is a government in which that attention is divided between many, who are all doing uninteresting actions. Accordingly, so long as the human heart is strong and the human reason weak, Royalty will be strong because it appeals to diffused feeling, and Republics weak because they appeal to the understanding.

The best reason why Monarchy is a strong government is, that it is an intelligible government. The mass of mankind understand it, and they hardly anywhere in the world understand any other.

The Sovereign has, under a constitutional monarch such as ours, three rights – the right to be consulted, the right to encourage, the right to warn.

The Queen . . . must sign her own death-warrant if the two Houses unanimously send it up to her.

Above all things our royalty is to be reverenced, and if you begin to poke about it you cannot reverence it . . . Its mystery is its life. We must not let daylight in upon magic.

The only fit material for a constitutional king is a prince who begins early to reign – who in his youth is superior to pleasure – who in his youth is willing to labour – who has by nature a genius for discretion. Such kings are among God's greatest gifts, but they are also among His rarest.

It is an inevitable defect, that bureaucrats will care more for routine than for results.

But would it not have been a miracle if the English people, directing their own policy, and being what they are, had directed a good policy? Are they not above all nations divided from the rest of the world, insular both in situation and in mind, both for good and for evil? Are they not out of the current of common European causes and affairs? Are they not a race contemptuous of others? Are they not a race with no special education or culture as to the modern world, and too often despising such culture? Who could expect such a people to comprehend the new and strange events of foreign places?

A bureaucracy is sure to think that its duty is to augment official power, official business, or official members, rather than to leave free the energies of mankind; it overdoes the quantity of government, as well as impairs its quality.

David Bailey 1938-
English photographer

I never cared for fashion much. Amusing little seams and witty little pleats. It was the girls I liked.
Independent 5 November 1990

Pearl Bailey 1918-90
American actress and singer

A man without ambition is dead. A man with ambition but no love is dead. A man with ambition and love for his blessings here on earth is ever so alive. Having been alive it won't be so hard in the end to lie down and rest.

Thomas Bailey Aldrich 1836-1907
American poet, novelist, traveller and editor

The possession of unlimited power will make a despot of almost any man. There is a possible **Nero** in the gentlest human being that walks.
Leaves from a Notebook (1903)

Kay Bailey Hutchison 1943-
American Republican politician

I would never waste time being offended by anything so trivial.
asked about being introduced as 'the pretty senator from Texas'

Ewen Bain 1925-89
Scottish cartoonist

No son – they're not the same – devolution takes longer.
father to his son, who is reading a book on evolution
cartoon caption
  in *Scots Independent* January 1978

Jacques Bainville 1879-1936
French historian

Written by Bible readers *for* Bible readers.
of the Treaty of Versailles
  Les Consequences Politiques de la Paix (1920)

James Baker 1930-
American politician

He's the only man I know who could look at the swimsuit issue of *Sports Illustrated* and complain because the bathing suits weren't flame retardant.
on Michael Dukakis

Kenneth Baker 1934-
Conservative Party politician

He has conferred on the practice of vacillation the aura of statesmanship.
on SDP Leader Dr David Owen

Why should Scottish and Welsh nationalism be seen as a noble thing, when in England it is seen as something dirty?
  Sunday Times 6 January 2000 'Talking Heads'

Michael Bakunin 1814-76
Russian revolutionary and anarchist

The urge for destruction is also a creative urge!
  Jahrbuch für Wissenschaft und Kunst (1842)

We wish, in a word, equality – equality in fact as corollary, or rather, as primordial condition of liberty. From each according to his faculties, to each according to his needs; that is what we wish sincerely and energetically.
  declaration signed by forty-seven anarchists on trial after the failure of their uprising at Lyons in 1870
  J Morrison Davidson *The Old Order and the New* (1890)

James Baldwin 1924-87
American novelist and essayist

Freedom is not something that anybody can be given; freedom is something people take and people are as free as they want to be.
  Nobody Knows My Name (1961) 'Notes for a Hypothetical Novel'

Money, it turned out, was exactly like sex, you thought of nothing else if you didn't have it and thought of other things if you did.

in *Esquire* May 1961 'Black Boy looks at the White Boy'

Stanley Baldwin 1867-1947
British Conservative statesman; Prime Minister, 1923-24, 1924-29

If there is going to be a war – and no one can say that there is not – we must keep him fresh to be our war Prime Minister.
*of his reasons for excluding **Churchill** from the Cabinet*
letter, 17 November 1935

Supposing I had gone to the country and said that Germany was rearming and that we must rearm, does anybody think that this pacific democracy would have rallied to that cry at the moment? I cannot think of anything that would have made the loss of the election from my point of view more certain.
speech in the House of Commons, 12 November 1936

I think it is well also for the man in the street to realise that there is no power on earth that can protect him from being bombed. Whatever people may tell him, the bomber will always get through. The only defence is in offence, which means that you have to kill more women and children more quickly than the enemy if you want to save yourselves.
speech in the House of Commons, 10 November 1932

Do not run up your nose dead against the Pope or the National Union of Mineworkers!
Lord Butler *The Art of Memory* (1982)

You will find in politics that you are much exposed to the attribution of false motive. Never complain and never explain.
Harold Nicolson 'Diary' (21 July 1943)

A statesman wants courage and vision, but after six months he wants first, second, third and all the time – patience.

I would rather be an opportunist and float than go to the bottom with my principles round my neck.

A. J. Balfour (1st Earl of Balfour) 1848-1930
British Conservative Prime Minister

Christianity, yes, but why journalism?
to Frank **Harris**, who had claimed that Christianity and journalism were the two main curses of civilisation

It is unfortunate, considering that enthusiasm moves the world, that so few enthusiasts can be trusted to speak the truth.
letter to Mrs **Drew**, 19 May 1891

His Majesty's Government view with favour the establishment in Palestine of a national home for the Jewish people, and will use their best endeavours to facilitate the achievement of this object, it being clearly understood that nothing shall be done which may prejudice the civil and religious rights of existing non-Jewish communities in Palestine, or the rights and political status enjoyed by Jews in any other country.
letter to Lord **Rothschild**, 2 November 1917

I thought he was a young man of promise, but it appears he was a young man of promises.
*on Winston **Churchill***

Winston Churchill *My Early Life* (1930)

I never forgive but I always forget.
  R. Blake *Conservative Party* (1970)

Zionism, be it right or wrong, good or bad, is rooted in age-long traditions, in present need, in future hopes, of far profounder import that the desires and prejudices of the seven hundred thousand Arabs who now inhabit that ancient land.
in August 1919
  Max Egremont *Balfour* (1980)

I am more or less happy when being praised, not very uncomfortable when being abused, but I have moments of uneasiness when being explained.
  K. Young *A. J. Balfour* (1963)

I would rather consult my valet than the Conservative conference.

I must follow them. I am their leader.

E. Digby Baltzell 1915-96
American sociologist, academic and author

There is a crisis in American leadership in the middle of the twentieth century that is partly due, I think, to the declining authority of an establishment which is now based on an increasingly castelike White-Anglo-Saxon-Protestant (WASP) upper class.
  The Protestant Establishment (1964)

Honoré de Balzac 1799-1850
French novelist and playwright

No man has ever yet discovered the way to give friendly advice to any woman, not even to his own wife.
  Petite misères de la vie conjugales (1846)

Despotism accomplishes great things illegally; liberty doesn't even go to the trouble of accomplishing small things legally.
  La Peau de Chagrin (1831)

Equality may perhaps be a right, but no power on earth can ever turn it into a fact.
  [Editor's note: true, but try telling that to Harriet Harman.]

This coffee plunges into the stomach . . . the mind is aroused, and ideas pour forth like the battalions of the Grand Army on the field of battle . . . Memories charge at full gallop . . . the light cavalry of comparisons deploys itself magnificently; the artillery of logic hurry in with their train of ammunition; flashes of wit pop up like sharp-shooters.
  [Editor's note: I'll have a cup of what *he's* having.]

Lord Bancroft 1922-96
British civil servant; Head of the Civil Service, 1978-81

Conviction politicians, certainly: conviction civil servants, no.
  'Whitehall: Some Personal Reflections', lecture at the London School of Economics, 1 December 1983

The Band Wagon American musical comedy film (1953)

We're not quarrelling! We're in complete agreement! We hate each other!

Tallulah Bankhead 1903-68
American actress

There is less in this than meets the eye.
Shouts and Murders (1922)

Don't bother to thank me. I know what a perfectly ghastly season it's been for you Spanish dancers.
encountering a group from the Salvation Army and dropping a $50 bill into one of their tambourines.

Cocaine habit-forming? Of course not. I ought to know. I've been using it for years.

W. N. P. Barbellion 1889-1919
English Essayist and diarist

On the bus the other day a woman with a baby sat opposite, the baby bawled, and the woman at once began to unlace herself, exposing a large red udder, which she swung into the baby's face. The infant, however, continued to cry and the woman said, 'Come on, there's a good boy – if you don't, I shall give it to the gentleman opposite.'
The Journal of a Disappointed Man (1919)

Pat Barker 1943-
English novelist

The Somme is like the Holocaust. It revealed things about mankind that we cannot come to terms with and cannot forget. It can never become the past.
on winning the Booker Prize 1995
in *Athens News* 9 November 1995

Alben W. Barkley 1877-1956
American Democrat politician

For six years profound silence was mistaken for profound wisdom.
on the Coolidge administration
speech, Democratic National Convention, 1932

The best audience is one that is intelligent, well-educated – and a little drunk.

Clive Barnes 1927-2008
British-born American writer and critic

Television is the first truly democratic culture   the first culture available to everybody and entirely governed by what the people want. The most terrifying thing is what the people *do* want.

Lord Barnett 1923-
Labour Party member of the House of Lords

A man explained inflation to his wife thus: 'When we married, you measured 36-24-36. Now you're 42-42-42. There's more of you, but you are not worth as much.'

Michael Barnier 1951-
French politician

Alliance is not allegiance.
on Europe's relations with America
   Independent 29 October 2004

P. T. Barnum 1810-91
American showman

Every crowd has a silver lining.

Roseanne Barr 1952-
American actress, comedian, writer, television producer and director

My hope is that gays will be running the world, because then there would be no war – just a greater emphasis on military apparel.

I do what it says on the aspirin bottle: take two and keep away from children.

Sir James M. Barrie 1860-1937
Scottish playwright

It is all very well to be able to write books, but can you waggle your ears?
   to H. G. Wells

There are few more impressive sights in the world than a Scotsman on the make.
   What Every Woman Knows (performed 1908, published 1918)

It's a sort of bloom on a woman. If you have it, you don't need to have anything else; and if you don't have it, it doesn't much matter what else you have.
   What Every Woman Knows (performed 1908, published 1918)

Ambition – it is the last infirmity of noble minds.

Dave Barry 1947-
American author and columnist

I can win an argument on any topic, against any opponent. People know this, and steer clear of me at parties. Often, as a sign of their great respect, they don't even invite me.

We Americans live in a world where the medical care system is second to none in the world, unless you count maybe 25 or 30 little scuzzball countries like Scotland that we could vaporize in seconds if we felt like it.

When trouble arises and things look bad, there is always one individual who perceives a solution and is willing to take command. Very often, that individual is crazy.

Gerald Barry 1898-1968
English editor and publicist

Democracy: in which you say what you like and do what you're told.

John Barrymore 1882-1942
American actor

Love . . . the delightful interval between meeting a beautiful girl and discovering that she looks like a haddock.

Busy yourselves with this, you damned walruses, while the rest of us proceed with the libretto.
   throwing a sea bass to a noisily coughing audience

C. A. Bartol

Good manners and good morals are sworn friends and fast allies.

Bruce Barton 1886-67
American author, advertising executive and politician

Nothing splendid has ever been achieved except by those who dared believe that something inside them was superior to circumstance.

Bernard Baruch 1870-1965
American financier and presidential adviser

Let us not be deceived – we are today in the midst of a cold war.
   speech to South Carolina Legislature,16 April 1947

You can talk about capitalism and communism and all that sort of thing, but the important thing is the struggle everybody is engaged in to get better living conditions, and they are not interested too much in government.
   The Times 20 August 1964

A political leader must keep looking over his shoulder all the time to see if the boys are still there. If they aren't still there, he's no longer a political leader.
   New York Times 21 June 1965

Age is only a number, a cipher for the records. A man can't retire his experience. He must use it. Experience achieves more with less energy and time.

Claude-Frédéric Bastiat 1801-50
French economist

All men's impulses, when motivated by legitimate self-interest, fall into a harmonious social pattern.
   Economic Harmonies (1964)

Once an abuse exists, everything is arranged on the assumption that it will last indefinitely; and, as more and more people come to depend upon it for their livelihood, and still others depend upon them, a superstructure is erected that soon comprises a formidable edifice.
   Journal des Economistes (1848)

Government is the great fiction, through which everybody endeavours to live at the expense of everybody else.
   Essays on Political Economy

Charles Baudelaire 1821-67
French poet, critic and translator

Poetry and progress are like two ambitious men who hate one another with an instinctive hatred, and when they meet upon the same road, one of them has to give place.

Lord Bauer 1915-2002
Hungarian-born British economist

Foreign aid is a system of taking money from poor people in rich countries and giving it to rich people in poor countries.
   attributed

Yehuda Bauer 1926-
Czech-born Israeli historian

I come from a people who gave the Ten Commandments to the world. Time has come to strengthen them by three additional ones, which we ought to adopt and commit ourselves to: thou shalt not be a perpetrator; thou shalt not be a victim; and thou shalt never, but never, be a bystander.
   speech to the German Bundestag, 1998, quoted in his own speech to the Stockholm International Forum on the Holocaust, 26 July 2000

Vicki Baum 1888-1960
Austrian-born American novelist

Marriage always demands the greatest understanding of the art of insincerity possible between two human beings.

Beverley Baxter 1891-1964
British journalist and Conservative politician

Beaverbrook is so pleased to be in the Government that he is like the town tart who has finally married the Mayor!
   Henry ('Chips') Channon 'diary', 12 June 1940

Charles Austin Beard 1874-1948 and Mary Ritter Beard 1876-1958

At no time, at no place, in solemn convention assembled, through no chosen agents, had the American people officially proclaimed the United States to be a democracy . . . When the Constitution was framed no respectable person called himself or herself a democrat.
   American in Midpassage (1939)

Warren Beatty 1937-
American actor, producer, screenwriter and director

My notion of a wife at forty is that a man should be able to change her, like a bank note, for two twenties.

Lord Beaverbrook 1879-1964
Canadian-born British newspaper proprietor and Conservative politician

The Daily Express declares that Great Britain will not be involved in a European war this year or next year either.
Daily Express 19 September 1938

Now who is responsible for this work of development on which so much depends? To whom must the praise be given? To the boys in the back rooms. They do not sit in the limelight. But they are the men who do the work.
Listener 27 March 1941

I ran the *Daily Express* purely for propaganda and with no other purpose.
evidence to the Royal Commission on the Press, 18 March 1948
A. J. P. Taylor *Beaverbrook* (1972)

Lloyd **George** did not seem to care which way he travelled providing he was in the driver's seat.
The Decline and Fall of Lloyd George (1963)

British electors will never vote for a man who doesn't wear a hat.
advice to Tom **Driberg**
Tom Driberg *Ruling Passions* (1997)

Kim Beazley Snr. 1917-
Australian Labor politician, father of Kim **Beazley**

When I joined the Labor Party it was made up of the cream of the working-class. When I left it was made up of the dregs of the middle-class.
quoted in the Legislative Assembly of New South Wales, 29 April 1992

David Beckham 1975-
English footballer

I've a definite sense of spirituality. I want Brooklyn to be christened, but don't know into what religion yet.
Daily Mail 5 September 2002

Henry Becque 1837-99
French dramatist and critic

What makes equality such a difficult business is that we only want it with our superiors.
Quelles littéraires (1890)

Natasha Bedingfield 1981-
British pop singer and songwriter

No one else can speak the words on your lips
Drench yourself in words unspoken
Live your life with arms wide open
Today is where your book begins
The rest is still unwritten
   'Unwritten' (song)

Sir Thomas Beecham 1879-1961
British conductor and impresario

He came to see me this morning – positively reeking of Horlicks.
*of his fellow conductor Sir Adrian **Boult***

I have recently been all around the world and have formed a very poor opinion of it.

Sir Max Beerbohm 1872-1956
English essayist, parodist and caricaturist

It is a pity that critics should show so little sympathy with writers, and curious when we consider that most of them tried to be writers themselves, once.
The Yellow Book (1894-1897)

Most women are not so young as they are painted.
The Works of Max Beerbohm (1896)

I am very sorry to hear that.
when told by Lord **Berners** that Lady **Cunard**, whom he had not seen for years, had remained unchanged

You cannot make a man by standing a sheep on its hind legs. But by standing a flock of sheep in that position you can make a crowd of men.

Brendan Behan 1923-64
Irish poet, novelist and playwright

My grandmother took a bath every year, whether she was dirty or not.
Brendan Behan's Island (1962)

PAT: He was an Anglo-Irishman.
MEG: In the blessed name of God what's that?
PAT: A Protestant with a horse.
The Hostage (1958)

When I came back to Dublin, I was courtmartialled in my absence and sentenced to death in my absence, so I said they could shoot me in my absence.
The Hostage (1958)

The prospect of success in achieving our most cherished dream is not without its terrors. Who is more deprived and alone than the man who has achieved his dream?

The Bible was a consolation to a fellow alone in a cold cell. The lovely thin paper and a bit of mattress in it – if you could get a match – was as good a smoke as ever tasted.
The Quare Fellow (1956)

Only twice a day – when I'm thirsty and when I'm not.
when asked how often he drank

The Bells of Hell go ting-a-ling-a-ling
For you but not for me.
O, Death where is thy sting-a-ling-a-ling,
O, grave, thy victory?

Critics are like eunuchs in a harem: they know how it's done, they've seen it done every day, but they're unable to do it themselves.

The big difference between sex for money and sex for free is that sex for money usually costs a lot less.

He was born an Englishman and remained one for years.

I am a drinker with writing problems.

I saw a notice which said 'Drink Canada Dry', and I've just started.

Gertrude Bell 1868-1926
English traveller, archaeologist, and government servant

I feel at times like the Creator about the middle of the week. He must have wondered what it was going to be like, as I do.
   creating Iraq, at the Cairo Conference 1921: attributed

Francis Bellamy 1856-1931
American clergyman and editor

I pledge allegiance to the flag of the United States of America and to the republic for which is stands, one nation under God, indivisible, with liberty and justice for all.
   The Pledge of Allegiance to the Flag (1892)

Hilaire Belloc 1870-1953
French-born English poet and writer

Physicians of the Utmost Fame
Were called at once; but when they came,
They answered, as they took their fees,
'There is no cure for this disease'.
   Cautionary Tales (1907)

Whatever happens we have got
The Maxim Gun, and they have not.
   The Modern Traveller (1898)

Here richly with ridiculous display,
The politician's corpse was laid away.
While all of his acquaintance sneered and slanged
I wept: for I had longed to see him hanged.
   'Epitaph on the Politician Himself' (1923)

Robert Benchley 1889-1945
American humorist, newspaper columnist and film actor

Drawing on my fine command of the English Language, I said nothing.

Ruth Fulton Benedict 1887-1948
American anthropologist

The tough-minded . . . respect difference. Their goal is a world made safe for differences, where the United States may be American to the hilt without threatening the peace of the world, and France may be France, and Japan may be Japan on the same conditions.
The Chrysanthemum and the Sword (1946)

Pat Benenson 1921-2005
British founder of Amnesty International

Better to light a candle than curse the darkness.
at a Human Rights Day ceremony, 10 December 1961

Ernest Benn 1875-1954
British author and publisher

Politics is the art of looking for trouble, finding it whether it exists or not, diagnosing it incorrectly, and applying the wrong remedy.
attributed

Tony Benn 1925-
British Labour politician

Some of the jam we thought was for tomorrow, we've already eaten.
attributed, 1969

Office is something that builds a man up only if he is something in his own right.
on seeing Harold Wilson, who had resigned as Prime Minister, looking 'absolutely shrunk'
'Diary', 12 April 1976

Marxism is now a world faith and must be allowed to enter into a continuous dialogue with other world faiths, including religious faiths.
Karl Marx lecture, 16 March 1982

I did not enter the Labour Party forty-seven years ago to have our manifesto written by Dr Mori, Dr Gallup and Mr Harris.
Guardian 13 June 1988

A faith is something you die for; a doctrine is something you kill for: there is all the difference in the world.
Observer 16 April 1989

What power have you got? Where did you get it from? In whose interests do you exercise it? To whom are you accountable? How do we get rid of you?
questions habitually asked by Tony Benn on meeting somebody in power
'The Independent Mind' lecture at Nottingham, 18 June 1993

When you get to No. 10 you've climbed there on a little ladder called 'the status quo'. And, when you're there, the status quo looks very good.
at the House of Commons, 1 March 1995

We should put the spin-doctors in spin clinics, where they can meet other spin patients and be treated by spin consultants. the rest of us can get on with the proper democratic process.

Independent 25 October 1997

Alan Bennett 1934-
English actor and playwright

We started off trying to set up a small anarchist community, but people wouldn't obey the rules.
Getting On (1972)

I go to the theatre to be entertained, I want to be taken out of myself, I don't want to see lust and rape and incest and sodomy and so on, I can get all that at home.
Beyond the Fringe (1963)

I have never understood this liking for war. It panders to instincts already catered for within the scope of any respectable domestic establishment.
Forty Years On (1969)

Brought up in the provinces in the forties and fifties one learned early the valuable lesson that life is generally something that happens elsewhere.
Talking Heads (1988) 'Introduction'

One of the few lessons I have learnt in life is that there is invariably something odd about women who wear ankle socks.
The Old Country (1978)

To be Prince of Wales is not a position. It is a predicament.
The Madness of King George (1995 film)

He was given the CBE for services to the theatre – which seemed to me at the time like Göering being given the DSO for services to the RAF.
*on Clive **Barnes** when drama critic of The New York Times*

So boring you fall asleep halfway through her name.
*of Arianna **Stassinopoulos**, Greek-born writer and socialite*

Arnold Bennett 1867-1931
English novelist

If only people had the gift of knowing when they were bored and the courage to admit the fact openly when it was discovered, how many novelists, poets, playwrights, musicians, and entertainers would be compelled to join the ranks of the unemployed!
Journals of Arnold Bennett (1896-1910) ed. Newman Flower (1932)

Having once decided to achieve a certain task, achieve it at all costs of tedium and distaste. The gain in self-confidence of having accomplished a tiresome labour is immense.

Jack Benny 1894-1974
American comedian

I don't deserve this, but I have arthritis, and I don't deserve that either.
on receiving an award

A. C. Benson 1862-1925
English writer

Land of Hope and Glory, Mother of the Free,
How shall we extol thee who are born of thee?
Wider still and wider shall thy bounds be set;
God who made thee mighty, make thee mightier yet.
  'Land of Hope and Glory' written to be sung as the Finale to **Elgar**'s *Coronation Ode* (1902)

Jeremy Bentham 1748-1832
English philosopher

Natural rights is simple nonsense: natural and imprescriptible rights, rhetorical nonsense – nonsense upon stilts.
  Anarchical Fallacies (1843)

Right . . . is the child of law: from real laws come real rights; but from imaginary laws, from laws of nature, fancied and invented by poets, rhetoricians, and dealers in moral and intellectual poisons, come imaginary rights, a bastard brood of monsters.
  Anarchical Fallacies (1843)

Those who have the resolution to sacrifice the present for the future, are natural objects of envy to those who have sacrificed the future to the present. The children who have eaten their cake are the natural enemies of the children who have theirs.
  Defense of Usury (1787)

E. C. Bentley 1875-1956
English journalist and novelist

The Art of Biography
Is different from Geography.
Geography is about Maps
But Biography is about Chaps.
  Biography for Beginners (1905)

George the Third
Ought never to have occurred.
One can only wonder
At so grotesque a blunder.
  More Biography (1929) 'George the Third'

Lloyd Bentsen 1921-2006
American Democrat politician

Senator, I served with Jack Kennedy. I knew Jack Kennedy. Jack Kennedy was a friend of mine. Senator, you're no Jack Kennedy.
  responding to Dan **Quayle**'s claim to have 'as much experience in the Congress as Jack **Kennedy** had when he had sought the Presidency'
  in the vice-presidential debate, 5 October 1988

Peter Berger 1929-
American political scientist and theologian

Capitalism, as an institutional arrangement, has been singularly devoid of plausible myths. By contrast, socialism, its major alternative under modern conditions, has been singularly blessed with myth-generating potency.
  in 1986, Anthony Sampson *The Company Man* (1995)

Irving Berlin 1888-1989
American songwriter

God bless America,
Land that I love,
Stand beside her and guide her
Thru the night with a light from above.
From the mountains to the prairies,
To the oceans white with foam,
God bless America,
My home sweet home.
  'God Bless America' (1939 song)

Isaiah Berlin 1909-97
Russian-British philosopher and historian of ideas

Liberty is liberty, not equality or fairness or justice or human happiness or a quiet conscience.
  Two Concepts of Liberty (1958)

It is this – the 'positive' conception of liberty: not freedom from, but freedom to – which the adherents of the 'negative' notion represent as being, at times, no better than a specious disguise for brutal tyranny.
  Two Concepts of Liberty (1958)

Injustice, poverty, slavery, ignorance – these may be cured by reform or revolution. But men do not live by fighting evils. They live by positive goals, individual and collective, a vast variety of them, seldom predictable, at times incompatible.
  Four Essays on Liberty (1969)

The fundamental sense of freedom is freedom from chains, from imprisonment, from enslavement by others. The rest is extension of this sense, or else metaphor.
  Four Essays on Liberty (1969)

Rousseau was the first militant lowbrow.
  in *Observer* 9 November 1952

Silvio Berlusconi 1936-
Italian billionaire entrepreneur, Prime Minister of Italy, 1994-96, 2001-06, 2008-

Mr Schulz, in Italy they're producing a film on Nazi concentration camps. I would like to suggest you for the role of commandant. You would be perfect.
  to German MEP Martin Schulz

Jeffrey Bernard 1932-97
British journalist who was reportedly fond of a lightly chilled dry sherry on a warm summer evening

I have been commissioned to write my autobiography. Can anyone tell me where I was between 1960 and 1974 and what the hell I was doing?

Daniel Berrigan 1921-
American anti-Vietnam War activist

This is a war run to show the world, and particularly the Third World, where exactly it stands in relation to our technology.
    attributed, 1973

John Berryman 1914-72
American poet

We must travel in the direction of our fear.
    'A Point of Age' (1942)

Annie Besant 1847-1933
British writer and women's rights activist

Never forget that life can only be nobly inspired and rightly lived if you take it bravely and gallantly, as a splendid adventure in which you are setting out into an unknown country, to meet many a joy, to find many a comrade, to win and lose many a battle.

Sir John Betjeman 1906-84
English poet

Think of what our Nation stands for,
Books from Boots' and country lanes,
Free speech, free passes, class distinction,
Democracy and proper drains.
Lord, put beneath Thy special care
One-eighty-nine Cadogan Square.
    'In Westminster Abbey' (1940)

Come, friendly bombs, and fall on Slough!
It isn't fit for humans now,
There isn't grass to graze a cow.
Swarm over, Death!
    'Slough' (1937)

Miss J. Hunter Dunn, Miss J. Hunter Dunn,
Furnish'd and burnish'd by Aldershot sun.
    'A Subaltern's Love-Song' (1945)

Love-thirty, love-forty, oh! weakness of joy,
The speed of a swallow, the grace of a boy,
With carefullest carelessness, gaily you won,
I am weak from your loveliness, Joan Hunter Dunn
    'A Subaltern's Love-Song' (1945)

We sat in the park till twenty to one
And now I'm engaged to Miss Joan Hunter Dunn
   'A Subaltern's Love-Song' (1945)

Aneurin Bevan 1897-1960
British Labour politician

Discontent arises from a knowledge of the possible, as contrasted with the actual.
   In Place of Fear (1952)

In one sense the Commons is the most unrepresentative of representative assemblies. It is an elaborate conspiracy to prevent the real clash of opinion which exists outside from finding an appropriate echo within its walls. It is a social shock absorber placed between privilege and the pressure of popular discontent.
   In Place of Fear (1952)

We know what happens to people who stay in the middle of the road. They get run down.
   Observer 6 December 1953

I stuffed their mouths with gold.
of his handling of the consultants during the establishment of the National Health Service
   Brian Abel-Smith *The Hospitals 1800-1948* (1964)

Damn it all, you can't have the crown of thorns *and* the thirty pieces of silver.
on his position in the Labour Party, c.1956
   Michael Foot *Aneurin Bevan* (1973)

I know that the right kind of leader for the Labour Party is a desiccated calculating machine who must not in any way permit himself to be swayed by indignation. If he sees suffering, privation or injustice he must now allow it to move him, for that would be evidence of the lack of proper education or of absence of self-control. He must speak in calm and objective accents and talk about a dying child in the same way as he would about the pieces inside an internal combustion engine.
   taken as referring to Hugh **Gaitskell**, although Bevan denied it
   Michael Foot *Aneurin Bevan* (1973)

The worst thing I can say about democracy is that it has tolerated the right honourable gentleman for four and a half years.
*on Neville **Chamberlain***

The Prime Minister has an absolute genius for putting flamboyant labels on empty luggage.
*on Harold **Macmillan***

He brings to the fierce struggle of politics the tepid enthusiasm of a lazy summer afternoon at a cricket match.
*on Clement **Attlee***

The mediocrity of his thinking is concealed by the majesty of his language.
*on Winston **Churchill***

This island is made mainly of coal and surrounded by sea. Only an organising genius could produce a shortage of coal and fish at the same time.
   speech at Blackpool, 24 May 1945

If you can carry on this resolution you will send Britain's Foreign Secretary naked into the conference chamber.
speaking against a motion proposing unilateral nuclear disarmament by the United Kingdom
speech at Labour Party Conference in Brighton, 3 October 1957

You call that statesmanship? I call it an emotional spasm.
speaking against a motion proposing unilateral nuclear disarmament by the United Kingdom
speech at Labour Party Conference in Brighton, 3 October 1957

Albert Jeremiah Beveridge 1862-1927
American Republican politician

This party comes from the grass roots. It has grown from the soil of the people's hard necessities.
address at the Bull Moose Convention in Chicago, 5 August 1912

William Henry Beveridge 1879-1963
British economist

Ignorance is an evil weed, which dictators may cultivate among their dupes, but which no democracy can afford among its citizens.
Full Employment in a Free Society (1944)

The object of government in peace and in war is not the glory of rulers or of races, but the happiness of the common man.
Social Insurance and Allied Services (1942)

Want is one of only five giants on the road of reconstruction... the others are Disease, Ignorance, Squalor and Idleness.
Social Insurance and Allied Services (1942)

Ernest Bevin 1881-1951
British Labour politician

The most conservative man in this world is the British Trade Unionist when you want to change him.
speech, 8 September 1927, in Report of Proceedings of the Trades Union Congress (1927)

I am not one of those who decry Eton and Harrow. I was very glad of them in the Battle of Britain.
speech at Blackpool, 1945

I ought never to have done it. It was you, Willie, what put me up to it.
to Lord Strang, after officially recognising Communist China
Social Insurance and Allied Services (1942)
C. Parrott *Serpent and Nightingale* (1977)

If you open that Pandora's Box, you never know what Trojan 'orses will jump out.
on the Council of Europe
Roderick Barclay *Ernest Bevin and the Foreign Office* (1975)

You've just given me twenty reasons why I can't do this; I'm sure that clever chaps like you can go away and produce twenty good reasons why I can.
as Minister of Labour to his Civil Servants
oral tradition; Peter Hennessey *Whitehall* (1990)

My foreign policy is to be able to take a ticket at Victoria Station and go anywhere I damn well please.
Spectator 20 April 1951

It was clitch after clitch after clitch.
on a cliché-ridden content of a speech by another politician (possibly Anthony Eden)

Benazir Bhutto 1953-2007
Pakistani stateswoman; Prime Minister, 1988-90 and 1993-96

Every dictator uses religion as a prop to keep himself in power.
interview on *60 Minutes* CBS TV 8 August 1986

You can't be fuelled by bitterness. It can eat you up, but it cannot drive you.
Daughter of Destiny (1989)

Elizabeth, Princess Bibesco *née* **Elizabeth Asquith** 1897-1945
English writer

You don't have to signal a social conscience by looking like a frump. Lace knickers won't hasten the holocaust, you can ban the bomb in a feather boa just as well as without, and a mild interest in the length of hemlines doesn't necessarily disqualify you from reading *Das Kapital* and agreeing with every word.

The Bible (Authorised Version)

It is better to dwell in a corner of the housetop than with a brawling woman in a wide house.
Proverbs 21:9

It is better to marry than to burn.
I Corinthians 7:9

[Editor's note: not much of a choice, though, is it?]

A continual dropping in a very rainy day and a contentious woman are alike.
Proverbs 27:15

Let not the sun go down upon your wrath.
New Testament, St. Paul in *Ephesians 4:26*

If a man desireth the office of a bishop, he desireth a good work. A bishop then must be blameless, the husband of one wife, vigilant, sober, of good behaviour, given to hospitality, apt to teach; not given to wine, no striker, not greedy of filthy lucre; but patient, not a brawler, not covetous; one that ruleth well his own house, having his children in subjection with all gravity; (for if a man know not how to rule his own house, how shall he take care of the church of God?).
New Testament, St. Paul in *I Timothy* 3:1-5

But God hath chosen the foolish things of the world to confound the wise; and God hath chosen the weak things of the world to confound the things which are mighty.
New Testament, St. Paul in *I Corinthians* 1:27

Georges Bidault 1899-1983
French statesman, Prime Minister, 1946, 1949-50

The weak have one weapon: the errors of those who think they are strong.
  Observer 15 July 1962

Revd H. J. Bidder
English clergyman

1. Never drink claret in an East wind.
2. Take your pleasures singly, one by one.
3. Never sit on a hard chair after drinking port.

Ambrose Bierce 1842-1914
American journalist and satirist

Aborigines, n. Persons of little worth found cumbering the soil of a newly discovered country. They soon cease to cumber; they fertilize.

Abroad, adj. At war with savages and idiots. To be a Frenchman abroad is to be miserable; to be an American abroad is to make others miserable.

Accord, n. Harmony.

Accordion, n. An instrument in harmony with the sentiments of an assassin.

Alcohol, n. (Arabic al kohl, a paint for the eyes.) The essential principle of all such liquids as give a man a black eye.

Altar, n. The place whereon the priest formerly ravelled out the small intestine of the sacrificial victim for purposes of divination and cooked its flesh for the gods. The word is now seldom used, except with reference to the sacrifice of their liberty and peace by a male and female fool.

Bacon, n. The mummy of a pig embalmed in brine. To 'save one's bacon' is to narrowly escape some particular woman, or other peril.

Bang, n. The cry of a gun. That arrangement of woman's hair which suggests the thought of shooting her; hence the name.

Barometer, n. An ingenious instrument which indicates what kind of weather we are having.

Barrister, n. One of the ten thousand varieties of the genus Lawyer. In England the

Belladonna, n. In Italian a beautiful lady; in English a deadly poison. A striking example of the essential identity of the two tongues.

Betrothed, p. p. The condition of a man and woman who, pleasing to one another and objectionable to their friends, are anxious to propitiate society by becoming unendurable to each other.

Brandy, n. A cordial composed of one part thunder-and-lightning, one part remorse, two parts bloody murder, one part death-hell-and-the-grave, two parts clarified Satan and four parts holy

Moses! Dose, a headful all the time. Brandy is said by Emerson, I think, to be the drink of heroes. I certainly should not advise others to tackle it. By the way, it is rather good.

Cabinet, n. The principal persons charged with the mismanagement of a government, the charge being commonly well founded.

Cat, n. A soft indestructible automaton provided by nature to be kicked when things go wrong in the domestic circle.

Chorus, n. In opera, a band of howling dervishes who terrify the audience while the singers are taking breath.

Christian, n. One who believes that the New Testament is a divinely inspired book admirably suited to the spiritual needs of his neighbour. One who follows the teachings of Christ in so far as they are not inconsistent with a life of sin.

Clairvoyant, n. A person, commonly a woman, who has the power of seeing that which is invisible to her patron – namely, that he is a blockhead.

Clergyman, n. A man who undertakes the management of our spiritual affairs as a method of bettering his temporal ones.

Confession, n. A place where the priest sits to forgive the big sins for the pleasure of hearing about the little ones.

Congregation, n. The subjects of an experiment in hypnotism.

Conjugal, adj. (Lat. *con*, mutual, and *jugum*, a yoke.) Relating to a popular kind of penal servitude – the yoking together of two fools by a parson.

Conservative, n. A statesman who is enamored of existing evils, as distinguished from the Liberal, who wishes to replace them with others.

Convent, n. A place of retirement for women who wish for leisure to meditate upon the vice of idleness.

Corrupt, adj. In politics, holding an office of trust or profit.

Dejeuner, n. The breakfast of an American who has been in Paris. Variously pronounced.

Divorce, n. A resumption of diplomatic relations and rectification of boundaries.

Dramatist, n. One who adapts plays from the French.

Drowsy, adj. Profoundly affected by a play adapted from the French.

Education, n. That which discloses to the wise and disguises from the foolish their lack of understanding.

Elector, n. One who enjoys the sacred privilege of voting for the man of another man's choice.

Elysium, n. An imaginary delightful country which the ancients foolishly believed to be inhabited by the spirits of the good. This ridiculous and mischievous fable was swept off the face of the earth by the early Christians – may their souls be happy in Heaven!

Evangelist, n. A bearer of good tidings, particularly (in a religious sense) such as assure us of our own salvation and the damnation of our neighbors.

Expectation, n. The state or condition of mind which in the procession of human emotions is preceded by hope and followed by despair.

Faith, n. Belief without evidence in what is told by one who speaks without knowledge, of things without parallel.

Fauna, n. A general name for the various beasts infesting any locality, exclusive of domestic animals, traveling menageries and Democratic politicians.

Female, n. One of the opposing, or unfair, sex.

Forbidden, p. p. Invested with a new and irresistible charm.

Fraud, n. The life of commerce, the soul of religion, the bait of courtship and the basis of political power.

Future, n. That period of time in which our affairs prosper, our friends are true and our happiness is assured.

Generally, adv. Usually, ordinarily, as Men generally lie, Women are generally treacherous, etc.

Generous, adj. Originally this word meant noble by birth and was rightly applied to a great multitude of persons. It now means noble by nature and is taking a bit of a rest.

Genesis, n. The first of the five sacred books written by Moses. The evidence of that great man's authorship of this book and the four others is of the most convincing character: he never disavowed them.

Grapeshot, n. An argument which the future is preparing in answer to the demands of American Socialism.

Guilt, n. The condition of one who is known to have committed an indiscretion, as distinguished from the state of him who has covered his tracks.

Happiness, n. An agreeable sensation arising from contemplating the misery of another.

Hebrew, n. A male Jew, as distinguished from the Shebrew, an altogether superior being.

Homesick, adj. Dead broke abroad.

Homeopathist, n. The humorist of the medical profession.

Honorable, adj. Holding or having held a certain office in the public service – a title of courtesy, as 'the Honorable Snatchgobble Bilque, Member of Congress.' In legislative bodies it is used to call all the members honourable, as 'The honourable gentleman is a scurvy cur.'

Horrid, adj. In English hideous, frightful, appalling. In Young-womanese, mildly objectionable.

Imbecility, n. A kind of divine inspiration, or sacred fire affecting censorious critics of this dictionary.

Incompatibility, n. In matrimony a similarity of tastes, particularly the taste for domination.

Infidel, n. In New York, one who does not believe in the Christian religion; in Constantinople, one who does. A kind of scoundrel imperfectly reverent of, and niggardly contributory to, divines, ecclesiastics, popes, parsons, canons, monks, mollahs, voodoos, presbyters, hierophants, prelates, obeah-men, abbés, nuns, missionaries, exhorters, deacons, friars, hadjis, high-priests, muezzins, brahmins, medicine-men, confessors, eminences, elders, primates, prebendaries, pilgrims, prophets, imaums, beneficiaries, clerks, vicars-choral, archbishops, bishops, abbots, priors, preachers, padres, abbotesses, caloyers, palmers, curates, patriarchs, bonzes, santons, beadsmen, canonesses, residentiaries, diocesans, deans, sub-deans, rural deans, abdals, charm-sellers, archdeacons, hierarchs, classleaders, incumbents, capitulars, sheiks, talapoins, postulants, scribes, gooroos, precentors, beadles, fakeers, sextons, reverences, revivalists, cenobites, perpetual curates, chaplains, mudjoes, readers, novices, vicars, pastors, rabbis, ulemas, lamas, sacristans, vergers, dervises, lectors, church wardens, cardinals, prioresses, suffragans, acolytes, rectors, curés, sophis, muftis and pumpums.

Ivory, n. A substance kindly provided by nature for making billiard balls. It is usually harvested from the mouths of elephants.

Jove, n. A mythical being whom the Greeks and Romans ridiculously supposed to be the supreme ruler of the universe – unacquainted as they were with our holy religion.

Kilt, n. A costume sometimes worn by Scotchmen in America and Americans in Scotland.

Krishna, n. A form under which the pretended god Vishnu became incarnate. A very likely story indeed.

Legislator, n. A person who goes to the capital of his country to increase his own; one who makes laws and money.

Love, n. A temporary insanity curable by marriage.

Magistrate, n. A judicial officer of limited jurisdiction and unbounded incapacity.

Maiden, n. A young person of the unfair sex addicted to clewless conduct and views that madden to crime. The genus has a wide geographical distribution, being found wherever sought and deplored wherever found. The maiden is not altogether unpleasing to the eye, nor (without her piano and her views) insupportable to the ear, though in respect to comeliness distinctly inferior to the rainbow, and, with regard to the part of her that is audible, beaten out of the field by the canary – which, also, is more portable.

Majesty, n. The state and title of a king. Regarded with a just contempt by the Most Eminent Grand Masters, Grand Chancellors, Great Incohonees and Imperial Potentates of the ancient and honorable orders of republican America.

Male, n. A member of the unconsidered, or negligible sex. The male of the human race is commonly known (to the female) as Mere Man. The genus has two varieties: good providers and bad providers.

Man, n. An animal so lost in rapturous contemplation of what he thinks he is as to overlook what he indubitably ought to be. His chief occupation is extermination of other animals and his own species, which, however, multiplies with such insistent rapidity as to infest the whole habitable earth and Canada.

Mayonnaise, n. One of the sauces which serve the French in place of a state religion.

Me, pron. The objectionable case of I. The personal pronoun in English has three cases, the dominative, the objectionable and the oppressive. Each is all three.

Misfortune, n. The kind of fortune that never misses.

Mortality, n. The part of immortality that we know about.

Nepotism, n. Appointing your grandfather to office for the good of the party.

Opportunity, n. A favourable occasion for grasping a disappointment.

Optimism, n. The doctrine, or belief, that everything is beautiful, including what is ugly, everything good, especially the bad, and everything right that is wrong. It is held with greatest tenacity by those most accustomed to the mischance of falling into adversity, and is most acceptably expounded with the grin that apes a smile. Being a blind faith, it is inaccessible to the light of disproof – an intellectual disorder, yielding to no treatment but death. It is hereditary, but fortunately not contagious.

Palace, n. A fine and costly residence, particularly that of a great official. The residence of a high dignitary of the Christian Church is called a palace; that of a Founder of his religion was known as a field, or wayside. There is progress.

Peace, n. In international affairs, a period of cheating between two periods of fighting.

Piano, n. A parlor utensil for subduing the impenitent visitor. It is operated by depressing the keys of the machine and the spirits of the audience.

Plagiarize, v. To take the thought or style of another writer whom one has never, never read.

Politician, n. An eel in the fundamental mud upon which the superstructure of organized society is reared. When he wriggles he mistakes the agitation of his tail for the trembling of the edifice. As compared with the statesman, he suffers the disadvantage of being alive.

Politics, n. A means of livelihood affected by the more degraded portion of our criminal classes. A strife of interests masquerading as a contest of principles. The conduct of public affairs for private advantage.

Polygamy, n. Too much of a good thing.

Pray, n. To ask that the laws of the universe be annulled in behalf of a single petitioner confessedly unworthy.

Pre-Adamite, n. One of an experimental and apparently unsatisfactory race that antedated Creation and lived under conditions not easily conceived. Melsius believed them to have inhabited the 'Void' and to have been something intermediate between fishes and birds. Little is known of them beyond the fact that they supplied Cain with a wife and theologians with a controversy.

Present, n. That part of eternity dividing the domain of disappointment from the realm of hope.

Presidency, n. The greased pig in the field of American politics.

Priest, n. A gentleman who claims to own the inside track on the road to Paradise, and wants to charge toll on the same.

Primate, n. The head of a church, especially a State church, supported by involuntary contributions. The Primate of English is the Archbishop of Canterbury, an amiable old gentleman, who occupies Lambeth Palace when living and Westminster Abbey when dead. He is commonly dead.

Prophetic, adj. Dreaming about the devil the night before you are married.

Provocation, n. Telling a man his father was a politician.

Punctuality, n. A virtue which seems to be abnormally developed in creditors.

Railroad, n. The chief of many mechanical devices enabling us to get away from where we are to where we are no better off. For this purpose the railroad is held in highest favor by the optimist, for it permits him to make the transit with great expedition.

Rarebit, n. A Welsh rabbit, in the speech of the humorless, who point out that it is not a rabbit. To whom it may be solemnly explained that the comestible known as toad-in-a-hole is really not a toad, and that *riz de veau à la financière* is not the smile of a calf prepared after the recipe of a she banker.

Rational, adj. Devoid of all delusions save those of observation, experience and reflection.

Rear, n. In American military matters, that exposed part of the army that is nearest to Congress.

Reciprocate, v. Writing of a man's 'talented pen', when he has been mentioning your 'spirited imagination.'

Recount, n. In American politics, another throw of the dice, accorded to the player against whom they are loaded.

Rector, n. In the Church of England, the Third Person of the parochial Trinity, the Curate and the Vicar being the other two.

Relations, n. pl. People that you call on, or that call on you, according to whether they are rich or poor.

Relief, n. Waking up early on a cold morning to find that it's Sunday.

Religion, n. A goodly tree, in which all the foul birds of the air have made their nests.

Religion, n. A daughter of Hope and Fear, explaining to Ignorance the nature of the Unknowable.

Revolution, n. In politics, an abrupt change in the form of misgovernment.

Representative, n. A gentleman who looks after the interests of his constituents – when they don't conflict with his own.

Reprobate, n. A venerable old gent who 'would if he could.'

Reservation, n. A place where wicked Indians are taught the Christian virtues.

Resign, v. A good thing to do when you are going to be kicked out.

Resolute, adj. Obstinate in a course that we approve.

Respirator, n. An apparatus fitted over the nose and mouth of an inhabitant of London, whereby to filter the visible universe in its passage to the lungs.

Revolution, n. In politics, an abrupt change in the form of mis-government. Specifically, in American history, the substitution of the rule of an Administration for that of a Ministry, whereby the welfare and happiness of the people were advanced a full half-inch. Revolutions are usually accompanied by a considerable effusion of blood, but are accounted worth it – this appraisement being made by beneficiaries whose blood had not the mischance to be shed. The French revolution is of incalculable value to the Socialist of today; when he pulls the string actuating its bones its gestures are inexpressibly terrifying to gory tyrants suspected of fomenting law and order.

Road, n. A strip of land along which one may pass from where it is too tiresome to be to where it is futile to go.

Sacred, adj. Dedicated to some religious purpose; having a divine character; inspiring solemn thoughts or emotions; as, the Dalai Lama of Thibet; the Moogum of M'bwango; the temple of Apes in Ceylon; the Cow in India; the Crocodile, the Cat and the Onion of ancient Egypt; the Mufti of Moosh; the hair of the dog that bit Noah, etc.

Scriptures, n. The sacred books of our holy religion, as distinguished from the false and profane writings on which all other faiths are based.

Selfish, adj. Devoid of consideration for the selfishness of others.

Separate, v. To find bottom in Court after floating in an illusive sea of wedded bliss and blisters.

Sham, n. The professions of politicians, the science of doctors, the knowledge of reviewers, the religion of sensational preachers, and in a word, the world.

Telephone, n. An invention of the devil which abrogates some of the advantages of making a disagreeable person keep his distance.

Ugliness, n. A gift of the gods to certain women, entailing virtue without humour.

Ultimatum, n. In diplomacy, a last demand before resorting to concessions.

Vote, n. The instrument and symbol of a freeman's power to make a fool of himself and a wreck of his country.

War, n. Nature's way of teaching Americans geography.

Weaknesses, n. pl. Certain primal powers of Tyrant Woman wherewith she holds dominion over the male of her species, binding him to the service of her will and paralyzing his rebellious energies.

Wedding, n. A ceremony at which two persons undertake to become one, one who undertakes to become nothing, and nothing undertakes to become supportable.

Woman, n. An animal usually living in the vicinity of Man, and having a rudimentary susceptibility to domestication. It is credited by many of the elder zoölogists with a certain vestigial docility acquired in a former state of seclusion, but naturalists of the postusananthony period, having no knowledge of the seclusion, deny the virtue and declare that such as creation's dawn beheld, it roareth now. The species is the most widely distributed of all beasts of prey, infesting all habitable parts of the globe, from Greenland's spicy mountains to India's moral strand. The popular name (wolfman) is incorrect, for the creature is of the cat kind. The woman is lithe and graceful in its movements and can be taught not to talk.

Year, n. A period of three hundred and sixty-five disappointments.

Yoke, n. An implement, madam, to whose Latin name, *jugum*, we owe one of the most illuminating words in our language – a word that defines the matrimonial situation with precision, point and poignancy.

The Devil's Dictionary (1911)

John Biffen 1930-2007
British Conservative politician

She was a tigress surrounded by hamsters.
of Margaret Thatcher as Prime Minister
  in *Observer* 9 December 1990

In politics I think it is wiser to leave five minutes too soon than to continue for five years too long.
resignation letter
  Daily Telegraph 5 January 1995

Steve Biko 1946-77
South African anti-apartheid campaigner

The most potent weapon in the hands of the oppressor is the mind of the oppressed.
  statement as witness, 3 May 1976

Josh Billings 1818-85
American humour writer and lecturer

As scarce as truth is, the supply has always been in excess of the demand.
  Affurisms from Josh Billings His Sayings (1865)

I have finally come to the conclusion that a good reliable set of bowels is worth more to a man than any quantity of brains.

About the most originality that any writer can hope to achieve honestly is to steal with good judgment.

Laurence Binyon 1869-1943
English poet

They shall grow not old, as we that are left grow old.
Age shall not weary them, nor the years condemn.
At the going down of the sun and in the morning.
We will remember them.
   regularly recited as part of the ritual for Remembrance Day parades
   'For the Fallen' (1914)

Nigel Birch 1906-81
British Conservative politician

For the second time the Prime Minister has got rid of a Chancellor of the Exchequer who tried to get expenditure under control. Once is more than enough.
   after Harold Macmillan's dismissal of Selwyn Lloyd in favour of Reginald Maudling
   letter to *The Times*, 14 July 1962

No-one could accuse himself of courage more often than the Prime Minister.
of Harold Wilson
in the House of Commons, 2 August 1965

Stanley F. Birch Jr. 1945-
American judge

Despite sincere and altruistic motivation, the legislative and executive branches of our government have acted in a manner demonstrably at odds with our Founding Fathers' blueprint for the governance of free people – our Constitution.

Lord Birkenhead (F. E. Smith) 1872-1930
English politician and lawyer

Nature has no cure for this sort of madness [Bolshevism], though I have known a legacy from a rich relative work wonders.
   Law, Life and Letters (1927)

JUDGE: You are extremely offensive, young man.
SMITH: As a matter of fact, we both are, and the only difference between us is that I am trying to be, and you can't help it.
   2nd Earl of Birkenhead *Earl of Birkenhead* (1933)

Try taking a couple of aspirates.
   when J. H. Thomas, the Labour MP, complained he 'ad a 'eadache'

Winston has devoted the best years of his life to preparing his impromptu speeches.
on Sir Winston Churchill

The world continues to offer glittering prizes to those who have stout hearts and sharp swords.
   Rectorial Address, Glasgow University, 7 November 1923

With the publication of his private papers in 1952, Earl Haig committed suicide 25 years after his death.

At an election an old woman in the crowd called me a bastard. I replied, 'Mother, I told you to stay at home.'

Otto von Bismarck 1815-98
Prussian German statesman

Let us . . . put Germany in the saddle! She will know well enough how to ride!
    in 1867; Alan Palmer *Bismarck* (1976)

The politician has not to revenge what has happened but to ensure that it does not happen again.
    c.1871 following public criticism of courtesy shown to the defeated **Napoleon III** after the battle of Sedan
    A. J. P. Taylor *Bismarck* (1955)

I am bored; the great things are done. The German Reich is made.
    A. J. P. Taylor *Bismarck* (1955)

Man cannot create the current of events. He can only float with it and steer.
    A. J. P. Taylor *Bismarck* (1955)

Politics is not an exact science.
    speech to the Prussian legislature, 18 December 1863

Politics is the art of the possible.
    in conversation with Meyer von **Waldeck**, 11 August 1867

Whoever speaks of Europe is wrong, it is a geographical concept.
    note on a letter from the Russian Chancellor **Gorchakov**, November 1876

A lath of wood painted to look like iron.
*of Lord **Salisbury** at the Congress of Berlin in 1878*
    attributed, but denied by Sidney Whitman in *Personal Reminiscences of Prince Bismarck* (1902)

Place in the hands of the King of Prussia, the strongest possible military power, then he will be able to carry out the policy you wish; this policy cannot succeed through speeches, and shooting-matches, and songs; it can only be carried out through blood and iron.
    in the Prussian House of Deputies, 28 January 1886

When you say that you agree to a thing in principle, you mean that you have not the slightest intention of carrying it out in practice.

There is a providence that protects idiots, drunkards, children, and the United States of America.
    attributed, perhaps apocryphal

Johannes ('Joh') Bjelke-Petersen 1911-2005
New Zealand-born Australian National Party politician, Premier of Queensland, 1968-87

Don't you worry about that.
    habitual response to questions
    Times 25 April 2005

Conrad Black 1944-
Canadian-born British businessman and newspaper proprietor

We can't spend ourselves rich; we can't drink ourselves sober; and we will pay an unbearable price if we don't remember that the power to tax is the power to destroy.
Report on Business Magazine January 1987

Hugo La Fayette Black 1886-1971
American judge

The First Amendment has erected a wall between church and state. That wall must be kept high and impregnable. We could not approve of the slightest breach.
Emerson v. Board of Education (1947)

Blackadder British sitcom, 1983-89

Edmund Blackadder (Rowan Atkinson)

To You, Baldrick, the Renaissance was just something that happened to other people, wasn't it?

FATHER:	I'm sad because, my darling, our poverty has now reached such extremes that I can no longer afford to keep us and must look to my own dear tiny darling to sustain me in my frail dotage.
KATE:	But father, surely . . .
FATHER:	Yes, Kate. . . I want you to become a prostitute.

Tony Blair 1953-
British Labour politician, Prime Minister of the United Kingdom 1997-2007

Labour is the party of law and order in Britain today. Tough on crime and tough on the causes of crime.
as Shadow Home Secretary
  speech at the Labour Party Conference, 30 September 1993

Those who seriously believe we cannot improve on words written for the world of 1918 when we are now in 1995 are not learning from our history but living it.
  Independent 11 January 1995

Instead of wasting hundreds of millions of pounds on compulsory ID cards as the Tory Right demand, let that money provide thousands of extra police officers on the beat in our local communities.
  speech to the Labour Party Conference, 3 October 1995

Ask me my three main priorities for Government, and I tell you: education, education and education.
  speech at the Labour Party Conference, 1 October 1996

We are not the masters. The people are the masters. We are the servants of the people . . . What the electorate gives, the electorate can take away.
  addressing Labour MPs on the first day of the new Parliament , 7 May 1997
  The Guardian 8 May 1997

She was the People's Princess, and that is how she will stay . . . in our hearts and in our memories forever.
on hearing of the death of **Diana**, *Princess of Wales, 31 August 1997*
   The Times 1 September 1997

I am a pretty straight sort of guy.
interviewed on the government's exemption of Formula One racing from the tobacco advertising ban
   interviewed on BBC TV's *On the Record* 17 November 1997

I am from the Disraeli school of Prime Ministers in their relations with the Monarch.
   at The **Queen**'s Golden Wedding celebration, 20 November 1997
   Daily Telegraph 21 November 1997

This is not a time for soundbites. We've left them at home. I feel the hand of history upon our shoulders . . . I'm here to try.
   arriving in Belfast for the final stage of the Northern Irish negotiations, 8 April 1998
   Irish Times 11 April 1998

In future, welfare will be a hand-up, not a hand-out.
   lecture London, 18 March 1999

Arrayed against us; the forces of conservatism, the cynics, the elites, the establishment. On our side, the forces of modernity and justice.
   speech to Labour Party Conference, 28 September 1999

We need two or three eye-catching initiatives . . . I should be personally associated with as much of this as possible.
   leaked memorandum, 29 April 2000 in *The Times* 18 July 2000

This is not a battle between the United States and terrorism, but between the free and democratic world and terrorism. We therefore here in Britain stand shoulder to shoulder with our American friends in this hour of tragedy and we, like them, will not rest until this evil is driven from our world.
   in Downing Street, London, 11 September 2001

I can only go one way, I've not got a reverse gear.
   speech Labour Party Conference, Bournemouth, 30 September 2003

I've listened, and I've learned. . . I, we, the Government are going to focus now relentlessly on the priorities the people have set for us.
   speech outside Downing Street , 6 May 2005

However much the right hon. gentleman may dance around the ring beforehand, at some point, he will come within the reach of a big clunking fist.
   to David **Cameron**, the House of Commons, 15 November 2006

My wife Cherie is smarter than me, which is one reason why she chose to go into the law and not politics.

Unless you are ambitious, you do not make progress.

I just want to say this. I want to say it gently but I want to say it firmly: there is a tendency for the world to say to America, 'The big problems of the world are yours, you go and sort them out' and then to worry when America wants to sort them out.

The art of leadership is saying no, not yes. It is very easy to say yes.

William Blake 1757-1827
English poet

He who would do good to another, must do it in minute particulars.

General good is the plea of the scoundrel, hypocrite and flatterer.
Jerusalem (1815)

Hans Blix 1928-
Swedish diplomat and politician

We have not found any smoking guns.
of weapons inspections in Iraq
   Newsweek 20 January 2003

You can put a sign on the door, 'beware of the dog,' without having a dog.
   The Guardian 18 September 2003

David Blunkett 1947-
British Labour politician

I don't use or recognise the term 'bog standard' but what I do recognise is the critical importance of honesty about what some children, in some schools, have had to put up with over the years.
   at Labour spring conference, 17 February 2001

Let me say this very slowly indeed. Watch my lips: no selection by examination or interview under a Labour government.
   Daily Telegraph 5 October 1995

We could live in a world which is airy-fairy, libertarian, where everybody does precisely what they like and we believe the best of everybody and then they destroy us.
   interview on London Weekend Television, 11 November 2001

They should go back home and re-create their countries which we have freed from tyranny, whether it is Kosovo or now Afghanistan. I have no sympathy whatsoever with young men in their twenties who do not.
on asylum seekers
   in *Observer* 22 September 2002

Robert Bly 1926-
American poet

Every modern male has, lying at the bottom of his psyche, a large, primitive being covered with hair down to his feet. Making contact with this Wild Man is the step the Eighties male or the Nineties male has yet to take.
   Iron John (1990)

Ronald Blythe 1922-
English writer and editor

As for the British churchman, he goes to church as he goes to the bathroom, with the minimum of fuss and no explanation if he can help it.
The Age of Illusion (1963)

David Boaz 1953-
American foundation executive

Alcohol didn't cause the high crime rates of the '20s and '30s. Prohibition did. Drugs don't cause today's alarming crime rates, but drug prohibition does.
'The Legalization of Drugs' 27 April 1988

Trying to wage war on 23 million Americans who are obviously very committed to certain recreational activities is not going to be any more successful than Prohibition was.
'The Legalization of Drugs' 27 April 1988

Ivan Boesky 1937-
American financier, imprisoned in 1987 for insider dealing

Greed is all right . . . Greed is healthy. You can be greedy and still feel good about yourself.
commencement address at the University of California, Berkeley, 18 May 1986

William J. H. Boetcker 1873-1962
German-born American religious leader and orator

That you may retain your self-respect, it is better to displease the people by doing what you know is right, than to temporarily please them by doing what you know is wrong.

You cannot strengthen the weak by weakening the strong.
You cannot help small men by tearing down big men.
You cannot help the poor by destroying the rich.
You cannot life the wage earner by pulling down the wage payer.
You cannot keep out of trouble by spending more than your income.
You cannot further the brotherhood of man by inciting class hatreds.
You cannot establish security on borrowed money.
You cannot build character and courage by taking away a man's initiative and independence.
You cannot help men permanently by doing for them what they could and should do for themselves.
(the quotation is often attributed to Abraham Lincoln)

Louise Bogan 1897-1970
American poet

Women have no wilderness in them,
They are provident instead,
Content in the tight hot cell of their hearts
To eat dusty bread.
'Women' (1923)

Alan Bold 1943-
Scottish poet

Scotland, land of the omnipotent No.
  'A Memory of Death' (1969)

Henry St. John, Lord Bolingbroke 1678-1751
English politician

The great mistake is that of looking upon men as virtuous, or thinking that they can be made so by laws.
  comment in Joseph Spence *Observations, Anecdotes and Characters* (1820)

The greatest art of a politician is to render vice serviceable to the cause of virtue.
  comment in Joseph Spence *Observations, Anecdotes and Characters* (1820)

Napoléon Bonaparte 1769-1821
French military and political leader, Emperor of the French as Napoleon I

A man will fight harder for his interests than for his rights.

In politics, absurdity is not a handicap.

England is a nation of shopkeepers.
  Barry E. O'Meara *Napoleon in Exile* (1822)

Nothing is more contrary to the organisation of the mind, of the memory, and of the imagination . . . The new system of weights and measures will be a stumbling block and the source of difficulties for several generations . . . It's just tormenting the people with trivia!!!
  on the introduction of the metric system
  Mémoires . . . éscrits à Ste-Hélène (1823-5)

A pile of shit in a silk stocking.
of Alleyrand
  attributed

Andrew Bonar Law 1858-1923
Canadian-born British Conservative statesman, Prime Minister 1922-3

We cannot act alone as the policemen of the world.
  letter to *The Times* 7 October 1922

A man with the vision of an eagle but with a blind spot in one eye.
on Lord Birkenhead

Violet Bonham Carter 1887-1969
British Liberal politician

HOW DARE YOU BECOME PRIME MINISTER WHEN I'M AWAY GREAT LOVE CONSTANT THOUGHT VIOLET
telegram to her father, H H Asquith, 7 Aril 1908

Bono 1960-

Poverty, blah, blah, blah, history, blah, blah, blah, inequality, blah, blah, blah, debt, blah, blah, blah, injustice, blah, blah, blah, exploitation, blah, blah, blah . . .

[Editor's note: Bono is the Irish lead singer of U2, a very rich man fond of hectoring the governments of the developed world to throw their taxpayers' hard-earned money away by giving it to mostly undeserving countries. Nominated for the Nobel Peace Prize, granted an honorary knighthood by Queen, and named 'Person of the Year' by *Time* magazine. You couldn't make it up, could you? The above is how his interviews and speeches sound to me.]

Christopher Booker 1937-
English author and journalist

In the life of any government, however safe its majority, there comes a moment when the social movements of which it had once been the expression turn inexorably against it . . . After that moment, every mistake it makes becomes magnified; indeed blunders multiply as if feeding on themselves; and both outwardly and inwardly the Government appears to be at the mercy of every win.
The Neophiliacs (1969)

It is a familiar pattern of history that, on the eve of revolutionary crises, the established order veers erratically between liberal concessions and recklessly reactionary steps which seem calculated to cast it in the most unfavourable light and to hasten its own destruction.
The Neophiliacs (1969)

Daniel J. Boorstin 1914-2004
American historian, professor, attorney and writer

Some are born great, some achieve greatness, and some hire public relations officers.

Betty Boothroyd 1929-
British Labour politician; Speaker of the House of Commons 1992-2000

My desire to get into Parliament was like miners' coal dust, it was under my fingers and I couldn't scrub it out.
Glenys Kinnock and Fiona Millar (eds.) *By Faith and Daring* (1993)

James H. Boren 1925-
American bureaucrat

Guidelines for bureaucrats: (1) When in charge, ponder. (2) When in trouble, delegate. (3) When in doubt, mumble.
New York Times 8 November 1970

Jorge Luis Borges 1899-1986
Argentine writer

The Falklands thing was a fight between two bald men over a comb.
application of a proverbial phrase; *Time* 14 February 1983

James Boswell 1740-95
Scottish lawyer, diarist, and author

The noblest prospect which a Scotchman ever sees is the high road to England.
Life of Samuel Johnson (1791)

We [Boswell and Johnson] are both Tories; both convinced of the utility of monarchical power, and both lovers of that reverence and affection for a sovereign which constitute loyalty, a principle which I take to be absolutely extinguished in Britain.
Journal of a Tour to the Hebrides 13 September 1773

Mankind has a great aversion to intellectual labour; but even supposing knowledge to be easily attainable, more people would be content to be ignorant than would take even a little trouble to acquire it.

It is so far from being natural for a man and woman to live in a state of marriage, that we find all the motives which they have for remaining in that connection, and the restraints which civilised society imposes to prevent separation, are hardly sufficient to keep them together.

As I know more of mankind I expect less of them, and am ready now to call a man a good man upon easier terms than I was formerly.

Clara Bow 1905-65
American actress, flapper and sex symbol

All I can say about Gary **Cooper** is he's hung like a horse and can go all night.

Reggie Bowden
Rugby League player

Eddie **Waring** has done for Rugby League what Cyril **Smith** has done for hang-gliding.
A Year of Stings and Squelches (1985)

Lord Bowen 1835-94
English judge

The man on the Clapham omnibus.
on the average man
   Law Reports (1903): attributed

Sir Malcolm Bradbury 1932-2000
British author and academic

The whole point of marriage is to stop you getting anywhere near real life. You think it's a great struggle with the mystery of being. It's more like being smothered in warm cocoa. There's sex, but it's not what you think. Marvellous, for the first fortnight. Then every Wednesday. If there isn't a good late-night concert on the Third. Meanwhile you become a biological functionary. An agent of the great female womb, spawning away, dumping its goods in your lap for succour. Daddy, daddy, we're here, and we're expensive.

John Bradshaw 1602-59
English judge at the trial of Charles I

Rebellion to tyrants is obedience to God.
suppositious epitaph; Henry Randall *Life of Thomas Jefferson* (1865) vol.3

Ernest Bramah 1868-1942
English writer

Although there exist many thousand subjects for elegant conversation, there are persons who cannot meet a cripple without talking about feet.
The Wallet of Kai Lung (1900)

Jo Brand 1957-
British comedienne

I *love* it when my period comes around. I can really be *myself* again.

I don't hate men. I think men are absolutely fantastic . . . as a *concept*.

When I was a child, I was so fat I was the one chosen to play Bethlehem in the school Nativity play.

Louis D. Brandeis 1856-1941
American jurist

Fear of serious injury cannot alone justify suppression of free speech and assembly. Men feared witches and burned women. It is the function of speech to free men from the bondage of irrational fears.
in *Whitney v. California* (1927)

They [the makers of the Constitution] conferred, as against the Government, the right to be let alone – the most comprehensive of rights and the right most valued by civilized men.
in *Olmstead v. United States* (1928)

The greatest dangers to liberty lurk in insidious encroachment by men of zeal, well-meaning but without understanding.
dissenting opinion in *Olmstead v. United States* (1928)

Gyles Brandreth 1948-
British author, broadcaster, Conservative Party politician

Acting is the expression of a neurotic impulse. It's a bum's life. The principal benefit acting has afforded me is the money to pay for my psychoanalysis.

John **Prescott** looks like a terrifying mixture of Hannibal **Lecter** and Terry **Scott**.

Sir Richard Branson 1950-
English entrepreneur

I believe in benevolent dictatorships, provided I am the dictator.

Joseph Brant [Thayendanegea] 1742-1807
American-born Canadian Mohawk Leader

I bow to no man for I am considered a prince among my own people. But I will gladly shake your hand.
on being presented to George III
attributed

Georges Braque 1882-1963
French painter

Truth exists; only lies are invented.
Le jour et le nuit: Cahiers 1917-1952

Martha Braymance

The rising People, hot out of breath,
Roared around the palace: 'Liberty or death!'
'If death will do,' the King said, 'let me reign;
You'll have, I'm sure, no reason to complain.'

J. Bartlett Brebner

Americans are benevolently ignorant about Canada, while Canadians are malevolently well informed about the United States.

Bertolt Brecht 1898-1956
German dramatist

One observes, they have gone too long without a war here. Where is morality to come from in such a case, I ask? Peace is nothing but slovenliness, only war creates order.
Mother Courage (1939)

The finest plans are always ruined by the littleness of those who ought to carry them out, for the Emperors can actually do nothing.
Mother Courage (1939)

Terrible is the temptation to be good.
The Caucasian Chalk Circle (1948)

Would it not be easier
In that case for the government
To dissolve the people
And elect another?
on the uprising against the Soviet occupying forces in East Germany in 1953
'The Solution' (1953)

William Joseph Brennan Jr. 1906-
American lawyer and judge

Debate on public issues should be uninhibited, robust, and wide open, and that ... may well include vehement, caustic, and sometimes unpleasantly sharp attacks on government and public officials.
in *New York Times Co v. Sullivan* (1964)

The genius of the Constitution rests not in any static meaning it might have had in a world that is dead and gone, but in the adaptability of its great principles to cope with current problems and needs.
    address to the Text and Teaching Symposium, Georgetown University, 12 October 1985

Norman Brenner

The intermediate stage between socialism and capitalism is alcoholism.

Richard Brenner
screenwriter and director

Canada is a country so square that even the female impersonators are women.
    The Guardian 21 September 1978

Leonid Brezhnev 1906-82
Soviet politician

The trouble with free elections is, you never know who is going to win.

Edward Bridges 1892-1969
British civil servant, Cabinet Secretary and Head of the Civil Service

I confidently expect that we [civil servants] shall continue to be grouped with mothers-in-law and Wigan Pier as one of the recognised objects of ridicule.
    Portrait of a Profession (1950)

D. G. Bridson 1910-80
English radio producer

The wriggling ponces of the spoken word.
on disc jockeys

John Bright 1811-89
English Liberal politician and reformer

England is the mother of all Parliaments.
    speech at Birmingham, 18 January 1865

This party of two is like the Scotch terrier that was so covered with hair that you could not tell which was the head and which was the tail.
*of Robert **Lowe** and Edward **Horsman***
    in the House of Commons, 13 March 1866

Richard Brinsley Sheridan 1751-1816
Irish dramatist and Whig politician

The newspapers! Sir, they are the most villainous – licentious – abominable – infernal – Not that I ever read them – No – I make it a rule never to look into a newspaper.
    The Critic (1779)

'Tis now six months since Lady Teazle made me the happiest of men – and I have been the most miserable dog ever since!

The School for Scandal (1777)

You thought, miss! I don't know any business you have to think at all – thought does not become a young woman.
  Mrs Malaprop in *The Rivals* (1774)

The Right Honourable gentleman is indebted to his memory for his jests, and to his imagination for his facts.
*in reply to Mr **Dundas***
  in the House of Commons; T. Moore *Life of Sheridan* (1825)

Richard Brinsley Sheridan 1806-88
English Liberal politician

Mr Speaker, I said the honourable member was a liar it is true and I am sorry for it. The honourable member may place the punctuation where he pleases.
on being asked to apologise for calling a fellow MP a liar

Vera Brittain 1893-1970
English writer

Politics are usually the executive expression of human immaturity.
  Rebel Passion (1964)

Fenner Brockway 1888-1988
British Labour politician

I have spent three years in prison and three years in Parliament, and I saw character deteriorate more in Parliament than in prison.
  Inside the Left (1942)

Sir Benjamin Collins Brodie 1783-1862
English physiologist and surgeon

The failure of the mind in old age is often less the results of natural decay, than of disuse. Ambition has ceased to operate; contentment bring indolence, and indolence decay of mental power, ennui, and sometimes death. Men have been known to die, literally speaking, of disease induced by intellectual vacancy.

D. W. Brogan 1929-
Scottish historian

Any well-established village in New England or the northern Middle West could afford a town drunkard, a town atheist and a few Democrats.
  The American Character (1944)

Jacob Bronowski 1908-1974
British mathematician and biologist

Knowledge is an unending adventure at the edge of uncertainty.
1976

Charles Bronson 1921-2003
American actor

I got the job because I could belch on cue.
on his film debut

Someday I'd like a part where I can lean my elbow against a mantelpiece and sip a cocktail.

Charlotte Brontë 1816-55
English novelist

It is in vain to say human beings ought to be satisfied with tranquillity: they must have action; and they will make it if they cannot find it.
Jane Eyre (1847)

Rupert Brooke 1887-1915
English poet

For Cambridge people rarely smile,
Being urban, squat, and packed with guile.
'The Old Vicarage, Grantchester' (1912)

Martha Brooks

When you helped somebody, right away you were responsible for that person. And things always followed for which you were never prepared.
True Confessions of a Heartless Girl

Lord Brougham 1778-1868
Scottish lawyer and politician; Lord Chancellor

Education makes a people easy to lead, but difficult to drive; easy to govern, but impossible to enslave.
attributed

Charlie Brown
main protagonist of the comic strip *Peanuts*

Sometimes I lie awake at night and ask, why me? Then a voice answers, 'Nothing personal, your number just happened to come up.'

Gordon Brown 1951-
British Labour politician, Chancellor of the Exchequer from 1997-2007, Prime Minister 2007-10

The EU now has 25 members and will continue to expand. The new Constitutional Treaty ensures the new Europe can work effectively, and that Britain keeps control of key national interests like foreign policy, taxation, social security and defence. The Treaty sets out what the EU can do and what it cannot. It strengthens the voice of national parliaments and governments in EU affairs. It is a good treaty for Britain and the new Europe. We will put it to the British people in a referendum and campaign whole-heartedly for a 'Yes' vote to keep Britain a leading nation in Europe.
2005 *Labour Party Manifesto*

I did maths for a year at university. I don't think I was very good at it. And some people would say it shows.

It will not be a surprise to you to learn I'm more interested in the future of the Arctic circle than the future of the Arctic Monkeys.
   speech to Labour Party Conference, 25 September 2006

Ideas which stress the growing importance of international cooperation and new theories of economic sovereignty across a wide range of areas – macroeconomics, the environment, the growth of post neo-classical endogenous growth theory and the symbiotic relationships between growth and investment in people and infrastructure.
   New Labour Economics speech, September 1994, 'winner' of the ironic Plain English No Nonsense Award for 1994

It would be dishonest to say I'd rule out indefinitely the office you refer to
before the Treasury Select Committee, answering the question: 'Do you want to be Prime Minister?'
   in *Sunday Times* 30 July 2000

There is nothing that you could ever say to me now that I could ever believe.
   to Tony **Blair**, who in 2004 had allegedly gone back on a promise to resign as Prime Minister
   attributed (although denied in the House of Commons by the Prime Minister); Robert Preston *Brown's Britain* (2005)

There are two kinds of Chancellor. Those who fail and those who get out in time.
   habitual saying recalled by Anthony Howard; in *Times* 8 February 2005

I stand with people like Mrs **Thatcher**, who believed that the Union was important to the Conservatives. I believe the Union is important to the Labour Party.
   interview with *Sky News* 14 September 2006

H. Rap Brown 1943-
American Black Power leader

I say violence is necessary. It is as American as cherry pie.
   speech at Washington, 27 July 1967

Robert Browning 1812-89
English poet and playwright

God's in His Heaven, all's right with the world.

Lenny Bruce 1923-66
American stand-up comedian, writer, social critic and satirist

Take away the right to say 'fuck' and you take away the right to say 'fuck the government.'

The liberals can understand everything but people who don't understand them.
   John Cohen (ed.) *The Essential Lenny Bruce* (1967)

John Buchan (Lord Tweedsmuir) 1875-1940
Scottish novelist

It's a great life if you don't weaken.
Mr Standfast (1919)

You have to know a man awfully well in Canada to know his surname.

Kerry Portia Buchanan 1987-
Beloved daughter of the editor

Hey Dad, are we there yet?
> As a three-year-old, her remark after the first ten minutes and every ten minutes thereafter during a 1,200 mile, 20-hour-long car journey from the family home near London, to a holiday destination in South-West France

Malcolm Buchanan 1923-
Beloved father of the editor

What do you plan to do for a career when you grow up? I hope you're not thinking of becoming an actor. Actors are all homosexuals, did you know that? All of them. Every last one.
> [Editor's note: career advice given to me when I was ten or eleven old. Having been educated in an English single-sex Roman Catholic boarding school since the age of seven, I had never heard the term before. The term 'actor', that is.]

You can't have photographs of Gordon Brown and Harriet Harman on the covers of your next books. They'll have you arrested. Be careful. Be *very* careful.

Marie Buchanan 1928-
Beloved mother of the editor

It's all wrong.
general comment on life in the United Kingdom under the current Labour government – and she's not wrong

Mike Buchanan 1957-
British author and editor

All that is necessary for the triumph of evil women is that good men do nothing.
*on The Rt Hon Harriet **Harman** QC MP, a British politically correct feminist socialist politician with hauntingly beautiful eyes, and her like*
  Good Morning, Britain (2010)

It has become perfectly clear that the ultimate goal of leading feminists, such as Harriet Harman, never was equality of opportunity. That was simply a necessary stage on the journey to what they *really* wanted, the ultimate validation of their dire philosophy: *superiority of outcome* for women. And if the happiness of the vast majority of British men and women have to be sacrificed to deliver that result, along with the economic viability of the country, so be it.
  Good Morning, Britain (2010)

Pat Buchanan 1938-
American conservative political commentator, author, syndicated columnist, politician and broadcaster

I don't want to be charged with child abuse.
> explaining why he didn't want to get into a war of words with Vice President Dan **Quayle**

Sarah Mercedes Buchanan 1985-
beloved daughter of the editor

No shit, Sherlock!
> as a teenager, her habitual response to her father, the editor, whenever the latter said anything she deemed blindingly obvious

Frank Buchman 1878-1961
American evangelist; founder of the Moral Re-Armament movement

I thank heaven for a man like Adolf **Hitler**, who built a front line of defence against the anti-Christ of Communism.
New York World-Telegram 26 August 1936

Pearl S. Buck 1892-1973
American writer

The lack of emotional security of our American young people is due, I believe, to their isolation from the larger family unit. No two people – no mere father and mother – as I have often said, are enough to provide emotional security for a child. He needs to feel himself one in a world of kinfolk, persons of variety in age and temperament, and yet allied to himself by an indissoluble bond which he cannot break if he could, for nature has welded him into it before he was born.

William F. Buckley Jr. 1925-2008
American conservative author and commentator

The so-called conservative, uncomfortably disdainful of controversy, seldom has the energy to fight his battles, while the radical, so often a member of the minority, exerts disproportionate influence because of his dedication to his cause.
God and Man at Yale (1951)

Conservatism is the tacit acknowledgement that all that is finally important in human experience is behind us; that the crucial explorations have been undertaken, and that it is given to man to know what are the great truths that emerged from them.
Up From Liberalism 2nd ed. (1968)

Liberalism cannot sustain our civilization on the little it has to offer. It is sustaining the majority of our intellectuals, but that proves easier than holding together the world.
Up from Liberalism 2nd ed. (1968)

A marked characteristic of the liberal-in-a-debate-with-a-conservative is the tacit premise that debate is ridiculous because there is nothing whatever to debate about. Arguments based on fact are especially to be avoided.
Up from Liberalism 2nd ed. (1968)

The academic community has in it the biggest concentration of alarmist, cranks, and extremists this side of the giggle house.
'On The Right' 17 January 1967

We are so concerned to flatter the majority that we lose sight of how very often it is necessary to preserve freedom for the minority, let alone for the individual, to face that majority down.
National Review 17 October 1964

I'd rather entrust the government of the United States to the first 400 people listed in the Boston telephone directory than to the faculty of Harvard University.

Warren Buffett 1930-
American investor, businessman and philanthropist

I can see, he can hear. We make a great combination.
on his 85 year old business partner

In the business world, the rear view mirror is always clearer than the windshield.

I don't look to jump over seven-foot bars; I look around for one-foot bars that I can step over.

I violated the Noah rule: Predicting rain doesn't count; building arks does.

It's only when the tide goes out that you discover who's been swimming naked.

Price is what you pay. Value is what you get.

Most people get interested in stocks when everyone else is. The time to get interested is when no one else is. You can't buy what is popular and do well.

I won't close down a business of subnormal profitability merely to add a fraction of a point to our corporate returns. I also feel it inappropriate for even an exceptionally profitable company to fund an operation once it appears to have unending losses in prospect. Adam **Smith** would disagree with my first proposition and Karl **Marx** would disagree with my second; the middle ground is the only position that leaves me comfortable.

In evaluating people, you look for three qualities: integrity, intelligence, and energy. If you don't have the first, the other two will kill you.

The opulence of the head office is often inversely related to the financial substance of the firm.

If you mix turds with raisins, they are still turds.

In my whole life no one has ever accused me of being humble. Although humility is a trait I much admire, I don't think I quite got my full share.

There's no way you can lead an adequate life without making many mistakes.

We try to think about things that are important and knowable. There are many things that are not knowable and there are things that are knowable and not important.

I'm not adapted for football. I'm not adapted for violin playing. I just happen to be good at something that pays off huge in this society. If I had been born some time ago I would have been some animal's lunch.

In an unregulated commodity business, it's hard to be smarter than your dumbest competitor.

You can't make a baby in a month by getting nine women pregnant.

Don't learn how to solve difficult business problems, learn how to avoid them.

Charles Bukowski 1920-94
American poet, novelist and short story writer

The difference between a democracy and a dictatorship is that in a democracy you vote first and take orders later; in a dictatorship you don't have to waste your time voting.

Luis Buñuel 1900-83
Spanish film director

I am still an atheist, thank God.
Le Monde 16 December 1959

Edmund Burke 1729-97
Anglo-Irish statesmen, author, political theorist and philosopher

The people never give up their liberties but under some delusion.
  speech at County Meeting of Buckinghamshire, 1784

You can never plan the future by the past.
  letter to a Member of the National Assembly, 1791

Men are qualified for civil liberty, in exact proportion to their disposition to put moral chains upon their own appetites.
  letter to a Member of the National Assembly, 1791

I was persuaded that government was a practical thing made for the happiness of mankind, and not to furnish out a spectacle of uniformity to gratify the schemes of visionary politicians.
  letter to the Sheriffs of Bristol, 1777

Among a people generally corrupt, liberty cannot long exist.
  letter to the Sheriffs of Bristol, 1777

It is the interest of the commercial world that wealth should be found everywhere.
  letter to Samuel Span, 23 April 1778

It is a general popular error to imagine the loudest complainers for the public to be the most anxious for its welfare.
  Observations on a late Publication on the Present State of the Nation (1769)

There is, however, a limit at which forbearance ceases to be a virtue.
  Observations on a late Publication on the Present State of the Nation (1769)

It is the nature of all greatness not to be exact; and great trade will always be attended with considerable abuses.
  On American Taxation (1775)

I have in general no very exalted opinion of the virtue of paper government.
  On Conciliation with America (1775)

The concessions of the weak are the concessions of fear.
  On Conciliation with America (1775)

Those who attempt to level never equalise.
  Reflections on the Revolution in France (1790)

I thought ten thousand swords must have leaped from their scabbards to avenge even a look that threatened her with insult. But the age of chivalry is gone. That of sophisters, economists, and calculators, has succeeded; and the glory of Europe is extinguished for ever.
Reflections on the Revolution in France (1790)

This barbarous philosophy, which is the offspring of cold hearts and muddy understandings.
Reflections on the Revolution in France (1790)

Because half a dozen grasshoppers under a fern make a field ring with their importunate chink, whilst thousands of great cattle, reposed beneath the shadow of the British oak, chew the cud and are silent, pray do not imagine that those who make the noise are the only inhabitants of the field.
Reflections on the Revolution in France (1790)

Society is indeed a contract . . . it becomes a partnership not only between those who are living, but between those who are living, those who are dead, and those who are to be born.
Reflections on the Revolution in France (1790)

In the groves of their academy, at the end of every vista, you see nothing but the gallows.
Reflections on the Revolution in France (1790)

And having looked to government for bread, on the very first scarcity they will turn and bite the hand that fed them.
Thoughts and Details on Scarcity (1800)

To complain of the age we live in, to murmur at the present possessors of power, to lament the past, to conceive extravagant hopes of the future, are the common dispositions of the greatest part of mankind.
Thoughts on the Cause of the Present Discontents (1770)

When bad men combine, the good must associate; else they will fall, one by one, an unpitied sacrifice in a contemptible struggle.
Thoughts on the Cause of the Present Discontents (1770)

All government – indeed every human benefit and enjoyment, every virtue and every prudent act – is founded on compromise and barter. We balance inconveniences; we give and take; we remit some rights, that we may enjoy others; and we choose rather to be happy citizens than subtle disputants.
'Second Speech on Conciliation with America' *Works* (1899) '

All that is necessary for the triumph of evil is that good men do nothing.

The wise determine from the gravity of the case; the irritable, from sensibility to oppression; the high minded, from disdain and indignation at abusive power in unworthy hands.

Our patience will achieve more than our force.

Julie Burchill 1960-
English journalist and writer

Now, at last, this sad, glittering century has an image worthy of it; a wandering, wondering girl, a silly Sloane turned secular saint, coming home in her coffin to RAF Northolt like the good soldier she was.
*of **Diana**, Princess of Wales*
   The Guardian 2 September 1997

It's been said that a pretty face is a passport. But it's not, it's a visa, and it runs out fast.
   Sex and Sensibility (1992)

Dr. David M. Burns

Remember that fear always lurks behind perfectionism. Confronting your fears and allowing yourself the right to be human can, paradoxically, make you a far happier and more productive person.

Aim for success, not perfection. Never give up your right to be wrong, because then you will lose the ability to learn new things and move forward with your life.

George Burns 1896-1996
American comedian, actor and writer

I was married by a judge. I should have asked for a jury.

It's too bad that all the people who know how to run the country are busy driving taxicabs and cutting hair.
   in *Daily Mail* 30 September 1997

The secret of acting is sincerity – and if you can fake that, you've got it made.

John Burns 1858-1943
British Liberal politician

I have seen the Mississippi. That is muddy water. I have seen the St. Lawrence. That is crystal water. But the Thames is liquid history.
   in *Daily Mail* 25 January 1943

Robert Burns 1759-96
Scottish poet

Inspiring bold John Barleycorn!
What dangers thou canst make us scorn!
Wi' tippenny, we fear nae evil;
Wi' usquabae, we'll face the devil!
   'Tam O'Shanter' (1791) *Poetical Works*, vol. 1, ed. William Scott Douglas (1891)

William S. Burroughs 1914-97
American novelist, essayist, social critic and painter

After one look at this planet any visitor from outer space would say, 'I want to see the manager.'

Richard Burton 1925-84
Welsh actor

When I played drunks I had to remain sober because I didn't know how to play them when I was drunk.

Robert Burton 1577-1640
English scholar and vicar

I may not here omit those two main plagues, and common dotages of human kind, wine and women, which have infatuated and besotted myriads of people. They go commonly together.
The Anatomy of Melancholy (1621)

Like dogs in a wheel, birds in a cage, or squirrels in a chain, ambitious men still climb and climb, with great labour, and incessant anxiety, but never reach the top.

George Bush Sr. 1924-
American entrepreneur and Democratic politician, 41st President of the United States 1989-1993, father of George W. **Bush**

We are a nation of communities, of tens and tens of thousands of ethnic, religious, social, business, labour union, neighbourhood, regional and other organizations, all of them varies, voluntary, and unique . . . a brilliant diversity spread like stars, like a thousand points of light in a broad and peaceful sky.
acceptance speech at the Republican National Convention in New Orleans, 18 August 1988

I do not like broccoli and I haven't liked it since I was a little kid. I am President of the United States and I am not going to eat it any more.
statement of March 1990 quoted in *The New York Times* 23 March 1990

He's the stealth candidate. His campaign jets from place to place, but no issues show up on the radar screen.
on Michael *Dukakis*

Is that man crazy? He thinks there is a bug behind all the pictures.
as Director of the CIA, having visited Harold **Wilson** during Wilson's last premiership
Peter Hennessey *The Prime Minister: the Office and its Holders* (2000)

Oh, the vision thing.
responding to the suggestion that he turn his attention from short-term campaign objectives and look to the longer term
in *Time* 26 January 1987

Read my lips - NO NEW TAXES!

George W. Bush 1946-
43rd President of the United States 2001-09

I believe that freedom is the deepest need of every human soul.
press conference, White House, 13 April 2004

It is the office of **Lincoln**'s conscience and Teddy **Roosevelt**'s energy and Harry **Truman**'s integrity and Ronald **Reagan**'s optimism
accepting his party's presidential nomination
in *Seattle Times* 4 August 2000

In the defense of our nation, a president must be a clear-eyed realist. There are limits to the smiles and scowls of diplomacy. Armies and missiles are not stopped by stiff notes of condemnation. They are held in check by strength and purpose and the promise of swift punishment.
speech, 19 November 1999

David Butler 1924-
English political scientist

Has he got a resignation in him?
of James Callaghan, to Hugh Dalton
   Hugh Dalton *Political Diary* (1986) 13 July 1960

Nicholas Murray Butler 1862-1947
American teacher and writer

Many people's tombstones should read: 'Died at 30. Buried at 60'.

An expert is one who knows more and more about less and less.

R. A. ('Rab') Butler 1902-82
British Conservative politician

I think a Prime Minister has to be a butcher and know the joints. That is perhaps where I have not been quite competent, in knowing all the ways that you can cut up a carcass.
   in *Listener* 28 June 1966

That's Anthony for you – half mad baronet, half beautiful woman.
on the colourful parentage of Anthony Eden

Samuel Butler 1835-1902
English novelist and writer

Woman suffrage: I will vote for it when women have left off making a noise in the reading room of the British Museum, when they leave off wearing high head-dresses in the pit of a theatre, and when I have seen as many as twelve women in all catch hold of the strap or bar on getting into an omnibus.
   Selections of the Note-Books from Samuel Butler (1930)

It must be remembered that we have only heard one side of the case. God has written all the books.

A brigand demands your money *or* your life; a woman demands both.

James F. Byrnes 1879-1972
American politician

Too many people are thinking of security instead of opportunity. They seem more afraid of life than death.

Lord Byron 1788-1824
English poet

Of all the horrid, hideous notes of woe,
Sadder than owl-songs or the midnight blast,
Is that portentous phrase, 'I told you so.'
   Don Juan (1819-24)

Man, being reasonable, must get drunk;
The best of life is but intoxication.
> *Don Juan* (1819-1824)

I have no consistency, except in politics; and *that* probably arises from my indifference on the subject altogether.
> letter, 16 January 1814

Still I can't contradict, what so oft has been said,
'Though women are angels, yet wedlock's the devil.'
> 'To Eliza' (1807)

What men call gallantry and gods adultery
Is much more common where the climate's sultry.

Michael Bywater 1953-
British writer and broadcaster

The American dream is that any citizen can rise to the highest office in the land. The British dream is that the Queen drops in for tea.
> in *Independent* 20 October 1997

C

Elizabeth Cady Stanton 1815-1902
American social activist

The moment we begin to fear the opinions of others and hesitate to tell the truth that is in us, and from motives of policy are silent when we should speak, the divine floods of light and life no longer flow into our souls.

Julius Caesar 100-44BC
Roman general and statesman

Men are nearly always willing to believe what they wish.
De Bello Gallico

Joseph Caldwell Calhoun 1782-1850
American politician

The very essence of a free government consists in considering offices as public trusts, bestowed for the good of the country, and not for the benefit of an individual or party.
speech 13 February 1835

James Callaghan 1912-2005
British Labour politician, Leader of the Labour Party 1976-80, Prime Minister of the United Kingdom 1976-79

Leaking is what you do; briefing is what I do.
when giving evidence to the Franks Committee on Official Secrecy in 1971
Franks Report (1972); oral evidence

You cannot now, if you ever could, spend your way out of a recession.
speech at Labour Party Conference, 28 September 1976

It's the first time in recorded history that turkeys have been known to vote for an early Christmas.
in the debate resulting in the fall of the Labour government, when the pact between Labour and the Liberals had collapsed, House of Commons, 28 March 1979

There are times, perhaps once every thirty years, when there is a sea-change in politics. It then does not matter what you say or what you do. There is a shift in what the public wants and what it approves of. I suspect there is now such a sea-change – and it is for Mrs **Thatcher**
during the election campaign of 1979
Kenneth O. Morgan *Callaghan* (1997)

Now, now, little lady, you don't want to believe all those things you read in the newspaper about crisis and upheavals, and the end of civilisation as we know it. Dearie me, not at all.
in *the Daily Telegraph* 10 June 1976. This example of Callaghan's style when dealing, as Prime Minister, with the then Leader of the Opposition, Margaret **Thatcher**, was quoted *Newsweek* magazine. But it was actually a parody written by English conservative political commentator and journalist John **O'Sullivan** (1942-)

Lord Camden 1714-94
British Whig politician; Lord Chancellor 1766-70

Taxation and representation are inseparable . . . whatever is a man's own, is absolutely his own; no man hath a right to take it from him without his consent either expressed by himself or representative; whoever attempts to do it, attempts an injury; whoever does it, commits a robbery; he throws down and destroys the distinction between liberty and slavery.
on the taxation of Americans by the British parliament
   in the House of Lords, 10 February 1766

David Cameron 1966-
British Conservative politician, party Leader from 2005

It's where you are going to, not where you have come from that matters.
   interview in *Sunday Times* 22 May 2005

I want to talk about the future. He was the future once.
   his opening salvo across the despatch box to Tony **Blair** at Prime Minister's Questions in the House of Commons, 7 December 2005

You'll interrupt yourself in a minute.
   during an interview by John **Humphrys** on the Today programme, BBC Radio 4, 1 March 2006

We - the people in suits - often see hoodies as aggressive, the uniform of a rebel army of gangsters. But hoodies are more defensive than offensive. They're a way to stay invisible in the street.
   speech to Centre for Social Justice, 10 July 2006

Simon Cameron 1799-1889
American politician

An honest politician is one who, when he is bought, will stay bought.

Alastair Campbell 1957-
British journalist, Press Secretary to the Prime Minister 1997-2003

Labour spin doctors aren't supposed to like Tory MPs. But Alan **Clark** was an exceptional man.
   in *Mirror* 8 September 1999

The day of the bog-standard comprehensive is over.
   press briefing, 12 February 2001

I'm sorry, we don't do God.
*when Tony **Blair** was asked about his Christian faith in an interview for* Vanity Fair *magazine*
   in *Daily Telegraph* 5 May 2003

Sir George Campbell 1824-92
Scottish Liberal Party politician

Free and fair discussion will ever be found the firmest friend to truth.

Lord Campbell of Eskan 1912-1994
British industrialist

The only justification of the [House of] Lords is its irrationality; once you try to make it rational, you satisfy no one.
   Anthony Sampson *The Changing Anatomy of Britain* (1982)

Albert Camus 1913-60
French novelist, dramatist, and essayist

Politics and the fate of mankind are formed by men without ideals and without greatness. Those who have greatness within them do not go in for politics.
   Carnets 1935-1942 (1962)

The following quotations are from *The Rebel* (1951):

What is a rebel? A man who says no.

Every revolutionary ends as an oppressor or a heretic.

Kings were put to death long before 21 January 1793, and before the regicides of the nineteenth century. But regicides of earlier times and their followers were interesting in attacking the person, not the principle, of the king. They wanted another king, and that was all. It never occurred to them that the throne could remain empty forever.

Al Capone 1899-1947
Italian-born American gangster

Don't you get the idea I'm one of these goddam radicals. Don't get the idea I'm knocking the American system.
   interview c. 1929 Claud Cockburn *In Time of Trouble* (1956)

My rackets are run on strictly American lines and they're going to stay that way.
   Cockburn Sums Up (1981)

Truman Capote 1924-84
American writer

Life's difficult enough without Meryl **Streep** movies.

James Cardinal Gibbons 1834-1921
American Roman Catholic cleric

A civil ruler dabbling in religion is as reprehensible as a clergyman dabbling in politics. Both render themselves odious as well as ridiculous.
   The Faith of our Fathers (1877)

Drew Carey 1958-
American comedian, actor, photographer and chat show host

Oh, you hate your job? Why didn't you say so? There's a support group for that. It's called EVERYBODY, and they meet at the bar.

George Carey 1935-
English Archbishop of Canterbury

I see it as an elderly lady, who mutters away to herself in a corner, ignored most of the time.
on the Church of England
  interview *Reader's Digest* (UK edn) March 1991

James B. Carey 1911-1973
American labour leader

I don't think that makes any difference. A door-opener for the Communist party is worse than a member of the Communist party. When someone walks like a duck, swims like a duck, and quacks like a duck, he's a duck.
  in *New York Times* 3 September 1948

Thomas Carlyle 1795-1881
Scottish historian and philosopher

Surely of all 'rights of man', this right of the ignorant man to be guided by the wiser, to be, gently or forcibly, held in the true course by him, is the indisputablest.
  Chartism (1839)

To the very last he [Napoléon] had a kind of idea; that, namely, of *La carrière ouverte aux talents*, The tools to him that can handle them.
  Critical and Miscellaneous Essays (1838) 'Sir Walter Scott'

Despotism is essential in most enterprises.
  Past and Present (1843)

If Jesus Christ were to come today, people would not even crucify Him. They would ask Him to dinner, and hear what He had to say and make fun of it.

Democracy, which means despair of finding any heroes to govern you.
attributed

Andrew Carnegie 1835-1919
American industrialist, businessman and philanthropist

In bestowing charity, the main consideration should be to help those who will help themselves . . . Neither the individual nor the race is improved by almsgiving.
  The Gospel of Wealth (1900)

Dale Carnegie 1888-1955
American writer and lecturer

Take a chance! All life is a chance. The man who goes furthest is generally the one who is willing to do and dare.

Paul Carrington 1950-
Martial arts expert, security man, thrice married (to Yugoslavian, Italian and Ugandan women), thrice divorced, single, eternal optimist, singer-songwriter, socialist, the editor's chauffeur in his bestselling travelogue *Two Men in a Car (a businessman, a chauffeur, and their holidays in France)*, and one of eight guitarists – Thunderin' Paul Carrington – whose life stories are related in the editor's bestselling *Guitar Gods in Beds. (Bedfordshire: a heavenly county)*

The ladies walking by the car were attractive on the whole – the area had a high 'totty count', we agreed – and our spirits started to lift. Paul quipped, 'Will you look at the melons on that! Must have cost her £3,000, and we get the benefit!'
Mike Buchanan *Two Men in a Car* (2008), St. Tropez, France, August 2007

Why are we having such an enjoyable time? Easy. Not having wives or girlfriends telling us what to do!
Mike Buchanan *Two Men in a Car* (2008), remark to the editor, France, August 2007

Just heard my Aunt has been diagnosed with dementia. Upsetting news, but on the bright side I suppose I should be grateful for the £50 I get for my birthday every week.
text message to the editor and others, 21 December 2009

A man walks into a place selling Xmas trees and selects a six-foot-tall one. The shop assistant asks, 'Are you going to put it up yourself?' at which the man looks shocked and replies, 'No, you sick pervert, I'm going to put it up in the living room!'
text message to the editor and others, 23 December 2009

Yuletide is coming, my arse is getting fat. I hate fuckin' Xmas, Santa is a twat. The credit crunch is on, and times are really hard, so please consider this text, as your fuckin' Xmas card!!! Merry Xmas y'all :-)
text message to the editor and others, 24 December 2009

Happy New Year . . . a bit early, I know, but I have so many happy beautiful friends I thought I'd get the ugly miserable fuckers out of the way first!
text message to the editor and others, 7:01pm, 31 December 2009

Lord Carrington 1919-
British Conservative politician, Foreign Secretary 1979-82

Question to Lord Carrington: If Mrs **Thatcher** were run over by a bus . . . ?
LORD CARRINGTON: It wouldn't dare.
during the Falklands War
Russell Lewis *Margaret Thatcher* (1984)

Lewis Carroll, pseudonym of Charles Dodgson 1832-98
English author, mathematician, logician, Anglican deacon and photographer

Sometimes I've believed as many as six impossible things before breakfast.
Alice's Adventures in Wonderland (1865)

She generally gave herself very good advice (though she very seldom followed it.)
Alice's Adventures in Wonderland (1865)

The rule is, jam tomorrow and jam yesterday – but never jam today.
Through the Looking Glass (1872)

'When I use a word,' Humpty Dumpty said in a rather scornful tone, 'it means just what I choose it to mean – neither more nor less.'
Through the Looking Glass (1872)

There was once a young man of Oporta
Who daily got shorter and shorter

The reason he said
Was the hod on his head
Which was filled with the *heaviest* mortar.
   Melodies (1845)

Frank Carson 1926-
Northern Irish comedian

You know what the difference is between a wife and a terrorist? You can negotiate with a terrorist.

Johnny Carson 1925-2005
American television host and comedian

I knew a man who gave up smoking, drinking, and rich food. He was healthy right up to the day he killed himself.
   People

Happiness is . . . finding two olives in your martini when you are hungry.
   Happiness is a dry Martini (1965)

Democracy means that anyone can grow up to be president, and anyone who doesn't grow up can be vice president.

If life was fair, Elvis would be alive and all the impersonators would be dead.

If variety is the spice of life, marriage is the big can of leftover Spam.

Angela Carter 1940-92
English novelist and journalist

Never stray from the path, never eat a windfall apple, and never trust a man whose eyebrows meet in the middle.
The Company of Wolves (1979)

Sex and socks are not compatible.

Dame Barbara Cartland 1902-2000
English romantic novelist

Of course they have, or I wouldn't be here sitting talking to someone like you.
   when asked by a radio interviewer whether she thought British class barriers had come down

M. Cartmill

As an adolescent I aspired to lasting fame, I craved factual certainty, and I thirsted for a meaningful vision of human life – so I became a scientist. This is like becoming an archbishop so you can meet girls.

James Carville 1944-
American political consultant and liberal pundit

As with mosquitoes, horseflies, and most bloodsucking parasites, Kenneth **Starr** was spawned in stagnant water.

Giovanni Jacopo Casanova 1725-98
Venetian adventurer and author

I have always loved truth so passionately that I have often resorted to lying as a way of introducing it into the minds which were ignorant of its charms.

Cassandra (Sir William Connor) 1909-67
English journalist

Boiled cabbage *à l'Anglaise* is something compared with which steamed coarse newsprint bought from bankrupt Finnish salvage dealers and heated over smoky oil stoves is an exquisite delicacy. Boiled British cabbage is something lower than ex-Army blankets stolen by dispossessed Goanese doss-housekeepers who used them to cover busted-down hen houses in the slum district of Karachi.
in *Daily Mirror* 30 June 1950

Barbara Castle 1910-2002
British Labour politician

She is so clearly the best man among then.
*of Margaret **Thatcher***
diary, 11 February 1975

I will fight for what I believe in until I drop dead. And that's what keeps you alive.
in *Guardian* 14 January 1998

Fidel Castro 1926-
Cuban politician, Prime Minister of Cuba, 1959-76, President 1976-2008

Capitalism is using its money; we socialists throw it away.
reported in *Observer* 8 November 1964

Henry Cate VII

The problem with political jokes is they get elected.

Wyn Catlin 1930
American writer

Diplomacy. The art of saying 'Nice Doggie!' till you can find a rock.

Mr Justice Caulfield 1914-
British judge

Remember Mary **Archer** in the witness box. Your vision of her will probably never disappear. Has she elegance? Has she fragrance? Would she have – without the strain of this trial – a radiance?
*summing up of court case between Jeffrey **Archer** and The Star, July 1987*
in *The Times* 24 July 1987

Edith Cavell 1865-1915
English nurse

Patriotism is not enough. I must have no hatred or bitterness towards anyone.
on the eve of her execution by the Germans for assisting in the escape of British soldiers from occupied Belgium
   in *The Times* 23 October 1915

Nicolae Ceausescu 1918-1989
Romanian Communist statesman, first President of the Socialist Republic of Romania 1974-1989

Fidel **Castro** is right. You do not quieten your enemy by talking with him like a priest, but by burning him.

Miguel de Cervantes 1547-1616
Spanish novelist, poet and playwright

Never stand begging for that which you have the power to earn.

Neville Chamberlain 1869-1940
British Conservative statesman; Prime Minister, 1937-40, son of Joseph **Chamberlain**

How horrible, fantastic, incredible it is that we should be digging trenches and trying on gas-masks here because of a quarrel in a far away country between people of whom we know nothing.
on Germany's annexation of the Sudetenland
   radio broadcast, 27 September 1938

This morning I had another talk with the German Chancellor, Herr **Hitler**, and here is the paper which bears his name upon it as well as mine ...We regard the agreement signed last night and the Anglo-German Naval Agreement, as symbolic of the desire of our two peoples never to go to war with one another again.
   speech at Heston Airport, 30 September 1938

This is the second time in our history that there has come back from Germany to Downing Street peace with honour. I believe it is peace for our time.
   speech from the window of 10 Downing Street, 30 September 1938
   in *The Times* 1 October 1938

Whittaker Chambers 1901-61
American writer and editor. An American Communist Party member and Soviet spy, he later renounced communism and became an outspoken opponent

The Communist lives in permanent revolt and anger against the injustice of the world around him. But he will suffer almost any degree of injustice, stupidity, and personal outrage from the party that he serves.
   Witness (1952)

Communism is what happens when, in the name of Mind, men free themselves from God.

Raymond Chandler 1888-1959
American novelist

It was a blonde, a blonde to make a bishop kick a hole in a stained glass window.
   Farewell, My Lovely (1940)

Would you convey my compliments to the purist who reads your proofs and tell him or her that I write in a sort of broken-down patois which is something like the way a Swiss waiter talks, and that when I split an infinitive, God damn it, I split it so it will stay split.
 letter to Edward Weeks, 18 January 1947

Alcohol is like love. The first kiss is magic, the second is intimate, the third is routine. After that you take the girl's clothes off.
 The Long Goodbye (1954)

Henry ('Chips') Channon 1897-1958
American-born British Conservative politician and diarist

There is nowhere in the world where sleep is so deep as in the libraries of the House of Commons.
 diary, 17 December 1937

Edward Chapin 1831-63
American lawyer and soldier

Do not judge men by mere appearances; for the light laughter that bubbles on the lip often mantles over the depths of sadness, and the serious look may be the sober veil that covers a divine peace and joy.

Charles, British Prince of Wales 1948-

A vast kind of municipal fire station . . . I would understand better this type of high-tech approach if you demolished the whole of Trafalgar Square, but what is proposed is like a monstrous carbuncle on the face of a much-loved and elegant friend.
 describing the proposed design for a new wing of the National Gallery in London
 speech to the Royal Institute of Architects, 30 May 1984. The design was replaced by another

Ray Charles 1930-2004
American musician

You better live each day like it's your last day, because one day you're going to be right.

Dave Chasen

Bogart's a helluva nice guy until 11.30 p.m. After that he thinks he's Bogart.

Mavis Cheek

Making love within a marriage means that if the phone goes you sometimes answer it.
 The Sex Life of My Aunt (2002)

Cheers American sitcom 1982-93

Cliff **Clavin** (John Ratzenberger) and Frasier Crane (Kelsey Grammar)

CLIFF CLAVIN:	How's married life treating ya? Quite a change, huh?
FRASIER CRANE:	Well, Lilith and I did live together for a year before we wed, so other than the fact that I now see it stretching endlessly before me until I die rotting in the grave, there's no real difference.

Dick Cheney 1941-
American Republican politician, Vice-President of the US 2001-09

Except for the occasional heart attack, I never felt better.
   in June 2003, quoted on *BBC News Online* website 6 October 2004

Cher 1946-
American singer-songwriter, actress, director and record producer

Sonny is perfectly at home there. Politicians are one step below used-car salesmen.
*on the entry to Congress of ex-husband Sonny **Bono***

Konstantin Chernenko 1911-85
Soviet politician, Premier 1984-85

Those who try to give us advice on matters of human rights do nothing but provoke an ironic smile among us. We will not permit anyone to interfere in our affairs.

Lord Chesterfield 1694-1773
English writer and politician

Women, then, are only children of a larger growth: they have an entertaining tattle, and sometimes wit; but for solid, reasoning good sense, I never knew in my life one that had it, or who reasoned or acted consequentially for four and twenty hours together.
   letter, 5 September 1748

I could not help reflecting in my way upon the singular ill-luck of this my dear country, which, as long as ever I remember it, and as far back as I have read, has always been governed by the only two or three people, out of two or three millions, totally incapable of governing, and unfit to be trusted.
   in *The World* 7 October 1756

G. K. Chesterton 1874-1936
English writer, journalist, philosopher, poet, biographer

The prime truth of woman, the universal mother . . . that if a thing is worth doing, it is worth doing badly.
   What's Wrong With The World? (1910) 'Folly and Female Education'

Tradition means giving votes to the most obscure of classes, our ancestors. It is the democracy of the dead. Tradition refuses to submit to the small and arrogant oligarchy of those who merely happen to be walking about.
   Orthodoxy (1908)

'My country, right or wrong' is a thing no patriot would ever think of saying except in a desperate case. It is like saying, 'My mother, drunk or sober.'
   The Defendant (1901)

For the great Gaels of Ireland
Are the men that God made mad,
For all their wars are merry,
And all their songs are sad.
   The Ballad of the White Horse (1911)

Lancashire merchants whenever they like
Can water the beer of a man in Klondike
Or poison the meat of a man in Bombay;
And that is the meaning of Empire Day.
  'Songs of Education: II Geography' (1922)

They have given us into the hand of new unhappy lords,
Lord without anger and honour, who dare not carry their swords.
They fight by shuffling papers; they have bright dead alien eyes;
They look at our labour and laughter as a tired man looks at flies.
  'The Secret People' (1915)

Democracy means government by the uneducated, while aristocracy means government by the badly educated.
  in *New York Times* 1 February 1931

The whole modern world has divided itself into Conservatives and Progressives. The business of Progressives is to go on making mistakes. The business of the Conservatives is to prevent the mistakes from being corrected.

You can never have a revolution to establish a democracy. You must have a democracy in order to have a revolution.

When men cease to believe in God, they will not believe in nothing, they will believe in anything.

Christianity has not been tried and found wanting: it has been found difficult and not tried.

I owe my success to having listened respectfully to the very best advice, and then going away and doing the exact opposite.

To have a right to do a thing is not at all the same as to be right in doing it.

Jacques Chirac 1932-
French statesman, Prime Minister 1974-1976 and 1986-1988, President 1995-2007

You have been very rude, and I have never been spoken to like this before.
  to **Tony Blair** at the EU enlargement summit in Brussels
  in *Guardian* online 29 October 2002

Frank Chodorov 1887-1966
American economic and writer

When people say 'let's do something about it,' they mean 'let's get hold of the political machinery so that we can do something to somebody else.' And that somebody else is invariably you.
  Freedom is Better (1949)

The only way to a world society is through free trade.
  One Worldism (1950)

Jean Chrétien 1934-
Canadian Liberal statesman; Prime Minister 1993-2003

What kind of a proof? A proof is a proof. And when you have a good proof, it's because it's proven.

asked about the kind of proof he needed to be convinced that Iraq had weapons of mass destruction
   interview on CBC News, 6 September 2002

Agatha Christie 1890-1976
English crime writer of novels, short stories and plays

Where large sums of money are concerned, it is advisable to trust nobody.

Clementine Churchill 1885-1977
British wife of Winston Churchill

Winston . . . has the supreme quality which I venture to say very few of your present or future Cabinet possess, the power, the imagination, the deadliness to fight Germany.
   letter to Asquith on Winston Churchill's dismissal from the Admiralty, May 1915
   Martin Gilbert *In Search of Churchill* (1994)

Randolph Churchill 1911-68
English journalist and politician

I expect you know my friend, Evelyn Waugh, who, like you, your holiness, is a Roman Catholic.
   during an audience with the Pope

Lady Randolph Churchill 1854-1921
née Jennie Jerome, wife of Lord Randolph Churchill and mother of British Prime Minister Winston Churchill

We owe something to extravagance, for thrift and adventure seldom go hand in hand.

Sir Winston Churchill 1874-1965
British Conservative politician, Prime Minister 1940-45, 1951-55, soldier, painter

To be conservative at 20 is heartless and to be a liberal at 60 is plain idiocy.

You can always trust the Americans. In the end they will do the right thing, after they have eliminated all the other possibilities.

Who will relieve me of this Wuthering Height?
of Cripps at dinner
   quoted in Leslie Frewin *Immortal Jester* (1973)

He is one of those orators of whom it was well said, 'Before they get up they do not know what they are going to say; when they are speaking they do not know what they are saying; and when they have sat down they do not know what they have said.'
on Lord Charles Beresford
   speech in the House of Commons, 20 December 1912

The difference between him and Arthur is that Arthur is wicked and moral, Asquith is good and immoral.
comparing H. H. Asquith with Arthur Balfour
   E. T. Raymond *Mr Balfour* (1920)

It drives on with a courage which is stronger than the storm. It drives on with a mercy which does not quail in the presence of death. It drives on as proof, a symbol, a testimony that man is created in the image of God and that valour and virtue have not perished in the English race.

speaking at the centenary of the Royal National Lifeboat Institution, 1924

Anyone can rat, but it takes a certain amount of ingenuity to re-rat.
on rejoining the Conservatives twenty years after leaving them for the Liberals, c.1924
Kay Halle *Irrepressible Churchill*

Mr **Gladstone** read Homer for fun, which I thought served him right.
My Early Life (1930)

I remember when I was a child, being taken to the celebrated Barnum's circus, which contained an exhibition of freaks and monstrosities, but the exhibit on the programme which I most desired to see was the one described as 'The Boneless Wonder'. My parents judged that that spectacle would be too revolting and demoralizing for my youthful eyes, and I have waited 50 years to see the boneless wonder sitting on the Treasury Bench.
*of Ramsay **MacDonald***
speech in the House of Commons, 28 January 1931

I do not like elections, but it is in many elections that I have learnt to know and honour the people of this island. They are good through and through.
Thoughts and Adventures (1932)

Virtuous motives, trammelled by inertia and timidity, are no match for armed and resolute wickedness. A sincere love of peace is no excuse for muddling hundreds of millions of humble folk into total war. The cheers of the weak, well-meaning assemblies soon cease to count. Doom marches on.
demanding British re-armament, March 1936

The Government go on in strange paradox, decided only to be undecided, resolved to be irresolute, adamant for drift, solid for fluidity, all-powerful to be impotent.
in the House of Commons, 12 November 1936

There is not much collective security in a flock of sheep on the way to the butcher.
speech at the New Commonwealth Society luncheon, Dorchester Hotel, 25 November 1936

Dictators ride to and fro upon tigers which they dare not dismount. And the tigers are getting hungry.
letter, 11 November 1937

I would say to the House, as I said to those who have joined this Government: 'I have nothing to offer but blood, toil, tears, and sweat.'

I cannot forecast to you the action of Russia. It is a riddle wrapped in a mystery inside an enigma.
radio broadcast, 1 October 1939

You ask, what is our policy? I will say: It is to wage war, by sea, land and air, with all our might and with all the strength that God can give us: to wage war against a monstrous tyranny, never surpassed in the dark lamentable catalogue of human crime. That is our policy. You ask, What is our aim? I can answer with one word: Victory – victory at all costs, victory in spite of all terror, victory however long and hard the road may be; for without victory there is no survival.
in his first address as the newly appointed Prime Minister, 1940

What General Weygand called the 'Battle of France' is over. I expect that the Battle of Britain is about to begin. Upon this battle depends the survival of Christian civilisation. Upon it depends our own British life and the long continuity of our institutions and our Empire. The whole fury and

might of the enemy must very soon be turned on us. Hitler knows that he will have to break us in this island or lose the war. If we can stand up to him all Europe may be free and the life of the world may move forward into broad, sunlit uplands; but if we fail then the whole world, including the United States, and all that we have known and cared for, will sink into the abyss of a new dark age made more sinister, and perhaps more prolonged, by the lights of a perverted science. Let us therefore brace ourselves to our duty, and so bear ourselves that, if the British Empire and its Commonwealth lasts for a thousand years, men will still say, 'This was their finest hour.'
   speech in the House of Commons, 18 June 1940

The people of London with one voice would say to Hitler: 'You have committed every crime under the sun . . . We will have no truce or parley with you, or the grisly gang who work your wicked will. You do your worst – and we will do our best.
   speech at County Hall, London, 14 July 1941

Never give in – never, never, never, never, in nothing great or small, large or petty, never give in except to convictions of honour and good sense. Never yield to force; never yield to the apparently overwhelming might of the enemy.

Here is the answer which I will give to President **Roosevelt** . . . We shall not fail or falter; we shall not weaken or tire. Neither the sudden shock of battle nor the long-drawn trials of vigilance and exertion will wear us down. Give us the tools and we will finish the job.

We shall defend our island, whatever the cost may be, we shall fight on the beaches, we shall fight on the landing grounds, we shall fight in the fields and in the streets, we shall fight in the hills; we shall never surrender.

Never in the history of mankind have so many owed so much to so few.
referring to Royal Air Force pilots

What kind of people do they think we are, do they think we will be bowed by their tyranny?
speaking of the Japanese invasion of British colonies in SE Asia

He looked like a female llama surprised in her bath.
*on Charles **de Gaulle***

Why should I accept the Order of the Garter from His Majesty when the people have just given me the order of the boot?
   after the General Election of 1945
   D. Bardens *Churchill in Parliament* (1967)

Unless the right hon. gentleman changes his policy and methods and moves without the slightest delay, he will be as great a curse to this country in time of peace, as he was a squalid nuisance in time of war.
*of Aneurin **Bevan***
   speech in the House of Commons, 6 December 1945

He occasionally stumbles over the truth, but he always hastily picks himself up and hurries on as if nothing has happened.
*on Stanley **Baldwin***

He has all of the virtues I dislike and none of the vices I admire.
*on Sir Stafford **Cripps***

As far as I can see, you have used every cliché except 'God is love' and 'Please adjust your dress before leaving'.
*on a long-winded memorandum by Anthony **Eden***

LADY ASTOR: Mr Churchill, you are drunk!
WINSTON CHURCHILL: Yes, and you Madam, are ugly. But tomorrow I shall be sober.

LADY ASTOR: If you were my husband, Winston, I'd put poison in your tea.
WINSTON CHURCHILL: If you were my wife, Nancy, I'd drink it.

It would be a great reform in politics if wisdom could be made to spread as easily and rapidly as folly.
speech at the Guildhall, London, 10 September 1947

This is the sort of English up with which I will not put.
after an official had gone through one of his papers moving prepositions away from the ends of sentences
Ernest Gowers *Plain Words* (1948) 'Troubles with Prepositions'

I do not suffer from any desire to be relieved of my responsibilities. All I wanted was compliance with my wishes after reasonable discussion.
The Second World War (1951)

In defeat unbeatable, in victory unbearable.
*of Lord **Montgomery***
Edward Marsh *Ambrosia and Small Beer* (1964)

So do many people – to begin with. It is, however, a prejudice that many have been able to overcome.
in reply to his wife's remark, 'I hate the taste of beer.'

Are you insinuating that I am a purveyor of terminological inexactitudes?
responding to a journalist

I should think it hardly possible to state the opposite of the truth with more precision.
*squashing a critic (Aneurin **Bevan**) in the House of Commons by replying thus to one of his questions*

The Prime Minister has nothing to hide from the President of the United States.
*on stepping from his bath in the presence of a startled President **Roosevelt***
as recalled by Roosevelt's son in *Churchill* (BBC television series presented by Martin Gilbert, 1992)

I wish Stanley Baldwin no ill, but it would have been much better if he had never lived.
*on being asked to send **Baldwin** an 80th birthday tribute*
Martin Gilbert *In Search of Churchill* (1994)

An empty taxi arrived at 10 Downing Street, and when the door was opened **Attlee** got out.

MacDonald has the gift of compressing the largest amount of words into the smallest amount of thoughts.

All great things are simple, and many can be expressed in single words: freedom, justice, honour, duty, mercy, hope.

A pessimist sees the difficulty in every opportunity; an optimist sees the opportunity in every difficulty.

Kites rise highest against the wind, not with it.

Success is never final.

The British nation is unique in this respect. They are the only people who like to be told how bad things are, who like to be told the worst.

The inherent vice of capitalism is the unequal sharing of blessings. The inherent virtue of socialism is the equal sharing of misery.

One ought never to turn one's back on a threatened danger and try to run away from it. If you do that, you will double the danger. But if you meet it promptly and without flinching, you will reduce the danger by half.

Broadly speaking, the short words are the best, and the old words best of all.

Success is the ability to go from one failure to another with no loss of enthusiasm.

An appeaser is one who feeds a crocodile, hoping it will eat him last.

A politician needs the ability to foretell what is going to happen tomorrow, next week, next month, and next year. And to have the ability afterwards to explain why it didn't happen.

It helps to write down half a dozen things which are worrying me. Two of them, say, disappear; about two, nothing can be done, so it's no use worrying, and two perhaps can be settled.

My wife and I tried to breakfast together, but we had to stop or our marriage would have been wrecked.

I like pigs. Dogs look up to us. Cats look down on us. Pigs treat us as equals.

Everybody said I was the worst Chancellor of the Exchequer there ever was. And I am inclined to agree with them.

I gather, young man, that you wish to be a Member of Parliament. The first lesson that you must learn is, when I call for statistics about the rate of infant mortality, what I want is proof that fewer babies died when I was Prime Minister than when anyone else was Prime Minister. That is a political statistic.

I have always felt that a politician is to be judged by the animosities he excites among his opponents.

However beautiful the strategy, you should occasionally look at the results.
When the eagles are silent, the parrots begin to jabber.

When I am abroad I always make it a rule never to attack the government of my country. I make up for lost time when I come home.

Golf is a game whose aim is to hit a very small ball into an even smaller hole, with weapons singularly ill-designed for the purpose.

When I was younger, I made it a rule never to take a strong drink before lunch. It is now my rule never to do so before breakfast.

I have taken more out of alcohol than alcohol has taken out of me.

It is a good thing for an uneducated man to read books of quotations. Bartlett's *Familiar Quotations* is an admirable work, and I studied it intently. The quotations when engraved upon the memory give you good thoughts. They also make you anxious to read the authors and look for more.

A communist is like a crocodile. When it opens its mouth you can't tell whether it's trying to smile or preparing to eat you up.

We make a living by what we get, we make a life by what we give.

I am not a pillar of the church but a buttress – I support it from the outside.

If you have ten thousand regulations you destroy all respect for the law.
attributed

Don't talk to me about naval tradition. It's nothing but rum, sodomy and the lash.
attributed

Black dog is back again.
of his recurring depression
attributed

They say he can't hear either.
an MP observed Churchill as a very old man paying one of his infrequent visits to the House of Commons and remarked, 'After all, they say he's potty', which resulted in the above muttered reply

Dead birds don't fall out of nests.
after being advised in old age that his flies were undone

I am prepared to meet my Maker. Whether my Maker is prepared for the great ordeal of meeting me is another matter.
shortly before he died

Count Galeazzo Ciano 1903-44
Italian fascist politician, son-in-law of **Mussolini**

Victory has a hundred fathers, but defeat is an orphan.
diary, 9 September 1942

John Ciardi 1916-86
American poet, translator, and etymologist

The Constitution gives every American the inalienable right to make a damn fool of himself.

Alan Clark 1928-99
British Conservative politician, son of Kenneth **Clark**

Like most Chief Whips he knew who the shits were.
of Michael Jopling
diary, 17 June 1987

If I can comport myself with the dignity and competence of Ms Mo **Mowlem**, I shall be very satisfied.
after surgery for a brain tumour
 in *Sunday Times* 6 June 1999 'Talking Heads'

A *deux* he is delightful, clever, funny, observant, dryly cynical. But get him any where on 'display mode' and he might as well have a corncob up his arse.
*on Douglas **Hurd***

Our old friend economical . . . with the *actualité*
under cross-examination at the Old Bailey during the Matrix Churchill case
 in *Independent* 10 November 1992

Everyone in public life should be arrested at least once.

I have so many skeletons in my cupboard I can hardly shut the door.

There are three things in this world you can do nothing about: getting AIDS, getting clamped and running out of Château Lafite 45.

There's nothing that improves the mood of the party as the imminent execution of a senior colleague.

There are no true friends in politics. We're all sharks, circling and waiting for traces of blood to appear in the water.

Sir Arthur C. Clarke 1917-2008
English science fiction writer

I don't believe in astrology; I'm a Sagittarian and we're sceptical.

Blake Clark 1946-
American stand-up comedian and actor

Being in the army is like being in the Boy Scouts, except that the Boy Scouts have adult supervision.

Kenneth Clarke 1940-
British Conservative politician

Every Labour government in my lifetime has run out of money.
in *Guardian* 25 April 2005

Gordon **Brown** bases his politics on the Dolly **Parton** School of Economics – an unbelievable figure blown out of all proportion, with no visible means of support.

I do not wear a bleeper. I can't speak in soundbites. I refuse to repeat slogans . . . I hate focus groups. I absolutely hate image consultants.

John Clark Ridpath 1840-1900
American educator, historian and editor

Mankind have been organized to death. The social, political and ecclesiastical forms which have been instituted have become so hard and cold and obdurate that the life, the emotion, the soul within, has been well-nigh extinguished.
History of the World (1890)

Henry Clay 1777-1852
American politician

I am for resistance by the *sword*. No man in the nation desires peace more than I. But I prefer the troubled ocean of war . . . to the tranquil, putrescent pool of ignominious peace.
speech in the US Senate on the Macon Bill, 22 February 1810

The arts of power and its minions are the same in all countries and in all ages. It marks a victim; denounces it; and excites the public odium and the public hatred, to conceal its own abuses and encroachments.
speech in Norfolk, Virginia, 22 April 1844

Adam Clayton Powell Jr. 1908-72
American politician and pastor

Unless man is committed to the belief that all mankind are his brothers, then he labors in vain and hypocritically in the vineyards of equality.
Black Power: A Form of Godly Power (1967)

John Cleese 1939-
English actor, comedian, writer and film producer

If life were fair, Dan **Quayle** would be making a living asking, 'Do you want fries with that?'

Georges Clemenceau 1841-1929
French statesman, physician, journalist, Prime Minister of France 1906-09, 1917-20

My home policy: I wage war; my foreign policy: I wage war. All the time I wage war.
speech to French Chamber of Deputies, 8 March 1918

What do you expect when I'm between two men of whom one [**Lloyd George**] thinks he is **Napoléon** and the other [**Woodrow Wilson**] thinks he is Jesus Christ?
*to André Tardieu, on being asked why he always gave in to **Lloyd George** at the Paris Peace Conference, 1918*
Harold **Nicolson** letter, 20 May 1919

Oh, to be seventy again!
on seeing a pretty girl on his eightieth birthday
James Agate diary, 19 April 1938; has also been attributed to Oliver **Wendell Holmes Jr.**

Not to be a socialist at twenty is proof of want of heart; to be one at thirty is proof of want of head.
attributed François Guizot

Grover Cleveland 1837-1908
American Democratic statesman, 22nd and 24th President of the US 1885-89 and 1893-97

The lessons of paternalism ought to be unlearned and the better lesson taught that, while the people should patriotically and cheerfully support their government, its functions do not include the support of the people.
  inaugural address, 4 March 1893

William Jefferson ('Bill') Clinton 1946-
American Democratic politician, 42nd President of the United States 1993-2001

No wonder Americans hate politics when, year in and year out, they hear politicians make promises that won't come true because they don't even mean them – campaign fantasies that win elections, but don't get nations moving again.
  speech to the Detroit Economic Club, 21 August 1992

The urgent question of our time is whether we can make change our friend and not our enemy.
  inaugural address, 1993

I did not have sexual relations with that woman.
on his relationship with Monica Lewinsky
  in a television interview, *Daily Telegraph* (electronic edition), 27 January 1998

I did have a relationship with Ms Lewinsky that was not appropriate. In fact, it was wrong.
  broadcast to the American people, 18 August 1998
  in *Times* 19 August 1998

It depends on what the meaning of 'is' is.
  videotaped evidence to the grand jury; tapes broadcast 21 September 1998
  in *Guardian* 22 September 1998

The American people have spoken – but it's going to take a little while to determine exactly what they said.
on the US presidential election
  in *Mail on Sunday* 12 November 2000

I tried to walk a fine line between acting lawfully and testifying falsely but I now recognize that I did not fully accomplish that goal.
  in *Daily Telegraph* 20 January 2001

I think I did something for the worst possible reason – just because I could.
on his relationship with Monica Lewinsky
  in *Sunday Times* 20 June 2004

When I was in England I experimented with marijuana a time or two and I didn't like it and didn't inhale and never tried it again.

There is nothing wrong with America that cannot be cured by what is right with America.

Lord Clive 1725-74
British general; Governor of Bengal

I feel that I am reserved for some end or other.
while attempting to take his own life, his pistol twice failed to fire

G. R. Gleig *The Life of Robert, First Lord Clive* (1848)

Arthur Hugh Clough 1819-61
British poet

Thou shalt not covet; but tradition
Approves all forms of competition.
'The Latest Decalogue' (1862)

Jacqueline Cochran 1910-80
American aviatrix

I have found adventure in flying, in world travel, in business, and even close at hand . . . Adventure is a state of mind – and spirit.

Sir Barnett Cocks 1907-89
English parliamentary official

A committee is a cul de sac down which ideas are lured and then quietly strangled.

Leonard Cohen 1934-
Canadian singer and writer

I don't consider myself a pessimist. I think of a pessimist as someone who is waiting for it to rain. And I feel soaked to the skin.
in *Observer* 2 May 1993

Al Cohn 1925-88
American saxophonist

A gentleman is a man who knows how to play the accordion, but doesn't.
attributed remark

Jean-Baptiste Colbert 1619-83
French minister of finance under King Louis XIV

The art of taxation consists in so plucking the goose as to obtain the largest possible amount of feathers with the smallest amount of hissing.

Vernon Coleman 1946-
English author, formerly a general practitioner

Gordon Brown's term as Chancellor will be remembered for poor decisions, prejudice, and Soviet-style attempts at social engineering. His stupidity and incompetence have weakened Britain for generations to come. No one has done more damage to the nation for half a century. If you share my horror at the lowering of quality and standards in public life you will, I suspect, also share my belief that no one exemplifies the lowering more dramatically than Gordon the Moron. What have we done to deserve public servants such as Brown? It must have been something pretty terrible.
Gordon is a Moron (The Definitive and Objective Analysis of Gordon Brown's Decade as Chancellor of the Exchequer) (2007).

From Mr. Coleman's website, www.vernoncoleman.com:

Vernon Coleman, born in Walsall, Staffordshire, England, is balding and widely disliked by members of the Establishment. He doesn't give a toss about either of these facts. He is married to Donna Antoinette, the totally adorable Welsh Princess, and is very pleased about this.

Richard Law, Lord Coleraine 1901-80
British writer, son of Andrew Bonar Law

When all is said, the floating vote lives up to its name. It floats with the tide; and whoever would influence it must first influence the tide.
For Conservatives Only (1970)

Samuel Taylor Coleridge 1772-1834
English poet, critic and philosopher

He who begins by loving Christianity better than truth, will proceed by loving his own sect or church better than Christianity, and end in loving himself better than all.
Aids to Reflection (1825)

State policy, a cyclops with one eye, and that in the back of the head!
On the Constitution of the Church and State (1839)

In politics, what begins in fear usually ends in folly.
Table Talk (1835) 5 October 1830

Advice is like snow; the softer it falls, the longer it dwells upon, and the deeper it sinks into, the mind.

Colette 1873-1954
French novelist

Don't eat too many almonds; they add weight to the breasts.
Gigi (1944)

Joan Collins 1933-
English actress and authoress

I've never yet met a man who could look after me. I don't need a husband. What I need is a wife.
in *Sunday Times* 27 December 1987

Mortimer Collins 1827-76
English writer

A man is as old as he's feeling, a woman as old as she looks.
The Unknown Quantity

John Robert Colombo 1936-
Canadian writer

Canada could have enjoyed:
English government,
French culture,

And American know-how.
Instead it ended up with:
English know-how,
French government,
And American culture.
> *The New Romans* (1968) ed. Al Purdy 'O Canada'

Charles Caleb Colton 1780-1832
English cleric, writer, collector and eccentric

There are two modes of establishing our reputation: to be praised by honest men, and to be abused by rogues. It is best, however, to secure the former, because it will invariably be accompanied by the latter.

Confucius 551-479 BC
Chinese thinker and social philosopher

Do not be desirous of having things done quickly. Do not look at small advantages. Desire to have things done quickly prevents their being done thoroughly. Looking at small advantages prevents great affairs from being accomplished.

The man who in view of gain thinks of righteousness; who in the view of danger is prepared to give up his life; and who does not forget an old agreement however far back it extends – such a man may be reckoned a complete man.

The superior man, when resting in safety, does not forget that danger may come. When in a state of security he does not forget the possibility of ruin. When all is orderly, he does not forget that disorder may come. Thus his person is not endangered, and his States and all their clans are preserved.

To see what is right, and not to do it, is want of courage or of principle.

William Congreve 1670-1729
English playwright

Courtship is to marriage, as a very witty prologue to a very dull play.
> *The Old Bachelor* (1693)

This grief still treads upon the heels of pleasure;
Married in haste, we may repent at leisure.
> *The Old Bachelor* (1693)

These articles subscrib'd, if I continue to endure you a little longer, I may by degrees dwindle into a wife.
> *The Way of the World* (1700)

I nauseate walking; 'tis a country diversion; I loathe the country.
> *The Way of the World* (1700)

All ambitions are lawful except those which climb upward on the miseries or credulities of mankind.

Billy Connolly 1942-
Scottish comedian, musician, presenter, actor

I don't want a Stormont. I don't want a wee pretendy government in Edinburgh.
on the prospective Scottish Parliament; interview on *Breakfast with Frost* (BBC TV), 9 February 1997

This is my second doctorate. I read that David Attenborough has 29, but I think two will do me.
receiving an honorary degree from the Royal Scottish Academy of Music and Drama
in *Sunday Times* (online edition) 24 December 2006

Hypocrisy is the vaseline of political intercourse.
ABC's *Head Of The Class*

Marriage is a wonderful invention; but, then again, so is a bicycle repair kit.
Duncan Campbell *Billy Connolly* (1976)

Don't vote for politicians. It just encourages them.

When you're involved in a major car accident, why does someone always ask, 'Are you alright?' Maybe so you can say, 'Yes, fine thanks, I'll just pick up my limbs and be off.'

Cyril Connolly 1903-74
English intellectual, literary critic and author

Sheep with a nasty side.
on the British

Shirley Conran 1932-
British designer and journalist

Life is too short to stuff a mushroom.
Superwoman (1975)

Peter Cook 1937-95
British satirist and performer

I have recently been travelling round the world – on your behalf, and at your expense – visiting some of the chaps with whom I hope to be shaping your future. I went first to Germany, and there I spoke with the German Foreign Minister, Herr ... Herr and there, and we exchanged many frank words in our respective languages.
sketch satirising the Prime Minister, Harold **Macmillan**
Beyond The Fringe (1961)

Robin Cook 1946-2005
British Labour politician

Our foreign policy must have an ethical dimension and must support the demands of other people for the democratic rights on which we insist for ourselves.
mission statement by the New Foreign Secretary, 12 May 1997
in *Times* 13 May 1997

Why is it now so urgent that we should take military action to disarm a military capacity that has been there for 20 years, and which we helped to create?

resigning from the government over Iraq
speech in the House of Commons, 17 March 2003

New Labour is so programmed to appeal to floating voters that it has forgotten the language with which to appeal to its core voters.
in *Guardian* 8 April 2005

Alistair Cooke 1908-2004
English-born American journalist and broadcaster

There are some things in every country that you must be born to endure; and another hundred years of general satisfaction with Americans and America could not reconcile this expatriate to cranberry sauce, peanut butter and drum majorettes.
quoted in *The Observer* 5 September 1999

Calvin Coolidge 1872-1933
Lawyer, Republican Party politician, 30th President of the United States 1923-29

'Sins,' he said. 'Well, what did he say about sin?' 'He was against it.'
when asked by Mrs Coolidge what a sermon had been about
John H McKee *Coolidge: Wit and Wisdom* (1933)

There is no right to strike against the public safety by anybody, anywhere, any time.
telegram to Samuel Gompers, 14 September 1919

Civilization and profits go hand in hand.
speech in New York, 27 November 1920

The man has offered me unsolicited advice for six years, all of it bad.
*in 1928, when asked to support the Presidential nomination of his eventual successor, Herbert **Hoover***
Donald R McCoy *Calvin Coolidge: the Quiet President* (1967)

Nothing in the world can take the place of Persistence. Talent will not; nothing is more common than unsuccessful men with talent. Genius will not; unrewarded genius is almost a proverb. Education will not; the world is full of educated derelicts. Persistence and determination alone are omnipotent. The slogan 'Press On' has solved and always will solve the problems of the human race.

I have found it advisable not to give too much heed to what people say when I am trying to accomplish something of consequence. Invariably they proclaim it can't be done. I deem that the very best time to make the effort.

The chief business of the America people is business.

Nothing is easier than spending the public money. It does not appear to belong to anybody. The temptation is overwhelming to bestow it on somebody.
attributed

Alice Cooper 1948-
American rock singer

The hippies wanted peace and love. We wanted Ferraris, blondes and switchblades.
in *Independent* 5 May 2001

I am past writing angst songs for kids. My angst is when I can't get my Porsche's roof up and when I can't get my golf handicap down.
in *Times* 27 October 2001

Jilly Cooper 1937-
English author

The male is a domestic animal which, if treated with firmness and kindness, can be trained to do most things.
Men and Supermen (1972)

Do you really feel, Clemency, m'dear, that it's worth leaving a tolerant husband, three lovely children and nine hundred acres for the sake of six inches of angry gristle?
Polo (1991)

Tommy Cooper 1921-84
British prop comedian and magician

I fell off the roof the other day. The insurance man told me the accident policy covered falling off the roof, but didn't cover hitting the ground.

I recently started on the whisky diet and it's working like a treat. I've already lost four days.

My wife and I were married in the toilet. It was a marriage of convenience.

Last night I dreamt I ate a ten-pound marshmallow. When I woke up the pillow was gone.

Bill Cosby 1937-
American comedian, actor, author, television producer, musician and activist

A word to the wise ain't necessary – it's the stupid ones who need the advice.

Alan Corenk

Democracy consists of choosing your dictators, after they've told you what you think it is you want to hear.

Simon Cotter
Canadian comedian

Apparently bears are attracted to women in their menstrual cycles. A 1,000lb grizzly against a 120lb woman with cramps. I say fair fight.

Sir Noël Coward 1899-1973
English entertainer and writer

I've sometimes thought of marrying, and then I've thought again.

Very flat, Norfolk.
Private Lives (1930) Act 1

Certain women should be struck regularly, like gongs.
Private Lives (1930)

I can take any amount of criticism, so long as it is unqualified praise.
quoted in Laurence J Peter, *Quotations for Our Time* (1977)

Mad dogs and Englishmen
Go out in the midday sun
The Japanese don't care to,
The Chinese wouldn't dare to,
The Hindus and Argentines sleep firmly from twelve to one,
But Englishmen detest a siesta.
'Mad Dogs and Englishmen' (1931 song)

The stately homes of England
How beautiful they stand
To prove the upper classes
Have still the upper hand.
'The Stately Homes of England' (song) in *Operette* (1937)

There are bad times just around the corner,
There are dark clouds travelling through the sky
And it's no good whining
About a silver lining
For we know from experience that they won't roll by.
'There are Bad Times just Around the Corner' (1953 song)

If you'd been any prettier it would have been 'Florence of Arabia.'
to Peter O'Toole on *Laurence of Arabia* (1962)

My dear boy, forget about the motivation. Just say the lines and don't trip over the furniture.
advice to a theatre actor

For God's sake, go and tell that young man to take the Rockingham tea service out of his tights.
to choreographer about male dancer with unsightly bulge

The food was so abominable that I used to cross myself before taking a mouthful . . . I used to say, 'Ian, it tastes like armpits.'
of Ian Fleming's hospitality

She couldn't get a laugh if she pulled a kipper out of her cunt.
of an actress unable to elicit comedy from his lines

I don't see why not; everyone else has.
passing a Leicester Square movie poster which proclaimed 'Michael Redgrave and Dirk Bogarde in *The Sea Shall Not Have Them*'

Doesn't everyone?
when asked why he drank champagne for breakfast

I suppose they'll give you custody of the Daimler?

I was delighted to see that you thought I was as good as I thought I was.

Michel Guillaume Jean de Crèvecoeur 1735-1813
French-born immigrant to America

What then is this American, this new man? He is either a European, or the descendent of a European, hence that strange mixture of blood, which you will find in no other country. Here individuals of all nations are melted into a new race of men, whose labours and posterity will one day cause great changes in the world.
Letters from an American Farmer (1782)

Ivor Crewe 1945-
British political scientist

The British public has always displayed a healthy cynicism of MPs. They have taken it for granted that MPs are self-serving imposters and hypocrites who put party before country and self before party.
addressing the Nolan inquiry into standards in public life
in *Guardian* 18 January 1995

Quentin Crisp 1908-1999
English writer and raconteur

I became one of the stately homos of England.
The Naked Civil Servant (1968)

Julian Critchley 1930-2000
British Conservative politician and journalist

He could not see a parapet without ducking beneath it.
of Michael **Heseltine**
Heseltine (1987)

She cannot see an institution without hitting it with her handbag.
on Margaret **Thatcher**

When I was a young man I was told that the two occupational hazards of the Palace of Varieties [Westminster] were alcohol and adultery. The hurroosh that follows the intermittent revelation of the sexual goings-on of an unlucky MP has convinced me that the only safe pleasure for a parliamentarian is a bag of boiled sweets.

I will never forget the '81 - or was it the '82? - honours list.

Humming, Hawing and Hesitation are the three graces of contemporary parliamentary oratory.

Colin Crompton 1931-1985
English stand-up comedian

You've got to get married, haven't you? You can't go through life being happy.
Laugh with the Comedians (1971)

Oliver Cromwell 1599-1658
English solider and statesman; Lord Protector from 1653

You have sat too long here for any good you have been doing. Depart, I say, and let us have done with you. In the name of God, go!
addressing the Rump Parliament, 20 April 1653
  oral tradition quoted by Leo Amery to Neville Chamberlain in the House of Commons, 7 May 1940
  Bulstrode Whitelock *Memorials of the English Affairs* (1732 ed.)

Anthony Crosland 1918-77
British Labour politician, author and socialist theorist, Secretary of State for Education and Science, 1965

If it's the last thing I do, I'm going to destroy every fucking grammar school in England. And Wales, and Northern Ireland.

Total abstinence and a good filing system are not now the right signposts to the socialist Utopia; or at least, if they are, some of us will fall by the wayside.
  The Future of Socialism (1956)

Harold knows best. Harold is a bastard, but he is a genius. He's like Odysseus. Odysseus was a bastard, but he managed to steer the ship between Scylla and Charybdis.
on Harold Wilson
  Susan Crosland *Tony Crosland* (1982)

The party's over.
cutting back central government's support for rates, as Minister of the Environment in the 1970s
  Anthony Sampson *The Changing Anatomy of Britain* (1982)

Paul Crum (Roger Pettiward) 1906-42
English cartoonist

I keep thinking it's Tuesday.
  caption to cartoon of two hippopotami lazing in the water
  drawn anonymously for *Punch* 21 July 1937

Geoffrey Crump 1891-84
English teacher

Their worship's over: God's returned to Heaven,
And stays there till next Sunday at eleven.
'Matins'

Victor Cousin 1792-1867
French philosopher

All men have an equal right to the free development of their faculties; they have an equal right to the impartial protection of the state; but it is not true, it is against all the laws of reason and equity, it is against the eternal nature of things, that the indolent man and the laborious man, the spendthrift and the economist, the imprudent and the wise, should obtain and enjoy an equal amount of goods.

E. E. Cummings 1894-1962
American poet, painter, essayist, author and playwright

Once we believe in ourselves, we can risk curiosity, wonder, spontaneous delight, or any experience that reveals the human spirit.

A politician is an arse upon which everyone has sat except a man.

Edwina Currie 1946-
British Conservative Party politician

I wasn't even in the index.
*taking offence at not being mentioned in John **Major's** autobiography*

The strongest possible piece of advice I would give any young woman is: Don't screw around, and don't smoke.

There's no smoke without mud being flung around.

You know what they say: Don't get mad, get angry.

d

James Dale Davidson
American investment newsletter writer and author, founder and former head of the National Taxpayers Union

The politicians don't just want your money. They want your soul. They want you to be worn down by taxes until you are dependent and helpless. When you subsidize poverty and failure, you get more of both.

Anthony J. D'Angelo

Transcend political correctness and strive for human righteousness.
  The College Blue Book (1995)

If you believe that discrimination exists, it will.

Walther Darre 1895-1953
German Minister of Agriculture under Adolf Hitler

The United States is at present so demoralised and so corrupted that, like England and France, it need not be taken into consideration as a military adversary. The United States will also be forced by Germany to complete and final capitulation.
  quoted in H. R. Knickerbocker's *Is Tomorrow Hitler's?* (1941)

Clarence Darrow 1857-1938
American lawyer, noted defence attorney

I do not consider it to be an insult, but rather a compliment to be called an agnostic. I do not pretend to know where many ignorant men are sure – that is all that agnosticism means.
  speech at trial of John Thomas Scopes for teaching Darwin's theory of evolution in school, 15 July 1925, popularly referred to as the 'Monkey Trial'

Rita Davenport

Money isn't everything, but it ranks right up there with oxygen.

Robertson Davies 1913-95
Canadian novelist, playwright, critic, journalist, and professor

Many a promising career has been wrecked by marrying the wrong sort of woman. The right sort of woman can distinguish between creative lassitude and plain shiftlessness.

Happiness is always a by-product. It is probably a matter of temperament, and for anything I know it may be glandular. But it is not something that can be demanded from life, and if you are not happy you had better stop worrying about it and see what treasures you can pluck from your own brand of unhappiness.

Bette Davis 1908-89
American actress of film, television and theatre

I am doomed to an eternity of compulsive work. No set goal achieved satisfies. Success only breeds a new goal. The golden apple devoured has seeds. It is endless.
The Lonely Life (1962)

It has been my experience that one cannot, in any shape or form, depend on human relations for lasting reward. It is only work that truly satisfies.
The Lonely Life (1962)

She's the original good time that was had by all.
on a starlet

I'd marry again if I found a man who had 15 million dollars and would sign over half of it to me before the marriage, and guarantee that he'd be dead within a year.

Jack Dawson (Leonardo DeCaprio)

I don't know about you, but I intend to write a strongly worded letter to the White Star Line about all this.
Titanic (1997)

Les Dawson 1931-93
English comedian

Last year my wife ran off with the fellow next door and I must admit, I still miss him.

I wouldn't say that my wife is fat. But she's got a fat arse.
The Malady Lingers On (1982)

You could see the dampness rising from the wet raincoats like mist on the marshes.
on playing to matinée audiences at Bridlington

Simone de Beauvoir 1908-86
French novelist and feminist

It is not in giving life but in risking life that man is raised above the animal; that is why superiority has been accorded in humanity not to the sex that brings forth but to that which kills.
The Second Sex (1949)

Eugene Victor Debs 1855-1926
American socialist and labour organiser

When great changes occur in history, when great principles are involved, as a rule the majority are wrong. The minority are right.
speech at his trial for sedition in Cleveland, Ohio, 11 September 1918

W. F. Deedes 1913-
British Conservative politician and journalist

The millennium is going to present us with a very sharp portrait of ourselves: drinking is to continue all night and religious observance, as far as possible, is to be kept at bay.

in *Sunday Times* 15 August 1999

The man who said nobody ever lost money by underrating public taste has been proved wrong.
on the Millennium Dome
  in *Mail on Sunday* 4 June 2000

Daniel Defoe 1660-1731
British, poet and journalist

And of all plagues with which mankind are cursed,
Ecclesiastic tyranny's the worst.
'The True-Born Englishman' (1701)

Charles de Gaulle 1890-1970
French general and statesman who led the Free French Forces (from London) during World War II. Founded the French Fifth Republic in 1958 and served as its first President from 1959 to 1969

The sword is the axis of the world and its power is absolute.
  Vers l'armée de métier (1934) 'Comment?'

Since a politician never believes what he says, he is quite surprised to be taken at his word.
  Ernest Mignon *Les Mots du Général* (1962)

How can you govern a country which has 246 varieties of cheese?
  Ernest Mignon *Les Mots du Général* (1962)

Politics are too serious a matter to be left to the politicians.
*replying to Clement **Attlee**'s remark that 'De Gaulle is a very good soldier and a very bad politician'*
  Clement Attlee *A Prime Minister Remembers* (1961)

And now she is like everyone else.
on the death of his daughter Anne, who had been born with Down's syndrome
  Jean Lacouture *De Gaulle* (1965)

The EEC is a horse and carriage: Germany is the horse and France is the coachman.
  attributed
  Bernard Connolly *The Rotten Heart of Europe* (1995)

I always thought I was Joan of Arc and **Bonaparte** – how little one knows oneself.
*on being compared to **Robespierre***
  quoted in *Figaro Littéraire* (1958)

One does not put Voltaire in the Bastille.
*when asked to arrest **Sartre**, in the 1960s*
  in *Encounter* June 1975

Faced by the bewilderment of my countrymen, by the disintegration of a government in thrall to the enemy, by the fact that the institutions of my country are incapable, at the moment, of functioning, I, General de Gaulle, a French soldier and military leader, realise that I now speak for France.
  speech in London, 19 June 1940

Treaties, you see, are like girls and roses: they last while they last.
  speech at Elysée Palace, 2 July 1963

In order to become the master, the politician poses as the servant.

The perfection preached in the Gospels never yet built up an empire. Every man of action has a strong dose of egotism, pride, hardness, and cunning. But all those things will be forgiven him, indeed, they will be regarded as high qualities, if he can make of them the means to achieve great ends.

Ellen DeGeneres 1958-
American stand-up comedienne, television hostess and actress

People always ask me, 'Were you funny as a child?' Well, no, I was an accountant.

I don't need a baby growing inside me for nine months. For one thing, there's morning sickness. If I'm going to feel nauseous and achy when I wake up, I want to achieve that state the old-fashioned way: getting good and drunk the night before.

The good psychic would pick up the phone before it rang. Of course it is possible there was nobody on the other line. Once she said 'God Bless you.' I said, 'I didn't sneeze.' She looked deep into my eyes and said, 'You will, eventually.' And damn it if she wasn't right. Two days later I sneezed.

Shelagh Delaney 1939-
English dramatist

Women never have young minds. They are born three thousand years old.
   A Taste of Honey (1959)

Floyd Dell 1887-1969
American author, literary critic and actor

There is no human reason why a child should not admire and emulate his teacher's ability to do sums, rather than the village bum's ability to whittle sticks and smoke cigarettes. The reason why the child does not is plain enough – the bum has put himself on an equality with him and the teacher has not.

Ivor Dembina
English socialist comedian

Love and marriage is like a horse and carriage; obsolete for a hundred years.
2003

Edward Stanley, 14th Earl of Derby 1799-1869
British Conservative statesman; Prime Minister 1852, 1858-59, 1866-68

The duty of an opposition is very simple – to oppose everything and propose nothing.
1841

10th Duke of Devonshire 1895-1950
English politician

I dreamt that I was making a speech in the House. I woke up, and by Jove, I was!

A. V. Dicey 1835-1922
British jurist

The beneficial effect of state intervention, especially in the form of legislation, is direct, immediate, and, so to speak, visible, while its evil effects are gradual and indirect, and lie out of sight ... Hence the majority of mankind must almost of necessity look with undue favour upon government intervention.
Lectures on the Relation between Law and Public Opinion (1914)

Philip K. Dick 1928-82
American novelist, short story writer and essayist

The basic tool for the manipulation of reality is the manipulation of words. If you can control the meaning of words, you can control the people who must use the words.
How To Build A Universe That Doesn't Fall Apart Two Days Later (1978)

Charles Dickens 1812-70
English novelist

'It's always best on these occasions to do what the mob do.'
'But suppose there are two mobs?' suggested Mr Snodgrass.
'Shout with the largest,' replied Mr Pickwick.
Pickwick Papers (1837)

When you have seen a man in his nightcap, you lose all respect for him.
Sketches by Boz (1836)

Annual income twenty pounds, annual expenditure nineteen nineteen six, result happiness. Annual income twenty pounds, annual expenditure twenty pounds ought and six, result misery.
David Copperfield (1850)

John Dickinson 1732-1808
American politician

We have counted the cost of this contest, and find nothing so dreadful as voluntary slavery . . . Our cause is just, our union is perfect.
declaration of reasons for taking up arms against England, presented to Congress, 8 July 1775
C. J. Stillé *The Life and Times of John Dickinson* (1891)

Clarissa Theresa Philomena Aileen Mary Josephine Agnes Elsie Trilby Louise Esmerelda Dickson Wright 1947-
English celebrity chef. Trained as a lawyer, she became the youngest woman ever to be called to the Bar

The feminist movement seems to have beaten the manners out of men, but I didn't see them put up a lot of resistance.
Mail on Sunday, 24 September 2000

Phyllis Diller 1917-
American actress and stand-up comedienne

Never go to bed mad. Stay up and fight.

John Dillon 1851-1927
Irish nationalist politician

Women's suffrage will, I believe, be the ruin of our Western civilisation. It will destroy the home, challenging the headship of men laid down by God. It may come in your time – I hope not in mine.
   c.1912, to a deputation led by Hanna **Sheehy Skeffington**
   Diana Norman *Terrible Beauty* (1987)

Chris Dillow

Government is every salesman's dream – an idiot with lots of money.
   Investors Chronicle

Isak Dinesen (Karen Blixen) 1885-1962
Danish novelist and short-story writer

What is man, when you come to think upon him, but a minutely set, ingenious machine for turning, with infinite artfulness, the red wine of Shiraz into urine?
   Seven Gothic Tales (1934) 'The Dreamers'

Everett Dirksen 1896-1969
American Republican politician

A billion here and a billion there, and pretty soon you're talking real money.
on federal spending
   attributed, perhaps apocryphal; in *United States, Senate Historical Minute Essays* (online edition) July 2006

Dirty Harry 1971 film

When a naked man is chasing a woman through an alley with a butcher's knife and a hard-on, I figure he isn't out collecting for the Red Cross.
   spoken by **Harry Callahan** (Clint Eastwood)

Benjamin Disraeli 1804-81
Conservative statesman and author, Prime Minister 1874-80

You know who the critics are? The men who have failed in literature and art.
   Lothair (1870)

My idea of an agreeable person is a person who agrees with me.
   Lothair (1870)

Man is not the creature of circumstances. Circumstances are the creatures of men.
   Vivian Grey (1826)

There is no fascination so irresistible to a boy as the smile of a married woman.
   Vivien Grey (1826)

What we anticipate seldom occurs; what we least expect generally happens.
   Henrietta Temple (1837)

The age of chivalry is past. Bores have succeeded to dragons.
   The Young Duke (1831)

An insular country, subject to fogs, and with a powerful middle class, requires grave statesmen.
  Endymion (1880)

Never complain and never explain.
  J Morley *Life of William Ewart Gladstone* (1903)

You will find as you grow older that courage is the rarest of all qualities to be found in public life.
  to Lady Gwendolen Cecil, telling her that her father Lord Salisbury was the only man of real courage with whom Disraeli had worked
  Lady Gwendolen Cecil *Life of Robert Marquis of Salisbury* (1931)

Increased means and increased leisure are the two civilisers of man.
  speech in Manchester, 3 April 1872
  Selected Speeches of the Late Right Honourable the Earl of Beaconsfield (1882) ed. T. E. Kebbes

I am a Conservative to preserve all that is good in our constitution, a Radical to remove all that is bad. I seek to preserve property and to respect order, and I equally decry the appeal to the passions of the many or the prejudices of the few.
  campaign speech at High Wycombe, England, 27 November 1832

There can be no economy where there is no efficiency.
  address to his constituents, 1 October 1868

Upon the education of the people of this country the fate of this country depends.
  in the House of Commons, 15 June 1874

Potatoes at the moment, Madam.
  to a lady at dinner who wanted action against Russia and asked him what he was waiting for

I have climbed to the top of the greasy pole.
  upon becoming Prime Minister

The right honourable gentleman is reminiscent of a poker. The only difference is that a poker gives off the occasional signs of warmth.
  on Sir Robert Peel

If a traveller were informed that such a man was Leader of the House of Commons, he might begin to comprehend how the Egyptians worshipped an insect.
  on Lord John Russell

A misfortune is if Gladstone fell into the Thames; a calamity would be if somebody pulled him out.
  quantifying disaster

Have you no ambition, man?
  to the Comte d'Orsay who had said he was born French, had lived French, and would die French

She is an excellent creature, but she never can remember which came first, the Greeks or the Romans.
  of his wife, Mary Anne

There are three kinds of lies: lies, damned lies and statistics.
  attributed to Disraeli in Mark Twain *Autobiography* (1924)

The right honourable gentleman's smile is like the silver fittings on a coffin.

Mr Speaker, I withdraw my statement that half the cabinet are asses. Half the cabinet are not asses.

Michael Dobbs 1948-
British writer

You might very well think that, I couldn't possibly comment.
the Chief Whip's habitual response to questioning
House of Cards (as dramatised for television, 1990)

Frank Dobson 1940-
British Labour politician

I trudge the streets rather than trudge the soundbite. I would not know a focus group if I met one. I am unspun.
in *Sunday Times* 27 February 2000

The ego has landed.
*of Ken **Livingstone**'s independent candidacy for Mayor of London*
in *Times* 7 March 2000

When she goes to the dentist, he's the one who needs the anaesthetic.
*on Edwina **Currie***

Ken Dodd 1927-
English comedian and singer-songwriter

What do you mean, this is a long show? My audiences generally go home on milk floats.

Freud's theory was that when a joke opens a window and all those bats and bogeymen fly out, you get a marvellous feeling of relief and elation. The trouble with Freud is that he never played the Glasgow Empire Saturday night after Rangers and Celtic had both lost.
in *Guardian* 30 April 1991

Bob Dole 1923-
American attorney and former Republican Senator

You read what **Disraeli** had to say. I don't remember what he said. He said something. He's no longer with us.

Ignatius Donnelly 1831-1901
American politician

The Democratic Party is like a mule – without pride of ancestry or hope of posterity.
attributed

Don Juan Donoso Cortés

Adoration is so imperative a necessity for man that we find socialists, who are atheists, and as such refusing to adore God, making gods of men, and in this way inventing a new form of adoration.
'An essay on Catholicism, Authority and Order' (1951), translated by M. V. Goddard

John Dos Passos 1896-1970
American novelist and artist

The world is becoming a museum of socialist failures.
Occasions and Protests (1964)

Fyodor Dostoevsky 1821-81
Russian writer, essayist and philosopher

Man is tormented by no greater anxiety than to find someone quickly to whom he can hand over that great gift of freedom with which the ill-fated creature is born.
The Brothers Karamazov (1880)

Mack R. Douglas

The achievement of your goal is assured the moment you commit yourself to it.

Justice William O. Douglas 1898-1980
United States Supreme Court Associate Justice

The right to be let alone is indeed the beginning of all freedom.

Alec Douglas Home, see **Lord Home**

Caroline Douglas Home, see Caroline Douglas Home

Robert Downey Jr. 1965-
American actor, film producer and musician

A self-important, boring, flash-in-the-pan Brit.
on Hugh Grant

Sir Arthur Conan Doyle 1859-1930
Scottish-born novelist

The husband was a teetotaller, there was no other woman, and the conduct complained of was that he had drifted into the habit of winding up every meal by taking out his false teeth and hurling them at his wife.
The Adventures of Sherlock Holmes (1892)

The lowest and vilest alleys of London do not present a more dreadful record of sin than does the smiling and beautiful countryside.
The Adventures of Sherlock Holmes (1892)

Margaret Drabble 1939-
English novelist

England's not a bad country . . . It's just a mean, cold, ugly, divided, tired, clapped-out, post-imperial, post-industrial, slag-heap covered in polystyrene hamburger cartons.
A Natural Curiosity (1989)

Francis Drake c.1540-96
English sailor and explorer

There is plenty of time to win this game, and to thrash the Spaniards too.
   attributed, in *Dictionary of National Biography* (1917-)

The Drew Carey Show American sitcom 1995-2004

Mimi Bobeck (Kathy Kinney)

Find out what she loves most in the world and kill it. That way you'll move up a step.

Dr. Strangelove 1964 film

Clemenceau once said that war is too important to be left to the generals. When he said that, 50 years ago, he may have been right . . . but now, war is too important to be left to the politicians. They have neither the time, the training, nor the inclination for strategic thought . . . And I can no longer sit around and allow Communist subversion, Communist corruption, and Communist infiltration of our precious bodily fluids.
Col Jack Ripper commander of Burpleson AFB to Group Capt. Mandrake (Peter Sellers)

Peter Drucker 1909-2005
American writer, management consultant and self-described 'social ecologist'

Far too many people – especially people with great expertise in one area – are contemptuous of knowledge in other areas or believe that being bright is a substitute for knowledge.
   Harvard Business Review

Hugh Drummond
British aristocrat

Ladies and gentlemen, I give you a toast; it is: Absinthe makes the tart grow fonder.
   quoted in Sir Seymour Hicks, *The Vintage Years* (1943)

John Dryden 1631-1700
English poet, critic, and dramatist

If by the people you understand the multitude, the *hoi polloi*, 'tis no matter what they think; they are sometimes in the right, sometimes in the wrong: their judgment is a mere lottery.
   An Essay of Dramatic Poesy (1668)

Happy the man, and happy he alone,
He who can call today his own;
He who, secure within, can say,
Tomorrow, do thy worst, for I have lived today.
   'Imitation of Horace' (1685)

Great wits are sure to madness near allied
And thin partitions do their bounds divide.

Duck Soup 1933 film with the **Marx Brothers**

MRS TEASDALE [of her husband]:	Why, he's dead.
FIREFLY:	I'll bet he's just using that as an excuse.
MRS TEASDALE:	I was with him to the very end.
FIREFLY:	No wonder he passed away.
MRS TEASDALE:	I held him in my arms and kissed him.
FIREFLY:	So it was murder!

Alan Duncan 1957-
Businessman and Conservative Party politician

Another glass of champagne, please.
> at the Conservative Party's 2009 conference in Manchester Alan Duncan was photographed holding a glass of champagne, in defiance of a general instruction to party politicians and delegates not to appear elitist in the middle of a recession, seven or so months before the next general election, which the Conservative Party were expected to win. The photograph was taken at the *New Statesman* party – it was, allegedly, the only drink on offer – and was published in a number of newspapers the following day

Nobody who has ever done anything useful in life will ever come into this place if they have to live on rations and are treated like shit.
> a comment on how MPs were being treated after the 2009 expenses scandal, covertly recorded by former child actor Heydon Prowse on the balcony of the House of Commons

Isadora Duncan 1878-1927
American dancer

Any intelligent woman who reads the marriage contract and then goes into it, deserves all the consequences.
> *My Life* (1927)

Finley Peter Dunne 1867-1936
American journalist, humorist

Alcohol is nicissary f'r a man so that now an' thin he can have a good opinion iv himsilf, ondisturbed be th' facts.
> *Chicago Tribune* 26 April 1914 'Dooley on Alcohol'

Will Durant 1885-1981
American author, historian and philosopher

It may be true that you can't fool all the people all the time, but you can fool enough of them to rule a large country.

Leo Durocher 1906-91
American baseball coach

Take a look at them. All nice guys. They'll finish last. Nice guys. Finish last.
> *referring to the New York Giants*, 6 July 1946

Will Durst 1952-
American political satirist

Well, we won the war with Iraq, so you know what that means – in forty years, we'll all be driving Iraqi-made automobiles.

Andrea Dworkin 1946-2005
American radical feminist

Marriage as an institution developed from rape as a practice. Rape, originally defined as abduction, became marriage by capture. Marriage meant the taking was to extend in time, to be not only use of but possession of, or ownership.
Pornography (1981)

No woman needs intercourse; few women escape it.
Right-Wing Women (1978)

Bob Dylan 1941-
American singer-songwriter, musician, painter and poet

I try my best to be just like I am,
But everybody wants you to be just like them.
Maggie's Farm (1965)

Ah, but I was so much older then,
I'm younger than that now.
My Back Pages (1964)

What's money? A man is a success if he gets up in the morning and goes to bed at night and in between does what he wants to do.

e

Amelia Earhart 1898-1937
American aviatrix

Would you *mind* if I flew the Atlantic?
    to her husband George **Putnam**; George P. Putnam *Soaring Wings (1939)*

Sir Anthony Eden 1897-1977
British Conservative statesman; Prime Minister 1955-57

We are in armed conflict; that is the phrase I have used. There has been no declaration of war.
on the Suez crisis
    in the House of Commons, 1 November 1956

Everybody is always in favour of general economy and particular expenditure.
    in *Observer* 17 June 1956

We are not at war with Egypt. We are in armed conflict.

Thomas A. Edison 1847-1931
American inventor, scientist and businessman

There is no expedient to which a man will not go to avoid the labor of thinking.

Genius is one percent inspiration, ninety-nine percent perspiration.

King Edward VIII 1894-1972
King of the United Kingdom and the British Dominions and Emperor of India (1901-1910)

The thing that impresses me the most about America is the way parents obey their children.

Bob Edwards 1925-
British journalist and editor

Now I know what a statesman is; he's a dead politician. We need more statesmen.

Eugene Edwards

If by saying that all men are born free and equal, you mean that they are all equally born; it is true, but true in no other sense; birth, talent, labour, virtue, and providence, are forever making differences.

Patrick H. Edwards

People frequently say that so and so 'died doing what they loved.' I hope that when I die it's right before I was about to do something that I hated to do so I could at least avoid doing it one more time.

Clive Egleton 1927-2006
British novelist

Governments and their civil servants are in a different league. When they pull a fast one, the scale of their underhand dealing is breathtaking.
  The Honey Trap

Albert Einstein 1879-1955
German-born theoretical physicist, author

Nationalism is an infantile sickness. It is the measles of the human race.
  Helen Dukas and Banesh Hoffman *Albert Einstein, the Human Side* (1979)

When I was young, I found that the big toe always ends up making a hole in a sock. So I stopped wearing socks.
  to Philippe Halsman; A. P. French *Einstein: A Centenary Volume* (1979)

Great spirits have always found violent opposition from mediocrities. The latter cannot understand it when a man does not thoughtlessly submit to hereditary prejudices, but honestly and courageously uses his intelligence and fulfils the duty to express the results of his thought in clear form.
  New York Times 19 March 1940

If A is a success in life, then A equals x plus y plus z. Work is x; y is play; and z is keeping your mouth shut.
  in *Observer* 15 January 1950

Insanity: doing the same things over and over again and expecting different results.

I feel that you are justified in looking into the future with true assurance, because you have a mode of living in which we find the joy of life and the joy of work harmoniously combined. Added to this is the spirit of ambition which pervades your very being, and seems to make the day's work like a happy child at play.
referring to America

Men marry women with the hope they will never change. Women marry men with the hope they will change. Invariably they are both disappointed.

All of us who are concerned for peace and triumph of reason and justice must be keenly aware how small an influence reason and honest good will exert upon events in the political field.

It is the duty of every citizen according to his best capacities to give validity to his convictions in political affairs.

We should take care not to make the intellect our god; it has, of course, powerful muscles, but no personality.

The hardest thing in the world to understand is income tax.

Too many of us look upon Americans as dollar chasers. This is a cruel libel, even if it is reiterated thoughtlessly by the American themselves.

Dwight D. Eisenhower 1890-1969
American Republican statesman, Five-star general in the United States Army and the 34th President of the United States 1953-61

There is nothing wrong with America that the faith, love of freedom, intelligence and energy of her citizens cannot cure.

Governments are far more stupid than their people.
   attributed 1958

Every gun that is made, every warship launched, every rocket fired signifies, in the final sense, a theft from those who hunger and are not fed, those who are cold and not clothed. This world in arms is not spending money alone. It is spending the sweat of its laborers, the genius of its scientists, the hopes of its children. This is not a way of life at all in any true sense. Under the cloud of threatening war, it is humanity hanging from a cross of iron.
   speech before the American Society of Newspaper Editors, 16 April 1953

William Ellery Channing 1780-1842
American Unitarian preacher

Difficulties are meant to rouse, not discourage. The human spirit is to grow strong by conflict.

George Eliot, pseudonym of Mary Anne Evans 1819-80
English novelist

Keep true, never be ashamed of doing right; decide on what you think is right and stick to it.

An election is coming. Universal peace is declared, and the foxes have a sincere interest in prolonging the lives of the poultry.
   Felix Holt (1866)

Plain women he regarded as he did the other severe facts of life, to be faced with philosophy and investigated by science.
   of Tertius Lydgate *Middlemarch (1871-2)*

T. S. Eliot 1888-1965
American poet, playwright and literary critic

Humankind cannot bear very much reality.
   Four Quartets 'Burnt Norton' (1936)

The professional politician has too much to do to have leisure for serious reading, even on politics. He has far too little time for exchange of ideas and information with men of distinction in other walks of life.
   Notes Towards the Definition of Culture (1948)

The years between fifty and seventy are the hardest. You are always being asked to do things, and yet you are not decrepit enough to turn them down.
   remark, 23 October 1950, quoted in *The Oxford Book of Ages* (1985)

The majority of mankind is lazy-minded, incurious, absorbed in vanities, and tepid in emotion, and is therefore incapable of either much doubt or much faith.
  Pascal's *Pensées* (1931) introduction

Elizabeth I 1533-1603
English monarch, Queen of England and Ireland from 1558

I know I have the body of a weak and feeble woman, but I have the heart and stomach of a king, and of a king of England too; and think foul scorn that Parma or Spain, or any prince of Europe, should dare to invade the borders of my realm.
  speech to the troops at Tilbury on the approach of the Armada, 1588
  Lord Somers *A Third Collection of Scarce and Valuable Tracts* (1751)

Elizabeth II 1926-
British monarch, Queen of the United Kingdom from 1952

I declare before you all that my whole life, whether it be long or short, shall be devoted to your service and the service of our great Imperial family to which we all belong.
  broadcast speech, as Princess Elizabeth, to the Commonwealth from Cape Town, 21 April 1947

Queen Elizabeth, the Queen Mother 1900-2002
British Queen Consort of George VI and mother of Elizabeth II

I'm glad we've been bombed. It makes me feel I can look the East End in the face.
  to a London policeman, 13 September 1940
  John Wheeler-Bennett *King George VI* (1958)

The Princesses would never leave without me and I couldn't leave without the King, and the King will never leave.
on the suggestion that the Royal Family be evacuated during the Blitz
  Penelope Mortimer *Queen Elizabeth* (1986)

Ebenezer Elliott 1781-1849
English poet

What is a communist? One who hath yearnings
For equal division of unequal earnings.
  'Epigram' (1850)

Havelock Ellis 1859-1939
English sexologist

What we call 'progress' is the exchange of one nuisance for another nuisance.
  Impressions and Comments (1914)

Ben Elton 1959-
English comedian, author, playwright and director

Sometimes I wonder if we don't actually prefer things a little crap.
on the British

People who get through life dependent on other people's possessions are always the first to lecture you on how little possessions count.

Stark (1989)

Ralph Waldo Emerson 1803-82
American essayist, philosopher and poet

A foolish consistency is the hobgoblin of little minds, adored by little statesmen and philosophers and divines. With consistency a great soul has simply nothing to do.
Essays: 'Self-Reliance' (1841)

A sect or a party is an elegant incognito, devised to save a man from the vexation of thinking.
Journals (1909-14)

The peril of every fine faculty is the delight of playing with it for pride. Talent is commonly developed at the expense of character, and the greater it grows, the more is the mischief. Talent is mistaken for genius, a dogma or system for truth, ambition for greatest, ingenuity for poetry, sensuality for art.

Whatever you do, you need courage. Whatever course you decide upon, there is always someone to tell you that you are wrong. There are always difficulties arising that tempt you to believe your critics are right. To map out a course of action and follow it to an end requires some of the same courage that a soldier needs. Peace has its victories, but it takes brave men and women to win them.

Truth is the summit of being; justice is the application of it to affairs.

Nothing great was ever achieved without enthusiasm.

The teaching of politics is that the Government, which was set for protection and comfort of all good citizens, becomes the principal obstruction and nuisance with which we have to contend . . . The cheat and bully and malefactor we meet everywhere is the Government.

Whosoever would be a man must be a nonconformist.

None of us will ever accomplish anything excellent or commanding except when he listens to this whisper which is heard by him alone.

Democracy becomes a government of bullies tempered by editors.

Ideas must work through the brains and arms of men, or they are no better than dreams.

Man was born to be rich, or grow rich by use of his faculties, by the union of thought with nature. Property is an intellectual production. The game requires coolness, right reasoning, promptness, and patience in the players. Cultivated labor drives out brute labor.

Misunderstood! It is a right fool's word. Is it so bad then to be misunderstood? Pythagoras was misunderstood, and Socrates, and Jesus, and Luther, and Copernicus, and Galileo, and Newton, and every pure and wise spirit that ever took flesh. To be great is to be misunderstood.

The louder he talked of his honour, the faster we counted our spoons.
The Conduct of Life (1860)

There is always a certain meanness in the argument of conservatism, joined with a certain superiority in its fact.
The Conservative (1849)

Nothing astonishes men so much as common sense and plain dealing.
> *Essays* (1841)

Without ambition one starts nothing. Without work one finishes nothing. The prize will not be sent to you. You have to win it. The man who knows how will always have a job. The man who also knows why will always be his boss. As to methods there may be a million and then some, but principles are few. The man who grasps principles can successfully select his own methods. The man who tries methods, ignoring principles, is sure to have trouble.

Harry Emerson Fosdick 1878-1969
American clergyman

Rebellion against your handicaps gets you nowhere. Self-pity gets you nowhere. One must have the adventurous daring to accept oneself as a bundle of possibilities and undertake the most interesting game in the world – making the most of one's best.

R. Emmett Tyrrell Jr. 1943-
American conservative magazine editor

In fevered depravity the last Liberals ran riot through the 1970s gibbering: consciousness-raising! self-realization! group-therapy! sexuality! human rights! animal rights! water beds! wheat grass enemas! sanitary napkins shaped from genuine sea sponges! . . . This is light years removed from the New Deal.

Friedrich Engels 1820-95
preface to Karl Marx's pamphlet *The Civil War in France* (1872)

The state is nothing but an instrument of oppression of one class by another – no less so in a democratic republic than in a monarchy.

English coach driver to a coachful of passengers, heard by the author in 1987

We are now crossing the Severn Bridge, and will shortly be crossing the border into Wales. Would English passengers please put their watches back 50 years.

Ennius 239-169BC
Roman writer

The Roman state survives by its ancient customs and its manhood.
> *Annals*

Epictetus 55-135AD
Greek Stoic philosopher

The good or ill of a man lies within his own will.

Erasmus c.1469-1536
Dutch Christian humorist

In the country of the blind the one-eyed man is king.
> *Adages*

Ludwig Erhard 1897-1977
German statesman, Chancellor of West Germany 1963-66

Without Britain Europe would remain only a torso.
 remark on W. German television, 27 May 1962
 in *The Times* 28 May 1962

Susan Ertz 1894-1985
American writer

Millions long for immortality who don't know what to do with themselves on a rainy Sunday afternoon.
 Anger in the Sky (1943)

Evan Esar 1899-1995
American humorist

Eloquence is the art of saying as little as possible but making it sound as much as possible.

Think twice before you speak, and then you may be able to say something more insulting than if you spoke right out at once.

Edward Everett 1794-1865
American politician and educator

Education is a better safeguard of liberty than a standing army.

Sam Ewing

The government deficit is the difference between the amount of money the government spends and the amount it has the nerve to collect.

Nothing is as frustrating as arguing with someone who knows what he's talking about.

f

Émile Faguet 1847-1916
French writer and critic

It would be equally correct to say that sheep are born carnivorous, and everywhere they nibble grass.
commenting on Rousseau's 'Man was born free, and everywhere he is in chains'

Henry P. Fairchild 1815-99
American Marxist sociologist

No amount of artificial reinforcement can offset the natural inequalities of human individuals.

Lucius Cary, Lord Falkland 1610-43
English royalist politician

When it is not necessary to change, it is necessary not to change.
Discourses of Infallibility (1660) 'A Speech concerning Episcopacy' delivered in 1641

Family Guy American animated television sitcom 1999-2010

[Editor's note: *Family Guy* is a work of genius, the genius being the American writer Seth **MacFarlane**. The following material is quoted by Brian Griffin, the Martini-quaffing dog who talks with an English accent. Stewie, the malevolent toddler, also speaks with an English accent, reminiscent of Noël Coward.]

Why I Love Dames:

The Way They Smell. Whether it's the subtle hint of Ivory soap on a suburban housewife or the not-so-subtle fragrance of cheap perfume and peach body spray on a Las Vegas stripper, women smell great. Or at least better than men.

Their Boobs. Okay, you got me – I'm a breast dog. I don't know what it is about boobs, and I can't go too far into detail or they won't sell my book at Wal-Mart, but there's nothing like staring at an ample rack while a woman's trying to hold a conversation with you.

The Way a Classy Dame Feels on Your Arm. Although, let's face it, if she's really hot and has nice breasts, you can make certain allowances in the class department.

The Way They Laugh. With the obvious exception of Fran Drescher, a woman's laugh is like music to a man's ears. Especially if she's laughing at an only moderately funny joke, because then the song she's singin' is called 'Keep Buyin' the Drinks, Cowboy, 'Cause You Might Have a Shot.'

The certain as the French put it *je ne sais quoi*. Which, loosely translated, means, 'I don't know what.' It's that indescribable, intangible, almost ethereal quality that true ladies possess. A certain charm, confidence, and femininity that defies the scope of normal, everyday language. Christopher Morley called it 'the vibrations of beauty'. I call it 'not having a penis.'

Why I Hit The Bottle:
My reasons are threefold:

Liquid courage: I sometimes feel a little, well, anxious in social situations, especially with members of the opposite sex. I think this is justified, given that I stand two and a half feet tall, have a retractable penis, and can't hear a high-pitched whistle without losing control of my central nervous system. A few drinks often help me overcome that initial apprehension and really be myself. A few more drinks often turn me into Pat **O'Brien**.

Liquid therapy: Frank **Sinatra** used to say, 'I'm for anything that gets you through the night, be it prayer, tranquilizers, or a bottle of Jack Daniel's.' Well, I'm an atheist, I don't do so well with pills, and a bottle of booze is a lot cheaper than therapy. Although, if you get cirrhosis, the costs start to even out.

When you've had a handle of Jack, every woman looks like Ava **Gardner**. Let's face it, most people out there are ugly. Too ugly to date. You don't believe me? Head down to your local post office some lunchtime and tell me what percentage of the people in line you'd have sex with sober. 'Beer goggles' or 'gin glasses' or 'absinthe binoculars' or whatever the heck you wanna call them, perpetuate the species and keep portly women from being lonely.
    Brian Griffin's Guide to Booze, Broads, and the Lost Art of Being a Man (2006)

Jerry Falwell 1933-2007
American Baptist cleric, televangelist and conservative commentator

I listen to feminists and all these radical gals – most of them are failures. They've blown it. Some of them have been married, but they married some Casper Milquetoast who asked permission to go to the bathroom. These women just need a man in the house. That's all they need. Most of the feminists need a man to tell them what time of day it is and to lead them home. And they blew it and they're mad at all men. Feminists hate men. They're sexist. They hate men – that's their problem.

Michael Faraday 1791-1867
English physicist and chemist

Why sir, there is every possibility that you will soon be able to tax it!
to **Gladstone**, when asked about the usefulness of electricity
    W. E. H. Lecky *Democracy and Liberty* (1899 ed.)

George Farquhar 1678-1707
Irish dramatist

I have fed purely upon ale, and I always sleep upon ale.
    the landlord Boniface in *The Beaux's Stratagem* (1707)

William Faulkner 1897-1962
American novelist

A man shouldn't fool with booze until he's fifty; then he's a damn fool if he doesn't.
    James M. Webb and A. Wigfall Green *William Faulkner of Oxford* (1965)

The writer must teach himself that the basest of all things is to be afraid and, teaching himself that, forget it forever, leaving no room in his workshop for anything but the old verities and truths of the

heart, the old universal truths lacking which any story is ephemeral and doomed – love and honor and pity and pride and compassion and sacrifice.
  Nobel Peace Prize acceptance speech, Stockholm , 10 December 1950

The poet's voice need not merely be the record of man; it can be one of the props, the pillars, to help him endure and prevail.
  Nobel Peace Prize acceptance speech, Stockholm , 10 December 1950

The writer's only responsibility is to his art. He will be completely ruthless if he is a good one . . . If a writer has to rob his mother, he will not hesitate; the *Ode on a Grecian Urn* is worth any number of old ladies.
  in *Paris Review* Spring 1956

Guy Fawkes 1570-1606
English conspirator in the Gunpowder Plot, 1605

A desperate disease requires a dangerous remedy.
  on 6 November 1605, in *Dictionary of National Biography* (1917-)

Fawlty Towers British sitcom 1975, 1979

Basil Fawlty (John Cleese)

Sybil, you'd do well on *Mastermind*, if you chose as your specialist subject, 'Stating the Bleeding Obvious.'

When I asked you to build me a wall, I was hoping that rather than just dumping the bricks in a pile, I was wondering if you could find the time to cement them together, you know, in the traditional fashion.
  to an inexpensive and incompetent Irish builder he'd hired in defiance of his wife's instructions, in her absence

SYBIL FAWLTY:	If I find out you've been gambling, Basil, you know what I'm going to do, don't you?
BASIL FAWLTY:	You'll have to sew them back on first!

So what were you talking to him about, Basil? Car strikes, was it?
  Sybil Fawlty (Prunella Scales) asks Basil **Fawlty** (John Cleese) what he'd said to a guest whilst serving him breakfast, after it emerged that the guest had earlier died in his sleep

Jules Feiffer 1929-
American cartoonist

Be warned against all 'good' advice because 'good' advice is necessarily 'safe' advice, and though it will undoubtedly follow a sane pattern, it will very likely lead one into total sterility – one of the crushing problems of our time.

Marty Feldman 1933-1982
English writer, comedian and actor

The pen is mightier than the sword, and considerably easier to write with.

Jerry Della Femina 1936-
American advertising executive

Everybody sat around thinking about Panasonic, the Japanese electronics account. Finally I decided what the hell, I'll throw a line to loosen them up . . . the headline is: 'From Those Wonderful Folks Who Gave You Pearl Harbour'. Complete silence.
   suggesting a slogan

James Fenimore Cooper 1789-1851
American novelist

Party leads to vicious, corrupt and unprofitable legislation, for the sole purpose of defeating party.
   The American Democrat (1838)

Adam Ferguson 1723-1818
Scottish philosopher and historian

The most perfect equality of rights can never exclude the ascendant of superior minds.
   History of Civil Society (1823)

Adam Ferrara
American actor and comedian

What if God's a woman? Not only am I going to hell, I'll never know why!

Paul Feyerabend 1924-94
Austrian-born American philosopher of science

Knowledge is not a series of self-consistent theories that converges toward an ideal view; it is rather an ever increasing ocean of mutually incompatible (and perhaps even incommensurable) alternatives, each single theory, each fairy tale, each myth that is part of the collection forcing the others into greater articulation and all of them contributing, via this process of competition, to the development of our consciousness.

The only principle that does not inhibit progress is: *anything goes*.
Against Method (1975)

Helen Fielding 1958-
British-born novelist and screenwriter

I will not sulk about having no boyfriend, but develop inner poise and authority and sense of self as woman of substance, complete *without* boyfriend, as best way to obtain boyfriend.
   Bridget Jones's Diary (1996)

Head is full of moony fantasies about . . . being trendy Smug Married instead of sheepish Singleton.
   Bridget Jones's Diary (1996)

Henry Fielding 1707-1754
English novelist and dramatist

What is commonly called love, namely the desire of satisfying a voracious appetite with a certain quantity of delicate white human flesh.
   Tom Jones (1749)

Suzanne Fields

A grass-roots black political conservatism is growing from an awareness that liberals have merely reorganized the plantation, creating a new Big Daddy called Big Government. The welfare state, for all its good intentions, undermined traditional black values of self-reliance, self-control, self-help, self-improvement, and personal responsibility.
syndicated column, 28 November 1994

W. C. Fields 1880-1946
American comedian, actor, juggler and writer

I was in love with a beautiful blonde once. She drove me to drink. 'Tis the one thing I'm indebted to her for.
Never Give a Sucker an Even Break (1941)

Some weasel took the cork out of my lunch.
in film *You Can't Cheat an Honest Man* (US 1939)

Fish fuck in it.
when asked why he didn't drink water

It reminds me of an aardvark's ass.
*of Jeanette **Macdonald**'s face*

I exercise strong self-control, I never drink anything stronger than gin before breakfast.

I believe in clubs for women, but only if every other form of persuasion fails.

I am free of all prejudice. I hate everyone equally.

I'd rather have a bottle in front of me than a frontal lobotomy.

Women are like elephants to me: nice to look at, but I wouldn't want to own one.

I always keep a supply of stimulants handy in case I see a snake . . . which I also keep handy.

Ah, the patter of little feet around the house. There's nothing like having a midget for a butler.
attributed

There's not a man in America who at one time or another hasn't had a secret desire to boot a child in the ass.
attributed

If at first you don't succeed, try, try again. Then quit. No use being a damned fool about it.
attributed

John Fischer 1930-
Belgian pianist, composer and visual artist

Let's assume that each person has an equal opportunity, not to become equal, but to become different. To realise whatever unique potential of body, mind and spirit he or she possesses.

Michael Fish 1944-
British weather forecaster

A woman rang to say she heard there was a hurricane on the way. Well don't worry, there isn't.
weather forecast on the night before serious destructive gales in southern England
BBC TV, 15 October 1987

Carrie Fisher 1956-
American actress, screenwriter and novelist

Here's how men think. Sex, work – and those are reversible, depending on age – sex, work, food, sports and lastly, begrudgingly, relationships. And here's how women think. Relationships, relationships, relationships, work, sex, shopping, weight, food.
Surrender the Pink (1990)

Sex was for men. Marriage, like lifeboats, was for women and children.

Eddie Fisher 1928-
American singer

She was indeed the girl next door. If you lived next door to a self-centred, driven, insecure and untruthful phoney.
*on Debbie **Reynolds***

H. A. L. Fisher 1856-1940
English historian

Purity of race does not exist. Europe is a continent of energetic mongrels.
A History of Europe (1935)

Nothing commends a radical change to an Englishman more than the belief that it is really conservative.
A History of Europe (1935)

John Arbuthnot Fisher 1841-1920
British admiral

Sack the lot!
on overmanning and overspending within government departments
letter to *The Times*, 2 September 1919

Never contradict
Never explain
Never apologise
letter to *The Times*, 5 September 1919

Marve Fisher
American songwriter

I want an old-fashioned house
With an old-fashioned fence
And an old-fashioned millionaire.

'An Old-Fashioned Girl' (1954 song)
F. Scott Fitzgerald 1896-1940
American novelist

Let me tell you about the very rich. They are different from you and me.
   *to which Ernest **Hemingway** replied, 'Yes, they have more money.'*
   All the Sad Young Men (1926) 'Rich Boy'

At eighteen our convictions are hills from which we look; at forty-five they are caves in which we hide.
   Bernice Bobs her Hair (1920)

Her voice is full of money.
of Daisy
   The Great Gatsby (1925)

They were careless people, Tom and Daisy – they smashed up things and creatures and then retreated back into their money or their vast carelessness, or whatever it was that kept them together, and let other people clean up the mess they had made.
   The Great Gatsby (1925)

The hangover became a part of the day as well allowed-for as the Spanish siesta.
   The Crack-Up (1945) ed. Edmund Wilson 'My Lost City'

No grand idea was ever born in a conference, but a lot of foolish ideas have died there.
   The Crack Up (1945) Edmund Wilson (ed.)

Peter Fleming 1907-71
English journalist and travel writer

São Paulo is like Reading, only much farther away.
   Brazilian Adventure (1933)

Errol Flynn 1909-59
Australian film actor

My problem lies in reconciling my gross habits with my net income.
   Great Lovers of the Movies (1975)

If there is anyone to whom I owe money, I am prepared to forget it if they are.

Ferdinand Foch 1851-1929
French soldier and marshal

My centre is giving way, my right is retreating, situation excellent, I am attacking.
   message during the first battle of the Marne, September 1914
   R. Recouly *Foch* (1919)

This is not a peace treaty, it is an armistice for twenty years.
   at the signing of the Treaty of Versailles, 1919
   P. Reynaud *Mémoires* (1963)

Michael Foot 1913-
British Labour politician, Leader of the Labour Party 1980-83, writer

It is not necessary that every time he rises he should give his famous imitation of a semi-housetrained polecat.
of Norman Tebbit
in the House of Commons, 2 March 1978

Think of it! A second Chamber selected by the Whips. A seraglio of eunuchs.
in the House of Commons, 3 February 1969

He's passed from rising hope to elder statesman without any intervening period whatsoever.
of David Steel, Leader of the Liberal Party
in the House of Commons, 28 March 1979

A speech from Ernest **Bevin** on a major occasion had all the horrific fascination of a public execution. If the mind was left immune, eyes and ears and emotions were riveted.
Aneurin Bevin (1962)

Barry Forbes

Do what's right. Do it right. Do it right now.

Miss C. F. Forbes 1817-1911
English writer

The sense of being well-dressed gives a feeling of inward tranquillity which religion is powerless to bestow.

Gerald Ford 1909-
American Republican statesman, 38th President of the US, 1974-77

If the Government is big enough to give you everything you want, it is big enough to take away everything you have.
John F. Parker *If Elected* (1960)

Harrison Ford 1942-
American film actor and producer.

I don't use any particular method. I'm from the let's pretend school of acting.

Henry Ford 1863-1947
American industrialist

Exercise is bunk. If you are healthy, you don't need it. If you are sick, you shouldn't take it.

Howell Forgy 1908-83
American naval chaplain

Praise the Lord and pass the ammunition.
at Pearl Harbor, 7 December 1941, as Forgy moved alone a line of sailors passing ammunition by hand to the deck (later the title of a song by Frank Loesser, 1942)
in *New York Times* 1 November 1942

E. M. Forster 1879-1970
English novelist

She felt that those who prepared for all the emergencies of life beforehand may equip themselves at the expense of joy.
Howards End (1910)

Frederick Forsyth 1938-
English novelist

Everyone seems to remember with great clarity what they were doing on 2 November 1963, at the precise moment they heard President Kennedy was dead.
The Odessa File (1972)

Jodie Foster 1962-
American actress, film producer and director

Normal is not something to aspire to, it's something to get away from.

John Foster Dulles 1888-1959
US Secretary of State under President Dwight D. Eisenhower from 1953 to 1959

The world will never have lasting peace so long as men reserve for war the finest human qualities. Peace, no less than war, requires idealism and self-sacrifice and a righteous and dynamic faith.

H. W. Fowler 1858-1933
English lexicographer and grammarian

The English speaking world may be divided into (1) those who neither know nor care what a split infinitive is; (2) those who do not know, but care very much; (3) those who know and condemn; (4) those who know and approve; and (5) those who know and distinguish. Those who neither know nor care are the vast majority and are a happy folk, to be envied by most of the minority classes.
Modern English Usage (1926)

Norman Fowler 1938-
British Conservative politician

I have a young family and for the next few years I should like to devote more time to them.
  often quoted as 'spend more time with my family'
  resignation letter to the Prime Minister, in *Guardian* 4 January 1990

Charles James Fox 1749-1806
English Whig politician

I will not close my politics in that foolish way.
  in the last year of his life Fox's friends suggested that he should accept a peerage
  in *Dictionary of National Biography* (1917-)

Jeff Foxworthy 1958-
American stand-up comedian and actor

If you ever start feeling like you have the goofiest, craziest, most dysfunctional family in the world, all you have to do is go to a state fair. Because five minutes at the fair, you'll be going, 'you know, we're alright. We are dang near royalty.'

Janet Frame 1924-2004
New Zealand writer

For your own good is a persuasive argument that will eventually make a man agree to his own destruction.
Faces in the Water (1961)

Anatole France 1844-1924
French poet, journalist and novelist

I have no objection on principle to make to the guillotine. Nature, my only mistress and my only instructress, certainly offers me no suggestion to the effect that a man's life is of any value; on the contrary, she teaches in all kinds of ways that it is of none. The sole end and object of living beings seems to be to serve as food for other beings destined to the same end. Murder is of natural right; therefore, the penalty of death is lawful, on condition it is exercised from no motives either of virtue or of justice, but by necessity or to gain some profit thereby. However, I must have perverse instincts, for I sicken to see blood flow, and this defect of character all my philosophy has failed so far to correct.
The Gods are Thirsty

If fifty million people say a foolish thing it is still a foolish thing.

Dick Francis 1920- 2010
British horse racing crime writer and retired jockey

Emotion is a rotten base for politics.

Anne Frank 1929-45
Dutch Jewish girl who died of typhus in the Nazi Bergen-Belsen concentration camp.

Parents can only advise their children or point them in the right direction. Ultimately people shape their own characters.
The Diary of a Young Girl (1952)

Lawrence K. Frank

We are living the events which for centuries to come will be minutely studied by scholars who will undoubtedly describe these days as probably the most exciting and creative in the history of mankind. But preoccupied with our daily chores, our worries and personal hopes and ambitions, few of us are actually living in the present.

Tellis Frank 1965-
American basketball player

The worst thing about Europe is that you can't go out in the middle of the night and get a Slurpee.

Al Franken 1951-
American writer, actor, television show host, political commentator, Democratic Party politician

When you encounter seemingly good advice that contradicts other seemingly good advice, ignore them both.
  Oh, The Things I Know (2002)

Mistakes are a part of being human. Appreciate your mistakes for what they are: precious life lessons that can only be learned the hard way. Unless it's a fatal mistake, which, at least, others can learn from.'
  Oh, The Things I Know (2002)

Felix Frankfurter 1882-1965
American judge and US Supreme Court justice

It is a fair summary of history to say that the safeguards of liberty have been forged in controversies involving not very nice people.
  dissenting opinion in *United States v. Rabinowitz* 1950

Viktor Frankl 1905-97
Austrian neurologist, psychiatrist and Holocaust survivor

Life ultimately means taking the responsibility to find the right answer to its problems and to fulfil the tasks which it constantly sets for each individual.
  Man's Search for Meaning (1946)

Benjamin Franklin 1706-90
one of the Founding Fathers of the United States of America. Author, printer, satirist, political theorist, politician, scientist, inventor, civic activist, statesman, soldier and diplomat

We must indeed all hang together, or, most assuredly, we shall all hang separately.
  remark, 4 July 1776 at the signing of the Declaration of Independence

In this world nothing can be said to be for certain, except death and taxes.
  letter to Jean Baptiste Le Roy, 13 November 1789

The Constitution only guarantees the American people the right to pursue happiness. You have to catch it yourself.

Creditors have better memories than debtors.

No man e'er was glorious, who was not laborious.

Alexander Fraser Tytler, Lord Woodhouselee 1747-1813
British lawyer and writer

A democracy cannot exist as a permanent form of government. It can only exist until the voters discover that they can vote themselves largesse from the public treasury. From that moment on, the majority always votes for the candidates promising the most benefits from the public treasury with the result that a democracy always collapses over lousy fiscal policy, always followed by a dictatorship. The average of the world's great civilizations before they decline has been 200 years. These nations have progressed in this sequence: From bondage to spiritual faith; from faith to great courage; from courage to liberty; from liberty to abundance; from abundance to selfishness; from selfishness to

complacency; from complacency to apathy; from apathy to dependency; from dependency back again to bondage.
'Cycle of Democracy' (1770)

Malcolm Fraser 1930-
Australian liberal statesman, Prime Minister 1975-83

Life is not meant to be easy.
5th Alfred Deakin Lecture, 20 July 1971

Frasier American sitcom 1993-2004

Niles Crane (David Hyde Pierce)

How strange. I usually get some sign that Lilith is in town: dogs forming into packs, blood weeping from the walls.

Sir James Frazer 1854-1941
Scottish classicist, anthropologist

The awe and dread with which the untutored savage contemplates his mother-in-law are amongst the most familiar facts of anthropology.
The Golden Bough (1922)

Frederick the Great 1712-86
Prussian monarch, King from 1740

My people and I have come to an agreement which satisfies us both. They are to say what they please, and I am to do what I please.
his interpretation of benevolent despotism
attributed

Diplomacy without arms is like music without instruments.

Dawn French 1957-
British comedy actress

If I were alive in Ruben's time, I'd be celebrated as a model. Kate **Moss** would be used as a paint brush.
in *Sunday Times* 13 August 2006

Marilyn French 1929-
American writer

Whatever they may be in public life, whatever their relations with men, in their relations with women, all men are rapists, and that's all they are. They rape us with their eyes, their laws, and their codes.
The Women's Room (1977)

'I hate discussions of feminism that end up with who does the dishes,' she said. So do I. But at the end, there are always the damned dishes.
The Women's Room (1977)

Sir Clement Freud 1924-2009
English humorist and politician

If you resolve to give up smoking, drinking and loving, you don't actually live longer; it just seems longer.
   quoted in *The Observer* 27 December 1964 and ascribed to 'a third-rate comedian in Sloane Square'

Sigmund Freud 1856-1939
Austrian neurologist who founded the psychoanalytic school of psychology

The great question that has never been answered and which I have not yet been able to answer, despite my 30 years of research into the feminine soul, is 'What does a woman want?'

We are so made, that we can only derive intense enjoyment from a contrast, and only very little from a state of things.
   Civilization and its Discontents (1930)

Intolerance of groups is often, strangely enough, exhibited more strongly against small differences than against fundamental ones.
   Moses and Monotheism (1938)

We believe that civilisation has been created under the pressure of the exigencies of life at the cost of satisfaction of the instincts.
   Introductory Lectures on Psycho-analysis, Complete Works, Standard Edition (1915)

Why do we, you and I and many another, protest so vehemently against war, instead of just accepting it as another of life's odious importunities? For it seems a natural enough thing, biologically sound and practically unavoidable.
   letter in 1931 to Albert Einstein, who had invited him to be one of 'an association of intellectuals' actively opposed to war

Kinky Friedman 1944-
American singer, writer and politician

I support gay marriage because I believe they have a right to be just as miserable as the rest of us.
   quoted on CBS News, 21 August 2005

Milton Friedman 1912-2006
American economist and statistician

Few trends could so thoroughly undermine the very foundations of our free society as the acceptance by corporate officials of a social responsibility other than to make as much money for their stockholders as possible.
   Capitalism and Freedom (1962)

History suggests that capitalism is a necessary condition for political freedom. Clearly it is not a sufficient condition for it.
   Capitalism and Freedom (1962)

A society that puts equality – in the sense of equality of outcome – ahead of freedom will end up with neither equality nor freedom.
   Free to Choose (1980)

There is no place for government to prohibit consumers from buying products the effect of which will be to harm themselves.
Free to Choose (1980)

There is an invisible hand in politics that operates in the opposite direction to the invisible hand in the market. In politics, individuals who seek to promote only the public good are led by an invisible hand to promote special interests that it was no part of their intention to promote.
Bright Promises, Dismal Performance: An Economist's Protest (1983)

There's no such thing as a free lunch.

I am in favour of cutting taxes under any circumstances and for any excuse, for any reason, whenever it's possible.

The government solution to a problem is usually as bad as the problem.

The possibility of co-ordination through voluntary co-operation rests on the elementary – yet frequently denied – proposition that both parties to an economic transaction benefit from it, provided the transaction is bi-laterally voluntary and informed. Exchange can therefore bring about co-ordination without coercion. A working model of a society organized through voluntary exchange is a free private enterprise exchange economy – what we have been calling competitive capitalism.

If I spend somebody else's money on somebody else, I'm not concerned about how much it is, and I'm not concerned about what I get. And that's government.

Everywhere, and at all times, economic progress has meant far more to the poor than to the rich.

If you pay people not to work and tax them when they do, don't be surprised if you get unemployment.

I say thank God for government waste. If government is doing bad things, it's only the waste that prevents the harm from being greater.

One of the great mistakes is to judge policies and programs by their intentions rather than by their results.

Max Frisch 1911-91
Swiss novelist and dramatist

Technology . . . the knack of so arranging the world that we need not experience it.
Homo Faber (1957)

Erich Fromm 1900-80
German social psychologist, psychoanalyst, humanistic philosopher and democratic socialist

In the nineteenth century the problem was that *God is dead*; in the twentieth century the problem is that *man is dead*. In the nineteenth century it means schizoid self-alienation. The danger of the past was that men became slaves. The danger of the future is that men may become robots.
The Sane Society (1955)

Man's main task in life is to give birth to himself, to become what he potentially is.

Sir David Frost 1939-
British journalist, writer, media personality

The creed of the Inland Revenue is simple: if we bring one little smile to one little face today, then somebody's slipped up somewhere.

Robert Frost 1874-1963
American poet

I never dared be radical when young
For fear it would make me conservative when old
   'Precaution' (1936)

I shall be telling this with a sigh
Somewhere ages and ages hence:
two roads diverged in a wood, and I -
I took the one less traveled by,
And that has made all the difference.
   Mountain Interval 'The Road Not Taken' (1916)

There is one thing more exasperating than a wife who can't cook and won't, and that's the wife who can't cook and will.

By working faithfully eight hours a day you may eventually get to be a boss and work twelve hours a day.

The reason why worry kills more people than work is that more people worry than work.

The brain is a wonderful organ. It starts working the moment you get up in the morning, and does not stop until you get into the office.

James A. Froude 1818-1894
English historian, novelist and biographer

History is a voice forever sounding across the centuries the laws of right and wrong. Opinions alter, manners change, creeds rise and fall, but the moral law is written on the tablets of eternity.

Stephen Fry 1957-
English actor, writer, comedian, television presenter and film director

I tried to say more, but the Cough had come upon me, as it does these days. It starts as the smallest tickle in the throat and can build, though I say so myself as shouldn't, into a not unimpressive display. Something between a vomiting donkey and an explosion at a custard factory.
   The Hippopotamus (1995)

At sixty-six I am entering . . . the last phase of my active physical life, My body, on the move, resembles in sight and sound nothing so much as a bin-liner full of yoghurt.
   The Hippopotamus (1995)

A gentleman approached me in the street earlier and asked, 'Have you got a light mac?' to which I replied, truthfully, 'No, but I've got a dark brown overcoat.'
   Paperweight (1992)

The email of the species is deadlier than the mail.
>   in *Sunday Telegraph* 23 December 2001

Carlos Fuentes 1928-
Mexican novelist and writer

High on the agenda for the 21st century will be the need to restore some kind of tragic consciousness.
>   Rushworth M. Kidder *An Agenda for the 21st Century* (1987)

Francis Fukuyama 1952-
American historian

What we may be witnessing is not just the end of the Cold War, but the end of history as such: that is, the end point of man's ideological evolution and the universalism of Western liberal democracy.
>   in *Independent* 20 September 1989

Dr. Thomas Fuller 1654-1734
British physician, preacher and intellectual

Get the facts, or the facts will get you. And when you get them, get them right, or they will get you wrong.
>   *Gnomologia* (1732)

Thomas Fuller 1608-61
British cleric

A little skill in antiquity inclines a man to Popery. But depth in that study brings him about again to our religion.
>   *The Holy State and the Profane State* (1642)

g

Zsa Zsa Gabor 1917-
Hungarian-American actress, socialite and beauty queen

You mean apart from my own?
when asked how many husbands she had had
  K. Edwards *I Wish I'd Said That* (1976)

Oh, what a pretty dress – and so cheap!
  to another woman

He taught me housekeeping; when we divorce I keep the house.

A man in love is incomplete until he is married. Then he is finished.

I want a man who's kind and understanding. Is that too much to ask of a millionaire?

I never hated a man enough to give him back his diamonds.

A girl must marry for love, and keep on marrying until she finds it.

Hugh Gaitskell 1906-63
British Labour politician

There are some of us . . . who will fight and fight and fight again to save the Party we love.
opposing the vote in favour of unilateral disarmament
  speech at Labour Party Conference, 5 October 1960

It means the end of a thousand years of history.
on a European federation
  speech at Labour Party Conference, 3 October 1962

John Kenneth Galbraith 1908-2006
Canadian-American economist

I am a great friend of Israel. Any country that can stand Milton **Friedman** as an adviser has nothing to fear from a few million Arabs.

When faced with the choice between changing and proving there's no need to do so, most people get busy on the proof.

Under capitalism, man exploits man. Under communism, it's just the opposite.

Politics is not the art of the possible. It consists in choosing between the disastrous and the unpalatable.

Nothing is so admirable in politics as a short memory.

The Great Wall, I've been told, is the only man-made structure on earth that is visible from the moon. For the life of me I cannot see why anyone would go to the moon to look at it, when, with almost the same difficulty, it can be viewed in China.
in *The Sunday Times Magazine*

The reduction of politics to a spectator sport . . . has been one of the more malign accomplishments of television. Television newsmen are breathless on how the game is being played, largely silent on what the game is all about.
A Life in our Times (1981)

The experience of being disastrously wrong is salutary; no economist should be denied it, and not many are.
A Life in our Times (1981)

In public administration good sense would seem to require the public expectation be kept at the lowest possible level in order to minimize eventual disappointment.
A Life in our Times (1981)

One of the recurrent and dangerous influences on our foreign policy – fear of the political consequences of doing the sensible thing, which in many cases is nothing much at all.
A Life in our Times (1981)

The conventional wisdom.
ironic term for 'the beliefs that are at any time assiduously, solemnly and mindlessly traded between the conventionally wise'
The Affluent Society (1958)

George Galloway 1954-
Scottish politician, expelled from the Labour Party in 2003 and now a member of Respect

Sir, I salute your courage, your strength, your indefatigability.
to Saddam **Hussein**
in Baghdad, 1994; quoted in *The Scotsman* (online edition) 20 October 2003

John Galsworthy 1867-1933
English novelist and playwright

He was afflicted by the thought that where Beauty was, nothing ever ran quite straight, which, no doubt, was why so many people looked on it as immoral.
In Chancery (1920)

Idealism increases in direct proportion to one's distance from the problem.

Mahatma Gandhi 1869-1948
Indian statesman

Please go on. It is my day of silence.
note passed to the British Cabinet Mission at a meeting in 1942
Peter Hennessey *Never Again* (1992)

That would be a good idea
on being asked what he thought of modern civilisation, while visiting England in 1930
E. F. Schumacher *Good Work* (1979)

The moment the slave resolves that he will no longer be a slave, his fetters fall. He frees himself and shows the way to others. Freedom and slavery are mental states.
   Non-Violence in Peace and War (1949)

In my humble opinion, non-cooperation with evil is as much a duty as is cooperation with good.
   speech in Ahmadabad, 23 March 1922

There are seven sins in the world: wealth without work, pleasure without conscience, knowledge without character, commerce without morality, science without humanity, worship without sacrifice and politics without principle.

Gabriel García Márquez 1928-
Colombian novelist

The world must be all fucked up when men travel first class and literature goes as freight.
   One Hundred Years of Solitude (1967)

James A. Garfield 1831-81
20th President of the United States

Next in importance to freedom and justice is popular education, without which neither freedom nor justice can be permanently maintained.

John Nance Garner 1868-1967
American Democratic politician, Vice-President 1933-41

The vice-presidency isn't worth a pitcher of warm piss.
   O. C. Fisher *Cactus Jack* (1978)

Janeane Garofalo 1964-
American stand-up comedienne, actress, political activist and writer

Many people feel that mass acceptance and smooth socialization are desirable life paths for a young adult . . . Many people are often wrong . . . Don't bother being nice. Being popular and well liked is not in your best interest. Let me be more clear; if you behave in a manner pleasing to most, then you are probably doing something wrong. The masses have never been arbiters of the sublime, and they often fail to recognize the truly great individual. Taking into account the public's regrettable lack of taste, it is incumbent upon you not to fit in.

David Garrick 1717-79
English actor

Any fool can play tragedy, but comedy, sir, is a damned serious business.

Elizabeth Gaskell 1810-65
British novelist

Your wife and I didn't hit it off the only time I ever saw her. I won't say she was silly, but I think one of us was silly, and it wasn't me.
   Wives and Daughters (1866)

Bill Gates 1955-
American computer entrepreneur

If they want we will give them a sleeping bag, but there is something romantic about sleeping under the desk. They want to do it.
on his young software programmers
  in *Independent* 18 November 1995 'Quote Unquote'

The world has had a tendency to focus a disproportionate amount of attention on me.
  announcing that he will move to concentrate on his charity work, in *Washington Post* (online edition) 16 June 2006

John Gay 1685-1732
English poet and dramatist

Do you think your mother and I should have lived comfortably so long together, if ever we had been married?
  The Beggar's Opera (1728)

Eric Geddes 1875-1937
British politician and administrator

The Germans, if this government is returned, are going to pay every penny; they are going to be squeezed as a lemon is squeezed – until the pips squeak.
  speech at Cambridge, 10 December 1918

Bob Geldof 1954-
Irish rock musician

Most people get into bands for three very simple rock and roll reasons; to get laid, to get fame, and to get rich.
  in *Melody Maker* 27 August 1977

Martha Gellhorn 1908-98
American journalist and war reporter, married to Ernest **Hemingway** 1940-45

Never believe governments, not any of them, not a word they say; keep an untrusting eye on all they do.
Daily Telegraph 17 February 1998 'Obituary'

Jean Genet 1910-86
French novelist, poet, and dramatist

What we need is hatred. From it our ideas are born.
  The Blacks (1959); epigraph

Genghis Khan (Temujin) 1162-1227
Mongol ruler

Happiness lies in conquering one's enemies, in driving them in front of oneself, in taking their property, in savouring their despair, in outraging their wives and daughters.
  Witold Rodzinski *The Walled Kingdom: A History of China* (1979)

Daniel George (Daniel George Bunting) 1890-1967
English writer

O Freedom, what liberties are taken in thy name!
referring to the words of the revolutionary Mme Roland (1754-93) before being guillotined: 'O liberty! what crimes are committed in thy name!'
   The Perpetual Pessimist (1963, with Sagittarius)

Henry George 1839-97
American writer, politician and political economist

Man is the only animal whose desires increase as they are fed; the only animal that is never satisfied.

W. L. George

Wars teach us not to love our enemies, but to hate our allies.

Lord George-Brown 1914-85
English Labour politician

Most British Statesmen have either drunk too much or womanised too much. I never fell into the second category.

King George III 1738-1820
British monarch, King of Great Britain and Ireland from 1760

Born and educated in this country, I glory in the name of Briton.
The King's Speech on Opening the Session 18 November 1760

When he has wearied me for two hours he looks at his watch, to see if he may not tire me for an hour more.
of George Grenville
   in 1765; Horace Walpole *The Reign of George III* (1845)

King George V 1865-1936
British monarch, King of Great Britain and Ireland from 1910

I venture to allude to the impression which seemed generally to prevail among their brethren across the seas, that the Old Country must wake up if she intends to maintain her old position of pre-eminence in her Colonial trade against foreign competitors.
   speech at Guildhall, 5 December 1901

The complex forms and balanced spirit of our constitution were not the discovery of a single era, still less of a single party or of a single person. They are the slow accretion of centuries, the outcome of patience, tradition and experience.
   the words of G. M. Trevelyan in the King's Silver Jubilee address to Parliament, 1935
   David Cannadine G. M. *Trevelyan: a Life in History* (1992)

I will not have another war. *I will not.* The last one was none of my doing and if there is another one and we are threatened with being brought into it, I will go to Trafalgar Square and wave a red flag myself sooner than allow this country to be brought in.
   c.1935 Andrew Roberts *Eminent Churchillians* (1994)

I said to your predecessor: 'You know what they're all saying, no more coals to Newcastle, no more Hoares to Paris.' The fellow didn't even cough.
*in conversation with Anthony **Eden**, 23 December 1935, following Samuel **Hoare**'s resignation as Foreign Secretary*
Earl of Avon *Facing the Dictators* (1962)

I may be uninspiring, but I'll be damned if I'm an alien!
*on H. G. **Wells**'s comment on an alien and uninspiring court*
Sarah Bradford *George VI* (1989); attributed

My father was frightened of his mother; I was frightened of my father, and I am damned well going to see to it that my children are frightened of me.
attributed in Randolph S. Churchill *Lord Derby* (1959)

King George VI 1895-1952
British monarch, King of Great Britain and Northern Ireland from 1936

Harry Truman: You've had a revolution.
George VI: Oh no, we don't have those here
 *during President **Truman**'s visit to Britain just after Labour's election victory*
 ***Hugh Dalton** Political Diary* (1986) 28 July 1945

I feel happier now that we have no allies to be polite to and pamper.
 to his mother **Queen Mary**, 27 June 1940
 J. Wheeler-Bennett *King George VI* (1958)

Ricky Gervais 1961-
English comedian, actor, film-maker and broadcaster

If at first you don't succeed, remove all evidence you ever tried.

Eagles may soar high, but weasels don't get sucked into jet engines.

Never do today that which will become someone else's responsibility tomorrow.

Accept that some days you are the pigeon and some days you are the statue.

If your boss is getting you down, look at him through the prongs of a fork and imagine him in jail.

You have to be 100% behind someone before you can stab them in the back.

J. Paul Getty 1892-1976
American industrialist, collector of art and antiquities

If you can actually count your money, then you are not really a rich man.
 in *Observer* 3 November 1957

The best form of charity I know is the art of meeting a payroll.
 Russell Miller *The House of Getty* (1985)

The meek shall inherit the Earth, but not its mineral rights.

Money isn't everything, but it sure keeps you in touch with your children.

No one can possibly achieve any real and lasting success or get rich in business by being a conformist.

Ghostbusters 1984 film

Dr Peter Venkman (Bill Murray)

I don't have to take this abuse from you. I've got hundreds of people waiting to abuse me.

Edward Gibbon 1737-94
English historian and politician

All that is human must retrograde if it does not advance.
The Decline and Fall of the Roman Empire (1776-88)

Persuasion is the resource of the feeble; and the feeble can seldom persuade.
The Decline and Fall of the Roman Empire (1776-88)

Lewis Grassic Gibbon 1901-35
Scottish novelist and journalist

Bleakness, not meanness or jollity, is the keynote to Aberdonian character ... For anyone passing their nights and days in The Silver City by the Sea . . . it is comparable to passing one's existence in a refrigerator.
Scottish Scene or the Intelligent Man's Guide to Albyn, 'Aberdeen' 1934

Kahlil Gibran 1883-1931
Lebanese-born American writer and painter

Work is love made visible. And if you cannot work with love but only with distaste, it is better that you should leave your work and sit at the gate of the temple and take alms of those who work with joy.
The Prophet (1923) 'On Work'

An exaggeration is a truth that has lost its temper.
Sand and Foam (1926)

To understand the heart and mind of a person, look not at what he has already achieved, but at what he aspires to do.

André Gide 1869-1951
French author

One must allow others to be right, it consoles them for not being anything else.
The Immoralist (1930)

There are admirable potentialities in every human being. Believe in your strength and your youth. Learn to repeat endlessly to yourself, 'It all depends on me.'

It is only in adventure that some people succeed in knowing themselves – in finding themselves.

Sir John Gielgud 1904-2000
English actor, director and producer

Dear Ingrid – speaks five languages and can't act in any of them.
on Ingrid Bergman

Sometimes I think people see it as an indecent race between me, the **Pope** and Boris **Yeltsin**.
at the age of 92, on death

Sir W. S. Gilbert 1836-1911
English writer and lyricist

She may very well pass for forty-three in the dusk with a light behind her!
Trial by Jury (1875)

I always voted at my party's call
And I never thought of thinking for myself at all
HMS Pinafore (1878)

No Englishman unmoved that statement hears,
Because, with all our faults, we love our House of Peers.
The Pirates of Penzance (1879)

I often think it's comical
How Nature always does contrive
That every boy and every gal,
That's born into the world alive,
Is either a little Liberal,
Or else a little Conservative!
Iolanthe (1882)

The House of Peers, throughout the war,
Did nothing in particular,
And did it very well
Iolanthe (1882)

When in that House MPs divide,
If they've a brain and cerebellum too,
They have to leave that brain outside,
And vote just as their leaders tell 'em to.
Iolanthe (1882)

The prospect of a lot
Of dull MPs in close proximity,
All thinking for themselves is what
No man can face with equanimity.
Iolanthe (1882)

All shall equal be.
The Earl, the Marquis, and the Dook,
The Groom, the Butler, and the Cook,
The Aristocrat who banks with Coutts,
The Aristocrat who cleans the boots.

The Gondoliers (1889)

In short, whoever you may be,
To this conclusion you'll agree,
When every one is somebodee,
Then no one's anybody.
   The Gondoliers (1889)

George Gilder 1939-
American writer, intellectual and Republican Party activist

A regulatory apparatus is a parasite that can grow larger than its host industry and become in turn a host itself, with the industry reduced to parasitism, dependent on the subsidies and protections of the very government body that initially sapped its strength.
   Wealth and Poverty (1981)

Excessive regulation to save us from risks will create the greatest danger of all: a stagnant society in a changing world. The choice is not between comfortable equilibrium and reckless progress. It is between random deterioration by time and change and creative destruction by human genius.
   Wealth and Poverty (1981)

Most successful entrepreneurs contribute far more to society than they ever recover, and most of them win no riches at all. They are the heroes of economic life, and those who begrudge them their rewards demonstrate a failure to understand their role and their promise.
   Wealth and Poverty (1981)

Not taking and consuming, but giving, risking, and creating are the characteristic roles of the capitalist, the key producer of the wealth of nations.
   The American Spectator, February 1982

Hermione Gingold 1897-1987
English actress

Contrary to popular belief, English women do not wear tweed nightgowns.
   in *Saturday Review* 16 April 1955

Newton Gingrich 1943-
American Republican politician; Speaker of the House of Representatives from 1995

No society can survive, no civilization can survive, with 12-year-olds having babies, with 15-year-olds killing each other, with 17-year-olds dying of Aids, with 18-year-olds getting diplomas they can't read.
in December 1994, after the Republican electoral victory
   in *The Times* 9 February 1995

One of the greatest intellectual failures of the welfare state is the penchant for sacrifice, so long as the only people being asked to sacrifice are working, tax-paying Americans.
   in *USA Today* 16 January 1995

Nikki Giovanni 1943-
American poet

Mistakes are a fact of life. It is the response to error that counts.
   'Of Liberation' (1970)

Rudi Giuliani 1944-
American Republican politician, Mayor of New York 1993-2001

The number of casualties will be more than any of us can bear.
in the aftermath of the terrorist attacks which destroyed the World Trade Center buildings in New York and damaged the Pentagon, 11 September 2001
in *The Times* 12 September 2001

Edna Gladney 1886-1961
American philanthropist

There are no illegitimate children, only illegitimate parents.
during her successful lobbying of the Texas legislature to expunge the word 'illegitimate' from birth certificates
A. Loos *Kiss Hollywood Good-Bye* (1978)

Catherine Gladstone 1812-1900
British wife of William Ewart Gladstone

Oh, William, dear, if you weren't such a great man you would be a terrible bore.
to her husband
Roy Jenkins *Gladstone* (1995)

William Ewart Gladstone 1809-98
British Liberal statesman, Prime Minister 1868-74, 1880-85, 1886, 1892-94

The love of freedom itself is hardly stronger in England than the love of aristocracy.
in *Nineteenth Century* 1877

I am sorry to say that I have a long speech fermenting in me, and I feel as a loaf might in the oven.
Roy Jenkins *Gladstone* (1995)

Thomas Glascock 1890-1941
American politician

No, sir! I am his adversary, and choose not to subject myself to his fascination.
when General Thomas Glascock of Georgia took his seat in the US Senate, a mutual friend expressed the wish to introduce him to Henry Clay of Virginia
Robert V. Remini *Henry Clay* (1991)

Victoria Glendinning 1937-
English biographer and novelist

There's no greater bliss in life than when the plumber eventually comes to unblock your drains. No writer can give that sort of pleasure.
in *Observer* 3 January 1993

Elinor Glyn 1864-1943
British novelist and scriptwriter who pioneered mass-market women's erotic fiction

American husbands are the best in the world; no other husbands are so generous to their wives, or can be so easily divorced.

Jean-Luc Godard 1930-
French film director

GEORGES FRANJU: Movies should have a beginning, a middle, and an end.
JEAN-LUC GODARD: Certainly, but not necessarily in that order.
   in *Time* 14 September 1981

Arthur Godfrey 1903-83
American radio and television broadcaster and entertainer

I'm proud to be paying taxes in the United States. The only thing is, I could be just as proud for half the money.

Joseph Goebbels 1897-1945
German politician and Propaganda Minister in Nazi Germany 1933-45

If you tell a lie big enough and keep repeating it, people will eventually come to believe it. The lie can be maintained only for such time as the State can shield the people from the political, economic and/or military consequences of the lie. It thus becomes vitally important for the State to use all of its powers to repress dissent, for the truth is the mortal enemy of the lie, and thus by extension, the truth is the greatest enemy of the State.

Hermann Göering 1893-1946
German politician, military leader, and a leading member of the Nazi Party. Among many offices, he was Hitler's designated successor, and commander of the Luftwaffe

Why, of course the people don't want war. Why would some poor slob on a farm want to risk his life in a war when the best that he can get out of it is to come back to his farm in one piece. Naturally, the common people don't want war; neither in Russia nor in England nor in America, nor for that matter in Germany. That is understood. But, after all, it is the leaders of the country who determine the policy and it is always a simple matter to drag the people along, whether it is a democracy or a fascist dictatorship or a Parliament or a Communist dictatorship . . . voice or no voice, the people can always be brought to the bidding of the leaders. That is easy. All you have to do is tell them they are being attacked and denounce the pacifists for lack of patriotism and exposing the country to danger. It works the same way in any country.
   from a conversation with psychologist Gustave Gilbert whilst jailed in Nuremburg, 1946, documented in Gilbert's book *Nuremburg Diary* (1948)

We have no butter . . . but I ask you – would you rather have butter or guns? . . . preparedness makes us powerful. Butter merely makes us fat.
   speech at Hamburg, 1936: W. Frischauer *Goering* (1951)

Johann Wolfgang von Goethe 1749-1832
German writer of books of poetry, drama, literature, theology, philosophy, humanism and science

The intelligent man finds almost everything ridiculous, the sensible man hardly anything.

There is nothing more frightful than ignorance in action.

There is a courtesy of the heart; it is allied to love. From its springs the purest courtesy in the outward behavior.

Ludwig Max Goldberger 1848-1913

America, land of unlimited possibilities.
Land of Unlimited Possibilities: Observations on Economic Life in the United States of America (1903)

William Golding 1911-93
English novelist

Anyone who moved through those years without understanding that man produces evil as a bee produces honey, must have been blind or wrong in the head.
The Hot Gates (1965) 'Fable'

Emma Goldman 1869-1940
Russian-born American anarchist

The free expression of the hopes and aspirations of a people is the greatest and only safety in a sane society.
Living My Life (1931)

William Goldman 1931-
American novelist, playwright and screenwriter

Life isn't fair. It's just fairer than death, that's all.
The Princess Bride (1973)

Oliver Goldsmith 1730-74
Anglo-Irish writer, poet and physician

Don't let us make imaginary evils, when you know we have so many real ones to encounter.

Barry Goldwater 1909-98
Republican Party politician

Let us then not blunt the noble impulses of mankind by reducing charity to a mechanical operation of the federal government.
The Conscience of a Conservative (1960)

The idea that a man who makes $100,000 a year should be forced to contribute ninety per cent of his income to the cost of government, while the man who makes $10,000 is made to pay twenty per cent is repugnant to my notions of justice. I do not believe in punishing success.
The Conscience of a Conservative (1960)

If he were any dumber, he'd be a tree.
on Senator William Scott of Virginia

I would remind you that extremism in the defence of liberty is no vice! And let me remind you also that moderation in the pursuit of justice is no virtue!
speech accepting the presidential nomination, 16 July 1964
in *New York Times* 17 July 1964

Edmond de Goncourt 1822-96
French novelist

Housewarming at Zola's. Very tasty dinner, including some grouse whose scented flesh Daudet compared to an old courtesan's flesh marinated in a bidet.
Journal for 3 April 1878

Richard Goodwin 1931-
American writer

People come to Washington believing it's the centre of power. I know I did. It was only much later that I learned that Washington is a steering wheel that's not connected to the engine.
Peter McWilliams *Ain't Nobody's Business If You Do* (1993)

Mikhail Gorbachev 1931-
Last head of state of the Soviet Union, serving from 1988 until its collapse in 1991

After leaving the Kremlin . . . my conscience was clear. The promise I gave to the people when I started the process of perestroika was kept: I gave them freedom.
Memoirs (1995)

The guilt of **Stalin** and his immediate entourage before the Party and the people for the mass repressions and lawlessness they committed is enormous and unforgiveable.
speech on the seventieth anniversary of the Russian Revolution, 2 November 1987

The market is not an invention of capitalism. It has existed for centuries. It is an invention of civilisation.

Giles Gordon 1840-1903
Scottish literary agent and writer

You cannot enjoy Mozart and choose to wear an anorak.
Aren't We Due a Royalty Statement? (1993) ch. 27

Albert Gore Jr. 1948-
American Democrat politician, Vice-President 1993-2001; presidential candidate 2000

I am Al Gore, and I used to be the next president of the United States of America.
in *Newsweek* 19 March 2001

Teresa Gorman 1931-
British Conservative politician

The Conservative establishment has always treated woman as nannies, grannies and fannies.

Philip Gould 1950-
British Labour Party strategist

The New Labour brand has been badly contaminated. It is the object of constant criticism and, even worse, ridicule.
internal memo, May 2000, leaked to the press in July; text printed in *Guardian* 20 July 2000

Stephen Jay Gould 1941-2002
American palaeontologist, evolutionary biologist, and historian of science

In science, 'fact' can only mean 'confirmed to such a degree that it would be perverse to withhold provisional assent'. I suppose that apples might start to rise tomorrow, but the possibility does not merit equal time in physics classrooms.

Science is an integral part of culture. It's not this foreign thing, done by an arcane priesthood. It's one of the glories of human intellectual tradition.
  in *Independent* 24 January 1990

Ernest Gowers 1880-1966
British public servant

It is not easy nowadays to remember anything so contrary to all appearances as that officials are the servants of the public; and the official must try not to foster the illusion that it is the other way round.
  Plain Words (1948)

Lord (Lew) Grade 1906-99
Russian-born British media tycoon

If you want an answer today, the answer's 'No.'
  a Grade family motto, according to Michael Grade on BBC Radio *Quote ... Unquote* 28 February 2000

The Graduate 1967 film

Benjamin Braddock (Dustin Hoffman) and Mrs Robinson (Anne Bancroft)

MRS ROBINSON: Do you find me undesirable?
BEN BRADDOCK: Oh no, Mrs Robinson. I think . . . I think you're the most attractive of all my parents' friends. I mean that.

D. M. Graham 1911-99
British broadcaster

That this House will in no circumstances fight for its King and Country.
  motion worded by Graham, when an undergraduate, for a debate at the Oxford Union, 9 February 1933; the proposition was carried by 275 votes to 153

Phil Gramm 1942-
American Republican politician

Balancing the budget is like going to heaven. Everybody wants to do it, but nobody wants to do what you have to do to get there.
  in a television interview, 16 September 1990

I did not come to Washington to be loved, and I have not been disappointed.
  Michael Barone and Grant Ujifusa *The American Political Almanac* (1994)

Antonio Gramsci 1891-1937
Italian political theorist and activist

Our motto is still alive and to the point: Pessimism of the intellect, optimism of the will.
   L'Ordine Nuovo 4 March 1921

Marquis de la Grange 1639-92

When we ask for advice, we are usually looking for an accomplice.

Jennifer Granholm 1959-
Canadian-born American Democratic politician

Her greatness lay in doing what everybody else could but doesn't. She was unexpected. She was untitled. (She was) an improbably warrior that was leading an unlikely army of waitresses and street sweepers and shopkeepers and auto mechanics.
   at Rosa Parks' funeral, CNN.com, 2 November 2005

Bernie Grant 1944-2000
British Labour politician

The police were to blame for what happened on Sunday night and what they got was a bloody good hiding.
after the Broadwater Farm riot in which a policeman was killed
   as leader of the Haringey Council outside Tottenham Town Hall, 8 October 1995

Hugh Grant 1960-
English actor and film producer

Women are frightening. If you get to forty as a man, you're quite battle-scarred.

My roles play into a certain fantasy of what people want English people to be, whereas half the time we're vomiting beer and beating people up.

Ulysses S. Grant 1822-85
American Unionist general and statesman, 18th President of the US 1869-77

Leave the matter of religion to the family altar, the church, and the private school, supported entirely by private contributions. Keep the church and state forever separate.
   speech at Des Moines, Iowa, 1875

Günther Grass 1927-
German novelist, poet, and dramatist

The citizen's first duty is unrest.
   The Citizen's First Duty address delivered 1967; in *Speak Out!* (1968)

Muriel Gray 1959-
Scottish writer and broadcaster

Of course I want political autonomy, but not cultural autonomy. You just have to watch the Scottish Baftas to want to kill yourself.
explaining her preference for devolution rather than full independence

in *Scotland on Sunday* 14 January 1996

Jeff Green 1964-
English comedian and writer

If they ever invent a vibrator that can open a pickle jar, we've had it.
on women
Mail on Sunday 21 March 1999 'Quotes of the Week'

Pauline Green 1948-
British socialist politician, leader of the Socialist Group in the European Parliament

The Commission has an established culture that is secretive and authoritarian.
in *Daily Mail* 17 March 1999

Graham Greene 1904-91
English novelist

Catholics and Communists have committed great crimes, but at least they have not stood aside, like an established society, and been indifferent. I would rather have blood on my hands than water like Pilate.
The Comedians (1966)

He felt the loyalty we all feel to unhappiness – the sense that that is where we really belong.
The Heart of the Matter (1948)

Goodness has only once found a perfect incarnation in a human body and never will again, but evil can always find a home there. Human nature is not black and white but black and grey.
The Lost Childhood and Other Essays (1951) title essay

Innocence always calls mutely for protection, when we would be so much wiser to guard ourselves against it. Innocence is like a dumb leper who has lost his bell, wandering the world meaning no harm.
The Quiet American (1955)

Alan Greenspan 1926-
American economist, Chairman of the Federal Reserve of the United States 1987-2006

Capitalism is based on self-interest and self-esteem; it holds integrity and trustworthiness as cardinal virtues and makes them pay off in the marketplace, thus demanding that men survive by means of virtue, not vices. It is this superlatively moral system that the welfare statists propose to improve upon by means of preventative law, snooping bureaucrats, and the chronic goad of fear.
The Assault on Integrity (1963)

The free lunch has still to be invented.
in *Independent* 7 May 2004

Germaine Greer 1939-
Australian feminist

I didn't fight to get women out from behind the vacuum cleaner to get them onto the board of Hoover.
in *Guardian* 27 October 1986

Dick Gregory 1932-
American comedian

You gotta say this for the white race – its self-confidence knows no bounds. Who else could go to a small island in the South Pacific where there's no poverty, no crime, no unemployment, no war and no worry – and call it a 'primitive society'?
From the Back of the Bus (1962)

Julian Grenfell 1888-1915
English soldier and poet, killed in action in the first World War

And Life is Colour and Warmth and Light
And a striving evermore for these;
And he is dead, who will not fight;
And who dies fighting has increase.
written during the second battle of Ypres
'Into Battle' in *Times* 28 May 1915

Lord Grey of Falladon 1862-1933
British Liberal politician

The lamps are going out all over Europe; we shall not see them lit again in our lifetime.
25 Years (1925)

Norman Grubb 1959-
Planning Manager of Revlon UK to the editor, a friend, when the latter was Purchasing Manager at the same company (1992):

You haven't exactly got a challenging job Mike, have you? You get three quotes for something the company needs, then pick the lowest. A monkey could be trained to do that.

The editor's snappy response (1994):

Ha, that's a bit rich, Norm. You ask the sales people what they think they're going to sell, then you tell the production people what to make. Why not cut out your function altogether and have the sales people speak directly to the production people? No need for a monkey. You could be replaced by a pot plant.

Elizabeth Grymeston

A fair woman is a paradise to the eye, a purgatory to the purse, and a hell to the soul.

Che Guevara 1928-67
Argentine Marxist revolutionary

Whenever death may surprise us, let it be welcome if our battle cry has reached even one receptive ear and another hand reaches out to take up our arms.

Sir Alec Guinness 1914-2000
English actor

Always remember before going on stage, wipe your nose and check your flies.
advice given to a young theatre actor

Albert Guinon 1863-1923
French playwright

When everyone is against you, it means that you are absolutely wrong – or absolutely right.

Nubar Gulbenkian 1896-1972
English industrialist and philanthropist

The best number for a dinner party is two: myself and a damned good head waiter.

Richard Guggenheimer

Unless a life is activated by sustained purpose it can become a depressingly haphazard affair.

John Gunther 1901-70
American journalist and writer

All happiness depends on a leisurely breakfast.

Woody Guthrie 1912-67
American folksinger and songwriter

I ain't a communist necessarily, but I been in the red all my life.
  Joe Klein *Woody Guthrie* (1988)

h

Charles Haddon Spurgeon 1834-92
British preacher

You cannot slander human nature; it is worse than words can paint it.

Larry Hagman 1931-
American film and television actor, producer and director

My definition of a redundancy is an air-bag in a politician's car.

The cardinal rule of politics: never get caught in bed with a live man or a dead woman.

William Hague 1961-
English Conservative Party politician, author, public speaker and pianist

[Editor's note: William Hague's Welsh wife Ffion **Hague**, like Hollywood actress Catherine **Zeta-Jones**, hails from Wales. They are typical of the beautiful women to be found there. For non-British readers: Wales is the westernmost county in England, Scotland the northernmost.]

The Foreign Office is being run like a Dad's Army outfit by a Foreign Secretary who combines the pomposity of Captain Mainwaring with the incompetence of Private Pike and the calm of Corporal Jones.
on Robin Cook

I was born in Rotherham. Around where I lived, people thought a Conservative was something you spread on your toast.

The Liberal Democrat leader has gone in a few short weeks from '*Have I Got News For You*' to '*I'm Sorry, I Haven't Got a Clue.*'

If all we needed to govern the country was someone who repeated everything we'd said before, we could have bought a parrot.
expressing his disgruntlement at the appointment of Tony **Blair** as prime minister in a Conservative Party speech in Blackpool on 7 October 1999

Let me take you on a journey to a foreign land – to Britain after a second term of Tony **Blair**.
speech to Conservative Party Spring Conference, Harrogate, 4 March 2001

There was so little English in that answer that President Chirac would have been happy with it.
confronting John **Prescott** at Prime Minister's questions in the House of Commons, 29 March 2006

Earl Haig 1861-1928
British general, Commander in France, 1915-18

A very weak-minded fellow I am afraid, and, like the feather pillow, bears the marks of the last person who has sat on him!
*describing the **17th Earl of Derby**, in a letter to Lady **Haig**, 14 January 1918*

R. Blake *Private Papers of Douglas Haig* (1952)

Lord Hailsham (Quentin Hogg) 1907-2001
British Conservative politician

A great party is not to be brought down because of a scandal by a woman of easy virtue and a proved liar.
*on the **Profumo** affair*

In a confrontation with the politics of power, the soft centre has always melted away.
in October 1981; Anthony Sampson *The Changing Anatomy of Britain* (1982)

A piratical old bruiser with a first-class mind and very bad manners.
*of Denis **Healey***
interview in *The Times* 2 June 1987

Conservatives do not believe that the political struggle is the most important thing in life . . . The simplest of them prefer fox-hunting – the wisest religion.
The Case for Conservatism (1947)

The elective dictatorship.
meaning that the capacity of the government to make laws depends on its parliamentary majority, rather than on countrywide support
title of the Dimbleby Lecture, 19 October 1976

I've known every Prime Minister to a greater or lesser extent since **Balfour**, and most of them have died unhappy.
attributed, 1997

Richard Burdon Haldane 1856-1982
British politician, lawyer, and philosopher

We have come to the conclusion . . . that in the sphere of civil government the duty of investigation and thought, as preliminary to action, might with great advantage be more definitely added.
Peter Hennessey *Whitehall* (1990)

Robert Half

No one can be right all of the time, but it helps to be right most of the time.

Free advice is worth the price.

Lord Halifax 1633-95
English politician and essayist

The following quotations are all from *Political, Moral and Miscellaneous Thoughts and Reflections* (1750)

After a revolution, you see the same men in the drawing-room, and within a week the same flatterers.

It is in a disorderly government as in a river, the lightest things swim at the top.

If the laws could speak for themselves, they would complain of the lawyers in the first place.

The best party is but a kind of conspiracy against the rest of the nation.

Party is a little less than an inquisition, where men are under such a discipline in carrying on the common cause, as leaves no liberty of private opinion.'

If none were to have liberty but those who understand what it is, there would not be many freed men in the world.

Wherever a knave is not punished, an honest man is laughed at.

Lord Halifax 1881-1959
British Conservative politician and Foreign Secretary

No, not exactly. But it spoils one's eye for the high birds.
on being asked immediately after the Munich crisis if he were not worn out by the late nights
   attributed

Jerry Hall 1956-
American actress and supermodel

My mother said it was simple to keep a man. You must be a maid in the living room, a cook in the kitchen, and a whore in the bedroom. I said I'd hire the other two and take care of the bedroom bit.
   in *Observer* 6 October 1985

Rich Hall 1954-
American comedian and writer

Women say they want a man who knows what a woman's worth. That's a pimp.

Margaret Halsey 1910-
American writer

The English never smash in a face. They merely refrain from asking it to dinner.
   With Malice Toward Some (1938)

Alexander Hamilton 1755 - 1804
American economist, a Founding Father and political philosopher

Is it not time to awake from the deceitful dream of a golden age and to adopt as a practical maxim for the direction of our political conduct that we, as well as the other inhabitants of the globe, are yet remote from the happy empire of perfect wisdom and perfect virtue?
   The Federalist No. 6 (1787)

Christopher Hampton 1946-
British playwright

Asking a working writer what he thinks about critics is like asking a lamp-post what it feels about dogs.
   Sunday Times Magazine 16 October 1977

Tony Hancock 1924-68
English comedian

I thought my mother was a bad cook, but at least her gravy used to move about.
   in BBC Radio's *Hancock's Half-Hour*, 'A Sunday Afternoon at Home'

Tom Hanks 1956-
American actor, producer, writer and director

I'm glad I didn't have to fight in any war. I'm glad I didn't have to pick up a gun. I'm glad I didn't et killed or kill somebody. I hope my kids enjoy the same lack of manhood.

William Harcourt 1827-1904
British lawyer, journalist and Liberal statesman

We are all socialists now.
during the passage of Lord Goschen's 1888 budget
   A. G. Gardiner *The Life of Sir William Harcourt* (1923)

Kier Hardie 1856-1915
Scottish Labour politician

Woman, even more than the working class, is the great unknown quantity of the race.
   speech at Bradford, 11 April 1914

Larry Hardiman

The word 'politics' is derived from the word 'poly', meaning 'many', and the word 'ticks', meaning 'blood sucking parasites.'

G. H. Hardy 1877-1947
English mathematician

It is not worth an intelligent man's time to be in the majority. By definition, there are already enough people to do that.

Jeremy Hardy 1961-
English socialist comedian, his socialism ensuring that he makes frequent appearances on BBC Television and Radio

Marriage is like the witness protection programme: you get all new clothes, you live in the suburbs, and you're not allowed to see your friends anymore.

Thomas Hardy 1840-1928
English novelist and poet

'Peace upon earth!' was said, We sing it,
And pay a million priests to bring it.
After two thousand years of mass
We've got as far as poison gas.
   'Christmas: 1924' (1928)

W. F. Hargreaves

I'm Burlington Bertie
I rise at ten thirty and saunter along like a toff,
I walk down the Strand with my gloves in my hand,
Then I walk down again with them off.
    'Burlington Bertie from Bow' (1915 song)

Richard Harkness 1907-1977
American radio and TV journalist

What is a committee? A group of the unwilling, picked from the unfit, to do the unnecessary.
    quoted in *The New York Herald Tribune* 15 June 1960

Harriet Harman 1950-
Deputy Leader of the British Labour Party, a politically correct feminist socialist politician (1982-) with hauntingly beautiful eyes

Equality, blah, blah, blah, fairness, blah, blah, blah, sexism, blah, blah, blah, discrimination, blah, blah, blah, ageism, blah, blah, blah . . .

[Editor's note: the above is what I recall of Harriet Harman's monologues, interviews and writings, 1982-]

What must men do . . . They will have to . . . They will have to . . . Then they will feel able to . . . They must begin to . . . They must dramatically increase . . . They must . . . Men must . . . They must . . . They must . . . they must . . .

[Editor's note: on behalf of men everywhere, might I respond feebly with, '*Why* must we, Mistress Harriet?']

Extracts from three successive paragraphs in Harriet Harman's *The Century Gap (20th Century Man, 21st Century Woman* (1993), in a section titled 'Men Contributing More.' Available from Amazon resellers for £0.01 (plus p&p)

Chris Harris 1978-
British businessman

Why aren't we marching on Parliament and ejecting the shower of idiots who have been running this country since 1997? Because we're British, that's why. So all we do is moan. But I've finally had enough of living in a socialist republic. I'm off with my daughter soon to live and work in Australia. I'd rather give my money to the Australian government than to the British one.
    conversation with the author, 25 January 2010

Sidney J. Harris 1917-1986
American journalist

Never take the advice of someone who has not had your kind of trouble.

Clyde Harrison

Last year, if you didn't eat, didn't drive to work, didn't heat your home, didn't visit a doctor, didn't buy a house, didn't buy insurance of any kind, didn't have a child in college and didn't pay taxes, your cost of living agrees with the Government's cost of living index.

Hal Hartley 1959-
American film director and writer

There's a right way and a wrong way to do things. If you make a chair, you want to make a nice chair. You want people to admire it. I think doing something well is a form of respect for humanity in general. I have found that all incompetence comes from not paying attention, which comes from people doing something that they don't want to do. And doing what you don't want to do means either you have no choice, or you don't think that the moments of your life are worth fighting for.

Sir Max Hastings 1945-
British journalist, former editor of the estimable British newspapers *The Daily Telegraph* and the *Evening Standard*, historian and author

He possesses fewer gifts of leadership than my Labrador.
*on Conservative Party leader Iain Duncan **Smith***

It would be naive not to recognise the near-unteachability of the most disadvantaged of our children. But there are many, many more who have the brains and energy and supportive parents to propel themselves upwards in society – if only their schools give them the chance. We need fewer bog-standard tests and more exams that mean something; teachers committed to competition and enabling clever children of all classes to fulfil their potential. Yet Harmanism is about levelling down, stuffing the middle classes. Oh yes, and with the dollop of hypocrisy that allowed Harriet **Harman** (herself educated at the famously elitist St Paul's Girls' School) to choose a grammar school outside her constituency for her children.
 in *Daily Mail* 28 January 2010

Roy Hattersley 1932-
British Labour politician

Opposition is four or five years' humiliation in which there is no escape from the indignity of no longer controlling events.
 in *Independent* 25 March 1995 'Quote Unquote'

Politicians are entitled to change their minds. But when they adjust their principles some explanation is necessary.
 in *Observer* 21 March 1999

Bob Hawke 1929-
Australian Labour Party politician, 23rd Prime Minister of Australia 1983-91

He's the cutlery man of Australian politics. He was born with a silver spoon in his mouth, speaks with a forked tongue, and knifes his colleagues in the back.
*on Malcolm **Fraser***

Ethan Hawke 1970-
American actor, writer and film director

You are more likely to find great leadership coming from a man who likes to have sex with a lot of women than one who doesn't.

Helen Hayes 1900-93
American actress

The love of liberty is the love of others; the love of power is the love of ourselves.

Every human being on this earth is born with a tragedy, and it isn't original sin. He's born with the tragedy that he has to grow up. That he has to leave the nest, the security, and go out to do battle. He has to lose everything that is lovely and fight for a new loveliness of his own making, and it's a tragedy. A lot of people don't have the courage to do it.

My mother drew a distinction between achievement and success. She said that 'achievement is the knowledge that you have studied and worked hard and done the best that is in you. Success is being praised by others, and that's nice, too, but not as important or satisfying. Always aim for achievement and forget about success.'

Friedrich August von Hayek 1899-1992
Austrian-born economist and political philosopher

I am certain that nothing has done so much to destroy the juridical safeguards of individual freedom as the striving after this miracle of social justice.
  Economic Freedom and Representative Government (1973)

The system of private property is the most important guarantee of freedom, not only for those who own property, but scarcely less for those who do not.
  The Road to Serfdom (1944)

Once government has embarked upon planning for the sake of justice, it cannot refuse responsibility for anybody's fate or position.
  The Road to Serfdom (1944)

Once you admit that the individual is merely a means to serve the ends of the higher entity called society or the nation, most of those features of totalitarian regimes which horrify us follow of necessity.
  The Road to Serfdom (1944)

One cannot help a country to maintain its standard of life by assisting people to consume more than they produce.
  in *Daily Telegraph* 26 August 1976

William Hazlitt 1778-1830
English writer, literary critic, essayist, grammarian and philosopher

If mankind had wished for what is right, they might have had it long ago.

Man is the only animal that laughs and weeps, for he is the only animal that is struck with the difference between what things are and what they ought to be.

Talk of mobs! Is there any body of people that has this character in a more consummate degree than the House of Commons? Is there any set of men that determines more by acclamation, and less by deliberation and individual conviction?
  'On the Difference between Writing and Speaking'; in London *Magazine* July 1820

The greatest test of courage I can conceive is to speak the truth in the House of Commons.

'On the Difference between Writing and Speaking'; in London *Magazine* July 1820

There is nothing good to be had in the country, or if there is, they will not let you have it.
'Observations on Wordsworth's *Excursion*' (1819)

Cuthbert Morley Headlam 1876-1964
British Conservative politician

We ought to have made up more to the political leaders and their wives – the latter are an unattractive lot, but their influence is greater than one supposes.
diary 28 July 1933

Denis Healey 1917-
British Labour Party politician

There are going to be howls of anguish from the 80,000 people who are rich enough to pay over 75% tax on the last slice of their income.
speech at the Labour Party Conference, 1 October 1973

And who is the great Mephistiopheles behind this shabby Faust [the Foreign Secretary, Geoffrey **Howe**]? . . . To quote her own backbenchers, the Great she-elephant, she who must be obeyed, Catherine the Great of Finchley, the Prime Minister herself.
*of Margaret **Thatcher***
in the House of Commons, 27 February 1984

The Fabians . . . found socialism wandering aimlessly in Cloud-cuckoo-land and set it working on the gas and water problems of the nearest town or village.
of the parochialism of the Fabians
New Fabian Essays (1952)

La Passionara of middle-class privilege.
*of Margaret **Thatcher***
Kenneth Minogue and **Michael Biddiss** *Thatcherism* (1987)

There is the noble Marquis. Like a pike at the bottom of a pool.
*of Lord **Hartington**, apparently asleep on the Opposition Bench*
Herbert Gladstone *After Thirty Years* (1928)

Tony **Blair** [then newly elected leader of the British Labour Party] is a fresh face in British politics and the sort of chap the country needs, whereas John **Prescott** [the deputy leader] has the face of a man who clubs baby seals to death, but is, none the less, extremely pragmatic.
quoted in *The Sunday Telegraph* 17 July 1994

Three things happen when you get to my age. First your memory starts to go ... and I have forgotten the other two.
quoted in *The Independent* 23 July 1994 'Quote Unquote'

Being attacked in the House by him is like being savaged by a dead sheep.
*on Geoffrey **Howe***

A mixture of **Rasputin** and Tommy **Cooper**.
*on Sir Keith **Joseph***

Edward Heath 1916-2005
British Conservative statesman; Prime Minister 1970-74

Rejoice, rejoice, rejoice.
*telephone call to his office on hearing of Margaret **Thatcher**'s fall from power in 1990*
   attributed; in *Daily Telegraph* (online edition) 24 September 1998

It was not totally inconceivable that she could have joined me as my wife at No. 10.
*of the starlet Jayne **Mansfield***
   in *Sunday Times* 6 February 2000 'Talking Heads' 24 September 1998

That would be difficult.
   replying to Margaret Thatcher when she asked him to sit on her right for a photograph

Music means everything to me when I'm alone. And it's the best way of getting that bloody man Wilson out of my hair.

I am not a product of privilege. I am a product of opportunity.

I do not often attack the Labour Party. They do it so well themselves.

Simon Heffer 1960-
British journalist, columnist and writer

For the first few years of an independent Scotland the deficit caused by losing the financial support of the English taxpayer would doubtless be made up by Europe, in the interests of Brussels acquiring a new and loyal client state and preserving stability in the region. Yet this kind of support cannot possibly continue indefinitely. Scotland will have to make a success of its own economy, and pay its own way. If it loses its best brains and best businesses through high taxation, it could quickly find itself reduced to the level of a cold-weather theme park. It was economic failure before that forced Scotland into the arms of the English: and it is far from certain that such circumstances might not come about again. Some years in the future, the Scots themselves might see that it is once more in Scotland's interests to unite with the English. If and when that time comes, the English will need to consider the prospects on a purely commercial basis.
on Scottish independence
   Nor Shall My Sword: the reinvention of England (1999)

Georg Hegel 1770-1831
German idealist philosopher

What experience and history teach is this – that nations and governments have never learned anything from history, or acted upon any lessons they might have drawn from it.
Lectures on the Philosophy of World History: Introduction (1830)

America is therefore the land of the future where, in the ages that lie before us, the burden of the world's history shall reveal itself.

Heinrich Heine 1797-1856
German poet

Wherever books will be burned, men also, in the end, are burned.
   Almansor (1823)

Robert A. Heinlein 1907-88
American science fiction writer

Be wary of strong drink. It can make you shoot at tax collectors and miss.
Time Enough for Love (1974)

The power to tax, once conceded, has no limits; it consumes until it destroys.
The Moon is a Harsh Mistress (1969)

No state has an inherent right to survive through conscript troops and in the long run no state ever has. Roman matrons used to say to their sons: 'Come back with your shield, or on it.' Later on, this custom declined. So did Rome.

Democracy is based on the assumption that a million men are wiser than one man. How's that again? I missed something.

An elephant - a mouse built to government specifications.

The United States has become a place where entertainers and professional athletes are mistaken for people of importance.

Anyone who clings to the historically untrue - and thoroughly immoral - doctrine that violence never settles anything I would advise to conjure up the ghosts of Napoleon **Bonaparte** and the **Duke of Wellington** and let them debate it. The ghost of **Hitler** would referee. Violence, naked force, has settled more issues in history than any other factor, and the contrary opinion is wishful thinking at its worst. Breeds that forgot this basic truth have always paid for it with their lives and their freedoms.

Joseph Heller 1923-99
American satirical novelist, short story writer and playwright

Some men are born mediocre, some men achieve mediocrity, and some men have mediocrity thrust upon them.
Catch-22

If I am going to be trivial, inconsequential, and deceitful ... then I might as well be in government.
Closing Time (1994)

Sir Robert Helpmann 1909-86
Australian dancer and choreographer

The trouble with nude dancing is that not everything stops when the music stops.
After the opening night of *Oh, Calcutta!*

Ernest Hemingway 1899-1961
American author

God knows people who are paid to have attitudes towards things, professional critics, make me sick; camp following eunuchs of literature. They won't even whore. They're all virtuous and sterile. And how well meaning and high minded. But they're all camp followers.
Selected Letters (1981)

Tony Hendra 1941-
English satirist and writer

Your liberal is an eternal sixteen-year-old, forever rebellious, forever oblivious to the nasty realities of life, forever looking *forward* to some impossible revolution in human nature.
The Book of Bad Virtues (1995)

Peter Hennessey 1947-
English historian

The model of a modern Prime Minister would be a kind of grotesque composite freak – someone with the dedication to duty of a **Peel**, the physical energy of a **Gladstone**, the detachment of a **Salisbury**, the brains of an **Asquith**, the balls of a **Lloyd George**, the word-power of a **Churchill**, the administrative gifts of an **Attlee**, the style of a **Macmillan**, the managerialism of a **Heath**, and the sleep requirements of a **Thatcher**. Human beings do not come like that.
The Hidden Wiring (1995)

MI5 is a job creation scheme for muscular underachievers from the ancient universities.
in *The Times* 1981, profile of Roger **Hollis**

He seemed like a benign and decent beached whale washed up on the harder shores of modern Conservatism.
*of Rab **Butler** in his last years*
in *Independent* 8 May 1987

William A. Henry III 1950-1994
American cultural critic and author

The following quotations are from *In Defence of Elitism* (1994):

There is nothing wrong with discontent at having a modest place in the scheme of things. That very discontent produced the ambition that built the culture of yesterday and today. But the discontent of those times was accompanied by discipline, willingness to work hard, and ready acceptance of a competitive society.

Every corner of human race may have something to contribute. That does not mean that all contributions are equal . . . It is scarcely the same thing to put a man on the moon as to put a bone in your nose.

The worst aspect of what gets called 'political correctness' these days is the erosion of the intellectual confidence needed to sort out, and rank, competing values.

A fair society is one in which some people fail – and they may fail in something other than precise, demographically representative proportions.

The problem in contemporary America is that our awareness of life's capriciousness has translated into guilt whenever things go well.

Henry II 1133-89
English monarch, King from 1154

Will no one rid me of this turbulent priest?
*of Thomas **Becket**, Archbishop of Canterbury, murdered in Canterbury Cathedral, 1170*

Henry IV (of Navarre) 1553-1610
French monarch, King from 1589

I want there to be no peasant in my kingdom so poor that he is unable to have a chicken in his pot every Sunday.
  in Hardouin de Péréfixe *Histoire de Henry Le Grand* (1861)

Henry VIII 1491-1547
English monarch, King from 1509

The King found her [Anne of **Cleves**] so different from her picture . . . that . . . he swore they had brought him a Flanders mare.
  Tobias Smollett *A Complete History of England* (3rd ed., 1759)

Patrick Henry 1736-99
a prominent figure in the American Revolution, one of the Founding Fathers of the United States

I know not what course others may take; but as for me, give me liberty, or give me death!
  speech in Virginia Convention, 23 March 1775

We are not weak if we make proper use of those means which the God of Nature has placed in our power . . . The battle, sir, is not to the strong alone; it is to the vigilant, the active, the brave.
  speech in Virginia Convention, 23 March 1775

Guard with jealous attention the public liberty. Suspect everyone who approaches that jewel. Unfortunately, nothing will preserve it but downright force. Whenever you give up that force, you are inevitably ruined.
  attributed

Jim Henson 1936-1990
American puppeteer and creator of The Muppets

When I was young, my ambition was to be one of the people who made a difference in this world. My hope still is to leave the world a little bit better for my having been there. It's a wonderful life and I love it.
  It's Not Easy Being Green And Other Things to Consider

Katharine Hepburn 1907-2003
American actress

Acting is the most minor of gifts and not a very high-class way to earn a living. Shirley **Temple** could do it at the age of four.

A. P. Herbert 1890-1971
English writer and humorist

This high official, all allow
Is grossly overpaid;
There wasn't any Board, and now
There isn't any Trade
  'The President of the Board of Trade' (2002)

The Common Law of England has been laboriously built about a mythical figure – the figure of 'The Reasonable Man'.
Uncommon Law (1935)

The critical time in matrimony is breakfast-time.
Uncommon Law (1935)

Frank Herbert 1920-86
American writer of science fiction

Humans live best when each has a place to stand, when each knows where he belongs in the scheme of things and what he may achieve. Destroy the place and you destroy the person.
Dune (1965)

If you think of yourselves as helpless and ineffectual, it is certain that you will create a despotic government to be your master. The wise despot, therefore, maintains among his subjects a popular sense that they are helpless and ineffectual.
The Dosadi Experiment (1978)

George Herbert 1593-1633
Welsh poet, orator and Anglican priest

The more women looke to their glasse, the lesse they looke to their house.
Outlandish Proverbs

Oliver Herford 1863-1935
American humorist

Actresses will happen in the best-regulated families.

What is my loftiest ambition? I've always wanted to throw an egg into an electric fan.

Alexander Ivanovich Herzen 1812-70
Russian writer and revolutionary

Russia's future will be a great danger for Europe and a great misfortune for Russia if there is no emancipation of the individual. One more century of present despotism will destroy all the good qualities of the Russian people.
The Development of Revolutionary Ideas in Russia (1851)

Andrew Heslop 1966-
Yorkshire-based writer and business consultant

LIFE COACHING IN YORKSHIRE
Lesson One: Keeping happy means keeping busy.

'What's up wi' you, yer miserable basterd?'
'I'm a bit fed up wi' life, like.'
'Well stop mopin' abart and piss off darn't chippie n gerrus a couple a scallops.'
'Aw, a'rayt then.'
'See, tha feels better awready, ye soft get.'

Practice this until you are comfortable that the technique has been effective. You will then be ready for lesson two: *A night at the dogs keeps the blues away*.
private communication to the editor, 2009

When a business person says something is being done to attain 'synergies' – usually at the time of a merger or takeover – he means there is no rational or financial reason for doing so. Realised cost savings always fall far short of expectations. And it's not just business: civil servants rely on 'synergies' to justify their very existence.
conversation with the editor, 25 January 2010

Holly Heslop 1990-
Beloved daughter of Andrew Heslop

Being at university is exactly like being on the dole – except your parents are proud of you.
[Note from Andrew Heslop: this sums up New Labour policies well. Send everyone to university, irrespective of academic ability, and keep dole queues artificially low.]

Michael Heseltine 1933-
British businessman and Conservative Party politician

The self-appointed king of the gutter.
on Neil Kinnock

I am humble enough to recognise that I have made mistakes, but politically astute enough to know that I have forgotten what they are.

He who wields the knife never wears the crown.
in *New Society* 14 February 1986

Charlton Heston 1923-2008
American actor

When I told an audience last year that white pride is just as valid as black pride or red pride or anyone else's pride, they called me a racist. I've worked with brilliantly talented homosexuals all my life. But when I told an audience that gay rights should extend no further than your rights or my rights, I was called a homophobe. I served in World War II against the Axis powers. But during a speech, when I drew an analogy between singling out innocent Jews and singling out innocent gun owners, I was called an anti-Semite. Everyone I know knows I would never raise a closed fist against my country. But when I asked an audience to oppose this cultural persecution, I was compared to Timothy McVeigh.
in a speech to the Harvard Law School on 16 February 1999

Jack Hibberd 1940-
Australian playwright

Absinthe makes the parts grow stronger.

Bill Hicks 1961-94
American stand-up comedian and social critic

Did you ever think maybe Jesus Christ isn't going to come back while he sees himself nailed to crosses everywhere? It's a bit like going up to Jackie **Onassis** with a rifle pendant on your chest and saying, 'We're thinking about John, baby.'

I'm sick of those damned trailer park trash having 'miracle babies' every year and expecting you and I, the taxpayers, to pay for their upkeep. Their babies are no more miracles than when I have a dump 24 hours after I eat a Big Mac and fries.

Cullen Hightower 1923-
American quote and quip writer

Those who agree with us may not be right, but we admire their astuteness.

Jim Hightower 1943-
American politician

There's nothing in the middle of the road but yellow stripes and dead armadillos.
   attributed, 1984

Benny Hill 1924-1992
English comedian, actor and singer

Why buy a book when you can join a lending library?

Joe Hill 1879-1915
Swedish-born American labour leader and songwriter

You will eat, bye and bye,
In that glorious land above the sky;
Work and pray, live on hay,
You'll get pie in the sky when you die.
   'Preacher and the Slave' in *Songs of the Workers* (1911)

Paul von Hindenburg 1847-1934
German Field Marshal and statesman, President of the Weimar Republic 1925-34

That man for a Chancellor? I'll make him a postmaster and he can lick the stamps with my head on them.
of Hitler
   to **Meissner**, 13 August 1932; J. W. Wheeler-Bennett *Hindenburg: the Wooden Titan* (1936)

Sir Alfred Hitchcock 1899-1980
English filmmaker and producer

These are bagpipes. I understand the inventor of the bagpipes was inspired when he saw a man carrying an indignant, asthmatic pig under his arm. Unfortunately, the man-made sound never equalled the purity of the sound achieved by the pig.

Adolf Hitler 1889-1945
Austrian-born German politician, leader of the National Socialist German Workers Party

By means of shrewd lies, unremittingly repeated, it is possible to make people believe that heaven is hell – and hell heaven. The greater the lie, the more readily it will be believed by the great masses.
   Mein Kampf (1925-26)

Rather than go through that again, I would prefer to have three or four teeth taken out.
   to **Mussolini**, having spent nine hours intermittently in Franco's company

Paul Preston *Franco* (1993)

Those who want to live, let them fight, and those who do not want to fight in this world of eternal struggle do not deserve to live.
   his third public speech after taking power

Well, he seemed such a nice old gentleman, I thought I would give him my autograph as a souvenir.
*on Neville **Chamberlain** and the Munich Agreement (1938)*

What luck for rulers that men do not think.

Obstacles do not exist to be surrendered to, but only to be broken.

Thomas Hobbes 1588-1679
English philosopher

The following quotations are from *Leviathan* (1651):

I put for a general declination of all mankind, a perpetual and restless desire of power after power, that ceaseth only in death.

For what reason go men armed, and have locks and keys to fasten their doors, if they be not naturally in a state of war?

A man's conscience and his judgment is the same thing; and as the judgment, so also the conscience, may be erroneous.

Edward Hodnett

If you don't ask the right questions, you don't get the right answers. A question asked in the right way often points to its own answer. Asking questions is the ABC of diagnosis. Only the inquiring mind solves problems.

Eric Hoffer 1902-83
American social writer and philosopher

Absolute faith corrupts as absolutely as absolute power.

Power corrupts the few, while weakness corrupts the many.

The link between ideas and action is rarely direct. There is almost always an intermediate step in which the idea is overcome. De **Tocqueville** points out that it is at times when passions start to govern human affairs that ideas are most obviously translated into political action. The translation of ideas into action is usually in the hands of people least likely to follow rational motives. Hence, it is that action is often the nemesis of ideas, and sometimes of the men who formulate them. One of the marks of the truly vigorous society is the ability to dispense with passion as a midwife of action – the ability to pass directly from thought to action.

They who lack talent expect things to happen without effort. They ascribe failure to a lack of inspiration or ability, or to misfortune, rather than to insufficient application. At the core of every true talent there is an awareness of the difficulties inherent in any achievement, and the confidence that by persistence and patience something worthwhile will be realized. Thus talent is a species of vigor.

Our achievements speak for themselves. What we have to keep track of are our failures, discouragements and doubts. We tend to forget the past difficulties, the many false starts, and the painful groping. We see our past achievements as the end results of a clean forward thrust, and our present difficulties as signs of decline and decay.

Abbie Hoffman 1936-89
American social and political activist

Democracy is not something that you believe in, or something that you hang your hat on. It's something that you do, you participate. Without participation, democracy crumbles and fails. If you participate, you win, and the future is yours.

Simon Hoggart 1946-
British journalist

Peter **Mandelson** is someone who can skulk in broad daylight.
   in *Guardian* 10 July 1998

Friedrich Hölderlin 1770-1843
German poet

What has always made the state a hell on earth has been precisely that man has tried to make it his heaven.

Alec Douglas-Home, Lord Home 1903-95
British Conservative statesman; Prime Minister, 1963-4

There are two problems in my life. The political ones are insoluble and the economic ones are incomprehensible.

Had a letter from your father [Sir Roy **Harrod**, the economist] today about inflation . . . or deflation . . . or something.
   to Dominic **Harrod** at a Downing Street party
   Peter Hennessey *The Prime Minister: the Office and its Holders since 1945* (2000)

Caroline Douglas Home 1937-
Daughter of the British Prime Minister Lord **Home**

He [Sir Alec Douglas **Home**] is used to dealing with estate workers. I cannot see how anyone can say he is out of touch.

Herbert Hoover 1874-1964
Mining engineer, author, Republican Party politician, 31st President of the United States 1929-33

Blessed are the young, for they will inherit the national debt.

What the world needs today is a definite, spiritual mobilization of the nations who believe in God against this tide of Red agnosticism . . . And in rejecting an atheistic other world, I am confident that the Almighty God will be with us.

in proposing the abolition of the United Nations, in favor of a 'cooperation of God-fearing free nations'
Address upon the American Road 1948-50

Bob Hope 1903-2003
American comedian and actor

I don't know what people have got against the government – they've done nothing.

I must say the Senator's victory in Wisconsin was a triumph for democracy. It proves that a millionaire has just as good a chance as anybody else.
of John F. Kennedy's electoral victory
in 1960; William Robert Faith *Bob Hope* (1983)

Mark Hoppus 1972-
American musician and record producer

I can name the newscaster on *The Simpsons* but I can't name my own congressman. And that's what makes America great.

Horace 65-8 BC
Roman poet

He who postpones the hour of living rightly is like the rustic who waits for the river to run out before he crosses.

O citizens, first acquire wealth; you can practise virtue afterwards.
Epistles

Nick Hornby 1957-
English novelist and essayist

Being gay was a bit like the Olympics; it disappeared in ancient times, and then they brought it back in the twentieth century.
Maureen in *A Long Way Down* (2005)

John Hoskyns 1927-
British businessman; head of the Prime Minister's Policy Unit 1979-82

The House of Commons is the greatest closed shop of all . . . For the purposes of government, a country of 55 million people is forced to depend on a talent pool which could not sustain a single multinational company.
'Conservatism is Not Enough', Institute of Directors Annual Lecture, 25 September 1983

The Tory party never panics, except in a crisis.
in *Sunday Times* 19 February 1989

Sam Houston 1793-1863
American statesmen, politician and soldier

He has all the characteristics of a dog except loyalty.
on fellow legislator Thomas Jefferson Green

The North is determined to preserve this Union. They are not a fiery, impulsive people as you are, for they live in colder climates. But when they begin to move in a given direction . . . they move with the steady momentum and perseverance of a mighty avalanche.
in 1861, warning the people of Texas against secession
  Geoffrey C. Ward *The Civil War* (1991)

Michael Howard 1941-
British Conservative politician, Party Leader 2003-2005

Blair goes one way, **Brown** goes the other, and bang goes the third way.

I do not believe that one person's poverty is caused by another's wealth.

I am happy to debate the past with the Prime Minister any day he likes. I have a big dossier on his past, and I did not even have to sex it up.
  at Prime Minister's Questions in the House of Commons, 12 November 2003

Edgar W. Howe 1853-1937
American novelist, magazine and newspaper editor

Don't abuse your fiends and expect them to consider it criticism.

Geoffrey Howe 1926-
British Conservative politician

It is rather like sending your opening batsman to the crease only for them to find the moment the first balls are bowled that their bats have been broken before the game by the team captain . . . The time has come for others to consider their own response to the tragic conflict of loyalties with which I have myself wrested for perhaps too long.
*resignation speech as deputy prime minister on 13 November 1990, on his difficulties with Margaret **Thatcher***
  in the House of Commons, 13 November 1990

Louis McHenry Howe 1871-1936
American Democrat politician

You can't adopt politics as a profession, and remain honest.
speech, 17 January 1933

James Howell 1594-1666
British historian and writer

Respect a man, he will do the more.

Elbert Hubbard 1856-1915
American writer, publisher, artist and philosopher

How many a man has thrown up his hands at a time when a little more effort, a little more patience would have achieved success?

Never explain – your friends do not need it and your enemies will not believe you anyway.
  The Motto Book (1907)

Kim Hubbard

It is going to be fun to watch and see how long the meek can keep the earth after they inherit it.
   quoted in *Abe Martin's Wisecracks* ed. E. V. Lucas (1930)

L. Ron Hubbard 1911-86
Science fiction author and founder of the Church of Scientology

Dreams, goals, ambitions – these are the stuff man uses for fuel.

Howard Hughes 1905-76
American aviator, engineer, industrialist, film producer, film director and philanthropist

To err is human. To blame it on someone else is politics.

You're like a pay toilet, aren't you? You don't give a shit for nothing.
   to Robert Mitchum

Robert Hughes

If the first law of American corporate life is that deadwood floats, the corresponding rule of liberation-talk is that hot air expands.
   Culture of Complaint (1993)

The all-pervasive claim to victimhood tops off America's long-cherished culture of therapeutics. To seem strong may only conceal a rickety scaffolding of denial, but to be vulnerable is to be invincible.
   Culture of Complaint (1993)

Her face was her chaperone.

Victor Hugo 1802-85
French poet, novelist, and dramatist

An invasion of armies can be resisted, but not an idea whose time has come.
   Histoire d'un Crime (written 1851-2, published 1877)

David Hume 1711-76
Scottish philosopher

Money . . . is none of the wheels of trade: it is the oil which renders the motion of the wheels more smooth and easy.
   Essays: Moral and Political (1741-2) 'Of Money'

I cannot but bless the memory of Julius Caesar, for the great esteem he expressed for fat men, and his aversion to lean ones.

Hubert Humphrey 1911-78
American Democratic politician

The right to be heard does not automatically include the right to be taken seriously.

Barry Humphries 1934-
Australian entertainer

Tell me the history of that frock, Judy. It's obviously an old favourite. You were wise to remove the curtain rings.
   as **Dame Edna Everage** in London Weekend Television show, *Another Audience with Dame Edna* (1984)
   to **Judy**, wife of Liberal politician David **Steel**

The prigs who attack Jeffrey **Archer** should bear in mind that we all, to some extent, reinvent ourselves. Jeffrey has just gone to a bit more trouble.
   in *Observer* on 19 December 1999 'They said what...?'

Lord Hunt of Tanworth 1919-
British civil servant; Secretary of the Cabinet 1973-9

It has got to be, so far as possible, a democratic and accountable shambles.
of British Cabinet government, described as 'a shambles'
   at a seminar at the Institute of Historical Research, 20 October 1993

Douglas Hurd 1930-
British Conservative politician; Foreign Secretary 1989-95

People in the forefront of environmental causes are destroying experimental crops. That's not logical. That's Luddite.
   in *Sunday Times* 19 September 1999

William Hurrell Mallock 1849-1923
English author

The human race progresses because and when the strongest human powers and the highest human faculties lead it . . . if all the ruling classes of today could be disposed of in a single massacre, and nobody left but those who at present call themselves the workers, these workers would be as helpless as a flock of shepherdless sheep.
Aristocracy and Evolution (1892)

Robert M. Hutchins 1899-1977
American educator

Whenever I feel like exercise, I lie down until the feeling passes.

Sir Robert Hutchinson 1873-1950
Scottish soldier and Liberal politician

Vegetarianism is harmless enough, though it is apt to fill a man with wind and self-righteousness.

Sir Len Hutton 1916-90
English cricketer

It's a bit like watching men knitting.
   on women playing cricket

Aldous Huxley 1894-1963
English humanist, pacifist, poet, travel writer, film script writer

That all men are equal is a proposition which, at ordinary times, no sane individual has ever given his assent.

At least two-thirds of our miseries spring from human stupidity, human malice and those great motivators and justifiers of malice and stupidity: idealism, dogmatism and proselytising zeal on behalf of religious or political ideas.

Most human beings have an almost infinite capacity for taking things for granted.

Happiness is not achieved by the conscious pursuit of happiness; it is generally the by-product of other activities.
   Vedanta for the Western World (1945)

Idealism is the noble toga that political gentlemen drape over their will to power.
   in *New York Herald Tribune* 25 November 1963

Consistency is contrary to nature, contrary to life. The only completely consistent people are the dead.
   'Wordsworth in the Tropics' (1929)

Thomas H. Huxley 1825-95
British biologist

It is not who is right, but what is right, that is of importance.

The deepest sin against the human mind is to believe things without evidence.

Agnosticism simply means that a man shall not say he knows or believes that for which he has no grounds for professing to believe.

Science . . . warns me to be careful how I adopt a view which jumps with my preconceptions, and to require stronger evidence for such belief than for one to which I was previously hostile. My business is to teach my aspirations to confirm themselves to fact, not to try to make facts harmonise with my aspirations.

Logical consequences are the scarecrows of fools and the beacons of wise men.
   Science and Culture (1881) 'On the Hypothesis that Animals are Automata'

I

Carol Iannone
American conservative writer and literary critic

One almost begins to feel that the reason some women worked feverishly to get into men's clubs is to have a respite from the womanised world feminists have created.
Good Order (1994) ed. Brad Miner 'The Feminist Perversion'

Henrik Ibsen 1828-1906
19th century Norwegian playwright, theatre director

The strongest man in the world is he who stands alone.
An Enemy of the People (1882)

The majority never has right on its side. Never I say! That is one of the social lies that a free, thinking man is bound to rebel against. Who makes up the majority in any given country? Is it the wise men or the fools? I think we must agree that the fools are in a terrible overwhelming majority, all the wide world over. But, damn it, it can surely never be right that the stupid should rule over the clever!
An Enemy of the People (1882)

It is inexcusable for scientists to torture animals; let them make their experiments on journalists and politicians.

Harold L. Ickes 1874-1952
American lawyer and administrator

The trouble with Senator Long . . . is that he's suffering from halitosis of the intellect. That's presuming Senator Long has an intellect.
of Huey Long
   speech, 1935; G. Wolfskill and J. A. Hudson *All But the People: Franklin D. Roosevelt and his Critics, 1933-39* (1969)

Takayuki Ikkaku, Arisa Hosaka and Toshihiro Kawabata

Give a man a fish, and he'll eat for a day. Give a fish a man, and he'll eat for weeks!
Animal Crossing: Wild World (2005)

Ivan Illich 1926-
American sociologist

In a consumer society there are inevitably two kinds of slaves: the prisoners of addiction and the prisoners of envy.
Tools for Conviviality (1973)

William Ralph Inge 1860-1954
English clergyman, writer and essayist; Dean of St Paul's 1911-34

It takes in reality only one to make a quarrel. It is useless for the sheep to pass resolutions in favour of vegetarianism, while the wolf remains of a different opinion.
Outspoken Essays: First Series (1919)

The nations which have put mankind and posterity most in their debt have been small states – Israel, Athens, Florence, Elizabethan England.
Outspoken Essays: Second Series (1922)

The enemies of Freedom do not argue; they shout and they shoot.
End of an Age (1948)

The effect of boredom on a large scale in history is underestimated. It is a main cause of revolutions, and would soon bring to an end all the static Utopians and the farmyard civilisation of the Fabians.
End of an Age (1948)

Robert Ingersoll 1833-99
Civil War veteran, American political leader, and orator during the Golden Age of Freethought in America, noted for his broad range of culture and his defense of agnosticism

Any doctrine that will not bear investigation is not a fit tenant for the mind of an honest man.

There is no slavery but ignorance.

I'd rather smoke one cigar than hear two sermons.

If a man would follow, today, the teachings of the Old Testament, he would be a criminal. If he would follow strictly the teachings of the New, he would be insane.

If we are immortal it is a fact in nature, and we are not indebted to priests for it, nor to bibles for it, and it cannot be destroyed by unbelief.

Give to every other human being every right that you claim for yourself.

Bernard Ingham 1932-
British journalist and public relations specialist; press secretary to Margaret Thatcher 1979-90

My God, I've been stabbed in the front.
at a meeting of the Parliamentary Lobby, noticing that he had a spot of blood on his shirt
  recalled in a letter to Antony Jay, January 1995

Christopher Isherwood 1905-86
British-born American novelist, his novel *Goodbye to Berlin* (1939) was filmed as *Cabaret* in 1972

The common cormorant (or shag)
Lays eggs inside a paper bag,
You follow the idea, no doubt?
It's to keep the lightning out.
But what these unobservant birds
Have never thought of, is that herds
Of wandering bears might come with buns

And steal the bags to hold the crumbs.
    'The Common Cormorant' (written c.1925)

Hastings Lionel ('Pug') Ismay 1887-1965
British general and Secretary to the Committee of Imperial Defence; first Secretary-General of NATO

NATO exists for three reasons – to keep the Russians out, the Americans in, and the Germans down.
    to a group of British Conservative backbenchers in 1949
    Peter Hennessy *Never Again* (1992); oral tradition

Alec Issigonis 1906-88
Turkish-born British car designer

A camel is a horse designed by a committee.
on his dislike of working in teams
    in *Guardian* 14 January 1991 'Notes and Queries'; attributed

Eddie Izzard 1962-
British stand-up comedian, actor and marathon runner

I grew up in Europe, where the history comes from.

'Cake or death?' 'Cake, please.'
imagining how a Church of England Inquisition might have worked
    Dress to Kill (stage show, San Francisco, 1998)

j

Andrew Jackson 1767-1845
American Democratic statesman; 7th President of the US, 1829-37

The brave man inattentive to his duty, is worth little more to his country, than the coward who deserts her in the hour of danger.
>to troops who had retreated from their lines during the battle of New Orleans, 8 January 1815
>attributed

One man with courage makes a majority.
>attributed

Glenda Jackson 1936-
English actress and Labour Party politician

The important thing in acting is being able to laugh and cry. If I have to laugh, I think of my sex life. If I have to cry, I think of my sex life.

If I am one of **Blair**'s babes, well, I've been called a damn sight worse.
>in *Independent on Sunday* 8 August 1999

Robert H. Jackson 1892-1954
American judge

It is not the function of government to keep the citizen from falling into error; it is the function of the citizen to stop the government from falling into error.
>*American Communications Association v. Douds* (May 1950)

Clive James 1939-
Australian critic, novelist, TV presenter, poet and essayist

Everyone has a right to a university degree in America, even if it's in Hamburger Technology.

Margaret **Thatcher** sounds like *The Book of Revelations* read out over a railway station public address system by a headmistress of a certain age wearing calico knickers.

Henry James 1843-1916
Anglo-American writer

Summer afternoon. The two most beautiful words in the English language.

P. D. James 1920-
English writer of detective stories

I believe that political correctness can be a form of linguistic fascism, and it sends shivers down the spine of my generation who went to war against fascism.
>in *Paris Review* 1995

William James 1843-1916
American psychologist, doctor, philosopher, writer

Human beings, by changing the inner attitudes of their minds, can change the outer aspects of their lives.

If merely 'feeling good' could decide, drunkenness would be the supremely valid human experience.
The Varieties of Religious Experience (1902)

Anna Jameson 1794-1860
British writer

What we truly and earnestly aspire to be, that in some sense, we are. The mere aspiration, by changing the frame of the mind, for the moment realizes itself.

Storm Jameson 1891-1986
English novelist

She did not so much cook, as assassinate food.
of a hostess

Randall Jarrell 1914-64
American poet and literary critic

To Americans, English manners are far more frightening than none at all.
Pictures from an Institution (1954)

It is better to entertain an idea than to take it home to live with you for the rest of your life.
Pictures from an Institution (1954)

Lord Jay (Douglas Jay) 1907-96
English Labour politician

He never used one syllable where none would do.

In the case of nutrition and health, just as in the case of education, the gentleman in Whitehall really does know better for people than the people know themselves.
The Socialist Case (1939)

Sir Antony Jay 1930-
English writer

All any author wants from a review is six thousand words of closely reasoned adulation.
speech at a booksellers' luncheon, Birmingham (1967)

Thomas Jefferson 1762-1826
Political philosopher, third President of the United States 1801-09, principal author of the American Declaration of Independence (1776)

When a long train of abuses and usurpations ... evinces a design to reduce them (the people) under absolute despotism, it is their right, it is their duty, to throw off such a government.
American Declaration of Independence

Were we directed from Washington when to sow, and when to reap, we should soon want bread.
  Autobiography

Millions of innocent men, women and children, since the introduction of Christianity, have been burnt, tortured, fined, imprisoned; yet we have not advanced one inch towards uniformity of opinion. What has been the effect of coercion? To make one half the world fools, and the other half hypocrites.
  Notes on the State of Virginia (1781-1785)

We hold these truths to be sacred and undeniable; that all men are created equal and independent, that from that equal creation they derive rights inherent and inalienable among which are the preservation of life, and liberty, and the pursuit of happiness.
  'Rough Draft' of the American Declaration of Independence; J. P. Boyd et al. *Papers of Thomas Jefferson* (1950)

A wise and frugal government, which shall restrain men from injuring one another, which shall leave them otherwise free to regulate their own pursuits of industry and improvement, and shall not take from the mouth of labour the bread it has earned. This is the sum of good government, and this is necessary to close the circle of our felicities.
  first inaugural address, 4 March 1801

There is natural aristocracy among men. The grounds of this are virtue and talent.
  letter to former President, John **Adams**, 28 October 1813, *The Writings of Thomas Jefferson* (1898) Paul L. Ford

A strict observance of the written laws is doubtless one of the high virtues of a good citizen, but it is not the highest. The laws of necessity, of self-preservation, of saving our country when in danger, are of higher obligation.
  letter, 20 September 1810, *The Writings of Thomas Jefferson* (1898) ed. Paul L. Ford

Were it left to me to decide whether we should have a government without newspapers or newspapers without a government, I should not hesitate for a moment to prefer the latter.
  letter to Colonel Edward **Carrington**, 16 January 1787

The tree of liberty must be refreshed from time to time with the blood of patriots and tyrants. It is its natural manure.
  letter to W. S. **Smith**, 13 November 1787

The natural progress of things is for liberty to yield and governments to gain ground.
  letter to Colonel Edward **Carrington**, 27 May 1788

Offices are acceptable here as elsewhere, and whenever a man has cast a longing eye on them [official positions], a rottenness begins in his conduct.
  letter to Trench **Coxe**, 21 May 1799

Advertisements contain the only truths to be relied on in a newspaper.
  letter (1819)

What an augmentation of the field for jobbing, speculating, plundering, office-building and office-hunting would be produced by an assumption of all the state powers into the hands of the general government.
  letter, 13 August 1800

If the principle were to prevail, of a common law [i.e. a single government] being in force in the U.S . . . it would become the most corrupt government on the earth.
  letter to Gideon **Granger**, 13 August 1800

The republican is the only form of government which is not eternally at open or secret war with the rights of mankind.
  letter to William Hunter, 11 March 1790

I know no safe depository of the ultimate powers of the society but the people themselves; and if we think them not enlightened enough to exercise their control with a wholesome discretion, the remedy is not to take it from them, but to inform their discretion by education.
  letter to William Charles Jarvis, 28 September 1820

If we can prevent the government from wasting the labours of the people, under the pretence of taking care of them, they must become happy.
  letter to Thomas Cooper, 29 November 1802

The care of human life and happiness, and not their destruction, is the first and only legitimate object of good government.
  to the Republican Citizens of Washington County, Maryland, 31 March 1809

Because religious belief, or non-belief, is such an important part of every person's life, freedom of religion affects every individual. State churches that use government power to support themselves and force their views on persons of other faiths undermine all our civil rights. Moreover, state support of the church tends to make the clergy unresponsive to the people and leads to corruption within religion. Erecting the wall of separation between church and state, therefore, is absolutely essential in a free society.

Whenever any form of government becomes destructive of these ends (life, liberty, and the pursuit of happiness) it is the right of the people to alter or abolish it, and to institute new government.

Democracy will cease to exist when you take away from those who are willing to work and give to those who would not.

Democracy is 51% of the people taking away the rights of the other 49%.

I predict future happiness for Americans if they can prevent the government from wasting the labours of the people under the pretense of taking care of them.

We in America do not have government by the majority, we have government by the majority who participate.

An honest man can feel no pleasure in the exercise of power over his fellow citizens.

I'm a great believer in luck, and I find the harder I work, the more I have of it.

Some people dream of success while others wake up and work hard at it.

On matters of style, swim with the current, on matters of principle, stand like a rock.

The spirit of resistance to government is so valuable on certain occasions that I wish it to be always kept alive.

I would rather be exposed to the inconveniences attending too much liberty than to those attending too small a degree of it.

If once the people become inattentive to the public affairs, you and I, and Congress and Assemblies, Judges and Governors, shall all become wolves. It seems to be the law of our general nature, in spite of individual exceptions.

Experience hath shewn, that even under the best forms (of government) those entrusted with power have, in time, and by slow operations, perverted it into tyranny.

Fix reason firmly in her seat, and call to her tribunal every fact, every opinion. Question with boldness even the existence of a god; because, if there be one, he must approve the homage of reason rather than of blind-folded fear. Do not be frightened from this inquiry by any fear of its consequences.

The policy of the American government is to leave their citizens free, neither restraining nor aiding them in their pursuits.
  attributed

I believe that banking institutions are more dangerous to our liberties than standing armies. If the American people ever allow private banks to control the issue of their currency, first by inflation, then by deflation, the banks and corporations that will grow up around [the banks] will deprive the people of all property until their children wake-up homeless on the continent their fathers conquered. The issuing power should be taken from the banks and restored to the people, to whom it properly belongs.
  attributed

George Jellinek 1851-1911
Austrian legal philosopher

The idea of legally establishing inalienable, inherent and sacred rights of the individual is not of political but religious origin.

Roy Jenkins 1920-2003
British politician; co-founder of the Social Democratic Party, 1981

The politics of the left and centre of this country are frozen in an out-of-date mould which is bad for the political and economic health of Britain and increasingly inhibiting for those who liven within the mould. Can it be broken?
  speech to Parliamentary Press Gallery, 9 June 1980

William Jennings Bryan 1860-1925
Democratic Party politician, lawyer, 41st Secretary of State under President Woodrow Wilson.

Destiny is no matter of chance. It is a matter of choice. It is not a thing to be waited for, it is a thing to be achieved.

Jerome K. Jerome 1859-1927
English writer and humorist

I like work: it fascinates me. I can sit and look at it for hours.

It is always the best policy to speak the truth – unless, of course, you are an exceptionally good liar.

They say – people who ought to be ashamed of themselves do – that a consciousness of being well dressed imparts a blissfulness to the human heart that religion is powerless to bestow. I am afraid these cynical persons are sometimes correct.
The Idle Thoughts of an Idle Fellow (1886)

Douglas Jerrold 1803-57
English humorist and editor

A conservative is a man who will not look at the new moon, out of respect for that ancient institution, the old one.
quoted in *The Treasury of Humorous Quotations* (1951) eds. Evan Esar & Nicolas Bentley

W. Stanley Jevons 1835-82
English economist

All classes of society are trades unionists at heart, and differ chiefly in the boldness, ability, and secrecy with which they pursue their respective interests.
The State in Relation to Labour (1882)

John Paul II 1920-2005
Polish cleric, Pope 1978-2005

It would be simplistic to say that Divine Providence caused the fall of communism. It fell by itself as a consequence of its own mistakes and abuses. It fell by itself because of its own inherent weaknesses.
when asked by the Italian writer Vittorio Missori if the fall of the USSR could be ascribed to God
Carl Bernstein and Marco Politi *His Holiness: John Paul II and the Hidden History of our Time* (1996)

Jilted John a character created by Graham Fellows (1959-), English comedy actor and musician

Gordon is a moron.
Gordon is a moron.
'Gordon is a Moron' (1978 song)

Boris Johnson 1964-
British Conservative Party politician, journalist and editor. Former Member of Parliament and Major of London 2008-

The Liberal Democrats are not just empty. They are a void within a vacuum, surrounded by a large inanition.

Tony **Blair** is a mixture of Harry **Houdini** and a greased piglet. Nailing him is like trying to pin jelly to a wall.

The dreadful truth is that when people come to see their MP they have run out of better ideas.

Lyndon B. Johnson 1908-73
American Democratic Party politician, 36th President of the United States 1963-69

I don't want loyalty. I want *loyalty*. I want him to kiss my ass in Macy's window at high noon and tell me it smells like roses. I want his pecker in my pocket.
discussing a prospective assistant
Richard Reeves *A Ford, not a Lincoln* (1975)

Better to have him inside the tent pissing out, than outside pissing in.
*of J. Edgar **Hoover**, Director of the FBI 1924-72*
   D. Halberstein *The Best and the Brightest* (1972)

Did you ever think, Ken, that making a speech on economics is a lot like pissing down your leg? It seems hot to you, but it never does to anyone else.
   to J. K. **Galbraith**

I may not know much, but I know chicken shit from chicken salad.
*on a Richard **Nixon** speech*

Gerry **Ford** is so dumb he can't fart and chew gum at the same time.

I have learned that only two things are necessary to keep one's wife happy. First, let her think she's having her way. And second, to let her have it.

Paul Johnson 1928-
English journalist, historian, speechwriter and author

It is one of the dismal lessons of the twentieth century that, once a state is allowed to expand, it is almost impossible to contract it.
   Modern Times (1992)

Those who pillory capitalism for 'creating artificial needs' strike me as timid and dismal souls. You might just as well denounce Monet for creating an 'artificial need' for Impressionism.
   The Quotable Paul Johnson (1995)

Nothing appeals to intellectuals more than the feeling that they represent 'the people'. Nothing, as a rule, is further from the truth.
   The Birth of the Modern (1991)

A man who hates America hates humanity.
   U. S. News & World Report 30 December 1985

The study of history is a powerful antidote to contemporary arrogance. It is humbling to discover how many of our glib assumptions, which seem to us novel and plausible, have been tested before, not once but many times and in innumerable guises; and discovered to be, at great human cost, wholly false.
   The Recovery of Freedom (1980)

The politics of pity, based on the notion of strengthening the weak and weakening the strong, must produce impoverishment; but the assault on elitism is still more socially destructive, for it overthrows the principle of leadership itself and reduces human societies to herds of Gadarene swine.
   The Recovery of Freedom (1980)

Samuel Johnson 1709-84
English writer and lexicographer

Oats: A grain, which in England is generally given to horses, but in Scotland supports the people.
   A Dictionary of the English Language (1755)

A man seldom thinks with more earnestness of anything than he does of his dinner.

Our aspirations are our possibilities.

Mankind are happier in a state of inequality and subordination. Were they to be in this pretty state of equality, they would soon degenerate into brutes.
    attributed

The remainder of the Samuel Johnson quotations are from James Boswell *Life of Samuel Johnson* (1791):

The noblest prospect a Scotchman ever sees, is the high road that leads him to England!

It has been a common saying of physicians in England, that a cucumber should be well sliced, and dressed with pepper and vinegar, and then thrown out, as good for nothing.

A man who exposes himself when he is intoxicated, has not the art of getting drunk.

Depend upon it, Sir, when a man knows he is to be hanged in a fortnight, it concentrates his mind wonderfully.

There is no private house in which people can enjoy themselves so well as at a capital tavern . . . No, Sir; there is nothing which has yet been contrived by man by which so much happiness is produced as by a good tavern or inn.

This merriment of parsons is mightily offensive.

There is, indeed, nothing that so much seduces reason from vigilance, as the thought of passing life with an amiable woman.

A woman's preaching is like a dog's walking on its hind legs. It is not done well, but you are surprised to find it done at all.

BOSWELL: So, Sir, you laugh at schemes of political improvement.
JOHNSON: Why, Sir, most schemes of political improvement are very laughable things.

There are few ways in which a man can be more innocently employed than in getting money.

Patriotism is the last refuge of a scoundrel.

Politics are now nothing more than means of rising in the world.

It is better than some should be unhappy than that none should be happy, which would be the case in a general state of equality.

As I know more of mankind I expect less of them.

Tom Johnston 1881-1965
Scottish Labour politician

I have become . . . uneasy lest we should get political power without our first having, or at least simultaneously having, an adequate economy to administer. What purport would there be in our getting a Scots parliament in Edinburgh if it has to administer an emigration system, a glorified Poor Law, and a graveyard!

Memories (1952)

Barry Owen Jones 1932-
Australian Labour politician

The sheer incompetence of Australia's current management is for the time being an asset in maintaining high employment levels. But we cannot count on that incompetence for ever.
Sleepers, Wake (1982)

Robert Jones 1960-2007
British Conservative politician

Margaret **Thatcher** and Ted **Heath** both have a great vision. The difference is that Thatcher has a vision that Britain will one day be great again, and Heath has a vision that one day Heath will be great again.

Steve Jones 1944-
English geneticist

The greenest political party there has ever been was the Nazi party. The Nazis were great believers in purity, that nature should not be interfered with.
in *Times Higher Education Supplement* 27 August 1999

Students accept astonishing things happening in human genetics without turning a hair but worry about GM soya beans.
in *Times Higher Education Supplement* 27 August 1999

Erica Jong 1942-
American author and teacher

Men and women. Women and men. It will never work.

Advice is what we ask for when we already know the answer but wish we didn't.

Sir Keith Joseph 1918-94
British Conservative politician

The balance of our population, our human stock, is threatened ... a high and rising proportion of children are being born to mothers least fitted to bring children into the world and bring them up.
speech in Birmingham, 19 October 1974

It needs to be said that the poor are poor because they don't have enough money.

If we are to be prosperous we need more millionaires and more bankrupts.
maiden speech in the House of Lords, 18 February 1988

Tony Judt 1948-
British historian and author

By March 1918 **Lenin**'s Bolshevik regime, then just five months old, had knowingly killed more of its political opponents than Czarist Russia had in the whole preceding century.
'The Longest Road To Hell', *New York Times*, December 22, 1997

Carl Jung 1875-1961
Swiss psychiatrist

The pendulum of the mind alternates between sense and nonsense, not between right and wrong.

Observance of customs and laws can very easily be a cloak for a lie so subtle that our fellow human beings are unable to detect it. It may help us to escape all criticism, we may even be able to deceive ourselves in the belief of our obvious righteousness. But deep down, below the surface of the average man's conscience, he hears a voice whispering, 'There is something not right,' no matter how much his rightness is supported by public opinion or by the moral code.

In studying the history of the human mind one is impressed again and again by the fact that the growth of the mind is the widening of the range of consciousness, and that each step forward has been a most painful and laborious achievement. One could almost say that nothing is more hateful to man than to give up even a particle of his unconsciousness. Ask those who have tried to introduce a new idea!

Every form of addiction is bad, no matter whether the narcotic be alcohol or morphine or idealism.
Memories, Dreams, Reflections (1962)

The afternoon of human life must also have a significance of its own and cannot be merely a pitiful appendage to life's morning.
The Stages of Life (1930)

Junius
English 18th century pseudonymous writer

There is a holy mistaken zeal in politics as well as in religion. By persuading others, we convince ourselves.
in *Public Advertiser* 19 December 1969, letter 35

John Junor 1919-97
British journalist

Such a graceful exit. And then he had to go and do this on the doorstep.
*on Harold **Wilson**'s 'Lavender List', the honours list he drew up on resigning the British premiership in 1976*
in *Observer* 23 January 1990

k

Immanuel Kant 1724-1804
German philosopher

Out of the crooked timber of humanity no straight thing was ever made.

Beatrice Kaufman 1895-1945
American writer, wife of George S. Kaufman

I've been rich, and I've been poor: rich is better.
    in *Washington Post* 12 May 1937; often associated with Sophie Tucker

Gerald Kaufman 1930-
British Labour politician

We would prefer to see the House [the Royal Opera House] run by a philistine with the requisite financial acumen than by the succession of opera and ballet lovers who have brought a great and valuable institution to its knees.
    report of the Commons' Culture Media and Sport Select Committee on Covent Garden, 3 December 1997

The longest suicide note in history.
on the Labour Party manifesto New Hope for Britain (1983).
Denis Healey *The Time of My Life* (1989)

Margo Kaufman
American writer

The only thing worse than a man you can't control is a man you can.

I once complained to my father that I didn't seem to be able to do things the same way other people did. Dad's advice? 'Margo, don't be a sheep. People hate sheep. They eat sheep.'

Peter Kay 1973-
British comedian

Garlic bread – it's the future, I've tasted it.
Brian Potter envisages a reborn Phoenix Club
    Phoenix Nights

All castles had one major weakness. The enemy used to get in through the gift shop.
    attributed; in *Nuts* May 2005

Paul Keating 1944-
Australian Labour Party politician, 24th Prime Minister of Australia 1991-96

I'm a bastard. But I'm a bastard who gets the mail through. And they appreciate that.
    in 1994, to a senior colleague

in *Sunday Telegraph* 20 November 1994

Leadership is not about being nice. Its about being right and being strong.
in *Time* 9 January 1995

He is the greatest job and investment destroyer since the bubonic plague.
on John **Howard**

What we have got is a dead carcass swinging in the breeze, but nobody will cut it down to replace him.
on Malcolm **Fraser**

Garrison Keillor 1942-
American humorous writer and broadcaster

Years ago, manhood was an opportunity for achievement, and now it is a problem to be overcome.
The Book of Guys (1994)

My ancestors were Puritans from England. They arrived here in 1648 in the hope of finding greater restrictions than were permissible under English law at that time.
attributed, 1993

Helen Keller 1880-1968
American deaf blind author, political activist and lecturer

Avoiding danger is no safer in the long run than outright exposure. The fearful are caught as often as the bold.
My Religion (1927)

Life is either a daring adventure or nothing. Security does not exist in nature, nor do the children of men as a whole experience it. Avoiding danger is no safer in the long run than exposure.

Character cannot be developed in ease and quiet. Only through experience of trial and suffering can the soul be strengthened, ambition inspired, and success achieved.

Science may have found a cure for most evils; but it has found no remedy for the worst of them all - the apathy of human beings.

Optimism is the faith that leads to achievement. Nothing can be done without hope and confidence.

Hope sees the invisible, feels the intangible, and achieves the impossible.

George F. Kennan 1904-2005
American diplomat and historian

Government . . . is simply not the channel through which men's noblest impulses are to be realized. Its task, on the contrary, is largely to see to it that the ignoble ones are kept under restraint and are not permitted to go too far.
Around the Cragged Hill (1993)

John F. Kennedy 1917-63
American Democratic Party politician, 35th President of the United States

Conformity is the jailer of freedom and the enemy of growth.
Public Papers of the Presidents of the United States: John F. Kennedy, 1961

Don't buy a single vote more than necessary. I'll be damned if I'm going to finance a landslide.
reading out a message supposedly from his father, 1958

Let the word go forth from this time and place, to friend and foe alike, that the torch has been passed to a new generation of Americans, born in this century, tempered by war, disciplined by a hard and bitter peace, proud of our ancient heritage, and unwilling to witness or permit the slow undoing of those human rights to which this nation has always been committed, and to which we are committed today, at home and around the world!
inaugural address (1961)

We shall pay any price, bear any burden, meet any hardship, support any friend, oppose any foe to assure the survival and the success of liberty.
inaugural address (1961)

When we got into office, the thing that surprised me most was to find that things were just as bad as we'd been saying they were.
speech at the White House, 26 May 1961

Our problems are man-made, therefore they may be solved by man. And man can be as big as he wants. No problem of human destiny is beyond human beings.
speech at The American University, Washington DC, June 10, 1963

The problem of power is how to achieve its responsible use rather than its irresponsible and indulgent use – of how to get men of power to live for the public rather than off the public.

The ignorance of one voter in a democracy impairs the security of all.

The American, by nature, is optimistic. He is experimental, and inventor and a builder who builds best when called upon to build greatly.

Joseph P. Kennedy 1888-1969
American financier and diplomat, father of John F. Kennedy and Robert Kennedy

We're going to sell Jack like soapflakes.
when his son John made his bid for the Presidency
John H. Davis *The Kennedy Clan* (1984)

Ludovic Kennedy 1919-2009
British journalist, broadcaster, humanist and author

Research men in advertising are really blind men groping in a dark room for a black cat that isn't there.

Robert F. Kennedy 1925-68
American Democratic politician

Only those who dare to fail greatly can ever achieve greatly.

Jomo Kenyatta 1889-1978
Prime Minister (1963-4) and President (1964-78) of Kenya

Originally, the Africans had the land and the English had the Bible. Then the missionaries came to Africa and got the Africans to close their eyes and fold their hands and pray. And when they opened their eyes, the English had the land and the Africans had the Bible.

Jack Kerouac 1922-69
American novelist and poet

This is the story of America. Everybody's doing what they think they're supposed to do.
   On The Road (1957)

Jean Kerr 1923-
American writer

As someone pointed out recently, if you can keep your head when all about you are losing theirs, it's just possible you haven't grasped the situation.
Please Don't Eat The Daisies (1958) Introduction

John Maynard Keynes 1883-1946
English economist

Marxian Socialism must always remain a portent to the historians of Opinion - how a doctrine so illogical and so dull can have exercised the minds of men, and, through them, the events of history.
   The End of the Laissez-Faire (1926)

I do not know which makes a man more conservative - to know nothing but the present, or nothing but the past.
   The End of the Laissez-Faire (1926)

But this *long run* is a misleading guide to current affairs. *In the long run* we are all dead.
   A Tract on Monetary Reform (1923)

Practical men, who believe themselves to be quite exempt from any intellectual influences, are usually the slaves of some defunct economist. Madmen in authority, who hear voices in the air, are distilling their frenzy from some academic scribbler of a few years back.
   General Theory (1947 ed.)

This goat-footed bard, this half-human visitor to our age from the hag-ridden magic and enchanted woods of Celtic antiquity.
on David Lloyd George

The avoidance of taxes is the only intellectual pursuit that still carries any reward.

Omar Khayyam 11th-12th century
Persian astronomer, poet

Drink! for you know not whence you came, nor why;
Drink! for you know not why you go, nor where.
   The Rubaiyat (1879)

Nikita Khrushchev 1894-1971
Soviet statesman; Premier, 1958-64

If anyone believes that our smiles involve abandonment of the teaching of Marx, **Engels** and Lenin he deceives himself. Those who wait for that must wait until a shrimp learns to whistle.
    speech in Moscow, 17 September 1955

We are going to make the imperialists dance like fishes in a saucepan, even without war.
    in Vienna, 2 July 1960

Anyone who believes that the worker can be lulled by fine revolutionary phrases is mistaken ... If no concern is shown for the growth of material and spiritual riches, the people will listen today, they will listen tomorrow, and then they may say: 'Why do you promise us everything for the future? You are talking, so to speak, about life beyond the grave. The priest has already told us about this.'
    speech at World Youth Forum, 19 September 1964

If we could have the revolution over again, we would carry it out more sensibly and with smaller losses. But history does not repeat itself. The situation is favourable for us. If God existed, we would thank him.
    speech to Western Ambassadors, Moscow, 18 November 1956

Politicians are the same all over. They promise to build a bridge even where there is no river.

About the capitalist states, it doesn't depend on you whether the Soviet Union exists. If you don't like us, don't accept our invitation, and don't invite us to come to see you. Whether you like it or not, history is on our side. We will bury you.

Søren Kierkegaard 1813-55
Danish philosopher, theologian and psychologist

Of all tyrannies democracy is the most agonizing, the most insane, the absolute fall of everything great and elevated.
    Journal (1848)

People demand freedom of speech as a compensation for the freedom of thought which they seldom use.

Brian Kiley

I love being married. I was single for a long time and I just got sick of finishing my own sentences.

Lord Kilmuir (David Maxwell Fyfe) 1900-67
British Conservative politician and lawyer

Loyalty is the Tory's secret weapon.
    Anthony Sampson *Anatomy of Britain* (1962)

Daren King
English novelist

My wife has a black belt in body language.
    Jim Giraffe (2004) 'Stretch Armlong'

Neil Kinnock 1942-
British Labour politician

I have a lot of sympathy with him. I too was once a young, bald Leader of the Opposition.
on William Hague as Tory Leader
   in *Independent* on 3 October 1999

Referendums produce results and results have got to be listened to.
on the French rejection of the European Constitution
   in *Guardian* (online edition) 1 June 2005

It's a pity others had to leave theirs on the ground at Goose Green to prove it.
   to a heckler who said that Mrs Thatcher 'showed guts' during the Falklands War
   television interview, 6 June 1983

The grotesque chaos of a Labour council hiring taxis to scuttle round the city handing out redundancy notices to its own workers.
of the actions of the city council in Liverpool
   speech at the Labour Party Conference, 1 October 1985

Michael Kinsley 1951-
American political journalist, commentator, television host, and pundit

A gaffe is when a politician tells the truth.

The moral arc of a Washington career could be divided into four parts: idealism, pragmatism, ambition and corruption.
   Washington Post

Rudyard Kipling 1865-1936
British author and poet

The Three in One, the One in Three? Not so!
To my own Gods I go.
It may be they shall give me greater ease
Than your cold Christ and tangled Trinities.
   Plain Tales from the Hills (1888)

Winds of the World, give answer! They are whimpering to and fro-
And what should they know of England who only England know?-
The poor little street-bred people that vapour and fume and brag.
   'The English Flag' (1892)

I've taken my fun where I've found it,
An' now I must pay for my fun,
For the more you 'ave known o' the others
The less you will settle to one.
   'The Ladies' (1896)

To take up the White Man's burden -
And reap his old reward -
The blame of those ye better,
The hate of those ye guard.
   'The White Man's Burden' (1899)

It is always a temptation to a rich and lazy nation,
To puff and look important and to say:-
'Though we know we should defeat you, we have not the time to meet you,
We will therefore pay you cash to go away.'
And that is called paying the Dane-geld;
But we've proved it again and again,
That if once you have paid him the Dane-geld
You never get rid of the Dane.
   'What Dane-geld Means' (1911)

I could not dig: I dared not rob:
Therefore I lied to please the mob.
Now all my lies are proved untrue
And I must face the men I slew.
What tale shall serve me here among
Mine angry and defrauded young?
   'Epitaphs of the War: A Dead Statesman' (1919)

The female of the species is more deadly than the male.
   'The Female of the Species' (1919)

Russell Kirk 1918 – 1994
American political theorist, historian, social critic, literary critic and fiction author

In ordinary usage, the word 'conservative' tends to imply a proclivity toward permanence, and 'liberal' to imply a proclivity toward progression. But the twentieth-century liberal has come to care less and less about variety, individuality, moral improvement, and the other subjects which, in the eyes of John Stuart Mill, were the ends of liberalism: instead, he is willing to settle for an eternal and equalitarian stability.
   Beyond the Dream of Avarice (1956)

Jeane J. Kirkpatrick 1926-2006
American diplomat and ardent anticommunist

Americans tend to judge the moral quality of government by the personal morality and motives of high officials, and to assume that when good men with good motives and good personal habits lead a government, good government results. But this is not necessarily the case.
   address at the Ethics and Public Policy Dinner, Washington D.C., 29 September 1982

For every goal towards which human beings have worked there is, in our time, a right. Neither nature nor experience nor probability informs these lists of entitlements . . . Rights are vested in persons or groups, but goals are achieved by human effort.
   address to the Council on Foreign Relations, New York City, 10 March 1981

The principal function of a human rights policy that emphasizes motives rather than consequences is, I believe, to make us feel good about ourselves. It feels good to feel good, to be sure. But one wonders about that as a goal of foreign policy.
   address to the Council on Foreign Relations, New York City, 10 March 1981

Henry Kissinger 1923-
German-born American politician, US Secretary of State 1973-7

The illegal we do immediately. The unconstitutional takes a little longer.

in *Washington Post* 20 January 1977
attributed

If I want to talk to Europe who do I call?
attributed
quoted by Crispin **Blunt** in *Minutes of the House of Commons Select Committee on Defence*, 16 February 2002

The main advantage of being famous is that when you bore people at dinner parties they think it is their fault.
James Naughtie in *Spectator* 1 April 1995
attributed

We always tend to think of historical tragedy as failing to get what we want, but if we study history we find that the worse tragedies occurred when people got what they wanted . . . and it turned out to be the wrong objective.
The Washington Quarterly, January 1978

Lord Kitchener 1850-1916
British soldier and statesman

You are ordered abroad as a soldier of the King to help our French comrades against the invasion of a common enemy . . . In this new experience you may find temptations both in wine and women. You must entirely resist both temptations, and, while treating all women with perfect courtesy, you should avoid any intimacy. Do your duty bravely. Fear God. Honour the King.
message to soldiers of the British Expeditionary Force (1914)
in *The Times* 19 August 1914

John Knox c.1505-72
Scottish Protestant reformer

The first blast of the trumpet against the monstrous regiment of women.
title of pamphlet (1558)
[Editor's note: 'regiment' means 'rule'.]

Arthur Koestler 1905-83
Hungarian-born British novelist and essayist

One may not regard the world as a sort of metaphysical brothel for emotions.
Darkness at Noon (1940) 'The Second Hearing'

Helmut Kohl 1930-
German statesman, Chancellor of West Germany, 1982-90, and first post-war Chancellor of united Germany, 1990-98

I have been underestimated for decades. I have done very well that way.
in *New York Times* 25 January 1987

Michael Korda 1933-
English novelist and editor

An ounce of hypocrisy is worth a pound of ambition.

Dean Krakel
Director of the National Cowboy Hall of Fame

Metric is definitely communist. One monetary system, one language, one weight and measurement system, one world – all communist! We know the West was won by the inch, foot, yard, and mile.

Jiddu Krishnamurti 1895-1986
Indian-born writer and speaker on philosophical and spiritual subjects

Truth is a pathless land, and you cannot approach it by any path whatsoever, by any religion, by any sect.
  speech in Holland, 3 August 1929

Irving Kristol 1820-2009
American columnist, journalist and writer

If you are extraordinarily high-minded in your political pronouncements, you are bound in the nature of things to be more than ordinarily hypocritical.
  New York Times Magazine, 14 November 1971

Stanley Kubrick 1928-99
American film director

The great nations have always acted like gangsters, and the small nations like prostitutes.
  in *Guardian* 5 June 1963

Irv Kupcinet 1912-2003
American newspaper columnist

What can you say about a society that says that God is dead and Elvis is alive?

Abraham Kuyper 1837-1920
Dutch politician, journalist, politician and theologian

A nation consisting of citizens who consciences are bruised is itself broken in its national strength.
  Lectures on Calvinism

1

Labour Party campaign slogan 1997

Things can only get better.

[Editor's note: Ha.]

R. D. Laing 1927-89
Scottish psychiatrist

The brotherhood of man is evoked by particular men according to their circumstances. But it seldom extends to all men. In the name of our freedom and our brotherhood we are prepared to blow up the other half of mankind and to be blown up in turn.
 The Politics of Experience (1967)

Madness need not be all breakdown. It may also be break-through.
 The Politics of Experience (1967)

Norman Lamont 1942-
British Conservative politician

My wife said she had never heard me sing in the bath before.
of the aftermath of sterling's exit from the ERM (Exchange Rate Mechanism)
 quoted in *Financial Times* 23 September 1992

Giuseppe de Lampedusa 1896-1957
Italian novelist

Love. Of course, love. Flames for a year, ashes for thirty.
 The Leopard (1957)

Ann Landers (Esther Pauline Friedman Lederer) 1918-2002
American advice columnist

At every party there are two kinds of people – those who want to go home and those who don't. The trouble is, they are usually married to each other.
 in *International Herald Tribune* 19 June 1991

Lao-tzu 604-531BC
Chinese philosopher

When armies are mobilised and issues are joined,
The man who is sorry over the fact will win.
 The Way of Lao-tzu

Arms are instruments of ill omen . . . When one is compelled to use them, it is best to do so without relish. There is no glory in victory, and to glorify it despite this is to exult in the killing of men . . .

When great numbers of people are killed, one should weep over them with sorrow. When victorious in war, one should observe mourning rites.

Ring Lardner 1885-1933
American humorist

'Are you lost Daddy?', I asked tenderly. 'Shut up', he explained.
  The Young Immigrunts (1920)

Philip Larkin 1922-85
English poet and librarian

Sexual intercourse began
In nineteen sixty-three
(Which was rather late for me) –
Between the end of the *Chatterley* ban
And the Beatles' first LP
  'Annus Mirabilis' (1974)

They fuck you up, your mum and dad.
They may not mean to, but they do.
They fill you up with the faults they had
And add some extra, just for you.
  'This be the Verse' (1974)

Man hands on misery to man.
It deepens like a coastal shelf.
Get out as early as you can,
And don't have any kids yourself.
  'This be the Verse' (1974)

The notion of expressing sentiments in short lines with similar sounds at their ends seems as remote as mangoes on the moon.
  letter to Barbara Pym, 22 January 1975

François de La Rochefoucauld 1613-80
French nobleman and author

Good advice is something a man gives when he is too old to set a bad example.

What seems to be generosity is often no more than disguised ambition, which overlooks a small interest in order to secure a great one.

Doug Larson 1926-
America journalist

The surprising thing about young fools is how many survive to become old fools.

Instead of giving a politician the keys to the city, it might be better to change the locks.

Harold Laski 1893-1950
British Labour politician

I respect fidelity to colleagues even though they are fit for the hangman.
   letter to Oliver **Wendell Holmes Jr**, 4 December 1926

Harry Lauder 1870-1950
Scottish music-hall entertainer

Keep right on to the end of the road,
Keep right on to the end.
Tho' the way be long, let your heart be strong,
Keep right on round the bend.
   'The End of the Road' (1924 song)

D. H. Lawrence 1885-1930
English author, poet, playwright, essayist and literary critic.

How beautiful maleness is, if it finds its right expression.

T. E. Lawrence 1888-1935
British soldier and author

All men dream: but not equally. Those who dream by night in the dusty recesses of their minds wake in the day to find that it was vanity: but the dreamers of the day are dangerous men, for they may act their dream with open eyes, to make it possible.
   The Seven Pillars of Wisdom (1935)

Many men would take the death-sentence without a whimper to escape the life-sentence which fate carries in her other hand.
   The Mint (1955)

Poets hope too much, and their politics . . . usually stink after twenty years.
   letter to Cecil **Day-Lewis**, November 1934

Mark Lawson 1962-
British writer and journalist

Office tends to confer a dreadful plausibility on even the most negligible of those who hold it.
   Joe Queenan *Imperial Caddy* (1992)

Nigel Lawson 1932-
British Conservative politician

It represented the top of a singularly ill-concealed iceberg, with all the destructive potential that icebergs possess.
*of an article by Alan **Waters**, the Prime Minister's economic adviser, criticising the Exchange Rate Mechanism*
   in the House of Commons following his resignation as Chancellor, 31 October 1989

Neil **Kinnock** walked backwards into socialism as the penniless man walked backwards into the cinema, in the hope that the attendant would think he was leaving it.

A politician should always appear stupider than he is.

Emma Lazarus 1849-87
American poet

Give me your tired, your poor,
Your huddled masses yearning to breathe free,
The wretched refuse of your teeming shore,
Send these, the homeless, tempest-tossed, to me,:
I lift my lamp beside the golden door.
'The New Colossus' (1883)
inscription on the Statue of Liberty, New York

Edmund Leach 1910-89
English social anthropologist

Far from being the basis of the good society, the family, with its narrow privacy and tawdry secrets, is the source of all our discontents.
BBC Reith Lectures, 1967, in *Listener* 30 November 1967

Edward Lear 1812-88
English poet and artist

There was an old man with a beard,
Who said, 'It is just as I feared!
Two Owls and a Hen,
Four Larks and a Wren
Have all built their nests in my beard.
A Book of Nonsense (1846)

Fran Lebowitz 1950-
American author

While clothes with pictures and/or writing on them are not entirely an invention of the modern age, they are an unpleasant indication of the state of things.
Metropolitan Life (1978)

All God's children are not beautiful. Most of God's children are, in fact, barely presentable.
Metropolitan Life (1978)

Being a woman is of special interest to aspiring male transexuals. To actual women it is simply a good excuse not to play football.

Stanislaw Lec 1909-66
Polish writer

One has to multiply thoughts to the point where there aren't enough policemen to control them.
Unkempt Thoughts (1962)

Harper Lee 1926-
American author

I wanted you to see what real courage is, instead of getting the idea that courage is a man with a gun in his hand. It's when you know you're licked before you begin but you begin anyway and you see it through no matter what.

To Kill a Mockingbird (1960)

Robert E. Lee 1807-70
American general, engineer

To be a good soldier you must love the army. To be a good commander, you must be willing to order the death of the thing you love.
   conversation with Gen. **Longstreet**

Duty then is the sublimest word in the English language. You should do your duty in all things. You can never do more, you should never wish to do less.

Tom Lehrer 1928-
American singer-songwriter, satirist, pianist and mathematician

The Army has carried the American ideal to its logical conclusion. Not only do they prohibit discrimination on the grounds of race, creed and color, but also on ability.

Vladimir Lenin 1870-1924
Bolshevik Leader of the 1917 October Revolution, first head of state of the Soviet Union, 1917-22

No, Democracy is not identical with majority rule. Democracy is a State which recognises the subjection of the minority to the majority, that is, an organisation for the systematic use of force by one class against the other, by one part of the population against another.
   State and Revolution (1919)

While the State exists, there can be no freedom. When there is freedom there will be no State.
   State and Revolution (1919)

John Lennon 1940-80
English pop singer and songwriter

Imagine there's no heaven,
It's easy if you try.
No hell below us,
Above us, only sky.
   'Imagine' (1971 song)

Jay Leno 1950-
American comedian and television host

Fishnet stockings are now considered appropriate for office wear. So how are men going to be able to tell the professional women from the professional women?

Hilary **Clinton** said in her book it was a challenge to forgive Bill, but she figured if Nelson **Mandela** could forgive, she could give it a try. Isn't that amazing? I didn't know Clinton hit on Mandela's wife.

John **Kerry** described his Republican critics as 'the most crooked, lying group I've ever seen.' Wow, that's saying something, because Kerry's both a lawyer and a politician.

Politics is show business for ugly people. The women aren't as attractive. The men aren't as handsome. The money is not as good. Being in politics is basically like being in B movies.

Elmore Leonard 1925-
American novelist and screenwriter

Erotic is when you do something sensitive and imaginative with a feather. Kinky is when you use the whole chicken.

Alan Jay Lerner 1918-86
American songwriter

Why can't a woman be more like a man?
Men are so honest, so thoroughly square;
Eternally noble, historically fair.
   'A Hymn to Him' from *My Fair Lady* (1956)

Doris Lessing 1919-
British novelist and short-story writer

There's only one real sin, and that is to persuade oneself that the second-best is anything but the second-best.

David Letterman 1947-
American television host and comedian

Overall Bush's European trip has been an overwhelming success. Not once has he gotten separated from his group.

Winifred Mary Letts 1882-1972
English writer

I saw the spires of Oxford
As I was passing by,
The grey spires of Oxford
Against a pearl-grey sky;
My heart was with the Oxford me
Who went abroad to die.
   'The Spires of Oxford' (1916)

Oscar Levant 1906-72
American pianist and actor

She has the answer to everything and the solution to nothing.
   Memoirs of an Amnesiac (1965)

Underneath this flabby exterior is an enormous lack of character.
   Memoirs of an Amnesiac (1965)

Self-pity? It's the only pity that counts.
   quoted in *American National Biography* (online edition)

Sam Levenson 1911-80
American humorist, writer, television host and journalist

What we should have fought for was representation without taxation.

You Don't Have to be in 'Who's Who' to Know What's What

It was on my fifth birthday that Papa put his hand on my shoulder and said, 'Remember, my son, if you ever need a helping hand, you'll find one at the end of your arm.'

Leslie Lever 1905-77
British Labour politician

Generosity is part of my character, and I therefore hasten to assure this Government that I will never make an allegation of dishonesty against it wherever a simple explanation of stupidity will suffice.
Leon Harris *The Fine Art of Political Wit* (1964)

Lord Leverhulme 1851-1925
English industrialist and philanthropist

Half the money I spend on advertising is wasted. The trouble is, I don't know which half.

Ada Leverson 1862-1933
British writer and novelist

Feminine intuition, a quality perhaps even rarer in women than in men.
quoted in *The Feminist Companion to Literature in English* ed. Virginia Blaine and others (1990)

Bernard Levin 1928-2004
English journalist, author and broadcaster

It was almost impossible to believe he was anything but a down-at-heel actor resting between engagements at the decrepit theatres of minor provincial towns.
*on Harold **Macmillan***

Tony **Benn** flung himself into the Sixties technology with the enthusiasm (not to say language) of a newly enrolled Boy Scout demonstrating knot-tying to his indulgent parents.
The Pendulum Years (1970)

Whom the mad would destroy, they first make gods.
*of **Mao** Zedong in 1967*
in *The Times* 21 September 1987

Kurt Lewin 1890-1947
German-American psychologist

A successful individual typically sets his next goal somewhat but not too much above his last achievement. In this way he steadily raises his level of aspiration.

C. S. Lewis 1898-1963
English scholar, religious writer and novelist

She's the sort of woman who lives for others – you can always tell the others by their hunted expressions.
The Screwtape Letters (1942)

Often when I pray I wonder if I am not posting letters to a non-existent address.
letter to Arthur **Greeves**, 24 December 1930

He that looketh on a plate of ham and eggs to lust after it, hath already committed breakfast with it in his heart.

Joe E. Lewis 1902-71
American comedian and singer

It doesn't matter if you're rich or poor, as long as you've got money.

The way taxes are, you might as well marry for love.

A mistress is what comes between a mister and a mattress.

Sinclair Lewis 1885-1951
American novelist, short-story writer, and playwright

Intellectually, I know that America is no better than any other country; emotionally I know that she is better than every other country.

Victor Lewis-Smith
British satirist, producer and critic

It is often said that safe sex in Wales means branding the sheep that kicks.
London *Evening Standard* 21 August 2003

Willmott Lewis 1877-1950
British journalist

Every government will do as much harm as it can and as much good as it must.
to Claud Cockburn
Claud Cockburn *In Time of Trouble* (1957)

Liberace 1918-87
American pianist and entertainer

I cried all the way to the bank.
on dealing with adverse criticism

Life of Brian 1979 film

Some things in life are bad,
They can really make you mad.
Other things just make you swear and curse.
When you're chewing on life's gristle,
Don't grumble, give a whistle,
And this'll help things turn out for the best,
And always look on the bright side of life.

Life's a piece of shit,
When you look at it.
Life's a laugh and death's a joke, it's true.
You'll see it's all a show,
Keep 'em laughing as you go.
Just remember that the last laugh is on you,

And always look on the bright side of life.
   'Always Look on the Bright Side of Life'

Rush Limbaugh 1951-
American radio host and conservative political commentator

I am weary and near my wits' end at having to listen to the complaint that the American safety net has holes in it and too many people are slipping through. The problem is that too many people are using that safety net as a hammock.
   The Way Things Ought To Be (1992)

Children need love and discipline. They need mothers and fathers. A welfare check is not a husband. The state is not a father.
   See, I Told You So (1993)

Feminism is just a way for ugly women to get into the mainstream of America.

Abraham Lincoln 1809-65
Lawyer, slave abolitionist. Republican Party politician, 16th President of the United States

The President tonight has a dream: He was in a party of plain people, and, as it became known who he was, they began to comment on his appearance. One of them said, 'He is a very common-looking man.' The President replied, 'The Lord prefers common-looking people. That is why He makes so many of them.'
   John Hay *Letters of John Hay and Extracts from Diary* (1908)

You may fool all the people some of the time; you can even fool some of the people all of the time; but you can't fool all of the people all of the time.
   Alexander K. McClure *Lincoln's Yarns and Stories* (1904); also attributed to Phineas **Barnum**

This country, with its institutions, belongs to the people who inhabit it. Whenever they shall grow weary of the existing government, they can exercise their constitutional right of amending it, or their revolutionary right to dismember or overthrow it.
   first inaugural address, 4 March 1861

Prohibition . . . goes beyond the bounds of reason in that it attempts to control a man's appetite by legislation, and makes a crime out of things that are not crimes. A Prohibition law strikes a blow at the very principles upon which our government was founded.
   speech in the Illinois House of Representatives, 18 December 1840

Any people, anywhere, being inclined and having the power, have the *right* to rise up, and shake off the existing government, and form a new one that suits them better.
   in the House of Representatives, 12 January 1848

What is conservatism? Is it not adherence to the old and tried, against the new and untried?
   speech, 27 February 1860

I desire so to conduct the affairs of this administration that if at the end, when I come to lay down the reins of power, I have lost every other friend on earth, I shall at least have one friend left, and that friend shall be down inside me.
   reply to the Missouri Committee of Seventy, 1864

Somewhat like that boy in Kentucky who stubbed his toe while running to see his sweetheart. The boy said he was too big to cry, and far too badly hurt to laugh.
when asked how he felt after a defeat in the New York elections

His argument is as thin as the homeopathic soup that was made by boiling the shadow of a pigeon that had been starved to death.
*of Stephen **Douglas***

If I were two-faced, would I be wearing this one?

Better to remain silent and be thought a fool than to speak out and remove all doubt.

With malice toward none, with charity for all ... let us strive on to finish the work we are in . . . to do all which may achieve and cherish a just and lasting peace among ourselves and with all nations.

You cannot help the poor by destroying the rich. You cannot lift the wage earner by pulling down the wage payer.
   attributed

Raymond Lindquist 1915-42
American ecologist

Courage is the power to let go of the familiar.

Walter Lippmann 1889-1974
American journalist

Mr Coolidge's genius for inactivity is developed to a very high point. It is far from being an indolent activity. It is a grim, determined, alert inactivity which keeps Mr Coolidge occupied, constantly. Nobody has ever worked harder at inactivity, with such force of character, with such unremitting attention to detail, with such conscientious devotion to the task.
   Men of Destiny (1927)

The will to be free is perpetually renewed in every individual who uses his faculties and affirms his manhood.
   Arthur Seldon *The State is Rolling Back* (1994)

The notion that every problem can be studied as such with an open and empty mind, without preconception, without knowing what has already been learned about it, must condemn men to a chronic childishness.
   address to the American Association for the Advancement of Science, University of Pennsylvania, 29 December 1940

Ken Livingstone 1945-
British Labour Party politician, Member of Parliament 1987-2000, Mayor of London 2000-08

If voting changed anything, they'd abolish it.
   title of book, 1987; recorded earlier as a saying

I feel like Galileo going before the Inquisition to explain that the sun doesn't revolve around the earth. I hope I have more success.
   at Millbank, prior to appearing before the Labour Party's selection panel for the Mayor of London. He was rejected, but stood as an independent and won
   in *Guardian* 17 November 1999

I've met serial killers and professional assassins and nobody scared me as much as Mrs T.
*on Margaret **Thatcher***
　in *Observer* 23 January 2000 'They Said What...?'

I have been forced to choose between the party I love and have given 31 years of my life to, and upholding the democratic rights of Londoners.
　announcing his independent candidacy for Mayor of London
　in *Times* 7 March 2000

When Mr **Blair** invited me down to Chequers two weeks ago to discuss what I would do if I was elected mayor, we had a very pleasant 50 minutes, whilst my nephew and niece wandered around the ground and did a bit of vandalism.
　in *Observer* 12 March 2000 'They Said What...?'

The problem is that many MPs never see the London that exists beyond the wine bars and brothels of Westminster.

David Lloyd George 1863-1945
British Liberal statesman, Prime Minister 1916-22

I would as soon go for a sunny evening stroll around Walton Heath with a grasshopper, as try to work with Northcliffe.
*of Lord **Northcliffe** c. 1916*
　Frank Owen *Tempestuous Journey* (1954)

Führer is the proper name for him. He is a great and wonderful leader.
　after meeting **Hitler** in 1936
　Frank Owen *Tempestuous Journey* (1954)

Truth against the world.
　Welsh proverb; motto taken on becoming Earl Lloyd-George of Dwyfor, January 1945
　Donald McCormick *The Mask of Merlin* (1963)

Of all the bigotries that savage the human temper there is non so stupid as the anti-Semitic.
　Is It Peace? (1923)

If you want to succeed in politics, you must keep your conscience well under control.
　Lord Riddell diary, 23 April 1919

Death is the most convenient time to tax rich people.
　in Lord Riddell *Intimate Diary of the Peace Conference and After, 1918-23* (1933)

The world is becoming like a lunatic asylum run by lunatics.
　in *Observer* 8 January 1933

Ah, on the water, I presume.
*on being told by Lord **Beaverbrook**'s butler that, 'The Lord is out walking.'*
　Lord Cudlipp letter in *Daily Telegraph* 13 September 1993

The Prime Minister should give an example of sacrifice, because there is nothing which can contribute more to victory than that he should sacrifice the seals of office.
*of Neville **Chamberlain***
　in the House of Commons, 7 May 1940

At eleven o'clock this morning came to an end the cruellest and most terrible war that has ever scourged mankind. I hope we may say that this, this fateful morning, came to an end all wars.
   in the House of Commons, 11 November 1918

What is our task? To make Britain a fit country for heroes to live in.
   speech at Wolverhampton, 23 November 1918

He would make a drum out of the skin of his mother the louder to sing his own praises.
*on Sir Winston **Churchill***

When they circumcised Herbert **Samuel**, they threw away the wrong bit.

Negotiating with **de Valera** is like trying to pick up mercury with a fork.

Brilliant – to the top of his boots.
*of Earl **Haig***
   attributed

Frank Lloyd Wright 1869-1959
American architect, interior designer, writer and educator

Noble life demands a noble architecture for noble uses of noble men. Lack of culture means what it has always meant: ignoble civilization and therefore imminent downfall.

John Locke 1632-1704
English philosopher

Man . . . hath by nature a power . . . to preserve his property – that is, his life, liberty, and estate, against the injuries and attempts of other men.
   Second Treatise of Civil Government (1690)

Vince Lombardi 1913-70
American football coach

Show me a good loser and I'll show you a loser.
   attributed

Jack London 1876-1916
American author

Man always gets less than he demands from life.
   The People of the Abyss (1903)

The Lone Ranger American radio (1933-54) and television series (1949-57)

Hi-yo, Silver, away! The Lone Ranger! With his faithful Indian companion, Tonto, the daring and resourceful masked rider of the plains led the fight for law and order in the West.
   voiceover

Russell Long 1918-2003
American Democratic Party politician

Tax reform means, 'Don't tax you, don't tax me, tax that fellow behind the tree.'

Henry Wadsworth Longfellow 1807-82
American poet

When you ask one friend to dine,
Give him your best wine!
When you ask two,
The second best will do!

Lives of great men all remind us
We can make our lives sublime,
And, departing, leave us behind,
Footprints on the sands of time.
    'A Psalm of Life' (1839)

Most people would succeed in small things if they were not troubled with great ambitions.
    Driftwood (1857) 'Table Talk'

Lord Longford 1905-2001
British Labour politician and philanthropist

You would get second raters, people who could not even get into the Commons or the European Parliament or even into the Scottish or Welsh Parliaments. You would get the dregs.
opposing an elected second chamber
    in *Observer* 12 March 2000 'They Said What...'

Alice Roosevelt Longworth 1884-1980
Oldest child of President Theodore Roosevelt

If you can't say anything good about someone, sit right here by me.

Though I yield to no one in my admiration for Mr Coolidge, I do wish he did not look as if he'd been weaned on a pickle.
*on Calvin **Coolidge***

Louis XIV (the 'Sun King') 1638-1715
French monarch, King from 1643

Every time I create an appointment, I create a hundred malcontents and one ingrate.
    Voltaire *Siècle de Louis XIV* (1768 ed.)

Louis XVI 1754-93
French monarch, King from 1774; deposed in 1789 on the outbreak of the French Revolution and executed in 1793

Rien
Nothing
    diary entry for 14 July 1789, the day of the storming of the Bastille
    Simon Schama *Citizens* (1989)

Louis XVIII 1755-1824
French monarch, King from 1814; titular king from 1795

Punctuality is the politeness of kings.

in *Souvenirs de. J. Lafitte* (1844)
attributed

Robert Lowe (Viscount Sherbrooke) 1811-92
British Liberal politician

The Chancellor of the Exchequer is a man whose duties make him more or less of a taxing machine. He is entrusted with a certain amount of misery which it is his duty to distribute as fairly as he can.
in the House of Commons, 11 April 1870

Alison Lurie 1926-
American novelist

There's a rule, I think. You get what you want in life, but not your second choice too.
Real People (1969)

Martin Luther 1483-1546
Initiator of the Protestant Reformation

I cannot and will not recant anything, for to go against conscience is neither right nor safe. Here I stand, I can do no other. God help me. Amen.
in front of his inquisitors at the Diet of Worms

If I had heard that as many devils would set on me in Worms as there are tiles on the roofs, I should none the less have ridden there.
to the Princes of Saxony, 21 August 1524

Who loves not women, wine, and song,
Remains a fool his whole life long.
attributed

Martin Luther King 1929-68
American clergyman, activist and prominent leader in the African-American civil rights movement

Nothing in all the world is more dangerous than sincere ignorance and conscientious stupidity.
Strength to Love (1963)

The time is always right to do what is right.

Cowardice asks the question - is it safe?
Expediency asks the question - is it politic?
Vanity asks the question - is it popular?
But conscience asks the question - is it right?
And there comes a time when one must take a position that is neither safe, nor politic, nor popular; but one must take it because it is right.

I believe that unarmed truth and unconditional love will have the final word in reality. That is why right, temporarily defeated, is stronger than evil triumphant.

When you are right you cannot be too radical; when you are wrong, you cannot be too conservative.

Our scientific power has outrun our spiritual power. We have guided missiles and misguided men.

If a man hasn't discovered something he will die for, he isn't fit to live.
   speech in Detroit, 23 June 1963

George Lyttleton

I am interested to see how many young women share the illusion that a woman goes any faster when she runs than she does walking.
   letter to Rupert Hart-Davis of 21 March 1956

m

General Douglas MacArthur 1880-1964
American general, Chief of Staff of the United States Army during the 1930s later played a prominent role in the Pacific theatre of World War II

Americans never quit.

The enemy is in front of us, the enemy is behind us, the enemy is to the right and to the left of us. They can't get away this time!

Lord Macaulay 1800-59
English Whig politician, historian and poet

An acre in Middlesex is better than a principality in Utopia.
Essays Contributed to the Edinburgh Review (1843)

The history of England is emphatically the history of progress.
Essays Contributed to the Edinburgh Review (1843)

The Puritan hated bear-baiting, not because it gave pain to the bear, but because it gave pleasure to the spectators.
History of England (1849)

The object of oratory alone is not truth, but persuasion.
Knight's Quarterly Magazine August 1824 'Essay on Athenian Orators'

Nothing is so galling to a people not broken in from the birth as a paternal, or in other words a meddling government, a government which tells them what to read and say and eat and drink and wear.
in *Edinburgh Review* January 1830

We must at present do our best to form a class who may be interpreters between us and the millions whom we govern; a class of persons, Indian in blood and colour, but English in taste, in opinions, in morals, and in intellect.
minute, as Member of Supreme Council of India, 2 February 1835

Dwight MacDonald 1906-1982
American writer, editor, social critic and philosopher

Doris Day is as wholesome as a bowl of cornflakes and at least as sexy.

John A. Macdonald 1815-91
Scottish-born Canadian Liberal-Conservative statesman, Prime Minister 1867-73 and 1878-91

When fortune empties her chamberpot on your head, smile – and say 'we are going to have a summer shower.'
spoken c.1875 when Leader of the Opposition

Ramsay MacDonald 1866-1937
British Labour statesman; Prime Minister, 1924, 1931-5

A terror decreed by a Secret Committee is child's play compared with a terror instituted by 'lawful authority.'
 in *Socialist Review* January-March 1921

A body representing the citizenship of the whole nation is charged with so much that it can do nothing swiftly and well.
 Carl Cohen *Parliament and Democracy* (1962)

Ian McEwan 1948-
English novelist

The committee divided between the theorists, who had done all their thinking long ago, or had had it done for them, and the pragmatists, who hoped to discover what it was they thought in the process of saying it.
 The Child in Time (1987)

No human society, from the hunter-gatherer to the postindustrialist, has come to the attention of anthropologists that did not have its leaders and the led; and no emergency was ever dealt with effectively by democratic process.
 Enduring Love (1987)

Niccolò Machiavelli 1469-1527
Italian philosopher, writer, political theorist and philosopher, diplomat, musician, playwright, civil servant

So as a prince is forced to know how to act like a beast, he must learn from the fox and the lion; because the lion is defenceless against traps and the fox is defenceless against wolves. Therefore one must be a fox in order to recognise traps and lion to frighten off wolves.
 The Prince (1513)

Let no one oppose this belief of mine with that well-worn proverb: 'He who builds on the people builds on mud.'
 The Prince (1513)

Ambition is so powerful a passion in the human breast, that however high we reach we are never satisfied.

He who blinded by ambition, raises himself to a position whence he cannot mount higher, must thereafter fall with the greatest loss.

Compton Mackenzie 1883-1972
English novelist

Women do not find it difficult nowadays to behave like men, but they often find it extremely difficult to behave like gentlemen.
 Literature in My Time (1933)

Love makes the world go round? Not at all. Whisky makes it go round twice as fast.
 Whisky Galore (1947)

James Mackintosh 1765-1832
Scottish philosopher and historian

The Commons, faithful to their system, remained in a wise and masterly inactivity.
of the French Commons
   Vindiciae Gallicae (1791)

Iain MacLeod 1913-70
British Conservative politician

Double talk is his mother tongue. He is a man whose vision is limited to tomorrow's headlines.

We now have the worst of both worlds – not just inflation on the one side or stagnation on the other, but both of them together. We have a sort of 'stagflation' situation.

The Tory Party only panics in a crisis.

The Conservative Party always in time forgives those who were wrong. Indeed often, in time, they forgive those who were right.
   in *The Spectator* 21 February 1964

I cannot help it if every time the Opposition are asked to name their weapons they pick boomerangs.
   in *Dictionary of National Biography* (1917-)

Harold Macmillan 1894-1986
Conservative Party politician and Prime Minister 1957-63

It is thinking about themselves that is really the curse of the younger generation – they appear to have no other subject which interests them at all.
   the 'Tuesday memorandum', a draft of a letter to The Queen, advising on his successor, but not sent, 1963
   D. R. Thorpe *Alec Douglas-Home* (1996)

Sometimes the strain is awful, you have to resort to Jane Austen.
   of the office of Prime Minister
   in the Butler Papers; Peter Hennessey *The Hidden Wiring* (1995)

Toryism has always been a form of paternal socialism.
   said in 1936
   Anthony Sampson *Macmillan* (1967)

I was determined that no British government should be brought down by the action of two tarts.
*on the **Profumo** affair, July 1963*
   Anthony Sampson *Macmillan* (1967)

He [Aneurin **Bevan**] enjoys prophesying the imminent fall of the capitalist system and is prepared to play a part, any part, in its burial, except that of mute.
   Michael Foot *Aneurin Bevan* attributed (1962)

I have never found, in a long experience of politics, that criticism is ever inhibited by ignorance.
   Wall Street Journal, Aug 13, 1963

A Foreign Secretary – and this applies also to a prospective Foreign Secretary – is always faced with this cruel dilemma. Nothing he can say can do very much good, and almost anything he may say may

do a great deal of harm. Anything he says that is not obvious is dangerous; whatever is not trite is risky. He is forever poised between the cliché and the indiscretion.
  speech, House of Commons, 27 July 1955

Let us be frank about it: most of our people have never had it so good. Go around the country, go to the industrial towns, go to the farms, and you'll see a state of prosperity such as we have never had in my lifetime – nor indeed ever in the history of this country. What is beginning to worry some of us is 'Is it too good to be true?' or perhaps I should say 'Is it too good to last?'
  speech in Bedford, 20 July 1957

After a few months learning geography, now I've got to learn arithmetic.
  on moving from the Foreign Office to the Treasury

As usual the Liberals offer a mixture of sound and original ideas. Unfortunately none of the sound ideas are original and none of the original ideas are sound.

I have often found that the man who trusts nobody is apt to be the kind of man nobody trusts.

If people want a sense of purpose they should get it from their archbishops. They should not hope to get it from their politicians.

Memorial services are the cocktail parties of the geriatric set.

Louis MacNeice 1907-63
Northern Irish poet

Better good authentic mammon than a bogus god.
  Autumn Journal (1939)

Lester Maddox 1915-2003
American Democratic Party politician

That's part of American greatness, is discrimination. Yes, sir. Inequality, I think, breeds freedom and gives a man opportunity.

James Madison 1751-1836
American politician and political philosopher who served as the fourth President of the United States, 1809-17

The accumulation of all powers, legislative, executive, and judiciary, in the same hands, whether of one, a few, or many, and whether hereditary, self-appointed, or elective, may justly be pronounced the very definition of tyranny.
  The Federalist (1787)

Democracies have ever been spectacles of turbulence and contention; have ever been found incompatible with personal security, or the rights of property; have in general been as short in their lives as they are violent in their deaths.

Madonna 1958-
American recording artist and actress

I'm tough, ambitious and I know exactly what I want. If that makes me a bitch, okay.

Rita Mae Brown 1944-
American writer

The statistics on sanity are that one of every four Americans is suffering from some form of mental illness. Think of your three best friends. If they're okay, it's you.

Bill Maher 1956-
American stand-up comedian, television host, social and political commentator, author

Dick **Cheney**. If he were any duller he'd be on *Big Brother*. He can explain to **George W.** the tricky stuff – like how a bill becomes a law. Cheney adds one thing to the Republican ticket: adult supervision.'

Derek Mahon 1941-
Northern Irish poet

Society is built on many people hurting many people, it is just who does the hurting, which is forever in dispute.
   Miami and the Siege of Chicago (1968)

David Mahoney 1981-

The function of socialism is to raise suffering to a higher level.

Our heroes are those who act above and beyond the call of duty and in so doing give definition to patriotism and elevate all of us . . . America is the land of the free because we are the land of the brave.

Norman Mailer 1923-2007
American novelist, journalist, essayist, poet, playwright, screenwriter and film director

There is no greater importance in all the world like knowing you are right and that the wave of the world is wrong, yet the wave crashes upon you.
   Armies Of The Night (1968)

Writing books is the closest men ever come to child-bearing.

Joseph de Maistre 1753-1821
French writer and diplomat

Every nation has the government it deserves.
   letter, 15 August 1811

Sir John Major 1943-
British Conservative statesman; Prime Minister 1990-7

Margaret had been at her happiest confronting political dragons: I chose consensus.
*contrasting himself with Margaret **Thatcher***
   John Major *The Autobiography* (1999)

Society needs to condemn a little more and understand a little less.
   interview with *Mail on Sunday* 21 February 1993

It is time to get back to basics: to self-discipline and respect for the law, to consideration for others, to accepting responsibility for yourself and your family, and not shuffling it off on the state.
    speech to the Conservative Party Conference, 8 October 1993

Fifty years on from now, Britain will still be the country of long shadows on county [cricket] grounds, warm beer, invincible green suburbs, dog lovers, and – as George **Orwell** said – old maids bicycling to Holy Communion through the morning mist.
    speech to the Conservative Group for Europe, 22 April 1993

If the policy isn't hurting, it isn't working.
    speech in Northampton, 27 October 1989

Neil **Kinnock**'s speeches go on for so long because he has nothing to say so he has no way of knowing when he's finished saying it.

I'm drawing a line under the sand.
on the Maastricht Treaty in 1992

He behaves like an agitated parrot with constipation.
on Frank Dobson

Robin **Cook** is the only Foreign Secretary in 700 years who has more trouble at home than he has abroad. But don't mock. One days his looks will go.

Sustainable growth is growth that is sustainable.

Something that I was not aware had happened suddenly turned out not to have happened.

George Leigh Mallory 1886-1924
British mountaineer

Because it's there.
on being asked why he wanted to climb Mount Everest
    in *New York Times* 18 March 1923

Maxwell Maltz 1899-1975
American cosmetic surgeon and author

We find no real satisfaction or happiness in life without obstacles to conquer and goals to achieve.
    Communication Bulletin for Managers & Supervisors (2004)

Lord Mancroft 1914-87
English writer

Cricket – a game which the English, not being a spiritual people, have invented in order to give themselves a conception of eternity.
    Sports Illustrated 11 November 1963 'Scorecard'
    Bees in Some Bonnets (1979)

Nelson Mandela 1918-
South African statesman; President 1994-9

No one is born hating another person because of the colour of his skin, or his background, or his religion. People must learn to hate, and if they can learn to hate, they can be taught to love, for love comes more naturally to the human heart than its opposite.
Long Walk to Freedom (1994)

I have dedicated my life to this struggle of the African people. I have fought against white domination, and I have fought against black domination. I have cherished the ideal of a democratic and free society in which all persons live together in harmony with equal opportunities. It is an ideal which I hope to live for, and to see realised. But my lord, if needs be, it is an ideal for which I am prepared to die.
speech in Pretoria, 20 April 1964, which he quoted on his release in Cape Town, 11 February 1990

Jack de Manio 1914-88
English broadcaster

She has a face to launch a thousand dredgers.
of actress Glenda Jackson in the film Women in Love

Herman J. Mankiewicz 1897-1953
American screenwriter

I think that's what they call professional courtesy.
when a Hollywood agent told him how he had been swimming unscathed in shark-infested waters
quoted by Dick Vosburgh on BBC Radio, 31 July 1979, *Quote ... Unquote*

Joseph L. Mankiewicz 1909-93
American film director, screenwriter, and producer

Funny business, a woman's career: the things you drop on the way up the ladder so you can move faster. You forget you'll need them again when you get back to being a woman. It's one career all females have in common, whether we like it or not: being a woman. Sooner or later, we've got to work at it, no matter how many other careers we've had or wanted.
lines from *All About Eve* (1950)

Stephen Mansfield 1958-
American author

There is a schizophrenic nature in modern politics. A leader is expected to have a religious faith but he is not supposed to let it influence him in his duties. Somehow, the truths that determine everything else about his existence are not allowed to influence how he conducts himself in public life. Not only that, his principles are usually considered so personal that the public is not even allowed to know for certain what they are. This passes for noble statecraft in our time. It was once thought cowardice.

Mao Zedong 1893-1976
Chinese revolutionary, political theorist and Communist leader, led the People's Republic of China from its establishment in 1949 until his death in 1976. Mao is officially held in high regard in China as a great revolutionary, political strategist, military mastermind, and saviour of the nation. Mao's social-political programs, such as the Great Leap Forward and the Cultural Revolution, are blamed for causing severe famine and damage to

the culture, society and economy of China. Mao's policies and political purges from 1949 to 1975 are widely believed to have caused the deaths of around 70 million people

Every Communist must grasp the truth, 'Political power grows out of the barrel of a gun.'
: speech, 6 November 1938

Communism is not love. Communism is a hammer which we use to crush the enemy.
: quoted in *Time* 18 December 1950

Bob Marley 1945-81
Jamaican reggae musician and singer

Get up, stand up,
Stand up for your right.
Get up, stand up,
Don't give up the fight.

Don Marquis 1878-1937
American humorist, novelist, poet, newspaper columnist and playwright

The chief obstacle to the progress of the human race is the human race.

did you ever
notice that when
a politician
gets an idea
he usually
gets it all wrong.
: *archys life of mehitable* (1933)

an optimist is a guy
that has never had
much experience
: *archys life of mehitable* (1933)

Lord Marsh (Richard Marsh) 1928-
English politician

If you subtracted the North Sea oil revenues you would realise that present policies are leading us to the state of a banana republic that has run out of bananas.
on the state of Britain in 1978
: quoted in *The Daily Telegraph* 6 September 1978

George C. Marshall 1880-1959
American general and statesman, who as US Secretary of State, 1947-9

If a man does find the solution for world peace it will be the most revolutionary reversal of his record we have ever known.
: biennial report of the Chief of Staff, United States Army, 1 September 1945

John Marshall 1755-1835
American jurist

The people made the Constitution, and the people can unmake it. It is the creature of their own will, and lives only by their will.
in *Cohens v. Virginia* (1821)

Reverend Peter Marshall 1902-49
Scottish-American preacher

The choice before us is plain: Christ or chaos, conviction or compromise, discipline or disintegration. I am rather tired of hearing about our rights and privileges as American citizens. The time is come – it now is – when we ought to hear about the duties and responsibilities of our citizenship. America's future depends upon her accepting and demonstrating God's government.
on being elected Chaplain of the US Senate, January 1947

S. L. A. Marshall 1900-77
US Army combat historian

The art of leading, in operations large or small, is the art of dealing with humanity, of working diligently on behalf of men, of being sympathetic with them, but equally, of insisting that they make a square facing toward their own problems.
Men Against Fire (1947)

Dean Martin 1917-95
Italian-American singer, film actor and comedian

I once shook hands with Pat Boone and my whole right side sobered up.

You're not drunk if you can lie on the floor without holding on.

I'd hate to be a teetotaller. Imagine getting up in the morning and knowing that's as good as you're going to feel all day.
attributed remark

Steve Martin 1945-
American actor, comedian, writer, playwright, producer, musician, and composer

I like a woman with a head on her shoulders. I hate necks.

I believe that sex is one of the most beautiful, natural, wholesome things that money can buy.

H. E. Martz

He who builds a better mousetrap these days runs into material shortages, patent-infringement suits, work stoppages, collusive bidding, discount discrimination and taxes.

Groucho Marx 1890-1977
American comedian and film actor

Those are my principles. If you don't like them, I have others.

I've been around so long, I knew Doris **Day** before she was a virgin.
Max Wilk *The Wit and Wisdom of Hollywood* (1932); also attributed to Oscar **Levant**

Remember, you're fighting for this woman's honour, which is probably more than she ever did.
Duck Soup (1933 film)

Please accept my resignation. I don't care to belong to any club that will have me as a member.
Groucho and Me (1959)

I never forget a face, but in your case I'll be glad to make an exception.
Leo Rosten *People I have Loved, Known or Admired* (1970)

They say a man is as old as the woman he feels. In that case I'm eighty-five.
The Secret Word is Groucho (1976)

Gentlemen, **Chicolini** may look like an idiot and talk like an idiot, but don't let that fool you. He really is an idiot.

The secret of life is honesty and fair dealing. If you can fake that, you've got it made.

Only one man in a thousand is a leader of men - the other 999 follow women.

In America you can go on the air and kid the politicians, and the politicians can go on the air and kid the people.

Politics doesn't make strange bedfellows. Marriage does.

I never go to movies where the hero's bust is bigger than the heroine's.

Karl Marx 1818-83
German philosopher, political economist, historian, political theorist, sociologist, communist, revolutionary

The theory of the Communists may be summed up in the single sentence: Abolition of private property.
The Communist Manifesto (1840)

Religion . . . is the opium of the people.
A Contribution to the Critique of Hegel's Philosophy of Right (1843-4) introduction

What I did that was new was to prove . . . that the class struggle necessarily leads to the dictatorship of the proletariat.
letter to Georg Weydemeyer, 5 March 1852

All I know is that I am not a Marxist.
attributed in a letter from Friedrich Engels to Conrad Schmidt, 5 August 1890

Capitalism contains the seeds of its own destruction.

The last capitalist we hang shall be the one who sold us the rope.

Karl Marx 1818-83 and Friedrich Engels 1820-95

A spectre is haunting Europe - the spectre of Communism.

the opening words of *The Communist Manifesto* (1848)

Jackie Mason 1936-
American stand-up comedian

80% of married men cheat in America. The rest cheat in Europe.

Walter Matthau 1920-2000
American actor

I never mind my wife having the last word. In fact, I'm delighted when she gets to it.

W. Somerset Maugham 1874-1965
English playwright, novelist and short story writer

Money is like a sixth sense, without which you cannot make a complete use of the other five.
Of Human Bondage (1915)

You know, of course, that the Tasmanians, who never committed adultery, are now extinct.
The Bread-Winner

You can't learn too soon that the most useful thing about a principle is that it can always be sacrificed to expediency.
The Circle (1921)

Make him [the reader] laugh and he will think you a trivial fellow, but bore him in the right way and your reputation is assured.
The Gentleman in the Parlour (1930)

It is not true that suffering ennobles the character; happiness does that sometimes, but suffering, for the most part, makes men petty and vindictive.
The Moon and Sixpence (1919)

Impropriety is the soul of wit.
The Moon and Sixpence (1919)

Unfortunately sometimes one can't do what one thinks is right without making someone else unhappy.
The Razor's Edge (1943)

Dying is a very dull, dreary affair. And my advice to you to is to have nothing whatever to do with it.
to his nephew Robin, in 1965
Robin Maugham *Conversations with Willie* (1978)

I am told that today rather more than 60 per cent of the men who go to the universities go on a Government grant. This is a new class that has entered upon the scene . . . They are scum.
in *Sunday Times* 25 December 1955

The fact that a great many people believe something is no guarantee of its truth.

'My country, right or wrong,' is a thing that no patriot would think of saying except in a desperate case. It is like saying, 'My mother, drunk or sober.'

American women expect to find in their husbands a perfection that English women only hope to find in their butlers.

Love is what happens to a man and woman who don't know each other.

It is a funny thing about life: if you refuse to accept anything but the best you very often get it.

To eat well in England , all you have to take is breakfast three times a day.

Love is a dirty trick played on us to achieve the continuation of the species.

Richard Mawrey 1942-
British judge

Anyone who has sat through the case I have just tried and listened to evidence of electoral fraud that would disgrace a banana republic would find this statement surprising.
commenting on the government's refusal to revise the rules for postal voting
   in *Guardian* 4 April 2005

Louisa May Alcott 1832-88
American novelist

Far away there in the sunshine are my brightest aspirations. I may not reach them, but I can look up and see their beauty, believe in them, and try to follow where they lead.

Robert Maynard Hutchins 1899-1977
American educational philosopher

The death of democracy is not likely to be an assassination from ambush. It will be a slow extinction from apathy, indifference, and undernourishment.

Charles H. Mayo 1865-1939
American doctor, co-founder of the Mayo Clinic

The definition of a specialist as one who 'knows more and more about less and less' is good and true.
   in *Modern Hospital* September 1939

William G. McAdoo 1853-1930
American Democratic Party politician

It is impossible to defeat an ignorant man in argument.

Charlie McCarthy (dummy of Edgar Bergen) 1903-78
American ventriloquist, actor and radio performer

Ambition is a poor excuse for not having enough sense to be lazy.

Eugene McCarthy 1916-2005
American Democratic Party politician, poet

Being in politics is like being a football coach. You have to be smart enough to understand the game, and dumb enough to think it's important.

Never trust a member [of the US House of Representatives] who quotes the Bible, the Internal Revenue Code or the Rules of the House.

Joseph McCarthy 1908-57
American politician and anti-Communist agitator

McCarthyism is Americanism with its sleeves rolled.
   speech in Wisconsin, 1952
   Richard Rovere *Senator Joe McCarthy* (1973)

Mary McCarthy 1912-89
American novelist

Bureaucracy, the rule of no one, has become the modern form of despotism.
   On the Contrary (1961) 'The *Vita Activa*'

Samuel McChord Crothers 1857-1927
American Unitarian Universalist minister

Try as hard as we may for perfection, the net result of our labors is an amazing variety of imperfectness. We are surprised at our own versatility in being able to fail in so many different ways.

Foster C. McClellan

Trust yourself. Create the kind of self that you will be happy to live with all your life. Make the most of yourself by fanning the tiny, inner sparks of possibility into flames of achievement.

Eric McCormack 1963-
Canadian-American actor, musician, writer and producer

I phoned my mum and said I had the lead in *Will and Grace*. When she asked me who Will was, I answered that he was a lawyer and he was gay. Then she said, 'Oh Eric, not a *lawyer* ...'

J. D. McCoughey

God is dead, but 50,000 social workers have risen to take his place.

Ian McEwan 1948-
English novelist

I love you ... That is what they were all saying down their phones, from the hijacked planes and the burning towers. There is only love, and then oblivion. Love was all they had to set against the hatred of their murderers.
   of the last messages received from those trapped by terrorist attach in buildings and planes, 11 September 2001
   in *Guardian* 15 September 2001

Alfred McFote

WIFE: Mr Watt next door blows his wife a kiss every morning as he leaves the house. I wish you'd do that.
HUSBAND: But I hardly know the woman!

Roger McGough 1937-
English poet

I wanna be the leader
I wanna be the leader
Can I be the leader?
Can I? Can I?
Promise? Promise?
Yippee, I'm the leader
I'm the leader
OK, what shall we do now?
   'I Wanna be the Leader'

Ewan McGregor 1971-
Scottish actor

He flies at 500mph 200ft above the ground, whereas I wear make-up for a living.
on his fighter pilot brother Colin

Robert J. McKain

Set priorities for your goals. A major part of successful living lies in the ability to put first things first. Indeed, the reason most major goals are not achieved is that we spend our time doing second things first.

Lois McMaster Bujold 1949-
American author

Any community's arm of force – military, police security – needs people in it who can do necessary evil, and yet not be made evil by it. To do only the necessary and no more. To constantly question the assumptions, to stop the slide into atrocity.
   Barrayar (1991)

Never, ever suggest they don't have to pay you. What they pay for, they'll value. What they get for free, they'll take for granted, and then demand as a right. Hold them up for all the market will bear.
   A Civil Campaign (1999)

If power was an illusion, wasn't weakness necessarily one also?
   A Civil Campaign (1999)

The will to be stupid is a very powerful force, but there are always alternatives.
   Brothers in Arms (1989)

Michael Meacher 1939-
British Labour Party politician

When I arrived at the Environment Ministry in 1997, John **Prescott** thought that biodiversity was a kind of washing powder.

Peter Medawar 1915-87
English immunologist and writer

A bishop wrote gravely to the *Times* inviting all nations to destroy 'the formula' of the atomic bomb. There is no simple remedy for ignorance so abysmal.
The Hope of Progress (1972)

Robert Megarry 1910-2006
British lawyer and judge

Whereas in England all is permitted that is not expressly prohibited, it has been said that in Germany all is prohibited unless expressly permitted and in France all is permitted that is expressly prohibited. In the European Common Market (as it then was) no-one knows what is permitted and it all costs more.
'Law and Lawyers in a Permissive Society', 5th Riddell Lecture delivered in Lincoln's Inn Hall, 22 March 1972

Golda Meir 1878-1978
Israeli stateswoman, Prime Minister 1969-74

Women's Liberation is just a lot of foolishness. It's the men who are discriminated against. They can't bear children. And no-one's likely to do anything about that.
in *Newsweek* 23 October 1972

Lord Melbourne

I like large features. People with small features and squeeny noses never do anything.
to Queen Victoria
quoted in *Lord M.* (1954) by David Cecil

David Mellor 1949-
British Conservative Party politician, barrister, broadcaster, journalist and football pundit

I cannot stay in a Tory Party led by a man who thinks that charisma is December 25.
on Iain Duncan Smith

H. L. Mencken 1880-1956
American journalist, essayist, magazine editor, satirist, critic of American life and culture

Conscience: the inner voice which warns us that somebody may be looking.
A Little Book in C Major (1916)

The final test of truth is ridicule. Very few dogmas have ever faced it and survived.
Damn! A Book of Calumny (1918)

Archbishop: a Christian ecclesiastic of a rank superior to that attained by Christ.
Sententiae (1912-48)

Say what you like about the Ten Commandments, you must always come back to the pleasant fact that there are only ten of them.
Sententiae (1916)

I long ago associated with the Chinese doctrine that it is foolish to do anything standing up that can be done sitting down, or anything sitting down that can be done lying down.
Happy Days (1940)

Love is the delusion that one woman differs from another.
Chrestomathy (1949)

Nothing is so abject and pathetic as a politician who has lost his job, save only a retired stud-horse.
Chrestomathy (1949)

An idealist is one who, on noticing that a rose smells better than a cabbage, concludes that it will also make better soup.
Chrestomathy (1949)

Puritanism. The haunting fear that someone, somewhere, may be happy.
Chrestomathy (1949)

A government can never be the impersonal thing described in text-books. It is simply a group of men like any other. In every 100 of the men composing it there are two who are honest and intelligent, ten obvious scoundrels, and 88 poor fish.
Minority Report (1956)

It is now quite lawful for a Catholic woman to avoid pregnancy by a resort to mathematics, though she is still forbidden to resort to physics and chemistry.
Notebooks (1956)

The worst government is often the most moral. One composed of cynics is often very tolerant and humane. But when fanatics are on top there is no limit to oppression.
Minority Report (1956)

Man, at his best, remains a sort of one-lunged animal, never completely rounded and perfect, as a cockroach, say, is perfect. If he shows one valuable quality, it is almost unheard of for him to show any other. Give him a head and he lacks a hear., Give him a heart of a gallon capacity, and his head holds scarcely a pint.
Smart Set (1923)

The truth has a horrible sweat to survive in this world, but a piece of nonsense, however absurd on its face, always seems to prosper.
Smart Set (1923)

No one in this world, so far as I know – and I have searched the records for years, and employed agents to help me – has ever lost money by underestimating the intelligence of the great masses of the plain people.
in *Chicago Tribune* 19 September 1926

If there had been any formidable body of cannibals in the country he would have promised to provide them with free missionaries fattened at the taxpayer's expense.
*of Harry **Truman** in the 1948 presidential campaign*
in *Baltimore Sun* 7 November 1948

The saddest life is that of a political aspirant under democracy. His failure is ignominious and his success is disgraceful.
  in *Baltimore Evening Sun* 9 December 1929

Here, indeed, was his one really notable talent. He slept more than any other President, whether by day or night . . . Nero fiddled, but Coolidge only snored . . . He had no ideas, and he was not a nuisance.
on Calvin Coolidge

He was as cool as an undertaker at a hanging.
of Henry Cabot Lodge at the Republican National Convention in Chicago
  in the *Baltimore Evening Sun* 15 June 1920

The only really happy folk are married women and single men.
  attributed

On one issue at least, men and women agree: they both distrust women.
  attributed

One hears that the 'women of the United States' are up in arms about this or that; the plain fact is that eight fat women, meeting in a hotel parlor, have decided to kick up some dust.
  1925

I've made it a rule never to drink by daylight and never to refuse a drink after dark.

God is the immemorial refuge of the incompetent, the helpless, the miserable. They find not only sanctuary in His arms, but also a kind of superiority, soothing to their macerated egos; He will set them above their betters.

A prohibitionist is the sort of man one wouldn't care to drink with – even if he drank.

Every decent man is ashamed of the government he lives under.

Democracy is the art of running the circus from the monkey cage.

It is hard to believe that a man is telling the truth when you know that you would lie if you were in his place.

College football would be more interesting if the faculty played instead of the students – there would be a great increase in broken arms, legs and necks.

The trouble with fighting for human freedom is that one spends most of one's time defending scoundrels. For it is against scoundrels that oppressive laws are first aimed, and oppression must be stopped at the beginning if it is to be stopped at all.

Under democracy the parties always devote their chief energies to trying to prove that the other parties are unfit to rule. They commonly succeed, and are right.

Democracy is the theory that the common people know what they want and deserve to get it good and hard.

Nobody ever went broke underestimating the intelligence of the American public.

As democracy is perfected, the office of president represents, more and more, the inner soul of the people. On some great and glorious day the plain folks of the land will reach their heart's desire at last, and the White House will be occupied by a downright moron.

If I had my way, any man guilty of golf would be ineligible for any office of trust in the United States.

The men the American public admire most extravagantly are the most daring liars; the men they detest most violently are those who try to tell them the truth.

Unquestionably, there is progress. The average American now pays out twice as much in taxes as he formerly got in wages.

A good politician is quite as unthinkable as an honest burglar.

It is a sin to believe evil of others, but it is seldom a mistake.

Opera in English is, in the main, just about as sensible as baseball in Italian.

The whole aim of practical politics is to keep the populace alarmed (and hence clamorous to be led to safety) by menacing it with an endless series of hobgoblins, all of them imaginary.

The most common of all follies is to believe passionately in the palpably not true. It is the chief occupation of mankind.

Sunday: A day given over by Americans to wishing they were dead and in heaven, and that their neighbours were dead and in hell.

The cynics are right, nine times out of ten.

A church is a place in which gentlemen who have never been to heaven brag about it to persons who will never get there.

Dr. Karl Menninger 1893-1990
American psychiatrist

The adjuration to be 'normal' seems shockingly repellent to me; I see neither hope nor comfort in sinking to that low level. I think it is ignorance that makes people think of abnormality only with horror and allows them to remain undismayed at the proximity of 'normal' to average and mediocre. For surely anyone who achieves anything is, essentially, abnormal.

Rick Mercer 1969-
Canadian comedian

America is our neighbour, our ally, our trading partner, and our friend. Still, sometimes you'd like to give them such a smack.
  This Hour Has 22 Minutes CBC television, 11 November 1996

George Meredith 1828-1909
English poet and novelist

I expect that Woman will be the last thing civilised by Man.

The Ordeal of Richard Feverel (1859)

Thomas Merton 1915-68
American Catholic writer, Trappist monk, poet and social activist

The truth that many people never understand, until it is too late, is that the more you try to avoid suffering the more you suffer because smaller and more insignificant things begin to torture you in proportion to your fear of being hurt.

Propaganda makes up our minds for us, but in such a way that it leaves us the sense of pride and satisfaction of men who have made up their own minds. And in the last analysis, propaganda achieves this effect because we want it to. This is one of the few real pleasures left to modern man: this illusion that he is thinking for himself when, in fact, someone else is doing his thinking for him.

Klemens von Metternich 1773-1859
German-Austrian politician and diplomat

To ruin those who possess something is not to come to the aid of those who possess nothing; it is only to render misery general.
Mémoires (1880)

Jules Michelet 1798-1874
French historian

What is the first part of politics? Education. The second? Education. And the third? Education.
Le Peuple (1846)

Bette Midler 1945-
American singer, actress and comedian

Self-esteem is something you have to earn! The only way to achieve self-esteem is to work hard. People have an obligation to live up to their potential.

George Mikes 1912-87
Hungarian-born British writer

An Englishman, even if he is alone, forms an orderly queue of one.
How to be an Alien (1946)

John Stuart Mill 1806-73
English philosopher, political theorist, political economist, Member of Parliament

The following quotations are from *On Liberty* (1956):

He who lets the world, or his own portion of it, choose his plan of life for him, has no need of any other faculty than the ape-like one of imitation. He who chooses his plan for himself, employs all his faculties. He must use observation to see, reasoning and judgment to foresee, activity to gather materials for decision, discrimination to decide, and when he has decided, firmness and self-control to hold to his deliberate decision.

The only purpose for which power can be rightfully exercised over any member of a civilised community, against his will, is to prevent harm to others. His own good, either physical or moral, is not sufficient warrant.

The only freedom worth the name, is that of pursuing our own good in our own way.

Liberty consists in doing what one desires.

A State which dwarfs its men, in order that they may be more docile instruments in its hands even for beneficial purposes, will find that with small men no great thing can really be accomplished.

Alice Duer Miller 1915-2005
American writer

I am American bred,
I have seen much to hate here – much to forgive,
But in a world where England is finished and dead,
I do not wish to live.
The White Cliffs (1940)

Dennis Miller 1953-
American stand-up comedian, political commentator, actor, sports commentator, television and radio personality

A good rule of thumb is if you've made it to 35 and your job still requires you to wear a name tag, you've probably made a serious vocational error.

Henry Miller 1891-1980
American novelist and painter

Even before the music begins there is that bored look on people's faces. A polite form of self-imposed torture, the concert.
The Tropic of Cancer (1934)

Living apart and at peace with myself, I came to realize more vividly the meaning of the doctrine of acceptance. To refrain from giving advice, to refrain from meddling in the affairs of others, to refrain, even though the motives be the highest, from tampering with another's way of life – so simple, yet so difficult for an active spirit. Hands off!

Sir Jonathan Miller 1934-
English entertainer, writer and director

I'm not really a *Jew*. Just *Jew-ish*. Not the whole hog, you know.
Beyond the Fringe (1960)

He looks like an explosion in a pubic hair factory.
on journalist Paul Johnson

Max Miller 1894-1963
English comedian

My wife's the ugliest woman in the world – I'd sooner take her with me than kiss her goodbye.
recorded at the Holborn Empire, London, October 1938

My wife's father said if you marry my daughter I'll give you three acres and a cow. I'm still waiting for the three acres.

Zell Miller 1932-
American Democratic Party politician

It is the soldier who salutes the flag, serves beneath the flag, whose coffin is draped by the flag who gives that protester the freedom to abuse and burn that flag.

Spike Milligan 1918-2002
Irish comedian, writer, musician, poet and playwright

Money couldn't buy you friends but you got a better class of enemy.
Puckoon (1963)

The mortuarial man entered the room. One was taller than the other, as is often the case in Ireland.
Puckoon (1963)

A bald man is a desperate man; but a bald *vain* man is a hairless Greek Tragedy.
Puckoon (1963)

I am a hero wid coward's legs. I'm a hero from the waist up.
Puckoon (1963)

Contraceptives should be used on every conceivable occasion.
The Last Goon Show of All (1972)

The ship is sinking. We must try and save it. Help me get it into the lifeboat.
The Goon Show

All I ask is the chance to prove that money can't make me happy.

Well, we can't stand around here doing nothing. People will think we're workmen.

There are holes in the sky,
where the rain gets in.
But they're ever so small,
that's why rain is thin.

The Grand Old Duke of York,
He had ten thousand men.
His case comes up next week.

I'm walking backwards for Christmas
Across the Irish sea.
I'm walking backwards for Christmas
It's the only thing for me.
'I'm Walking Backwards for Christmas' (1956 song)

Robert Millikan 1868-1953
American physicist

I conceive the essential task of religion to be 'to develop the consciences, the ideals, and the aspirations of mankind.'

Lord Milner 1854-1925
British colonial administrator

If we believe a thing to be bad, and if we have a right to prevent it, it is our duty to try to prevent it and to damn the consequences.
　speech in Glasgow, 26 November 1909

John Milton 1608-74
English poet

Let not England forget her precedence of teaching nations how to live
　The Doctrine and Discipline of Divorce (1643) 'To the Parliament of England'

Ludwig von Mises 1881-1973
Austrian economist, philosopher and author

It is always the individual who thinks. Society does not think any more than it eats or drinks.
　Human Action (1966)

What makes many men feel unhappy under capitalism is the fact that capitalism grants to each the opportunity to attain the most desirable positions which, of course, can only be attained by a few.
　The Anti-Capitalist Mentality (1956)

Daydreams of a 'fair' world which would treat him according to his 'real worth' are the refuge of all those plagued by a lack of self-knowledge.
　The Anti-Capitalist Mentality (1956)

Austin Mitchell 1934-
British Labour politician

Welcome to Britain's New Political Order. No passion . . . No Right. No Left. Just multi-hued blancmange.
　in *Observer* 11 April 1999 'Sayings of the Week'

George Mitchell 1933-
American politician, chairman of the Northern Ireland peace talks 1996-99

Although he is regularly asked to do so, God does not take sides in American politics.
　comment during the hearing of the Senate Select Committee on the Iran-Contra affair, July 1987

John Mitchell 1913-88
Lawyer, US Attorney-General to the Nixon administration

Katie **Graham**'s gonna get her tit caught in a big fat wringer if that's published.
on hearing that Katherine Graham's Washington Post *was to reveal the connection between Watergate and the campaign funding for the Committee to Re-Elect the President*
　in 1973; Katherine Graham *Personal History* (1997)

Margaret Mitchell 1900-49
American novelist

I wish I could care what you do or where you go but I can't . . . My dear, I don't give a damn.
　Gone with the Wind (1936), lines spoken by Rhett Butler

Warren Mitchell 1926-
British actor

You don't retire in this business. You just notice the phone hasn't rung for ten years.
   in *Guardian* 30 December 2000

Nancy Mitford 1904-73
English writer

Abroad is unutterably bloody and foreigners are fiends.
   The Pursuit of Love (1945)

François Mitterrand 1916-96
French socialist statesman; President of France 1981-95

She has the eyes of Caligula, but the mouth of Marilyn **Monroe**.
   *of Margaret **Thatcher**, briefing his new European Minister Roland Dumas*
   in *Observer* 25 November 1990

Wilson Mizner 1876-1933
American playwright

Treat a whore like a lady and a lady like a whore.
   quoted in Bob Chieger *Was It Good For You Too?* (1983)

Molière, stage name of Jean-Baptiste Poquelin (1622-73)
French playwright and actor

Everyone has a right to his own course of action.

Bob Monkhouse 1928-2003
English comedy writer, comedian, actor, British television presenter and game show host

People always say, 'You're a comedian. Tell us a joke.' They don't say, 'You're a politician, tell us a lie.'

Marilyn Monroe 1926-1962
America actress, singer and model

Ever noticed that 'what the hell' is always the right decision?

Lady Mary Wortley Montagu 1689-1762
English aristocrat and writer

I have never had any great esteem for the generality of the fair sex, and my only consolation for being of that gender has been the assurance it gave me of never being married to anyone amongst them.
   letter to Mrs **Calthorpe** of 7 December 1723

I give myself, sometimes, admirable advice, but I am incapable of taking it.

Michel de Montaigne 1533-92
Statesman and author

We cannot do without it (marriage) and yet we disgrace and vilify the same. It may be compared to a cage, the birds without despair to get in, and those within despair to get out.
Essays (1595)

To set a mark we can seldom hit is not an honest game. We take good care not to be righteous according to the laws of God, and we make it impossible to be righteous according to our own. From the same sheet of paper on which a judge writes his sentence against an adulterer, he tears off a piece to scribble a love note to his colleague's wife.

I will follow the right side even to the fire, but excluding the fire if I can.

No man is exempt from saying silly things; the mischief is to say them deliberately.

Ambition is not a vice of little people.

Charles de Montesquieu 1689-1755
French social commentator and political thinker

The principle of democracy is corrupted not only when the spirit of equality is lost but also when the spirit of extreme equality is taken up and each one wants to be the equal of those chosen to command.
The Spirit of the Laws (1748)

It has been eternally observed that any man who has power is led to abuse it.
The Spirit of the Laws (1748)

In the state of nature . . . all men are born equal, but they cannot continue in this equality. Society makes them lose it, and they recover it only by the protection of the law.

Robert Montgomery 1904-1981
American actor and director

If you achieve success, you will get applause, and if you get applause, you will hear it. My advice to you concerning applause is this; enjoy it but never quite believe it.

Monty Python and the Holy Grail 1975 film

I fart in your general direction! Your mother was a hamster and your father smelt of elderberries.
French sentry to King Arthur

Monty Python's Flying Circus British BBC television comedy series 1969-1974

Your report here says you are an extremely dull person. You see, our experts describe you as an appallingly dull fellow, unimaginative, timid, lacking in initiative, spineless, easily dominated, no sense of humour, tedious company and irrepressibly drab and awful. And whereas in most professions these would be considered drawbacks, in chartered accountancy they are a positive boon.
Monty Python's Flying Circus

It's not pining, it's passed on. This parrot is no more. It's ceased to be. It's expired. It's gone to meet its maker. This is a late parrot. It's a stiff. Bereft of life it rests in peace. It would be pushing up the daisies if you hadn't nailed it to the perch. It's rung down the curtain and joined the choir invisible. It's an ex-parrot.
   man registering a complaint with a pet-shop owner
   lines from BBC TV *Monty Python's Flying Circus*, 7 December 1969, 'The Parrot Sketch'

George Moore 1873-1958
English philosopher

A man travels the world over in search of what he needs and returns home to find it.

Jo Moore 1963-
British government adviser

It is now a very good day to get out anything we want to bury.
   email sent in the aftermath of the terrorist action in America, 11 September 2001
   in *Daily Telegraph* 10 October 2001

Sir Roger Moore 1927-
British actor and film producer, secret agent James Bond 1973-85

My acting range? Left eyebrow raised, right eyebrow raised.

Ed Moran

California, noun: From the Latin '*calor*', meaning 'heat' (as in English 'calorie' or in Spanish '*caliente*'); and 'fornia', for 'sexual intercourse' or 'fornication'. Hence: Terra de California, 'the land of hot sex.'

Eric Morecambe 1926-1984 and Ernie Wise 1925-1999
English comedians

[Eric of his wife] I'm not saying she's fat but we've been married for six years, and I still haven't seen all of her.
   The Morecambe and Wise Jokebook (1979)

ERNIE: But I thought you said she had a million-dollar figure?
ERIC: She has, but it's all in loose change.

Ted Morgan
French-American writer, biographer, journalist and historian

Howard **Hughes** was able to afford the luxury of madness, like a man who not only thinks he is **Napoléon** but hires an army to prove it.

Christopher Morley 1890-1957
American journalist, novelist, essayist and poet

Maybe this world is another planet's hell.

John Morley 1838-1923
British Liberal politician

Having the singular peculiarity of being neither business nor rest.
of parliamentary life
Recollection (1917)

Robert Morley 1908-92
English actor

The British tourist is always happy abroad as long as the natives are waiters.
in *Observer* 20 April 1958

I asked my accountant if anything could get me out of the financial mess I'm in now. He thought for a long time and then said, Yes, death would help.'

Morrissey 1959-
English singer and songwriter

I was looking for a job,
and then I found a job,
and heaven knows I'm miserable now.
'Heaven Knows I'm Miserable Now' (1984 song, The Smiths)

Girlfriend in a coma,
I know, I know,
it's really serious.
'Girlfriend in a Coma' (1987 song, The Smiths)

Sir John Mortimer 1923-2009
English barrister, dramatist, screenwriter, author and *bon viveur*, a self-declared 'champagne socialist'

Our homosexuality was dictated by necessity rather than choice. We were like a generation of diners condemned to cold cuts because the steak and kidney was 'off'.
of his schoolboy 'homosexuality'
Clinging to the Wreckage (1982)

The worst fault of the working classes is telling their children they're not going to succeed, saying: 'There is life, but it's not for you.'
in *Daily Mail* 31 May 1988

I suppose true sexual equality will come when a general called Anthea is found having an unwise lunch with a young, unreliable model from Spain.
The Spectator, 26 March 1994

I refuse to spend my life worrying about what I eat. There is no pleasure worth foregoing just for an extra three years in the geriatric ward.

J. B. Morton 1893-1979
English humorous writer

Erratum. In my article on the Price of Milk, 'Horses' should have read 'Cows' throughout.
The Best of Beachcomber (1963)

Every decent man carries a pencil behind his ear to write down the price of fish.

Oswald Mosley 1896-1980
British politician, founder of the British Union of Fascists

I am not, and never have been, a man of the right. My position was on the left, and is now in the centre of politics.
  letter to *The Times* 26 April 1968

The Mrs Merton Show British television spoof talk show 1994-8

Mrs Merton (Caroline Aherne)
So, Debbie **McGee**, what first attracted you to millionaire Paul **Daniels**?

Robert Mugabe 1924-
African statesman; Prime Minister of Zimbabwe 1980-8, President 1987-

Blair, keep your England and let me keep my Zimbabwe.
  at the Earth Summit on Johannesburg, 2 September 2002

Cricket civilises people and creates good gentlemen. I want everyone to play cricket in Zimbabwe; I want ours to be a nation of gentlemen.
  in *Sunday Times* 26 February 1984

Our present state of mind is that you are now our enemies.
  to white farmers in Zimbabwe, against the background of Mugabe's land reforms
  television broadcast, 18 April 2000

Malcolm Muggeridge 1903-90
British journalist, author, satirist, media personality, soldier, spy

There is no indication that he was in any way troubled by the Apostle Paul's strictures on homosexual practices.
  review in *The Observer* of *Ruling Passions* by Tom Driberg (1977)

He is not only a bore, but he bores for England.
*on Anthony **Eden***

Harold **Macmillan** seemed in his very person to embody the national decay he supposed himself to be confuting. He exuded an aroma of mothballs.

Frank Muir 1920-98
English comedy writer, radio and television personality, raconteur

It has been said that a bride's attitude towards her betrothed can be summed up in three words: Aisle, Altar, Hymn.
  Upon My Word!

The thinking man's crumpet.
*of TV presenter Joan **Bakewell***

Martin Mull 1943-
American actor, comedian, satirist, painter and recording artist

It's hard to decide if TV makes morons out of everyone or if it mirrors Americans who are morons to begin with.

Adam Müller 1779-1829
German publicist, literary critic and political economist

No trace will remain of the political castles in the air which our century has erected.
   On the Necessity of a Theological Basis for All Political Science and Political Economy in Particular (1819)

Haruki Murakami 1949-
Japanese writer and translator

Is it possible, finally, for one human being to achieve perfect understanding of another? We can invest enormous time and energy in serious efforts to know another person, but in the end, how close are we able to come to that person's essence? We convince ourselves that we know the other person well, but do we really know anything important about anyone?
   The Wind Up Bird Chronicle (1999)

Iris Murdoch 1919-99
English author and philosopher

Dora Greenfield left her husband because she was afraid of him. She decided six months later to return to him for the same reason.
   The Bell (1958)

Well, what's wrong, for political purposes, with . . . a relaxed individual, a person of habit and tradition, with a reasonably decent sense of order, but without any lofty moral aspirations? After all, if one appeals to a general notion of human nature, must one not agree that we are on the whole *not* framed to be particularly good?
   Metaphysics as a Guide to Morals (1992)

The cry of equality pulls everyone down.

Christy Murphy

I understand life isn't fair, but why couldn't it just once be unfair in my favour?

Maureen Murphy 1952-2008
American Republican politician

The reason there are so few female politicians is that it is too much trouble to put makeup on two faces.

Edward R. Murrow 1908-65
American broadcast journalist

He mobilized the English language and sent it into battle to steady his fellow countrymen and hearten those Europeans upon whom the long dark night of tyranny had descended.
*of Winston **Churchill***
   broadcast, 30 November 1954; *In Search of Light* (1967)

No one can terrorize a whole nation, unless we are all his accomplices.
*of Joseph **McCarthy***
  'See It Now' broadcast, 9 March 1954

Anyone who isn't confused doesn't really understand the situation.
on the Vietnam War
  Water Bryan *The Improbable Irish* (1969)

When the politicians complain that TV turns the proceedings into a circus, it should be made clear that the circus was already there, and that TV has merely demonstrated that not all the performers are well trained.

Benito Mussolini 1883-45
Italian politician, leader of the National Fascist Party

If every age has its own characteristic doctrine, there are a thousand signs which point to Fascism as the characteristic doctrine of our time.
  The Political and Social Doctrine of Fascism (1935)

Mike Myers 1963-
Canadian actor, comedian, screenwriter and film producer

My theory is that all of Scottish cuisine is based on a dare.

Canada is the essence of not being. Not English, not American, it is the mathematic of not being. And a subtle flavour – we're more like celery as a flavour.

Garth, marriage is punishment for shoplifting, in some countries.
  comedy sketch (1989)

n

Ralph Nader 1934-
American attorney, author, lecturer, political activist, four-time candidate for President of the United States

The only place where democracy comes before work is in the dictionary.
speech to the National Association for the Advancement of Colored People, 2000

Sarojini Naidu 1879-1949
Indian politician

If only Bapu [Gandhi] knew the cost of setting him up in poverty!
    A. Campbell-Johnson *Mission with Mountbatten* (1951)

Ogden Nash 1902-71
American poet

He tells you when you've got on too much lipstick,
And helps you with your girdle when your hips stick.
    'The Perfect Husband' (1949)

I test my bath before I sit,
And I'm always moved to wonderment
That what chills the finger not a bit
Is so frigid on the fundament
    'Samson Agnoistes' (1942)

I believe a little incompatibility is the spice of life, particularly if he has income and she is pattable.
    'I Do, I Will, I Have' (1949)

Any kiddie in school can love like a fool,
But hating, my boy, is an art.
    'Pleas for Less Malice Toward None' (1931)

Candy
Is dandy
But Liquor
Is quicker
    Hard Lines (1931)

A bit of talcum
Is always walcum
    'The Baby' (1931)

Let us pause to consider the English,
Who when they pause to consider themselves they get all reticently thrilled and tinglish,
Because every Englishman is convinced of one thing, viz.:

That to be an Englishman is to belong to the most exclusive club there is.
 'England Expects'

Progress might have been all right once, but it went on too long.

To keep your marriage brimming,
With love in the loving cup,
Whenever you're wrong, admit it;
Whenever you're right, shut up.

George Jean Nathan 1882-1958
American drama critic and editor

Politics is the pursuit of trivial men who, when they succeed at it, become important in the eyes of more trivial men.

I only drink to make other people seem more interesting.

Jawaharlal Nehru 1889-1964
Indian statesman, first Prime Minister of India (1944-64)

The policy of being too cautious is the greatest risk of all.

Vice-Admiral Horatio Nelson 1758-1805
British naval officer

Desperate affairs require desperate remedies.

Howard Nemerov 1920-91
American poet and novelist, poet laureate 1988-91

Praise without end the go-ahead zeal of
of whoever it was invented the wheel;
but never a word for the poor soul's sake
that thought ahead, and invented the brake.
 'To the Congress of the United States, Entering its Third Century' 26 February 1989

Johann von Neumann 1903-57
Austro-Hungarian-born American mathematician and scientist

The Ten Commandments contain 297 words, the Bill of Rights 463 words, and Lincoln's Gettysburg Address 266 words. A recent federal directive regulating the price of cabbage contains 26,911 words.
 New York Times

It would appear that we have reached the limits of what it is possible to achieve with computer technology, although one should be careful with such statements, as they tend to sound pretty silly in 5 years.

Alfred E. Newman
Fictional mascot and cover boy of *Mad* magazine

Crime does not pay . . . as well as politics.

Paul Newman 1925-2008
American actor, film director, entrepreneur, humanitarian and auto racing enthusiast

The embarrassing thing is that the salad dressing is out-grossing my films.

Randy Newman 1943-
American singer-songwriter, arranger, composer and pianist

That's a hell of an ambition, to be mellow. It's like wanting to be senile.
on middle of the road music

Jack Nicklaus 1940-
American golfer

Achievement is largely the product of steadily raising one's levels of aspiration and expectation.
My Story (1997)

Harold Nicolson 1886-1968
British Labour Party politician, diplomat, author, diarist and politician

Like a village fiddler after Paganini.
comparing Clement **Attlee** as a public speaker with Sir Winston **Churchill**

Friedrich Nietzsche 1844-1900
German philosopher and philologist

For men are not equal: thus speaks justice.
Thus Spake Zarathustra (1883-1885)

The individual has always had to struggle to keep from being overwhelmed by the tribe. If you try it, you will be lonely often, and sometimes frightened. But no price is too high to pay for the privilege of owning yourself.
The Gay Science (1882)

God is dead.
Nietzsche (1844-1900)

Nietzsche is dead.
God (0-)
Graffito seen by the editor on the external wall of a church in England in the 1960s

David Niven 1909-83
English actor

The great thing about **Errol** was – you always knew precisely where you stood with him because he *always* let you down. He let himself down too, from time to time, but that was his prerogative.
on Errol Flynn
Bring on the Empty Horses (1975)

Richard Milhous Nixon 1913-94
American Republican statesman, 37th President of the US

When the President does it, that means that it is not illegal.

in conversation: David Frost *I Gave Them a Sword* (1978)

My own view is that taping of conversations for historical purposes was a bad decision.
attributed, 1974

Grover Norquist 1956-
American lobbyist, founder of Americans for Tax Reform

I don't want to abolish government. I simply want to reduce it to the size where I can drag it into the bathroom and drown it in the bathtub.
interview on National Public Radio, Morning Edition, 25 May 2001

Steven Norris 1945-
British Conservative politician

You have your own company, your own temperature control, your own music – and don't have to put up with dreadful human beings sitting alongside you.
on cars compared to public transport
comment to Commons Environment Select Committee, in *Daily Telegraph* 9 February 1995

Whenever I want a good read I get one of Jeffrey Archer's novels and stand on it so I can reach the good books.

Not Only . . . But Also British television series 1965-70

Have you seen that bloody Leonard da Vinci cartoon? I couldn't see the bloody joke . . . The sense of humour must have changed over the years. I bet when that da Vinci cartoon first came out, I bet people were killing themselves. I bet old da Vinci had an accident when he done it . . . Apart from that, Pete, it's a different culture. It's Italian y'see, we don't understand it. For instance, *The Mousetrap* did terribly in Pakistan.

Denis Norden 1922-
English humorist

If all the world's a stage, and all the men and women merely players, where do all the audiences come from?

Ted Nugent 1948-
American guitarist and vocalist, noted for his vocal conservative political views

God gave us the gift of life. It is the most precious gift ever. To be unarmed is to be helpless to protect that gift; that is outright irresponsible.

Diana Nyad 1949-
American long-distance swimmer

There is . . . nothing greater than touching the shore after crossing some great body of water knowing that I've done it with my own two arms and legs.

O

Michael Oakeshott 1901-1990
English philosopher

The pursuit of perfection as the crow flies is an activity both impious and unavoidable in human life. It involved the penalties of impiety (the anger of the gods and social isolation), and its reward is not that of achievement but that of having made the attempt.
   'The Tower of Babel' (1948)

To be conservative, then, is to prefer the familiar to the unknown, to prefer the tried to the untried, fact to mystery, the actual to the possible, the limited to the unbounded, the near to the distant, the sufficient to the superabundant, the convenient to the perfect, present laughter to utopian bliss.
   'On Being Conservative' (1956)

Barack Obama 1961-
American President 2008-

If there is anyone out there who still doubts that America is a place where all things are possible, who still wonders if the dream of our founders is alive in this time, who still questions the power of our democracy, tonight is your answer.
   election night speech in Chicago

Conan O'Brien 1963-
American television host, comedian, comedy writer

Yesterday American and British troops handed out food to hundreds of Iraqis. Not surprisingly, the Iraqis handed the British food back.

At Microsoft a minority employee is one who has a girlfriend.

Edna O'Brien 1932-
Irish novelist and short story writer

The vote, I think, means nothing to women. We should be armed.

John O'Farrell 1962-
British author, broadcaster and comedy scriptwriter

If men were shouted down for being sexist when they used the word 'postman', then asking if there was any chance of a quick shag seemed like a bit of a non-starter.
   Things Can Only Get Better (1998)

The Office British comedy series 2001-2

David Brent (Ricky Gervais) and **Dawn Tilsley** (Lucy David)

David Brent:	This is Dawn, our receptionist. I'd say that at one time or another every man in the office has woken up at the crack of dawn (sniggers)
Dawn Tinsley:	What!?
David: (sheepishly)	Can I have the mail please?

How can I hate women? My mother's one.

This is the accounts department, the number bods. Don't be fooled by their job descriptions, they are absolutely mad, all of 'em. Especially that one, he's mental. Not literally of course, that wouldn't work.

There may be no 'I' in team but there's a 'me' if you look hard enough.

David Ogilvy 1911-1999
British-born advertising executive

The consumer isn't a moron; she is your wife.
Confessions of an Advertising Man (1963)

Marvin Olasky 1950-
American journalist

We do not increase compassion by expanding it to cover anything. Instead, we kill a good word by making it mean too much, and nothing.
The Tragedy of American Compassion (1993)

Vic Oliver 1898-1964
English actor and radio comedian

If a man is after money, he's money mad; if he keeps it, he's a capitalist; if he spends it, he's a playboy; if he doesn't get it, he's a ne'er-do-well; if he doesn't try to get it, he lacks ambition. If he gets it without working for it; he's a parasite; and if he accumulates it after a life time of hard work, people call him a fool who never got anything out of life.

Sir Lawrence Olivier 1907-1989
English actor

Dear boy, why not try *acting*?
to Dustin Hoffman during the filming of *Marathon Man* (1976). Hoffman had stayed up for three nights in order to portray a sleepless character

1. Never hunt south of the Thames.
2. Never drink port after champagne.
3. Never have your wife in the morning lest something better should turn up during the day.
Confessions of an Actor (1982)

Lord Onslow

I oppose the plan to reform the House of Lords. I will be sad if I look down after my death and don't see my son asleep on the same benches on which I slept.

James Oppenheim 1882-1932
American poet, novelist, editor and lay psychoanalyst

The foolish man seeks happiness in the distance, the wise grows it under his feet.

Robert Orben 1927-
American magician and comedy writer

Illegal aliens have always been a problem in the United States. Ask any Indian.

Shaquille O'Neal 1972-
American professional basketball player, rapper, actor, reserve police officer and US Deputy Marshal

I'm tired of hearing about money, money, money. I just want to play the game, drink Pepsi, wear Reebok.

P. J. O'Rourke 1947-
American political satirist, journalist and writer

Always read something that will make you look good if you die in the middle of it.

That doesn't mean that you should just sit back and let accidents happen to you. No, you have to go out and cause them yourself. That way, you're in control of the situation.

There are a number of mechanical devices which increase sexual arousal, especially in women. Chief among these is the Mercedes-Benz 380SL convertible.

Giving money and power to government is like giving whisky and car keys to teenage boys.

Politics are a lousy way for a free man to get things done. Politics are, like God's infinite mercy, a last resort.

Feeling good about government is like looking on the bright side of any catastrophe. When you quit looking on the bright side, the catastrophe is still there.

Every government is a parliament of whores. The trouble is, in a democracy, the whores are us.
Parliament of Whores (1991)

Politicians are wonderful people as long as they stay away from things they don't understand, such as working for a living.

The mystery of government is not how Washington works but how to make it stop.

No drug, nor alcohol, causes the fundamental ills of society. If we're looking for the sources of our troubles, we shouldn't test people for drugs; we should test them for stupidity, ignorance, greed and (especially) love of power.

How much fame, money, and power does a woman have to achieve on her own before you can punch her in the face?

Joe Orton 1933-1967
English playwright

You were born with your legs apart. They'll send you to your grave in a 'Y'-shaped coffin.
  What The Butler Saw (1969)

George Orwell 1903-1950
English novelist, journalist, literary critic, poet

Political language – and with variations this is true of all political parties, from Conservatives to Anarchists – is designed to make lies sound truthful and murder respectable, and to give an appearance of solidity to pure wind.

Roast beef and Yorkshire, or roast pork and apple sauce, followed by suet pudding and driven home, as it were, by a cup of mahogany-brown tea, have put you in just the right mood . . . In these blissful circumstances, what is it that you want to read about? Naturally, about a murder.
  Decline of the English Murder and other essays (1965) title essay, written 1946

All animals are equal but some animals are more equal than others.
  Animal Farm (1945)

It was a bright cold day in April, and the clocks were striking thirteen.
  First sentence of *Nineteen Eighty-Four* (1949)

If you want a picture of the future, imagine a boot stamping on a human face – forever.

War is peace. Freedom is slavery. Ignorance is strength.

Don't you see that the whole aim of Newspeak is to narrow the range of thought? In the end we shall make thought crime literally impossible, because there will be no words in which to express it.
  Nineteen Eighty-Four (1949)

If liberty means anything at all, it means the right to tell people what they do not want to hear.

In a Lancashire cotton-town you could probably go for months on end without once hearing an 'educated' accent, whereas there can hardly be a town in the South of England where you could throw a brick without hitting the niece of a bishop.
  The Road to Wigan Pier (1937)

Advertising is the rattling of a stick inside a swill bucket.
  quoted in Laurence J. Peter, *Quotations for our Time* (1977)

We of the sinking middle class ... may sink without further struggles into the working class where we belong, and probably when we get there it will not be so dreadful as we feared, for, after all, we have nothing to lose but our aitches.
  The Road to Wigan Pier (1937)

As with the Christian religion, the worst advertisement for Socialism is its adherents.
  The Road to Wigan Pier (1937)

A typical Socialist is . . . a prim little man with a white-collar job, usually a secret teetotaller and not often with vegetarian leanings, with a history of Nonconformity behind him, and, above all, with a social position which he has no intention of forfeiting.
The Road to Wigan Pier (1937)

The Catholic and the Communist are alike in assuming that an opponent cannot be both honest and intelligent.
in *Polemic* January 1946 'The Prevention of Literature'

In our time, political speech and writing are largely the defence of the indefensible.
Shooting an Elephant (1950)

The creatures outside looked from pig to man, and from man to pig, and from pig to man again, but already it was impossible to say which was which.
Animal Farm (1945)

England is not the jewelled isle of Shakespeare's much-quoted passage, nor is it the inferno depicted by Dr Goebbels. More than either it resembles a family, a rather stuffy Victorian family, with not many black sheep in it but with all its cupboards bursting with skeletons . . . A family with the wrong members in control.
The Lion and the Unicorn (1941) 'England Your England.

George Osborne 1971-
British Conservative politician

There are now enough tax inspectors in Britain to fill every seat in the Olympic Stadium in Berlin where the World Cup Final was held – and you'd still have 30,000 waiting outside for tickets.

Sound money is the oldest Conservative principle of all.
speech to Conservative Party Conference, 3 October 2006

John Osborne 1929-94
English dramatist

There aren't any good, brave causes left. If the big bang does come, and we all get killed off, it won't be in aid of the old-fashioned, grand design. It'll be just for the Brave New-nothing-very-much-thank-you. About as pointless and inglorious as stepping in front of a bus.
Look Back in Anger (1956)

Charles Osgood 1933-

Being politically correct means always having to say you're sorry.

Sir William Osler 1849-1919
Canadian physician

Live neither in the past nor in the future, but let each day's work absorb your entire energies, and satisfy your widest ambition.

John L O'Sullivan 1813-95
American journalist and diplomat

Understood as a central consolidated power, managing and directing the various interests of society, all government is evil, and the parent of evil . . . The best government is that which governs least.
United States Magazine and Democratic Review (1837)

A torchlight procession marching down your throat.
Collections and Recollections G. W. E. Russell (1898)

James Otis 1725-1783
American lawyer

Taxation without representation is tyranny.

Dr. David Owen (Lord Owen) 1938-
British Social Democrat politician

We are fed up with fudging and mudging, with mush and slush. We need courage, conviction, and hard work.
speech to his supporters at Labour Party Conference in Blackpool, 2 October 1980

Robert Owen 1771-1858
Welsh-born socialist and philanthropist

All the world is queer save thee and me, and even thou art a little queer.
to his partner W. Allen, on severing business relations at New Lanark, 1828 (attributed)

Count Oxenstierna 1583-1654
Swedish statesman

Dost thou not know, my son, with how little wisdom the world is governed?
letter to his son, 1648; *Table Talk* (1689)

P

Walter Page 1855-1918
American journalist, publisher and diplomat

The air currents of the world never ventilated his mind.
on Woodrow Wilson

The English have three vegetables and two of them are cabbage.

Thomas Paine 1737-1809
English political theorist

It is necessary to the happiness of man that he be mentally faithful to himself. Infidelity does not consist in believing, or in disbelieving, it consists in professing to believe what one does not believe.
The Age of Reason (1794)

Government, even in its best state, is but a necessary evil; in its worst state, an intolerable one. Government, like dress, is the badge of lost innocence; the palaces of kings are built upon the ruins of the bowers of paradise.
Common Sense (1776)

What we obtain too cheaply, we esteem too lightly.
The Crisis (1776)

I do not believe that any two men, on what are called doctrinal points, think alike who think at all. It is only those who have not thought that appear to agree.
The Rights of Man pt. 2 (1792)

Sarah Palin 1964-
American Republican politician

President Obama has been in office for a year. I'd like to ask him, 'So, Mr President, how's the hopey, changey stuff been working out?'
speech February 2010

Gwyneth Paltrow 1972-
American actress

I love men, even though they're lying, cheating scumbags.

Dorothy Parker 1893 – 1967
American writer

Three highballs, and I think I'm St Francis of Assisi.
Just a Little One (1929)

Guns aren't lawful;

Nooses give;
Gas smells awful;
You might as well live.
   Résumé (1937)

Oh, life is a glorious cycle of song,
A medley of extemporanea;
And love is a thing that can never go wrong –
And I am Marie of Roumania
   Not So Deep as a Well (1937)

By the time you say you're his,
Shivering and sighing,
And he vows his passion is
Infinite, undying –
Lady, make a note of this:
One of you is lying.
   Unfortunate Coincidence (1937)

Woman lives but in her lord;
Count to ten, and man is bored.
With this the gist and sum of it,
What earthly good can come of it?
   General Review of the Sex Situation (1937)

I hate women. They get on my nerves.
   quoted in *Women's Wicked Wit* ed. Michelle Lovric (2000)

Tell him I've been too fucking busy, or vice versa.
*on hearing that Harold **Ross** editor of* The New Yorker *had called while she was on honeymoon, demanding late copy*

How can they tell?
when told Coolidge had died

Pearls before swine.
*in response to Clare **Booth** Luce's use of the customary phrase 'Age before beauty' when going through a swing-door together*

Because he spills his seed on the ground.
on why she named her canary 'Onan'

C. Northcote Parkinson 1909-93
English writer

The following quotations are from *Parkinson's Law* (1958):

A committee is organic rather than mechanical in its nature: it is not a structure but a plant. It takes root and grows. It flowers, wilts, and dies, scattering the seed from which other committees will bloom in their turn.

Expenditure rises to meet income.

Work expands so as to fill the time available for its completion.

Men enter politics solely as a result of being unhappily married.

The man who is denied the opportunity of taking decisions of importance begins to regard as important the decisions he is allowed to take.

Matthew Parris 1949-
British journalist and former Conservative politician

A big cat detained briefly in a poodle parlour, sharpening her claws on the velvet.
describing Margaret Thatcher in the House of Lords
   Look Behind You! (1993)

Being an MP feeds your vanity and starves your self-respect.
   in *The Times* 9 February 1994

Why waste it on some vanilla-flavoured pixie. Bring on the fruitcakes, we want a fruitcake for an unlosable seat. They enliven the Commons.
   the day before the Kensington and Chelsea association chose Alan Clark as their parliamentary candidate
   in *Mail on Sunday* 26 January 1997

My name is Mandy: Peter B;
I'm back in charge – don't mess with me.
My cheeks are drawn, my face is bony,
The line I take comes straight from Tony.
on Peter Mandelson's return to government
   in *Times* 21 October 1999

Since the dawn of time every politician has been torn between a wish to say something memorable and a terror of saying something which is remembered.

New Labour doesn't do candour. Mr Blair will find humility when the hippopotamus finds grace.

Geoffrey Parsons

To feel the right emotions is fully as important as to hold the right ideas, and the great service of religion is the development of the right emotions.

Blaise Pascal 1623-62
French mathematician, physicist and religious philosopher

Men never do evil so fully and cheerfully as when we do it out of conscience.
   Pensées (1670)

Man is but a reed, the most feeble thing in nature, but he is a thinking reed. The entire universe need not arm itself to crush him. A vapour, a drop of water, suffices to kill him. But if the universe were to crush him, man would still be more noble than that which killed him, because he knows that he dies and the advantage which the universe has over him; the universe knows nothing of this.
   quoted by Rebecca West *Black Lamb and Grey Falcon: A Journey Through Yugoslavia* (1941)

Boris Pasternak 1890-1960
Russian novelist and poet

I don't like people who have never fallen or stumbled. Their virtue is lifeless and it isn't of much value. Life hasn't revealed its beauty to them.
Doctor Zhivago (1958)

Man is born to live, not to prepare for life.
Doctor Zhivago (1958)

John Patrick 1905-95
American playwright and screenwriter

Pain makes man think. Thought makes man wise. Wisdom makes life endurable.

Chris Patten 1944-
British Conservative politician

A kind of walking obituary for the Labour Party.
*on Michael **Foot***

Attacking the Liberals is a difficult business, involving all the hazards of wrestling with a greased pig at a village fair, and then insulting the vicar.
attributed, 1996

Pat Paulsen 1927-97
American comedian and satirist

Assuming either the Left Wing or the Right Wing gained control of the country, it would probably fly around in circles.

Jeremy Paxman 1950-
British journalist and broadcaster

Did you threaten to overrule him?
*question asked 14 times of Michael **Howard**, referring to the sacking of a prison governor by Derek **Lewis**, Director of the Prison Service*
   interview, *Newsnight* 13 May 1997

No government in history has been as obsessed with public relations as this one ... Speaking for myself, if there is a message I want to be off it.
*after criticism from Alastair **Campbell** of interviewing tactics in* The World at One *and* Newsnight
   Daily Telegraph 3 July 1998

Labour's attack dog.
*description of the Labour politician John **Reid**, to which Reid took great exception*
   on *Newsnight* programme, 8 March 2005

Down here we live under a sort of Scottish Raj . . . I don't see why there is need for them to feel chippy.
on the influence of Scottish MPs at Westminster
   in *Scotsman* 14 March 2005

Logan Pearsall Smith 1865-1946
American essayist and critic

There are two things to aim at in life: first, to get what you want; and, after that, to enjoy it. Only the wisest of mankind achieve the second.
Afterthoughts (1931)

What music is more enchanting than the voices of young people, when you can't hear what they say?
Afterthoughts (1931) 'Age and Death'

People say that life is the thing, but I prefer reading.
Afterthoughts (1931) 'Myself'

Robert Peel 1788-1850
British Conservative statesman; Prime Minister 1834-5, 1841-6

No man attached to his country could always acquiesce in the opinions of the majority.
in the House of Commons, 1831

I am not sure that those who clamour most, suffer most.
in the House of Commons, 1834

Of all vulgar arts of government, that of solving every difficulty which might arise by thrusting the hand into the public purse is the most delusory and contemptible.
in the House of Commons, 1834

There are those who seem to have nothing else to do but to suggest modes of taxation to men in office.
in the House of Commons, 1842

Claiborne Pell 1918-2009
American Democratic Party senator

The strength of the United States is not the gold at Fort Knox or the weapons of mass destruction that we have, but the sum total of the education and the character of our people.

Claude D. Pepper 1900-89
American Democratic Party politician

The mistake a lot of politicians make is forgetting they've been appointed and thinking they've been anointed.

Samuel Pepys 1633-1703
English civil servant and diarist

To the Theatre, where I saw again *The Lost Lady*, which doth now please me better than before. And here, I sitting behind in a dark place, a lady spat backward on me by mistake, not seeing me. But after seeing her to be a very pretty lady, I was not troubled at it at all.
Diary entry for 28 January 1661

I went out to Charing Cross, to see Major-General **Harrison** hanged, drawn and quartered: which was done there, he looking as cheerful as any man could do in that condition.

Diary entry for 13 October 1660. Thomas Harrison signed the death warrant of King Charles I in 1649. Pepys had also seen the King beheaded in 1660

And strange to see what delight we married people have to see those poor fools decoyed into our condition.
Diary entry for 25 December 1665. Pepys had been watching a Christmas Day wedding

Shimon Peres 1923-
Polish-born Israeli statesman; Prime Minister 1984-6 and 1995-6

Television has made dictatorship impossible, but a democracy unbearable.
at a Davos meeting, in *Financial Times* 31 January 1995

Marko Peric

I used to think that all the king's horses and all the king's men to fix one guy was a bit excessive. Then I realised they must have had a really strong union.

H. Ross Perot 1930-
American businessman

Equal opportunity means everyone will have a fair chance at being incompetent.

Democracy is a process by which the people are free to choose the man who will get the blame.

If you see a snake, just kill it. Don't appoint a committee on snakes.

Laurence J. Peter 1919-90
Canadian/American educationalist, author

In a hierarchy every employee tends to rise to his level of incompetence . . . In time every post tends to be occupied by an employee who is incompetent to carry out its duties . . . Work is accomplished by those employees who have not yet reached their level of incompetence.
The Peter Principle (1968)

Mike Peters 1943-
American cartoonist

When I go into the voting booth, do I vote for the person who will be the best President? Or the slime bucket who will make my life as a cartoonist wonderful?
Wall Street Journal 20 January 1993

Lord Peyton 1919-
British Conservative politician

The great thing about Alec Home is that he was not media driven. He would have had some difficulty in spelling the word 'image.'
of Lord Home
in conversation, 1997; Peter Hennessey *The Prime Minister: the Office and its Holders since 1945* (2000)

Arthur Phelps 1881-1944
Austro-Hungarian-born Romanian and German army officer

Conscience has nothing to do as lawgiver or judge; but is a witness against me if I do wrong, and which approves if I do right. To act against conscience is to act against reason and God's Law.

Prince Philip 1921-
British Prince, husband of Elizabeth II

If you stay here much longer you'll all be slitty-eyed.
> remark to Edinburgh University students in Peking, 16 October 1986

Just at this moment we are suffering a national defeat comparable to any lost military campaign, and what is more it is self-inflicted. . . Gentlemen, I think it is about time we pulled our fingers out . . . If we want to be more prosperous we've simply got to get down to it and work for it. The rest of the world does not owe us a living.
> speech in London to businessmen, 17 October 1961

Tolerance is the one essential ingredient . . . You can take it from me that The Queen has the recipe for tolerance in abundance.
his recipe for a successful marriage, during celebrations for their golden wedding anniversary
> in *Times* 20 November 1997

Emo Philips 1956-
American comedian

Grandmother's brain was dead, but her heart was still beating. It was the first time we ever had a Democrat in the family.

Women: you can't live with them, and you can't get them to dress up in a skimpy Nazi uniform and beat you with a warm squash.

I discovered my wife in bed with another man, and I was crushed. So I said, 'Get off me, you two!'

John Pienaar 1956-
British journalist

She is a loose cannon with a sense of direction.
of Clare Short
> in *Observer* 29 February 2004

Albert Pike 1809-91
American attorney, soldier, writer and Freemason

He who endeavors to serve, to benefit, and improve the world, is like a swimmer, who struggles against a rapid current, in a river lashed into angry waves by the winds. Often they roar over his head, often they beat him back and baffle him. Most men yield to the stress of the current . . . Only here and there do the stout strong heart and vigorous arms struggle on toward ultimate success.

Sir Arthur Wing Pinero 1855-1934
English playwright

Pinero always said that the only way to get anything across to an English audience was first to say, 'I'm going to hit this man on the head', then 'I'm hitting this man on the head', and finally, 'I *have* hit this man on the head.

Harold Pinter 1930-2008
English dramatist, actor and director

Apart from the known and the unknown, what else is there?
   The Homecoming (1965)

William Pitt 1759-1806
British Tory statesman; Prime Minister, 1783-1801, 1804-6

Lord **North** will, I hope, in a very little time make room for me in Downing Street, which is the best summer Town House possible.
as newly appointed Chancellor of the Exchequer, 16 July 1782

Pius XII 1876-1958
Italian cleric; Pope from 1939

One Galileo in two thousand years is enough.
on being asking to proscribe the works of Teilhard de Chardin
   attributed; Stafford Beer *Platform for Change* (1975)

Plato 427-347BC
Greek philosopher, mathematician, writer of philosophical dialogues

Those who are able to see beyond the shadows and lies of their culture will never be understood, let alone believed, by the masses.

One of the penalties for refusing to participate in politics is that you end up being governed by your inferiors.

The price good men pay for indifference to public affairs is to be ruled by evil men.

We are twice armed if we fight with faith.

Plutarch 46-120AD
Greek historian, biographer, essayist, later a Roman citizen

When the candles are out all women are fair.
   Morals

Written laws are like spider's webs; they will catch, it is true, the weak and the poor, but would be torn into pieces by the rich and powerful.
   Parallel Lives

The real destroyer of the liberties of the people is he who spreads among them bounties, donations and benefits.

Edgar Allan Poe 1809-49
American writer, poet, editor and literary critic

Those who dream by day are cognizant of many things which escape those who dream only by night.
  Eleanora (1842)

Roman Polanski 1933-
French-born and resident Polish film director, producer, writer and actor

Sometimes I'm charmed by the fact that there are women with whom you can discuss the theory of light all evening, and at the end they will ask you what is your birth sign.

Channing Pollock 1880-1946
American writer and critic

A critic is a legless man who teaches running.
  The Green Book

Jack Pomeroy

A communist is a person who publicly airs his dirty **Lenin**.

Georges Pompidou 1911-74
French politician, Prime Minister 1962-68, President of France 1969-74

A statesman is a politician who places himself at the service of the nation. A politician is a statesman who places the nation at his service.

Alexander Pope 1688-1744
English poet

Blessed is the man who expects nothing, for he shall never be disappointed.
  in a joint letter to William **Fortescue**, 23 September 1725

Sir Karl Popper 1902-94
Austrian and British philosopher

We may become the makers of our fate when we have ceased to pose as its prophets.
  The Open Society and its Enemies (1945) Introduction

Marxism is only an episode - one of the many mistakes we have made in the perennial and dangerous struggle for building a better and a freer world.
  The Open Society and its Enemies (rev. ed. 1952)

We should therefore claim, in the name of tolerance, the right not to tolerate the intolerant.
  The Open Society and its Enemies (1945)

Philosophers should consider the fact that the greatest happiness principle can easily be made an excuse for a benevolent dictatorship. We should replace it by a more modest and more realistic principle - the principle that the fight against avoidable misery should be a recognized aim of public policy, while the increase of happiness should be left, in the main, to private initiative.

Michael Portillo 1953-
British Conservative politician and broadcaster

Gordon **Brown** has the charisma of a coffin lid.

Dennis Potter 1935-94
English television dramatist

Religion to me has always been the wound, not the bandage.
   interview with Melvyn **Bragg** on Channel 4, March 1994

Stephen Potter 1900-69
British writer and radio producer

'Yes, but not in the South,' with slight adjustments, will do for any argument about any place, if not about any person.
   Lifemanship (1950)

How to be one up – how to make the other man feel that something has gone wrong, however slightly.
   Lifemanship (1950)

Ezra Pound 1885-1972
American expatriate poet, critic and intellectual

Properly, we should read for power. Man reading should be man intensely alive. The book should be a ball of light in one's hand.

Jerry Pournelle 1933-
American science fiction writer, essayist and journalist

You won't learn much about capitalism at a university. How could you? Capitalism is a matter of risks and rewards, and a tenured professor doesn't have much to do with either.

Anthony Powell 1905-2000
English novelist

Parents – especially step-parents – are sometimes a bit of a disappointment to their children. They don't fulfil the promise of their early years.
   A Buyer's Market (1952)

He's so wet you could shoot snipe off him.
   A Question of Upbringing (1951)

She was the sort of woman who, if she had been taken in adultery, would have caught the first stone and thrown it back.
   A Writer's Notebook (2001)

'Dinner at the Huntercombes' possessed only two dramatic features – the wine was a farce and the food a tragedy.'
   The Acceptance World (1955)

Growing old is like being increasingly penalised for a crime you haven't committed.
   Temporary Kings (1973)

Enoch Powell 1912-98
English Conservative then Ulster Unionist politician

Those whom the gods wish to destroy, they first make mad. We must be mad, literally mad, as a nation to be permitting the annual inflow of some 50,000 dependents, who are for the most part the material of the future growth of the immigrant descended population. It is like watching a nation busily engaged in heaping up its own funeral pyre.
  speech at Annual Meeting of West Midlands Area Conservative Political Centre, Birmingham, 20 April 1968

ANNE BROWN: How would you like to be remembered?
ENOCH POWELL: I should like to have been killed in the war.
  in a radio interview, 13 April 1986

To pretend that you cannot exchange goods and services freely with a Frenchman or an Italian, unless there is an identical standard of bathing beaches or tap water in the different countries is not logic. It is naked aggression.
  in *Guardian* 22 May 1990

To write a diary every day is like returning to one's own vomit.

The amateur in politics is the person who's always sure he knows the result of the next General Election.

History is littered with wars which everybody knew would never happen.

All political lives, unless they are cut off in midstream at a happy juncture, end in failure.

Politicians who complain about the media are like ships' captains who complain about the sea.

Above any other position of eminence, that of prime minister is filled by fluke.

There is a mania in legislation in detecting discrimination. But all life is about discrimination.
  attributed 1975

Lift the curtain and 'the State' reveals itself as a little group of fallible men in Whitehall, making guesses about the future, influenced by political prejudices and partisan prejudices, and working on projections drawn from the past by a staff of economists.
  attributed

Sir William Preece 1834-1913
Chief engineer of the British Post Office

The Americans have need of the telephone, but we do not. We have plenty of messenger boys.

John Prescott 1938-
British Labour Party politician, Deputy Prime Minister of the United Kingdom (1997-2007), accomplished croquet player

Here we have a government disintegrating between our eyes.
*on the Conservative administration under John **Major**'s government*

I mean that's an example of this Government that believes in the private sector and is in fact damaged the public sector's handling within the public sector in a number of these areas and you can go on with them in another areas.
> in the House of Commons, 18 May 1992

Hansard's translation into English:
The Government's insistence on private sector terms has damaged the public sector.

So I think the basic point that it is necessary in order to have private capital in our industries to get the extra resources that we do want that you have to be privatised is not borne out by the facts, in other countries, and neither we should have it here also and if he's any doubts about that go and have a look at the reports that talk about it.
> in the House of Commons, 18 May 1992
> Matthew Parris reports that Hansard gave up, and did not even attempt to report the last passage

We did it! Let's wallow in our victory!
> a speech to the Labour Party Conference, 29 September 1997, following Tony Blair's warning that the Labour Party should not be triumphalist in victory

During the election I met this chap who said, 'You've got to help me, John. I've never had sex under a Labour government.' If you're listening, mate, I hope the first hundred days were good for you!
> 3 October 1997

I'm not going to defend any fucking hypocrites.
> on Harriet *Harman* in June 1998, after he was asked to defend her decision to send her child to a selective school, then against Labour policy

It was a bit windy, and the wife doesn't like getting her hair blown about.
> on taking a ministerial limousine for the 100-yard trip to the conference centre where he was to make a speech on the need to use cars less, 29 September 1999

JOHN PRESCOTT:	Bear in mind that it's something like 70 to 80 per cent of the actual demand are single-parent households or single youngsters or people who are living in a single house – can we do that again? People who are living in a single house – can we do that again? I made that crap.
NICK ROBINSON:	We are actually live at the moment.
7 March 2000	

The Prime Minister has made clear, when he was asked about this, that in fact a decision about the Europe and the consultations would be in the early part of the parliament, he's now defined it in that it could be in that two-year period when we will use the criteria established by the Chancellor for which governments will assess whether that's been achieved. I don't think anything has changed in that sense.
> clarifying the Euro, 9 February 2001

Macho man, *moi?*
> *After an accusation of overbearingly masculine behaviour by the female French environment minister, November 2001*

[Editor's note: In his biography of John Prescott, Colin Brown records that while making a short TV film at King's Cross station, a man reeled past waving a can of cider, and the following exchange took place.]

MAN:	That's a nice silk tie you have on, comrade!
PRESCOTT:	If you don't get out of this shot, I'll stick one on your chin.

All that glitters isn't Gould.
*on Labour Party pollster Philip **Gould***

It's great to be back on the terra cotta.
on landing at an airport after a bumpy ride

It's true, they made a savage attack in words, and language.
*on Stephen **Byers**, the transport secretary who resigned after being attacked by a select committee, 30 May 2002*

There's that bloody idiot . . .
*on seeing Simon **Hoggart**, the English journalist and broadcaster, author of a book of quotations by Prescott, behind the stage at the 2002 Labour conference in Blackpool*

You're a terrible man for asking the questions and not giving an answer.
   to Edward Stourton, 31 October 2002

I mean IDS – cor blimey, he's the man – what did he say? – 'unite or die'? – I think it's more likely to be 'Die Another Day' the way he's going.
*on Iain Duncan **Smith**, 31 December 2002*

I don't say it, I mumble it. It's one of my little compromises.
on the oath of allegiance to the Queen

I have changed. I no longer keep coal in the bath, I keep it in the bidet.

I'm meant to be the bloke who walks around looking like he's about to club a baby seal.

I saw in the paper today, how many Transport ministers, Barbara **Castle**, they said, was popular, when Barbara Castle brought in seat belts and drink driving, she was very unpopular.

That was by alternative governments, so don't make that particular point, but we are now actually taking proper, putting the amount of resources and investment to move what we call extreme conditions which must now regard as normal.

The green belt is a Labour policy, and we intend to build on it.

For the first time in 50 years, bus passenger numbers have risen to their highest level ever.

My position is that I want to make our position clear . . . the example in Germany is just one example, for example.

The global alliance I'm calling for is as much for peace as well as war, and these two things need to be done if we're to sort out this problem.

That's precisely true now and more so this four more years on.

[Editor's note: in October 2002, the Fire Brigades Union announced a series of strikes. John Prescott, Deputy Prime Minister, was put in charge of the negotiations. The crisis lasted until the summer of 2003.]

It was hey-diddle-diddle, the man in the middle, it was 25,000 instead of 30,000, and we can see how they probably arrived at that.
asked whether firefighters had been offered a rise of 16 per cent

There are 400 engines, some without an engine, some without wheels, I mean, I don't know what you mean by that.
in response to the question, 'Why don't ministers make sure the military can use the 400 fire engines which are available but are standing idle?'

In regard to the 4 per cent wage increase, that of course was for the first year, which was generally offered by the employers and indeed was referred to by the Bain inquiry. The 11 per cent, the 1.3, later the 7.3, to which you refer, added to the 4 per cent . . . the overall part of the pay bill is the 7.4 per cent!
in response to the question, 'Exactly how much had the firefighters been offered?'

I've already mentioned quite frankly there may be a 100, previously, then it was down to one yesterday, now it's no, not. And I think we should welcome that as a fact.
in response to the question, 'Will the Government use the law to stop London tube drivers taking secondary action?'

Some children need a kick up the backside. Others need a carrot.
   reflection on how best to motivate children to study harder at school
   attributed

JOHN HUMPHREYS: Does it worry you that a lot of expectations haven't been met?
JOHN PRESCOTT: Well, it does if it was a lot. I mean our judgment of, often it's reflected in targets and there's a lot of attention to whether the target's actually achieved. Sometimes it only fails by 2 per cent and that's considered to be a failure . . . was critical of targets when they first came in because I think if you fail to achieve by them by 1 or 2 per cent the media will interpret that as failure. That's what I was saying years ago, and unfortunately it's still the case . . . targets are a way of how you can improve delivery when the electorate were not believing governments who were making promises and then aren't delivered.
BBC radio interview

Elvis Presley 1935-77
American actor and musician

Ambition is a dream with a V8 engine.

Bill Price
Quality Director of Revlon UK in the 1990s, when the editor worked there

I've never heard such a load of *merde de torot* in all my life!
*disagreeing on a point made by his French colleague Véronique **Robert** during a large meeting of senior executives, 1992*

Richard Price 1723-91
English nonconformist minister

Now, methinks, I see the ardour for liberty catching and spreading; a general amendment beginning in human affairs; the dominion of kings changed for the dominion of laws, and the dominion of priests giving way to the dominion of reason and conscience.
   A Discourse on the Love of our Country (1790)

J. B. Priestley 1894-1984
English novelist, playwright, literary and social critic, broadcaster

Like its politicians and its wars, society has the teenagers it deserves.

God can stand being told by Professor Ayer and Marghanita Laski that he doesn't exist.

Romano Prodi 1939-
Italian statesman, President of the European Commission 1999-2004

I know very well that the stability pact is stupid, like all decisions that are rigid.
on the rules underpinning the single currency
   interview in *Le Monde* (electronic edition) 17 October 2002

The pillars of the nation states are the sword and the currency, and we changed that. The euro-decision changed the concept of the nation state.
   in *Daily Telegraph* 7 April 1999

The Producers 1968 film

Max Bialystock (Zero Mostel)

Bloom, do me a favour. Move a few decimal points around. You can do it. You're an accountant. You're in a noble profession. The word 'count' is part of your title.

Greg Proops 1959-
American stand-up comedian, actor, voice actor and producer

If this election had gone down in another country we'd be invading them right now to install a democracy.
referring to George W. Bush's 2000 election victory

Richard Pryor 1940-2005
American stand-up comedian, actor and writer

Marriage is really tough because you have to deal with feelings and lawyers.

Joseph Pulitzer 1847-1911
Hungarian-born American newspaper proprietor and editor

A cynical, mercenary, demagogic, corrupt press will produce in time a people as base as itself.
inscribed on the gateway to the Columbia School of Journalism in New York
   W. J. Granberg *The World of Joseph Pulitzer* (1965)

Philip Pullman 1946-
English writer

I thought physics could be done to the glory of God, till I saw there wasn't any God at all and that physics was more interesting anyway.
   Amber Spyglass (2000), Mary Malone speaking

q

Dan Quayle 1947-
American Republican Party politician

A mind is a terrible thing to waste . . . You take the UNCF model that what a waste it is to lose one's mind or not to have a mind is being very wasteful. How true that is.
addressing the United Negro College Fund

I believe we are on an irreversible trend towards more freedom and democracy. But that could change.

Republicans understand the importance of bondage between a mother and child.

We're going to have the best-educated American people in the world.

The holocaust was an obscene period in our nation's history . . . No, not our nation's, but in World War II. I mean, we all lived in this century. I didn't live in this century, but in this century's history.

I have made good judgments in the past. I have made good judgments in the future.

It isn't pollution that's harming the environment. It's the impurities in our air and water that are doing it.

Quintilian 35-100
Roman rhetorician from Hispania

Though ambition itself be a vice, yet it is often times the cause of virtues.

r

The Belzer Rabbi

Let a good man do good deeds with the same zeal that the evil man does bad ones.

François Rabelais (c. 1494-1553)
French writer, doctor and Renaissance humanist

I owe much; I have nothing; the rest I leave to the poor.

Few and signally blessed are those whom Jupiter has destined to be cabbage-planters. For they've always one foot on the ground and the other not far from it. Anyone is welcome to argue about felicity and supreme happiness. But the man who plants cabbages I now positively declare to be the happiest of mortals.
Gargantua and Pantagruel (1548)

Lord Radcliffe 1899-1977
British lawyer and public servant

Society has become used to the standing armies of power – the permanent Civil Service, the police force, the tax-gatherer – organised on a scale which was unknown to earlier centuries.
Power and the State (BBC Reith Lectures, 1951)

Walter Raleigh 1861-1922
English lecturer and critic

I wish I loved the Human Race;
I wish I loved its silly face;
I wish I liked the way it walks;
I wish I liked the way it talks;
And when I'm introduced to one
I wish I thought *What Jolly Fun!*
'Wishes of an Elderly Man' (1923)

Ayn Rand 1905-82
Russian-American novelist, philosopher, playwright and screenwriter

Morality is judgement to distinguish right and wrong, vision to see the truth, courage to act upon it, dedication to that which is good, and integrity to stand by it at any price.
The Fountainhead (1943)

My philosophy, in essence, is the concept of man as a heroic being, with his own happiness as the moral purpose of his life, with productive achievement as his noblest activity, and reason as his only absolute.

If you choose to help a man who suffers, do it only on the ground of his virtues, of his fight to recover, of his rational record, or of the fact that he suffers unjustly; then your action is still a trade, and his virtue is the payment for your help. But to help a man who has no virtues, to help him on the ground of his suffering as such, to accept his faults, his *need*, as a claim - is to accept the mortgage of a zero on your values.
Atlas Shrugged (1957)

The worse guilt is to accept an undeserved guilt.
Atlas Shrugged (1957)

The right to life is the source of all rights - and the right to property is their only implementation. Without property rights, no other rights are possible. Since man has to sustain his life by his own effort, the man who has no right to the product of his effort has no means to sustain his life. The man who produces while others dispose of his product, is a slave.
Capitalism: The Unknown Ideal (1966)

It is not the free market, but government patronage that corrupts.
The Ayn Rand Letter, 1 January 1973

The right to vote is a consequence, not a primary cause, of a free social system. And its value depends on the constitutional structure implementing and strictly delimiting the voters' power; unlimited majority rule is an instance of the principle of tyranny.

Happiness is that state of consciousness which proceeds from the achievement of one's values.

We are fast approaching the stage of the ultimate inversion: the stage where the government is free to do anything it pleases, while citizens may act only by permission which is the stage of the darkest periods of human history, the stage of rule by brute force.

In the case of some liberals' clamor for public TV, nothing more may be involved than some hack's desire to see his epic produced at public expense.

John Randolph 1773-1833
Congressman from Virginia, serving in the House of Representatives, Minister to Russia 1830

The principle of liberty and equality, if coupled with mere selfishness, will make men only devils, each trying to be independent that he may fight only for his own interest. And here is the need of religion and its power, to bring in the principle of benevolence and love to men.

Never were abilities so much below mediocrity so well rewarded; no, not when Caligula's horse was made Consul.
*on John Quincy **Adams**'s appointment of Richard **Rush** as Secretary of the Treasury*
speech, 1 February 1828

He is a man of splendid abilities but utterly corrupt. He shines and stinks like rotten mackerel by moonlight.
*of Edward **Livingston***
W. Cabell Bruce *John Randolph of Roanoke* (1923)

That most delicious of all privileges - spending other people's money.
W. Cabell Bruce *John Randolph of Roanoke* (1923)

Herbert Rappaport 1908-
Austro-Hungarian-born screenwriter, music editor and director

I hope that while so many people are out smelling the flowers, someone is taking the time to plant some.

William Raspberry 1935-

You cannot claim both full equality and special dispensation.
Washington Post 20 September 1989

Rawhide American Western television series 1959-66

Head 'em up, move 'em out, rope 'em in, head 'em off, pull 'em down, move 'em on.
theme song, lyrics by Ned Washington, music by Dimitri Tiomkin

F. J. Raymond

Next to being shot at and missed, nothing is really quite as satisfying as an income tax refund.

Nancy Reagan 1921-
widow of former United States President Ronald Reagan

I didn't intend for this to take on a political tone. I'm here for the drugs.
on being asked a political question at a 'Just Say No' rally

Ronald Reagan 1911-89
Actor, American Democratic Party then Republican Party politician, 40th President of the United States 1981-89

It isn't so much that Liberals are ignorant. It's just that they know so much that isn't so.
televised speech, eve of the 1964 election

Today there is an increasing number who can't see a fat man standing beside a thin one without automatically coming to the conclusion that the fat man got that way by taking advantage of the thin one.
televised speech, eve of the 1964 election

Government is like a big baby – an alimentary canal with a big appetite at one end and no responsibility at the other.
campaigning for the governorship of California, 1965
attributed

We're the party that wants to see an America in which people can still get rich.
at a Republican congressional dinner, 4 May 1982

I will not make age an issue of this campaign. I am not going to exploit for political purposes my opponent's youth and inexperience.
TV debate, 22 October 1984

My fellow Americans, I am pleased to tell you I just signed legislation which outlaws Russia forever. The bombing begins in five minutes.
radio microphone test, 1984

We are especially not going to tolerate these attacks from outlaw states run by the strangest collection of misfits, Looney Tunes, and squalid criminals since the advent of the Third Reich.
　　speech following the hijack of an American plane, 8 July 1985

The taxpayer – that's someone who works for the federal government but doesn't have to take a Civil Service examination.
　　attributed, 1985

I now begin the journey that will lead me into the sunset of my life. I know that for America there will always be a bright dawn ahead.
statement to the American people revealing that he had Alzheimer's disease
　in *Daily Telegraph* 5 January 1995

What makes him think a middle-aged actor, who's played with a chimp, could have a future in politics?
*on Clint **Eastwood**'s bid to be elected Mayor of Carmel*

Politics is supposed to be the second oldest profession. I have come to realise that it bears a very close resemblance to the first.

The nine most terrifying words in the English language are, 'I'm from the government and I'm here to help.'

How do you tell a communist? Well, it's someone who reads Marx and Lenin. And how do you tell an anti-Communist? It's someone who *understands* Marx and Lenin.

The government's view of the economy could be summed up in a few short phrases. If it moves, tax it. If it keeps moving, regulate it. And if it stops moving, subsidize it.

Freedom is never more than one generation away from extinction. We didn't pass it on to our children in the bloodstream. It must be fought for, protected, and handed on for them to do the same, or one day we will spend our sunset years telling our children and our children's children what it was once like in the United States where men were free.

Entrepreneurs and their small enterprises are responsible for almost all the economic growth in the United States.

I never drink coffee at lunch. I find it keeps me awake for the afternoon.

Nigel Rees 1944 -
English writer and broadcaster

To be a bore is to have halitosis of the mind, as someone should probably have said before me.
　Best Behaviour

Christopher Reeve 1952-2004
American actor, film director, producer, screenwriter, Superman.

So many of our dreams at first seem impossible, then they seem improbable, and then, when we summon the will, they soon become inevitable.
　speech at the Democratic National Convention, August 1996

Max Reger 1873-1916
German composer

I am sitting in the smallest room of my house. I have your review before me. In a moment it will be behind me.
in a letter to the music critic Rudolph **Louis,** 1906

John Reid 1947-
British Labour politician

What enjoyment does a single mother of three living in a council estate get? The only enjoyment sometimes is a cigarette.
in *Sunday Times* 13 June 2004

If you have a PhD and a posh accent from a school like yours, you are regarded as a sophisticate . . . You called me an attack dog because I've got a Glasgow accent.
to Jeremy **Paxman**
Newsnight, 8 March 2005

Our system is not fit for purpose.
on the Home Office Immigration and Nationality Directorate (IND)
speaking to the Commons Home Affairs Committee, 23 May 2006, in *Times* (online edition) 23 May 2006

George Reisman 1937-
American economist

Capitalism is a social system based on private ownership of the means of production. It is characterized by the pursuit of material self-interest under freedom and it rests on a foundation of the cultural influence of reason.
A Treatise on Economics (1996)

Jean-François Paul de Gondi, Cardinal de Retz 1613-79
French cardinal

Fear is, of all passions, that which weakens the judgment most.
Mémoires (1717)

Walter Reuther 1907-70
American labour leader

If it looks like a duck, walks like a duck and quacks like a duck, then it just may be a duck.
usually ascribed to Reuther during the McCarthyite witch-hunts of the 1950s. He came up with it as a test of whether someone was a Communist.

Burt Reynolds 1936-
American film actor

I haven't had a hit film since Joan **Collins** was a virgin.
in *The Observer* 27 March 1988 'Sayings of the Week'

Cecil Rhodes 1853-1902
South African statesman

Being an Englishman is the greatest prize in the lottery of life.
  A. W. Jarvis *Jottings from an Active Life* (1928)

John Rhys c.1890-1979
British novelist and short-story writer

The perpetual hunger to be beautiful and that thirst to be loved which is the real curse of Eve.
  The Left Bank (1927)

We can't all be happy, we can't all be rich, we can't all be lucky – and it would be so much less fun if we were . . . Some must cry so that others may be able to laugh the more heartily.
  Good Morning, Midnight (1939)

Grantland Rice 1880-1954
American sports journalist

For when the One Great Scorer comes to make against your name,
He writes – not that you won or lost – but how you played the Game.
  'Alumnus Football'

Adrienne Rich 1929-
American poet

We assume that politicians are without honor. We read their statements trying to crack the code. The scandals of their politics: not so much that men in high places lie, only that they do so with such indifference, so endlessly, still expecting to be believed. We are accustomed to the contempt inherent in the political lie.
  On Lies, Secrets, and Silence (1980)

Jean Paul Richter 1763-1825
German writer

A timid person is frightened before a danger, a coward during the time, and a courageous person afterward.

In later life, as in earlier, only a few persons influence the formation of our character; the multitude pass us by like a distant army. One friend, one teacher, one beloved, one club, one dining table, one work table are the means by which one's nation and the spirit of one's nation affect the character.

Hyman G. Rickover 1900-86
American four-star admiral, inventor of the nuclear submarine

Trying to make things work in government is sometimes like trying to sew a button onto a custard pie.

Adam Ridley 1942-
British economist, former Director of the Conservative Research Department

Parties come to power with silly, inconsistent and impossible policies because they have spent their whole period in opposition forgetting about the real world, destroying the lessons they learnt in government and clambering slowly back on to the ideological plain where they feel happiest.
in *RIPA Report* Winter 1985

Nicholas Ridley 1929-93
British Conservative politician

This is all a German racket designed to take over the whole of Europe
of the European monetary union
in an interview with Dominic Lawson, in the aftermath of which Ridley resigned from the Government
Spectator 14 July 1990

Seventeen unelected reject politicians with no accountability to anybody, who are not responsible for raising taxes, just spending money, who are pandered to by a supine parliament which also is not responsible for raising taxes.
of the European Commission
Spectator 14 July 1990

David Riesman 1909-2002
American sociologist, attorney and educator

The idea that men are created free and equal is both true and misleading: men are created different; they lose their social freedom and their individual autonomy in seeking to become like each other.

César Ritz 1850-1918
Swiss hotel proprietor, founder of the Paris Ritz (1890) and other Ritz hotels

The customer is never wrong.
R. Nevill and C. E. Jerningham *Piccadilly to Pall Mall* (1908)

Joan Rivers 1937-
American entertainer

Boy George is all England needs – another queen who can't dress.

Tom Robbins 1936-
American author

Humanity has advanced, when it has advanced, not because it has been sober, responsible, and cautious, but because it has been playful, rebellious, and immature.

Véronique Robert 1965-
French friend of the editor

We all have our bears to cross.
1987

Ugh, there are semen stains all over the carpets in the living room, the dining room, up the stairs and in all the bedrooms. Semen. Semen. There's even some on the walls! Can't you see it? Why are you all looking at me that way? What's that? It's pronounced 'cement'? So what's semen?
 to an open-mouthed group of friends, whilst showing them around her new flat, 1992

Andrew Roberts 1963-
English historian

Had the Conservative elite of the immediate post-war period shown half the energy and enterprise in peacetime as it has in war, it is hard to believe that Britain would have been reduced to her present stature of Italy with rockets.
 Eminent Churchillians (1994) Introduction

Frank Roberts 1907-98
British diplomat

Eden . . . was rather like an Arab horse. He used to get terribly het up and excited and he had to be sort of kept down.
 What has Become of Us? television series, 29 March 1994

He just didn't understand Hitler or his ruthlessness. We in the Foreign Office kept telling him it was all in *Mein Kampf*, but he wouldn't believe it.
 on Neville **Chamberlain**
  in *Daily Telegraph* 10 January 1998; obituary

Frederick William Robertson 1816-1853
English divine

The true aim of everyone who aspires to be a teacher should be, not to impart his own opinions, but to kindle minds.

Maximilien Robespierre 1758-94
One of the most influential figures of the French Revolution

What is the end of our revolution? The tranquil enjoyment of liberty and equality; the reign of that eternal justice, the laws of which are graven, not on marble or stone, but in the hearts of men, even in the heart of the slave who has forgotten them, and in that of the tyrant who disowns them.

Edward G. Robinson 1893-1973
Romanian-born American actor

The sitting around on set is awful, but I always figure that's what they pay me for. The acting I do for free.

Narenda Rocherolle

Aspiring to a small business that does what it does very well is a noble pursuit.
 Cashing In or Selling Out, SXSW (2006)

David Rockefeller 1915-
American banker, statesman, globalist, and the current patriarch of the Rockefeller family

Success in business requires training and discipline and hard work. But if you're not frightened by these things, the opportunities are just as great today as they ever were.

Sue Rodriguez 1951-94
Canadian activist for the legalisation of assisted suicide

If I cannot give consent to my own death, then whose body is this? Who owns my life?
appealing to a subcommittee of the Canadian Commons, November 1992, as the victim of a terminal illness
 in *Globe and Mail* 5 December 1992

Scott Roeben

Sex is like art. Most of it is pretty bad, and the good stuff is out of your price range.

Roy Rogers 1911-98
American singer and cowboy actor

There are two theories about arguing with women. Neither one works.

Will Rogers 1879-1935
American cowboy, comedian, humorist, social commentator, vaudeville performer and actor

Communism is like prohibition. It's a good idea but it won't work.
 Weekly Articles (1881)

I don't know jokes – I just watch the government and report the facts.
 Weekly Articles (1981)

The more you read and observe about this politics thing, you got to admit that each party is worse than the other. The one that's out always looks the best.
 Illiterate Digest (1924)

Half our life is spent trying to find something to do with the time we have rushed through life trying to save.
 letter in *New York Times* 29 April 1930

I see a good deal of talk from Washington about lowering taxes. I hope they do get 'em lowered enough so people can afford to pay 'em.'

Income tax has made more liars out of the American people than golf.

On account of being a democracy and run by the people, we are the only nation in the world that has to keep a government for four years, no matter what it does.

Advertising is the art of convincing people to spend money they don't have on something they don't need.

America is a nation that conceives many odd inventions for getting somewhere but can think of nothing to do when it gets there.

I am not a member of any organized political party. I'm a Democrat.

Jean Rook 1931-91
English journalist

Listen to him, and it's like sitting on wet seaweed on Land's End at the end of February.
*on Francis **Wilson**, TV weatherman*

Eleanor Roosevelt 1884-1962
First Lady of the United States 1933-45

Do what you feel in your heart to be right – for you'll be criticized anyway. You'll be damned if you do, and damned if you don't.

It is not fair to ask of others what you are unwilling to do yourself.

Where, after all, do universal human rights begin? In small places, close to home – so close and so small that they cannot be seen on any map of the world. Yet they are the world of the individual person: The neighbourhood he lives in; the school or college he attends; the factory, farm or office where he works. Such are the places where every man, woman and child seeks equal justice, equal opportunity, equal dignity without discrimination. Unless these rights have meaning there, they have little meaning anywhere. Without concerted citizen action to uphold them close to home, we shall look in vain for progress in the larger world.

Franklin D. Roosevelt 1882-1945
32nd President of the United States

These unhappy times call for the building of plans that . . . build from the bottom up and not from the top down, that put their faith once more in the forgotten man at the bottom of the economic pyramid.
   radio address, 7 April 1932

The only thing we have to fear is fear itself.
   inaugural address, 4 March 1933

The only sure bulwark of continuing liberty is a government strong enough to protect the interests of people, and a people strong enough and well enough informed to maintain its sovereign control over its government.
   'Fireside Chat' radio broadcast, 14 April 1938

The American people are quite competent to judge a political party that works both sides of the street.
   campaign speech in Boston, 4 November 1944

If you treat people right they will treat you right . . . 90% of the time.

In the truest sense, freedom cannot be bestowed; it must be achieved.

Theodore Roosevelt 1858-1919
Naturalist, explorer, hunter, author, soldier, Democratic Party then Republican Party politician, 26th President of the United States 1901-1909

It is not the critic who counts; not the man who points out how the strong man stumbles, or where the doer of deeds could have done them better. The credit belongs to the man who is actually in the arena, whose face is marred by dust and sweat and blood, who strives valiantly; who errs and comes short again and again; because there is not effort without error and shortcomings; but who does actually strive to do the deed; who knows the great enthusiasm, the great devotion, who spends himself in a worthy cause, who at the best knows in the end the triumph of high achievement and who at the worst, if he fails, at least he fails while daring greatly. So that his place shall never be with those cold and timid souls who know neither victory nor defeat.
'Man in the Arena' speech, 23 April 1910

I wish to preach, not the doctrine of ignoble ease, but the doctrine of the strenuous life.
speech to the Hamilton Club, Chicago, 10 April 1899

The first requisite of a good citizen in this Republic of ours is that he shall be able and willing to pull his weight.
speech in New York, 11 November 1902

Far and away the best prize that life offers is the chance to work hard at work worth doing.
address at the State Fair, Syracuse, New York Labour Day, 7 September 1903

Speak softly and carry a big stick; you will go far.
quoting an 'old adage'
speech in Chicago, 3 April 1903

To announce that there must be no criticism of the president, right or wrong, is not only unpatriotic and servile, but is morally treasonable to the American public.
on John Tyler

If I must choose between righteousness and peace, I choose righteousness.

While my interest in natural history has added very little to my sum of achievement, it has added immeasurably to my sum of enjoyment in life.

Justice consists not in being neutral between right and wrong, but in finding out the right and upholding it, wherever found, against the wrong.

When I say I believe in a square deal I do not mean . . . to give every man the best hand. If the cards do not come to any man, or if they do come, and he has not got the power to play them, that is his affair. All I mean is that there shall be no crookedness in the dealing.

5th Earl of Rosebery (Archibald Philip Primrose) 1847-1929
British Liberal Prime Minister

I am leaving tonight; Hannah and the rest of the heavy baggage will follow later.

Dick Ross
British economist, former Deputy Director of the Central Policy Review Staff

You must think the unthinkable, but always wear a dark suit when presenting the results.

in the early 1970s; Peter Hennessey *Whitehall* (1990)

Clinton Rossiter 1917-1970
American historian and political scientist

Government, in the conservative view, is something like fire. Under control, it is the most useful of servants; out of control, it is a ravaging tyrant.
Conservatism in America, 2nd ed. (1962)

Man's nature is essentially immutable, and the immutable strain is one of deep-seated wickedness.
Conservatism in America, 2nd ed. (1962)

Leo Rosten 1908-97
American writer

The only thing I can say about W. C. Fields, whom I have admired since the day he advanced upon Baby LeRoy with an ice pick, is this: any man who hates dogs and babies can't be all bad.
of W. C. Fields

Jean-Jacques Rousseau 1712-78
Swiss philosopher, political theorist, writer, and composer

Man is born free, but everywhere he is in chains.
The Social Contract (1762)

Slaves become so debased by their chains as to lose even the desire of breaking from them.
The Social Contract (1762)

To renounce liberty is to renounce being a man, to surrender the rights of humanity and even its duties. For he who renounces everything no indemnity is possible. Such a renunciation is incompatible with man's nature; to remove all liberty from his will is to remove all morality from his acts.

Every law the people has not ratified in person is null and void – is, in fact, not a law.

As soon as any man says of the affairs of the State, 'What does it matter to me?', the State may be given up for lost.

Helen Rowland 1875-1950
American humorist

Nowadays most women grow old gracefully; most men, disgracefully.

J. K. Rowling 1965-

Remember, if the time should come when you have to make a choice between what is right and what is easy.
Harry Potter and the Goblet of Fire (2000)

Maude Royden 1876-1956
English religious writer

The Church of England should go forward along the path of progress and be no longer satisfied only to represent the Conservative Party at prayer.
  in *Times* 17 July 1917

Mike Royko 1932-97
American newspaper columnist

Anyone who is different today faces harassment, whether it is in the way he dresses, or in the position he takes on important issues. And when the price of being different is a cold fear, with good reason, then freedom as we peddle it in our international publicity releases is gone. If and when it disappears, it won't be stolen by big government, the tax collector, or the Supreme Court. Fascism will be the people's choice. It usually is. We've managed to avoid it so far only because nobody nutty enough to give the people what they want has come along. Yet.
  For the Love of Mike (2001)

Rita Rudner 1953-
American comedienne, writer and actress

I love being married. It's so great to find that one special person you want to annoy for the rest of your life.

Someday I want to be rich. Some people get so rich they lose all respect for humanity. That's how rich I want to be.

Donald Rumsfeld 1932-
American aviator, businessman and politician

It's less important to have unanimity than it is to be making the right decisions and doing the right thing, even though at the outset it may seem lonesome.

Going to war without France is like going duck hunting without your accordion.

There are known knowns. These are thing we know that we know. There are known unknowns. That is to say, there are things we know we don't know. But there are also unknown unknowns. These are things we don't know we don't know.

Osama **Bin Laden** is either alive and well, or alive and not well, or not alive.

John Ruskin 1819-1900
English art critic, social thinker, poet and artist

Of all the pulpits from which human voice is ever sent forth, there is none from which it reaches so far as from the grave.
  The Seven Lamps of Architecture (1849)

The force of the guinea you have in your pocket depends wholly on the default of a guinea in your neighbour's pocket. If he did not want it, it would be of no use to you.
  Unto this Last (1862)

Lord Bertrand Russell 1872-1970
British philosopher, logician, mathematician, historian, free trade champion, pacifist and social critic

I was told by the Chinese that they would bury me by the Western Lake and build a shrine to my memory. I have some slight regret that this did not happen as I might have become a god, which would have been very *chic* for an atheist.
   Autobiography (1968)

One should as a rule respect public opinion in so far as is necessary to avoid starvation and to keep out of prison, but anything that goes beyond this is voluntary submission to an unnecessary tyrant.
   The Conquest of Happiness (1930)

One of the symptoms of approaching nervous breakdown is the belief that one's work is terribly important, and that to take a holiday would bring all kinds of disaster.
   The Conquest of Happiness (1930)

Envy is the basis of democracy.
   The Conquest of Happiness (1930)

A sense of duty is useful in work, but offensive in personal relations. People wish to be liked, not to be endured with patient resignation.
   The Conquest of Happiness (1930)

The man who has fed the chicken every day throughout its life at last wrings its neck instead, showing that a more refined view as to the uniformity of nature would have been useful to the chicken.
   The Problems of Philosophy (1912)

Next to enjoying ourselves, the next greatest pleasure consists in preventing others from enjoying themselves, or, more generally, in the acquisition of power.
   Sceptical Essays (1928)

The opinions that are held with passion are always those for which no good ground exists; indeed the passion is the measure of the holder's lack of rational conviction.
   Sceptical Essays (1928)

The infliction of cruelty with a good conscience is a delight to moralists. That is why they invented Hell.
   Sceptical Essays (1928) 'On the Value of Scepticism'

Every man, wherever he goes, is encompassed by a cloud of comforting convictions, which move with him like flies on a summer day.
   Sceptical Essays (1928) 'Dreams and Facts'

Work is of two kinds: first, altering the position of matter at or near the earth's surface relatively to other such matter; second, telling other people to do it. The first kind is unpleasant and ill paid; the second is pleasant and highly paid.
   In Praise of Idleness and Other Essays (1986) title essay (1932)

Man is a credulous animal, and must believe something; in the absence of good grounds for belief, he will be satisfied with bad ones.
   Unpopular Essays (1950)

The fact that an opinion has been widely held is no evidence whatever that it is not utterly absurd; indeed in view of the silliness of the majority of mankind, a widespread belief is more likely to be foolish than sensible.
Marriage and Morals (1929)

If I were to suggest that between the Earth and Mars there is a china teapot revolving about the sun in an elliptical orbit, nobody would be able to disprove my assertion provided I were careful to add that the teapot is too small to be revealed even by our most powerful telescopes. But if I were to go on to say that, since my assertion cannot be disproved, it is intolerable presumption on the part of human reason to doubt it, I should rightly be thought to be talking nonsense.
'Is there a God?' commissioned (but not published) by *The Illustrated Magazine*, 1952; first published in *Collected Papers* (1997) vol. 11

Men fear thought as they fear nothing else on earth – more than ruin – more even than death . . . Thought is subversive and revolutionary, destructive and terrible, thought is merciless to privilege, established institutions, and comfortable habit. Thought looks into the pit of hell and is not afraid. Thought is great and swift and free, the light of the world, and the chief glory of man.

Many people would sooner die than think; In fact, they do so.

If a man is offered a fact which goes against his instincts, he will scrutinise it closely, and unless the evidence is overwhelming, he will refuse to believe it. If, on the other hand, he is offered something which affords a reason for acting in accordance to his instincts, he will accept it even on the slightest evidence. The origin of myths is explained in this way.

It has been said that man is a rational animal. All my life I have been searching for evidence which could support this.

The whole problem with the world is that fools and fanatics are always so certain of themselves, but wiser people so full of doubts.

All movements go too far.

There is no nonsense so arrant that it cannot be made the creed of the vast majority by adequate governmental action.

If there were in the world today any large number of people who desired their own happiness more than they desired the unhappiness of others, we could have paradise in a few years.

This is one of those views which are so absolutely absurd that only very learned men could possibly adopt them.

Our great democracies still tend to think that a stupid man is more likely to be honest than a clever man.

Passive acceptance of the teacher's wisdom is easy to most boys and girls. It involves no effort of independent thought, and seems rational because the teacher knows more than his pupils; it is moreover the way to win the favour of the teacher unless he is a very exceptional man. Yet the habit of passive acceptance is a disastrous one in later life. It causes man to seek and to accept a leader, and to accept as a leader whoever is established in that position.

Few people can be happy unless they hate some other person, nation, or creed.

Men are born ignorant, not stupid; they are made stupid by education.

It is possible that mankind is on the threshold of a golden age; but, if so, it will be necessary first to slay the dragon that guards the door. And that dragon is religion.

Admiration of the proletariat, like that of dams, power stations, and aeroplanes, is part of the ideology of the machine age.

Drunkenness is temporary suicide: the happiness that it brings is merely negative, a momentary cessation of unhappiness.

I am as drunk as a lord, but then, I am one, so what does it matter?

Whereas in art nothing worth doing can be done without genius, in science even a very moderate capacity can contribute to a supreme achievement.

It is because modern education is so seldom inspired by a great hope that it so seldom achieves great results. The wish to preserve the past rather that the hope of creating the future dominates the minds of those who control the teaching of the young.

Lord John Russell 1792-1878
British Whig statesman; Prime Minister, 1846-52, 1865-6

Among the defects of the Bill, which were numerous, one provision was conspicuous by its presence and another by its absence.
   speech to the electors of the City of London, April 1859

Lord Russell of Killowen 1832-1900
English jurist

Two mothers-in-law.
   when asked, as Lord Chief Justice, what was the maximum punishment for bigamy

S

William Safire 1929-
American author, columnist, journalist and presidential speechwriter

The right to do something does not mean that doing it is right.

Carl Sagan 1934-96
American astronomer, astrochemist and author

In science it often happens that scientists say, 'You know, that's a really good argument; my position is mistaken', and then they would actually change their minds and you never hear that old view from them again. They really do it. It doesn't happen as often as it should, because scientists are human and change is sometimes painful. But it happens every day. I cannot recall the last time something like that happened in politics or religion.
  1987 CSICOP Keynote Address

In every country, we should be teaching our children the scientific method and the reasons for a Bill of Rights. With it comes a certain decency, humility and community spirit. In the demon-haunted world that we inhabit by virtue of being human, this may be all that stands between us and the enveloping darkness.

The universe is not required to be in perfect harmony with human ambition.

All of the books in the world contain no more information than is broadcast as video in a single large American city in a single year. Not all bits have equal value.

We make our world significant by the courage of our questions and by the depth of our answers.

Mort Sahl 1927-
Canadian-born American comedian, actor and speechwriter

A conservative is someone who believes in reform. But not now.

Antoine de Saint-Exupéry 1900-44
French writer and aviator

Perfection is achieved, not when there is nothing more to add, but when there is nothing left to take away.

Augustus Homer Saint-Gaudens 1848-1907
Irish-born American sculptor

What garlic is to salad, insanity is to art.
  Reminiscences (1913)

Saki pseudonym of Hector Hugo Munro 1870-1916
British writer

I'm living so far beyond my income that we may almost be said to be living apart.
   The Unbearable Bassington (1912)

We all know that Prime Ministers are wedded to the truth, but like other married couples they sometimes live apart.
   The Unbearable Bassington (1912)

His shoes exhaled the right *soupçon* of harness-room; his socks compelled one's attention without losing one's respect.
   The Chronicles of Clovis (1911)

The young have aspirations that never come to pass, the old have reminiscences of what never happened.

J. D. Salinger 1919-
American author

If you really want to hear about it, the first thing you'll probably want to know is where I was born and what my lousy childhood was like, and how my parents were occupied and all before they had me, and all that David Copperfield kind of crap.
   The Catcher in the Rye (1951), opening words

Lord Salisbury (Robert Arthur Talbot Gascoyne-Cecil, third Marquess of Salisbury) 1830-1903
British Conservative statesman; Prime Minister 1855-6, 1886-92, 1985-1902

They believe intensely in amiable theories, they loved the sympathy and applause of their fellow men, they were kind-hearted, and charitably fancied everybody as well meaning as themselves; and therefore – so far as it can be said of any single man – they were the proximate causes of a civil convulsion which, for the horror of its calamities, stands alone in the history of the world.
of those he regarded as weak-willed liberals
   in *Saturday Review* 10 March 1860

Free institutions, carried beyond the point which the culture of the nation justifies, cease to produce freedom. There is the freedom that makes each man free; and there is the freedom, so called, which makes each man the slave of the majority.
   in *Saturday Review* 10 March 1860

We do not care to scrutinise too closely, the moral boundary which separates a reckless hustings pledge from premeditated fraud.
   in *Saturday Review* February 1861

It is the same with all efforts to root up any evil by the expenditure of money. To attach a money value to the existence of an evil, even for the purpose of extirpating it, can have no other end than that of multiplying the evil.
   in *Saturday Review* 10 January 1863

The politician who 'yields' to public opinion is simply a dishonourable man. No 'voice of the people', however distinct and powerful, can absolve a man from the guilt of professing doctrines in which he does not believe.
   in *Saturday Review* 31 October 1863

Parliament is a potent engine, and its enactments must always do something, but they very seldom do what the originators of these enactments meant. Therefore most legislation will have the effect of surrounding the industry which it touches with precautions and investigations, inspections and regulations, in which it will be slowly enveloped and stifled.
  in *Times* March 1891

First rate men will not canvas mobs: and mobs will not elect first rate men.
  Andrew Roberts *Salisbury: Victorian Titan* (1999)

I have a profound distrust of government inspectors, and I am generally disposed to finding them wrong.
  Andrew Roberts *Salisbury: Victorian Titan* (1999)

Whatever happens will be for the worse, and therefore it is in our interest that as little should happen as possible.
  said to Lord **Dufferin** about events in Persia, December 1879; Andrew Roberts *Salisbury: Victorian Titan* (1999)

The Italians have very much the huffiness which you see occasionally in the governess of a family. They are always thinking themselves slighted.
  Andrew Roberts *Salisbury: Victorian Titan* (1999)

To those who have found breakfast with difficulty and do not know where to find dinner, intricate questions of politics are a matter of comparatively secondary interest.
  Andrew Roberts *Salisbury: Victorian Titan* (1999)

It may wear the appearance of some religious movement or pretend to the authority of some great moral effect. But underneath that cloak there is concealed that steady enemy of human liberty – the desire of men, whenever they may grasp a bit of power, to force others to conform their ideas to their own.
  warning to the Primrose League about the spirit of tyranny, May 1889; Andrew Roberts *Salisbury: Victorian Titan* (1999)

The use of Conservatism was to delay changes 'til they became harmless.
  Andrew Roberts *Salisbury: Victorian Titan* (1999)

In making appointments I can count on a Scotchman not falling below a certain level, they may not be very clever, but they are safe not to be stupid. There is a strong resemblance between the Scotch and the Jews. They both begin as fighters, then become very religious and finally are devoted to money-making.
  in Lady Rayleigh diary, 1900: Andrew Roberts *Salisbury: Victorian Titan* (1999)

The Admiralty would always follow the progress of science at a respectable distance, always arriving at an appreciation of each successive intervention just soon enough to find that it is obsolete, and never yielding their adhesion to anything new until the time has come to defend it against the claims of something newer.
  Andrew Roberts *Salisbury: Victorian Titan* (1999)

To loot somebody or something is the common object, under a thick varnish of pious phrases.
  rediscovering his fear of socialism
  Andrew Roberts *Salisbury: Victorian Titan* (1999)

A very useful institution. It fosters a wholesome taste for bright colours, and gives old men who have good legs an excuse for showing them.
  of the Order of the Garter, which had been awarded to both his father and grandfather as well as the early Cecils

Andrew Roberts *Salisbury: Victorian Titan* (1999)

When a man says that he agrees with me in principle, I am quite certain that he does not agree with me in practice.
Andrew Roberts *Salisbury: Victorian Titan* (1999)

When great men get drunk with a theory, it is the little men who have the headache.
on political theorists
Andrew Roberts *Salisbury: Victorian Titan* (1999)

Whitehall will create business for itself surely as a new railway will create traffic.
Andrew Roberts *Salisbury: Victorian Titan* (1999)

By office boys for office boys.
of the Daily Mail
H. Hamilton Fyfe *Northcliffe, an Intimate Biography* (1930)

I wish party government was at the bottom of the sea. It is only insincerity codified.
Arthur Hardinge *Life of Henry Herbert, 4th Earl of Carnarvon* (1925)

A party whose mission is to live entirely upon the discovering of grievances are apt to manufacture the element upon which they subsist.
speech at Edinburgh, 24 November 1882

Sobriety is a very good thing and philanthropy is a very good thing, but freedom is better than either.
speech at Kingston-upon-Thames, 15 June 1883

By a free country, I mean a country where people are allowed, so long as they do not hurt their neighbours, to do as they like. I do not mean a country where six men may make five men do exactly as they like.
speech to the Kingston and District Working Men's Conservative Association, June 1883

The duty was to represent the permanent as opposed to the passing feeling of the English nation.
on the House of Lords
speech to Hackney Conservative Club, November 1880

People imagine that where an evil exists, The Queen, the Lords and the Commons should stop it. I wonder they have not brought in an Act of Parliament to stop unfavourable weather on the occasion of political demonstrations.
speech at Newport, 7 October 1885

English policy is to float lazily downstream, occasionally putting out a diplomatic boathook to avoid collisions.
letter to Lord **Lytton**, 9 March 1877

One of the nuisances of the ballot is that when the oracle has spoken you never know what it means.
to G. M. **Sandford**, October 1877

The agonies of a man who has to finish a difficult negotiation, and at the same time to entertain four royalties at a country house can be better imagined than described.
letter to Lord **Lyons**, 5 June 1878

There are marks of hurry which in so old a man are inexplicable. I suppose he still cherishes his belief in an early monastic retreat from this wicked world – and is feverishly anxious to annihilate all his enemies before he takes it.
on Gladstone
letter to Arthur **Balfour**, 16 June 1880

I wish the English arm may be equal to all the work his peace-loving policy has given it.
of Gladstone
letter to the Rev. Charles **Conybeare**, February 1881

As a rule I observe that the places where we win seats are the places where no Tory Leader has spoken.
letter to Arthur **Balfour**, 22 September 1881

My epitaph must be: 'Died of writing inane letters to empty-headed Conservative Associations.' It is a miserable death to look forward to.
letter to Lady Janetta **Manners**, 1884

I had secretly indulged the hope that we should be beaten in this election. A spell in Opposition is so good for bracing up the Conservative fibre of our party.
letter to Lord **Granby**, 6 October 1900

Alex Salmond 1954-
Scottish Nationalist politician

I do not want to be separate from anything. I want my country to be joined in co-operation and mutual respect – on a footing of equality – with all the nations of Europe.
in *Scotsman* 27 November 1998

Sharon Salzberg
American teacher of Asian meditation practices

Often we can achieve an even better result when we stumble yet are willing to start over, when we don't give up after a mistake, when something doesn't come easily but we throw ourselves into trying, when we're not afraid to appear less than perfectly polished.
O Magazine (2004)

Herbert Samuel (1st Viscount Samuel) 1870-1963
British Liberal Party politician and diplomat

A difficulty for every solution.
on the Civil Service

Jim Samuels

The United States is like the guy at the party who gives cocaine to everybody and still nobody likes him.

George Santayana 1863-1952
Spanish-born philosopher and critic

Those who cannot remember the past are condemned to repeat it.
The Life of Reason (1905)

Nathalie Sarraute 1902-99
French novelist

Radio and television, to which we devote so many of the leisure hours once spent listening to parlour chatter and parlour music, have succeeded in lifting the manufacture of banality out of the sphere of handicraft and placed it in that of a major industry.
  in *Times Literary Supplement* 10 June 1960

Jean-Paul Charles Aymard Sartre 1905-80
French existentialist philosopher, playwright, novelist, screenwriter, political activist, biographer, and literary critic

She believed in nothing; only her scepticism kept her from being an atheist.
  Huis Clos (1944)

Hell is other people.
  Huis Clos (1944)

Erik Satie 1866-1925
French composer

When I was young I was told: 'You'll see, when you're fifty.' I am fifty and I haven't seen a thing.

Alexei Sayle 1952-
English stand-up comedian, actor and author

Americans have different ways of saying things. They say 'elevator', we say 'lift'. They say 'President', we say 'stupid psychopathic git'.

I genuinely try as hard as I can to buy British. In consequence, my house is full of slightly second-rate crap. Imagine if there were no Japanese, and the British had invented the Walkman. It would be a big teak box covered in leatherette, with the headphones out of a Lancaster bomber.

Dorothy L. Sayers 1893-1957
English novelist and dramatist

Those who prefer their English sloppy have only themselves to thank if the advertisement writer uses his mastery of vocabulary and syntax to mislead their weak minds . . . The moral of all this . . . is that we have the kind of advertising we deserve.
  in *Spectator* 19 November 1936 'The Psychology of Advertising'

Hugh Scanlon 1911-2004
British trade union leader

Of course liberty is not licence. Liberty in my view is conforming to majority opinion.
  television interview, 9 August 1977

Arthur Scargill 1938-
British trade union leader

I wouldn't vote for Ken Livingstone if he were running for mayor of Toytown.
  in *Guardian* 3 May 2000

Lord Scarman 1911-2004
British judge

A government above the law is a menace to be defeated.
Why Britain needs a Written Constitution 1992

No bevy of men, not even parliament, could always be trusted to safeguard human rights.
on the need for a written constitution
Anthony Sampson *The Essential Anatomy of Britain* (1992)

Friedrich von Schiller 1759-1805
German poet, philosopher, historian and playwright

It does not prove a thing to be right because the majority say it is so.

Dr. Laura Schlessinger 1947-
American talk radio host, commentator and authoress

The reward for doing right is mostly an internal phenomenon: self-respect, dignity, integrity, and self-esteem.

Artur Schnabel 1882-1951
Austrian-born American pianist

The notes I handle no better than many pianists. But the pauses between the notes – ah, that's where the art resides!
in *Chicago Daily News* 11 June 1958

Arthur Schopenhauer 1788-1860
German philosopher

In our part of the world where monogamy is the rule, to marry means to halve one's rights and double one's duties.

Charles M. Schulz 1922-2000
American cartoonist best known for the *Peanuts* comic strip

My life has no purpose, no direction, no aim, no meaning, and yet I'm happy. I can't figure it out. What am I doing right?

J. L. Schumpeter 1883-1950
Austrian-born American economist

Early in life I had three ambitions: to be the greatest economist in the world, the greatest horseman in Austria, and the best lover in Vienna. Well, in one of those goals I have failed.
Richard Swedberg *Schumpeter: a Biography* (1991)

The cold metal of economic theory is in Marx's pages immersed in such a wealth of steaming phrases as to acquire a temperature not naturally its own.
Capitalism, Socialism and Democracy (1942)

Carl Schurz 1829-1906
German revolutionary, American statesman and reformer, Union Army General in the American Civil War, journalist, newspaper editor and orator

Our country, right or wrong. When right, to be kept right, when wrong to be put right.

Ideals are like stars: you will not succeed in touching them with your hands, but like the seafaring man on the ocean desert of waters, you choose them as your guides, and following them, you reach your destiny.

Arnold Schwarzenegger 1947-
Austrian-American bodybuilder, actor, model, businessman, and Republican Party politician

Money doesn't make you happy. I now have $50 million but I was just as happy when I had $48 million.

H. Norman Schwartzkopf III 1934-
American general, Commander of US forces in the Gulf War

Seven months ago I could give a single command and 541,000 people would immediately obey it. Today I can't get a plumber to come to my house.
   in *Newsweek* 11 November 1991

Albert Schweitzer 1875-1965
Alsatian German-French theologian, musician, philosopher and physician

Man is a clever animal who behaves like an imbecile.

C. P. Scott 1846-1932
British newspaper editor and proprietor; editor of the *Manchester Guardian*, 1872-1929

Television? The word is half Greek, half Latin. No good can come of it.
   Asa Briggs *The BBC: the First Fifty Years* (1985)

Robert Falcon Scott 1868-1912
English explorer

We took risks, we knew we took them: things have come out against us, and therefore we have no cause for complaint.
   'The Last Message' in *Scott's Last Expedition* (1913)

Sir Walter Scott 1771-1832
Scottish historical novelist and poet, particularly associated with Toryism

He that climbs the tall tree has won the right to the fruit.

Roger Scruton 1944-
English philosopher, writer and composer

The doctrine of the 'quality' of all rational beings - unless read in the spirit of some philosophical abstraction - is so manifestly false that it seldom attempts to translate itself from the language of slogans into a description of reality.
   The Meaning of Conservatism (1980)

John Sedgewick 1813-64
American general

They couldn't hit an elephant at this dist-.
    last words before being shot by a sniper at the Battle of Spotsylvania in the American Civil War

Jerry Seinfeld 1954-
American stand-up comedian, actor and writer

I do not understand how you can pour wax on your upper thigh, rip the hair out by the root, and still be afraid of a spider.
  I'm Telling You for the Last Time (1998)

There's very little advice in men's magazines, because men think, I know what I'm doing. Just show me somebody naked.

Arthur Seldon 1916-2005
British economist, co-founder of the Institute for Economic Affairs

Government of the busy by the bossy for the bully.
on over-government
  Capitalism (1990)

Seneca c. 5-65
Roman writer, philosopher, statesman

Drunkenness is nothing but voluntary madness.
  Epistulae ad Lucilium

Sex and the City American cable television series 1998-2004

'The thing that really drives me crazy,' said the artist, 'is when I see a women wearing one of those tartan skirts with high knee socks. I can't work all day.'

Tokyo Sexwale 1953-
South African politician and businessman

The president's shoes are huge and Thabo has tiny feet.
of Thabo Mbeke as President of South Africa
  quoted on *BBC News Online* website, 7 August 2001

Sgt Bilko 1996 film

Master Sgt. Ernest G. Bilko (Steve Martin)
All I've ever wanted was an honest week's pay for an honest day's work.
  inspired by the CBS television series *The Phil Silvers Show* (1955-1959)

William Shakespeare 1564-1616
English poet and playwright

Be not afraid of greatness: some men are born great, some achieve greatness and some have greatness thrust upon them.
  Twelfth Night (1601)

Once more unto the breach, dear friends, once more,
Or close the wall up with our English dead!
In peace there's nothing so much becomes a man
As modest stillness and humility;
But when the blast of war blows in our ears,
Then imitate the action of the tiger:
Stiffen the sinews, summon up the blood.
   Henry V (1599)

Discuss unto me; art thou officer?
Or art thou base, common and popular?
   Henry V (1599)

Why should we pay tribute? If Caesar can hide the sun from us with a blanket, or put the moon in his pocket, we will pay him tribute for light; else, sir, no more tribute.
   Cymbeline (1609-10)

And where the offence is let the great axe fall.
   Hamlet (1601)

Diseases desperate grown,
By desperate appliances are relieved,
Or not at all.
   Hamlet (1601)

It was always yet the trick of our English nation, if they have a good thing, to make it too common.
   Henry IV, Part 2 (1599)

The first thing we do, let's kill all the lawyers.
   Henry VI, Part 2 (1599)

Why, man, he doth bestride the narrow world
Like a Colossus; and we petty men
Walk under his huge legs, and peep about
To find ourselves dishonourable graves.
Men at some time are masters of their fates:
The fault, dear Brutus, is not in our stars,
But in ourselves, that we are underlings.
   Julius Caesar (1599)

Let me have men about me that are fat;
Sleek-headed men and such as sleep o' nights;
Yond' Cassius has a lean and hungry look;
He thinks too much: such men are dangerous.
   Julius Caesar (1599)

There is a tide in the affairs of men,
Which, taken at the flood, leads on to fortune;
Omitted, all the voyage of their life
Is bound in shallows and in miseries.
On such a full sea are we now afloat,
And we must take the current when it serves,
Or lose our ventures.

Julius Caesar (1599)

A dog's obeyed in office.
   King Lear (1605-6)

Get thee glass eyes;
And, like a scurvy politician, seem
To see the things thou dost not
   King Lear (1605-6)

Man, proud man,
Drest in a little brief authority,
Most ignorant of what he's most assured,
His glassy essence, like an angry ape,
Plays such fantastic tricks before high heaven,
As make the angels weep.
   Measure for Measure (1604)

This royal throne of kings, this sceptered isle,
This earth of majesty, this seat of Mars,
This other Eden, demi-paradise,
This fortress built by Nature for herself
Against infection and the hand of war,
This happy breed of men, this little world,
This precious stone set in the silver sea,
Which serves it in the office of a wall,
Or as a moat defensive to a house,
Against the envy of less happier lands,
This blessed plot, this earth, this realm, this England.
   Richard II (1595)

A young man married is a man that's marred.
   All's Well that Ends Well (1603-4)

CLEOPATRA:	Thou eunuch Mardian.
MARDIAN:	What's your Highness' pleasure?
CLEOPATRA:	Not to hear thee sing.
	I take no pleasure
	In aught a eunuch has . . .

   Antony and Cleopatra (1606-7)

How my achievements mock me!
   Troilus and Cressida (1602)

He has not so much brain as earwax.
   Troilus and Cressida (1602)

The world must be peopled. When I said I would die a bachelor, I did not think I should live till I were married.
   Much Ado About Nothing (1600)

William Shatner 1931-
American actor, 'Captain Kirk' in *Star Trek*

Get a life!
> *to Star Trek fans on* Saturday Night Live, *1986*
> William Shatner *Get a Life!* (1999)

George Bernard Shaw 1856-1950
Irish playwright

I'm only a beer teetotaller, not a champagne teetotaller.
> *Candida* (1898)

We have no more right to consume happiness without producing it than to consume wealth without producing it.
> *Candida* (1898)

The following quotations are from *Man and Superman* (1903):

He who can, does. He who cannot, teaches.

Do not do unto others as you would that they should do unto you. Their tastes may not be the same.

A lifetime of happiness! No man alive could bear it: it would be hell on earth.

If you strike a child take care that you strike it in anger, even at the risk of maiming it for life. A blow in cold blood neither can nor should be forgiven.

The reasonable man adapts himself to the world; the unreasonable one persists in trying to adapt the world to himself. Therefore all progress depends on the unreasonable man.

Englishmen never will be slaves; they are free to do whatever the Government and public opinion allow them to do.

Revolutions have never lighted the burden of tyranny: they have only shifted it to another shoulder.

Liberty means responsibility. That is why most men dread it.

Beauty is all very well at first sight; but who ever looks at it when it has been in the house for three days?

Money is indeed the most important thing in the world; and all sound and successful personal and national morality should have this fact for its basis.
> *The Irrational Knot* (1905)

He knows nothing; and he thinks he knows everything. That points clearly to a political career.
> *Major Barbara* (1907)

An Irishman's heart is nothing but his imagination.
> *John Bull's Other Island* (1907)

Remember that you are a human being with a soul and the divine gift of articulate speech: that your native language is the language of Shakespeare and Milton and The Bible; and don't sit there crooning like a bilious pigeon.
  Pygmalion (1916)

All great truths begin as blasphemies.
  Annajanska (1919)

It is evident that if the incomes of the rich were taken from them and divided among the poor as we stand at present, the poor would be very little less poor, the supply of capital would cease because nobody could afford to save; the country houses would fall into ruins; and learning and science and art and literature and all the rest of what we call culture would perish.
  The Intelligent Woman's Guide to Socialism and Capitalism (1928)

What Englishman will give his mind to politics as long as he can afford to keep a motor car?
  The Apple Cart (1930)

One man that has a mind and knows it can always beat ten men who haven't and don't.
  The Apple Cart (1930)

Life is not meant to be easy, my child; but take courage: it can be delightful.
  Back to Methuselah (rev. ed., 1930)

Democracy substitutes election by the incompetent many for appointment by the corrupt few.

Democracy is a device that ensures we shall be governed no better than we deserve.

An Englishman thinks he is moral when he is only uncomfortable.

It is impossible for an Englishman to open his mouth without making some other Englishman hate or despise him.

I make a fortune from criticising the policy of the government, and then hand it over to the government in taxes to keep it going.

Americans adore me and will go on adoring me until I say something nice about them.

We learn from experience that men never learn anything from experience.

The power of accurate observation is commonly called cynicism by those who have not got it.

The English have no respect for their language, and will not teach their children to speak it.

Patriotism is the conviction that your country is superior to all others because you were born in it.

If the lesser mind could measure the greater as a footrule can measure a pyramid, there would be finality in universal suffrage. As it is, the political problem remains unsolved.

Alcohol is the anaesthesia by which we endure the operation of life.

Alcohol is a very necessary article . . . It makes life bearable to millions of people who could not endure their existence if they were quite sober. It enables Parliament to do things at eleven at night that no sane person would do at eleven in the morning.

The fact that a believer is happier than a sceptic is no more to the point than the fact that a drunken man is happier than a sober one.

You have to choose (as a voter) between trusting the natural stability of gold and the honest and intelligence of members of government. And with due respect to those gentlemen, I advise you, as long as the capitalist system lasts, to vote for gold.

Hartley Shawcross 1902-2003
British Labour politician

I don't think it was right. It was victors' justice.
of the Nuremberg Trials
> interviewed on his 95th birthday, in *Daily Telegraph* 10 February 1997

Lord Shelburne 1737-1805
British Whig politician, Prime Minister

The country will neither be united at home nor respected abroad, till the reins of government are lodged with men who have some little pretensions to common sense and common honesty.
> in the House of Lords, 22 November 1770

The sun of Great Britain will set whenever she acknowledges the independence of America . . . the independence of America would end in the ruin of England.
> in the House of Lords, October 1782

Percy Bysshe Shelley 1792-1822
One of the major English Romantic poets, critically regarded among the finest lyric poets in the English language

A system could not well have been devised more studiously hostile to human happiness than marriage.
> Notes to 'Queen Mab' (1813)

As a bankrupt thief turns thief-taker, so an unsuccessful author turns critic.
> *Adonais*, Preface (1821)

Gillian Shepherd 1940-
British Conservative politician

John **Major**'s self-control in cabinet was rigid. The most angry thing he would ever do was throw down his pencil.

The trend in the rise in unemployment is downward.

William Tecumseh Sherman 1820-91
American general

I will never again command an army in America if we must carry along paid spies. I will banish myself to some foreign country first.
a reference to war correspondents
> letter to his wife, February 1863

Emanuel Shinwell 1884-1986
British Labour politician

We know that the organised workers of the country are our friends. As for the rest, they don't matter a tinker's cuss.
speech to the Electrical Trades Union conference at Margate, 7 May 1947

Jonathan Shipley 1714-88
English clergyman, Bishop of St Asaph

I look upon North America as the only great nursery of freemen left on the face of the earth.
1774

Clare Short 1946-
British Labour politician

I sometimes call them the people who live in the dark. Everything they do is in hiding . . . Everything we do is in the light. They live in the dark.
comparing Tony Blair's political advisers with elected politicians
New Statesman 9 August 1996

It will be golden elephants next.
suggesting that the government of Montserrat was 'talking mad money' in claiming assistance for evacuating the island
Observer 24 August 1997

Reckless with our government; reckless with his own future, position and place in history. It's extraordinarily reckless.
when asked if she thought that Tony Blair was acting recklessly on Iraq
interview on *Westminster Hour*, 9 March 2003

I think everyone agrees we would have done better with a different leader.
comment, 6 May 2005, the morning after the British general election

Jean Sibelius 1865-1957
Finnish composer

Pay no attention to what the critics say. No statue has ever been put up to a critic.

John Silber 1926-
American academic and politician

It is a striking paradox that democracy places the highest value upon the development of the individual, yet is frequently indifferent and hostile to greatness.
Straight Shooting (1989)

Ignazio Silone, pseudonym of Secondo Tranquilli 1900-78
Italian author

Liberty is the possibility of doubting, the possibility of making a mistake, the possibility of searching and experimenting, the possibility of saying No to any authority - literary, artistic, philosophic, religious, social and even political.
The God That Failed (1950)

John Simon 1818-97
British sergeant at law and Liberal Party politician

Democracy encourages the majority to decide things about which the majority is blissfully ignorant.

Kirke Simpson
American journalist

Warren **Harding** of Ohio was chosen by a group of men in a smoke-filled room early today as Republican candidate for President.
   news report, 12 June 1920

The Simpsons American animated television sitcom 1987-

What good is money, if it can't inspire terror in your fellow man?
   Montgomery burns, business tycoon

I'll keep it short and sweet. Family, Religion, Friendship. These are the three demons you must slay if you wish to succeed in business.
   Montgomery Burns, business tycoon

BART SIMPSON: I'm through with working. Working is for chumps.
HOMER SIMPSON: Son, I'm proud of you. I was twice your age before I figured that out.

The following are all spoken by Homer Simpson:

Marge, the reason we have elected officials is so we don't have to think!

English? Who needs that? I'm never going to England.

You don't like your job, you don't strike. You go in every day and do it really half-assed. That's the American way.

You tried your best and you failed miserably. The lesson is 'never try.'

Trying is the first step towards failure.

Marge, don't discourage the boy! Weaseling out of things is important to learn. It's what separates us from the animals. Except the weasel.'

I think Mr Smithers picked me for my motivational skills. Everyone always says they have to work twice as hard when I'm around.

Hey, just because I don't care doesn't mean I'm not listening.

If you really want something in life, you have to work for it. Now quiet, they're about to announce the lottery numbers.

If you really need money, you can sell your kidney or even your car.

All right, brain, you don't like me, and I don't like you, but let's just get me through this, and I can get back to killing you with beer.

Kill my boss? Do I dare live out the American dream?

Kids are the best, Apu. You can teach them to hate the things you hate. And they practically raise themselves, what with the internet and all.

Upton Sinclair 1878-1968
American author

It is difficult to get a man to understand something when his job depends on not understanding it.

C. H. Sisson 1914-2003
English poet

Here lies a civil servant. He was civil
To everyone, and servant to the devil.
   The London Zoo (1961)

Dame Edith Sitwell 1887-1964
British poet and critic

Eccentricity is not, as dull people would have us believe, a form of madness. It is often a kind of innocent pride, and the man of genius and the aristocrat are frequently regarded as eccentrics because genius and aristocrat are entirely unafraid of and uninfluenced by the opinions and vagaries of the crowd.

I enjoyed talking to her, but thought *nothing* of her writing. I considered her 'a beautiful little knitter.'
on Virginia Woolf
   letter to G. Singleton, 11 July 1955

I am one of those unhappy persons who inspires bores to the highest flights of art.
   quoted in *The Observer* 8 March 1998

Noel Skelton 1880-1935
British Conservative politician

To state as clearly as may be what means lie ready to develop a property-owning democracy, to bring the industrial and economic status of the wage-earner abreast of his political and educational, to make democracy stable and four-square.
   in *The Spectator* 19 May 1923

'Red' Skelton 1917-97
American actor and comedian

Well, it only proves what they always say – give the public something they want to see, and they'll come out for it.
on crowds attending the funeral of Harry Cohn
   comment, 2 March 1958; Bob Thomas *King Cohn* (1967)

B. F. Skinner 1904-90
American psychologist

The real question is not whether machines think but whether men do.

Contingencies of Reinforcement (1969)

Joan Sloan
Since we have to speak well of the dead, let's knock them while they're alive.

Samuel Smiles 1812-1904
Scottish author and reformer

It is a mistake to suppose that men succeed through success; they much oftener succeed through failures. Precept, study, advice, and example could never have taught them so well as failure has done.

Yakov Smirnoff 1951-
Ukrainian-born American comedian, painter and teacher

Many people are surprised to hear that we have comedians in Russia, but they are there. They are dead, but they are there.

I like American women. They do things sexually that Russian girls never dream of doing – like showering.

Adam Smith 1723-90
Scottish philosopher and economist

Little else is requisite to carry a state to the highest degree of opulence from the lowest barbarism, but peace, easy taxes, and a tolerable administration of justice; all the rest being brought about by the natural course of things.
Essays on Philosophical Subjects (1759)

The man of system seems to imagine that he can arrange the different members of a great society with as much ease as the hand arranges the different pieces upon a chessboard; he does not consider that the pieces upon the chessboard have no other principle of motion besides that which the hand impresses upon them; but that, in the great chessboard of human society, every single piece has a principle of motion of his own, altogether different from that which the legislator might choose to impress upon it.
Theory of Moral Sentiments (1759)

The following quotations are from *The Wealth of Nations* (1776):

It is not from the benevolence of the butcher, the brewer, or the baker, that we expect our dinner, but from their regard to their own interests. We address ourselves not to their humanity but their self love, and never talk to them of our necessities but of their advantages.

Great nations are never impoverished by private, though they sometimes are by public prodigality and misconduct. The whole, or almost the whole, public revenue, is in most countries employed in maintaining unproductive hands.

What is prudence in the conduct of every private family, can scarce be folly in that of a great kingdom. If a foreign country can supply us with a commodity cheaper than we ourselves can make it, better buy it of them with some part of the produce of our own industry, employed in a way in which we have some advantage.

Every individual necessarily labours to render the annual revenue of society as great as he can. He generally, indeed, neither intends to promote the public interest, nor knows how much he is promoting it. By preferring the support of domestic to that of foreign industry, he intends only his own security; and by directing that industry in such a manner as its produce may be of the greatest value, and he is in this, as in many other cases, led by an invisible hand to promote an end which was no part of his intention.

The natural effort of every individual to better his own condition . . . is so powerful, that it is alone, and without any assistance, not only capable of carrying on the society to wealth and prosperity, but of surmounting a hundred impertinent obstructions with which the folly of human laws too often encumbers its operations.

There is no art which one government sooner learns from another than that of draining money from the pockets of the people.

Alfred E. Smith 1873-1944
American politician

Well, down here in New York, we think it's quite fun, too, but we don't think it's everything.
when told by the Mayor of Boston: 'Of course, up in Boston, we think breeding is everything.'

Arthur Smith 1954-
English comedian

For millions of years, we men have been able to get away with being useless fathers, doing nothing around the house, and being terrible in bed. Now we're expected to be brilliant at all those things. It's so unfair.

Sir Cyril Smith 1928-
British Liberal Party then Labour Party then Liberal Party again politician. Believed to be the heaviest-ever MP, his weight peaking at 29st 12oz, about 190kg, which might explain the joke 'Cyril Smith has had more hot dinners than you've had hot dinners'

If he's going to take up pop singing, I'm going to take up belly dancing.
of Liberal leader David Steel's rap record 'I Feel Liberal'

Parliament is the longest running farce in the West End.

Dodie Smith 1896-1990
English novelist and playwright

I don't like the sound of all those lists he's making – it's like taking too many notes at school; you feel you've achieved something when you haven't.
   I Capture the Castle (1948)

Godfrey Smith 1926-
English journalist and columnist

In a world full of audio visual marvels, may words matter to you and be full of magic.
   letter to a new grandchild, in *Sunday Times* 5 July 1987

Ian Smith 1919-2007
Rhodesian statesman; Prime Minister of Rhodesia (now Zimbabwe) 1965-79

I don't believe in black majority rule in Rhodesia – not in a thousand years.
   broadcast speech, 20 March 1976

Iain Duncan Smith 1954-
English Conservative politician

Do not underestimate the determination of a quiet man.
   speech to the Conservative Party Conference, 10 October 2002

He's done more U-turns than a dodgy plumber.
*on Tony **Blair***

John Alexander Smith 1863-1939
British philosopher

Gentlemen, you are now about to embark on a course of studies which will occupy you for two years. Together, they form a noble adventure. But I would like to remind you of an important point. Nothing that you will learn in the course of your studies will be of the slightest possible use to you in after life, save only this, that if you work hard and intelligently you should be able to detect when a man is talking rot, and that, in my view, is the main, if not the sole, purpose of education.
   speech to Oxford University students, 1914

Linda Smith 1958-2006
British comedian

I play all my country and western music backwards. Your lover returns, your dog comes back to life and you cease to be an alcoholic.
   in *Daily Telegraph* 1 March 2006 Obituary

Dame Maggie Smith 1934-
English actress

Glenn **Close** is not an actress – she's an address.

Marion Smith

One of the advantages of living alone is that you don't have to wake up in the arms of a loved one.

Stevie Smith 1902-71
English poetess and novelist

People who are always praising the past
And especially the times of faith as best
Ought to go and live in the Middle Ages
And be burnt at the stake as witches and sages.
   'The Past' (1957)

I was much too far out all my life
And not waving but drowning.
   'Not Waving But Drowning' (1957)

If there wasn't death, I think you wouldn't go on.
  in *Observer* 9 November 1969

Sydney Smith 1771-1845
English writer and Anglican clergyman

What two ideas are more inseparable than beer and Britannia?
  H. Pearson *The Smith of Smiths* (1934)

Minorities . . . are almost always in the right.
  H. Pearson *The Smith of Smiths* (1934)

The summer and the country have no charms for me. I look forward anxiously to the return of bad weather, coal fires, and good society in a crowded city. I have no relish for the country: it is a kind of healthy grave.
  letter to Miss G. Harcourt, 1838

You call me in your speech 'my facetious friend', and I hasten to denominate you 'my solemn friend'; but you and I must not run into common-place errors; you must not think me necessarily foolish because I am facetious, nor will I consider you necessarily wise because you are grave.
  letter to Bishop **Bloomfield**, 1840

My living in Yorkshire was so far out of the way that it was actually twelve miles from a lemon.
  A Memoir of Sydney Smith (1855)

Don't you know, as the French say, that there are three sexes – men, women, and clergymen.
  A Memoir of Sydney Smith (1855)

He has occasional flashes of silence, that make his conversation perfectly delightful.
  A Memoir of Sydney Smith (1855)

There is one piece of advice, in a life of study, which I think no one will object to; and that is, every now and then to be completely idle - to do nothing at all.

Never try to reason the prejudice out of a man. It was not reasoned into him, and cannot be reasoned out.

Tobias Smollett 1721-71
Scottish novelist

I think for my part one half of the nation is mad – and the other not very sound.
  The Great Adventures of Sir Lancelot Greaves (1762)

A man may be very entertaining and instructive upon paper (said he), and exceedingly dull in common discourse. I have observed, that those who shine most in private company, are but secondary stars in the constellation of genius – A small stock of ideas is more easily managed, and sooner displayed, than a great quantity crowded together.
  The Expedition of Humphry Clinker (1771)

John Snagge 1904-97
English sports commentator

I can't see who is in the lead but it's either Oxford or Cambridge.

commentary on the 1949 Boat Race
  C. Dodd *Oxford and Cambridge Boat Race* (1983)

C. P. Snow 1905-80
English physicist, novelist and politician

The great edifice of modern physics goes up, and the majority of the cleverest people in the western world have about as much insight into it as their Neolithic ancestors would have had.
  The Two Cultures (1959)

When you think of the long and gloomy history of man, you will find more hideous crimes have been committed in the name of obedience than have ever been committed in the name of rebellion.
of Dodie Smith

Philip Snowden 1864-1937
British Labour politician

This is not Socialism. It is Bolshevism run mad.
on the Labour Party's 1931 election programme
  radio broadcast, 17 October 1931

Senator Soaper

Democracy is a form of government in which it is permitted to wonder aloud what the country could do under first-class management.

Socrates 469-399BC
Greek philosopher

And I tell you that virtue does not come from money, but from virtue comes money and all other good things to man, both to the individual and to the state.

Robert Solow 1924-
American economist

It is a good idea to be ambitious, to have goals, to want to be good at what you do, but it is a terrible mistake to let drive and ambition get in the way of treating people with kindness and decency. The point is not that they will then be nice to you. It is that you will feel better about yourself.

Aleksandr Solzhenitsyn 1918-2008
Soviet and Russian novelist, dramatist, and historian

How can you expect a man who's warm to understand one who's cold?
  One Day in the Life of Ivan Denisovich (1962)

If decade after decade the truth cannot be told, each person's mind begins to roam irretrievably. One's fellow countrymen become harder to understand than Martians.
  Cancer Ward (1968)

You only have power over people as long as you don't take *everything* away from them. But when you've robbed a man of *everything* he's no longer in your power – he's free again.
  The First Circle (1968)

In our country the lie has become not just a moral category but a pillar of the State.
   interview in 1974; in appendix to *The Oak and the Calf* (1975)

A decline in courage may be the most striking feature that an outside observer notices in the West today. The Western world has lost its civic courage, both as a whole and separately, in each country, in each government, in each political party, and, of course, in the United Nations. Such a decline in courage is particularly noticeable among the ruling and intellectual elites.
   commencement address at Harvard University, 8 June 1978

After the suffering of decades of violence and oppression, the human soul longs for higher things, warmer and purer than those offered by today's mass living habits, introduced as a calling card by the revolting invasion of commercial advertising, by TV stupor and intolerable music.
   commencement address at Harvard University, 8 June 1978

Yes, we are still prisoners of communism, and yet, for us in Russia, Communism is a dead dog, while for many people in the West it is still a living lion.
   broadcast on BBC Russian Service, in *Listener* 15 February 1979

The Iron Curtain did not reach the ground and under it flowed liquid manure from the West.
   speaking at Far Eastern Technical University, Vladivostok, 30 May 1994

Stephen Sondheim 1930-
American songwriter

I like to be in America!
OK by me in America!
Ev'rything free in America
For a small fee in America!
   'America' (1957 song), from *West Side Story*

A toast to that invincible bunch
The dinosaurs surviving the crunch
Let's hear it for the ladies who lunch.
   'The Ladies who Lunch' (1970), from *Company*

The concerts you enjoy together
Neighbours you enjoy together
Children you destroy together
That make marriage a joy.
   'The Little Things you do Together' (1970 song)

The same person you fucked to get in.
   to an actor who wailed, 'Who do I have to fuck to get out of this show?'

Lord Soper 1903-98
British peer and Methodist minister

It is, I think, good evidence of life after death.
of the quality of debate in the House of Lords
   Listener 17 August 1978

Charles Sorenson

It isn't the incompetent who destroy an organization. It is those who have achieved something and want to rest upon their achievements who are forever clogging things up.

Robert Southey 1774-1843
English poet and writer

The death of Nelson was felt in England as something more than a public calamity; men started at the intelligence, and turned pale, as if they had heard of the loss of a dear friend.
The Life of Nelson (1813)

It is not for man to rest in absolute contentment. He is born to hopes and aspirations as the sparks fly upward, unless he has brutified his nature and quenched the spirit of immortality which is his portion.

Thomas Sowell 1930-
African-American economist and social commentator

Much of the social history of the Western world over the past three decades has involved replacing what worked with what sounded good. In area after area - crime, education, housing, race relations - the situation has gotten worse after the bright new theories were put into operation. The amazing thing is that this history of failure and disaster has neither discouraged the social engineers nor discredited them.
Is Reality Optional? (1993)

When intellectuals discover that the world does not behave according to their theories, the conclusion they invariably draw is that the world must be changed. It must be awfully hard to change theories.
syndicated column, 10 December 1985

To build a beautiful world of ideals takes only an active imagination, some free time, and a nice vocabulary.
syndicated column, 1 July 1986

Understanding the limitations of human beings is the beginning of wisdom.
syndicated column, 2 December 1986

Wole Soyinka 1934-
Nigerian dramatist, novelist, and critic

The man dies in all who keep silent in the face of tyranny.
The Man Died (1972)

Books and all forms of writing have always been objects of terror to those who seek to suppress truth.
The Man Died (1972)

Art Spander
American sports writer

The great thing about democracy is that it gives every voter a chance to do something stupid.

Muriel Spark 1918-2006
British novelist

I am putting old heads on your young shoulders . . . all my pupils are the *crème de la crème*.
The Prime of Miss Jean Brodie (1961)

Long ago in 1945 all the nice people in England were poor, allowing for exceptions.
The Girls of Slender Means (1963), opening line

John Sparrow 1906-92
English academic, Warden of All Souls College, Oxford

That indefatigable and unsavoury engine of pollution, the dog.
letter to *Times* 30 September 1975

Grace Speare

Think and feel yourself there! To achieve any aim in life, you need to project the end-result. Think of the elation, the satisfaction, the joy! Carrying the ecstatic feeling will bring the desired goal into view.

Herbert Spencer 1820-1903
English philosopher and political theorist

The rule of the many by the few we call tyranny: the rule of the few by the many is tyranny also, only of a less intense kind.
Social Statics (1892)

Lord Spencer 1964-
English peer, brother of Diana, Princess of Wales

I always believed the press would kill her in the end. But not even I could believe they would take such a direct hand in her death as seems to be the case . . . Every proprietor and editor of every publication that has paid for intrusive and exploitative photographs of her . . . has blood on their hands today.
on the death of Diana, Princess of Wales, in a car crash while being pursued by photographers, 31 August 1997

Stephen Spender 1909-95
English poet and critic

I think continually of those who were truly great.
'I think continually of those who were truly great' (1933)

Oswald Spengler 1880-1936
German historian and philosopher

Socialism is nothing but the capitalism of the lower classes.
The Hour of Decision (1933)

Stephen Spielberg 1947-
American film director and producer

I think that today's youth have a tendency to live in the present and work for the future – and to be totally ignorant of the past.
Independent on Sunday 22 August 1999

Cecil Spring-Rice 1859-1918
British diplomat; Ambassador to Washington 1912-18

I vow to thee, my country – all earthly things above –
Entire and whole and perfect, the service of my love,
The love that asks no question; the love that stands the test,
That lays upon the altar the dearest and the best:
The love that never falters, the love that pays the price,
The love that makes undaunted the final sacrifice.
'I Vow to Thee, My Country' (written on the eve of his departure from Washington, 12 January 1918)

J. C. Squire 1884-1958
English man of letters

I'm not so think as you drunk I am.
'Ballad of Soporific Absorption' (1931)

God heard the embattled nations sing and shout
'Gott strafe England!' and 'God save the King!'
God this, God that, and God the other thing –
'Good God!' said God, 'I've got my work cut out.'
'The Dilemma' (1916)

Josef Stalin 1878-1953
Russian politician and leader of the Soviet Union. Over 20 million Soviet citizens are estimated to have died during his regime as a result of famine and other causes of death resulting from his administration

The State is an instrument in the hands of the ruling class, used to break the resistance of the adversaries of that class.
Foundations of Leninism (1924)

The Pope! How many divisions has *he* got?
on being asked to encourage Catholicism in Russia by way of conciliating the Pope, 13 May 1935
W. S. Churchill *The Gathering Storm* (1948)

Those who cast the votes decide nothing. Those who count the votes decide everything.

A single death is a tragedy, a million deaths is a statistic.

Bessie A. Stanley 1900-
American poetess

He has achieved success who has lived well, laughed often, and loved much.
'Success' (1904), opening line

Vivian Stanshall 1943-95
English singer-songwriter, painter, musician, author, poet and wit

If I had all the money I've spent on drink, I'd spend it on drink.
Sir Henry at Rawlinson End (1980)

Barbara Stanwyck 1907-90
American actress

My only problem is finding a way to play my fortieth fallen female in a different way from my thirty-ninth.

Freya Stark 1893-1993
English writer and traveller

The great and almost only comfort of being a woman is that one can always pretend to be more stupid than one is and no one is surprised.
The Valleys of the Assassins (1934)

Jim Stark

Women: you can't live with them, you can't live without them. That's probably why you can rent one for the evening.

Enid Starkie 1897-1970
English academic

Unhurt people are not much good in the world.
letter, 18 June 1943; Joanna Richardson *Enid Starkie* (1973)

Roger Starr

Those who seek to avoid the responsibilities of individual choice by assigning them to others are missing the essence of what it means to be human.
1979

David Steel 1938-
British Liberal politician; Leader of the Liberal Party 1976-88

I have the good fortune to be the first Liberal leader for over half a century who is able to say to you at the end of our annual assembly: go back to your constituencies and prepare for government.
speech to the Liberal Party Assembly, 18 September 1981

Mr Salmond is looking increasingly like a maiden in distress waiting to be rescued by James Bond. I do not think it is going to happen.
*referring to Sean **Connery**'s support for the Scottish National Party*
Daily Telegraph 27 April 1999

Richard Steele 1672-1729
British dramatist, essayist and editor

The married state, with and without the affection suitable to it, is the most complete image of heaven and hell we are capable of receiving in this life.

Spectator 9 September 1712

Shelby Steele 1946-
American author, academic, columnist, documentary film maker

I believe affirmative action is problematic in our society because it tries to function like a social program. Rather than ask it to ensure equal opportunity we have demanded that it create parity between the races.
The Content of our Character (1990)

Henry Steele Commager 1902-98
American historian, editor, essayist and reviewer

If our democracy is to flourish, it must have criticism; if our government is to function it must have dissent.

Change does not necessarily assure progress, but progress implacably requires change. Education is essential to change, for education creates both new wants and the ability to satisfy them.

Lincoln Steffens 1866-1936
American journalist

I have seen the future; and it works.
following a visit to the Soviet Union in 1919
  Letters (1938)

Gertrude Stein 1874-1946
American writer

In the United States there is more space where nobody is than where anybody is. That is what makes America what it is.
The Geographical History of America (1936)

John Steinbeck 1902-68
American writer

Man, unlike any other thing organic or inorganic in the universe, grows beyond his work, walks up the stairs of his concepts, emerges ahead of his accomplishments.
The Grapes of Wrath (1939)

I know this - a man got to do what he got to do.
The Grapes of Wrath (1939)

How can you frighten a man whose hunger is not only in his own cramped stomach but also in the wretched bellies of his children? You can't scare him - he has known a fear beyond every other.
The Grapes of Wrath (1939)

All the world's greats have been little boys who wanted the moon.
Cup of Gold (1953)

Unless the bastards have the courage to give you unqualified praise, I say ignore them.
on critics

Gloria Steinem 1934-
American feminist, journalist, social and political activist

Most American children suffer too much mother and too little father.

We are becoming the men we wanted to marry.

James Fitzjames Stephen 1928-94
English lawyer

The way in which the man of genius rules is by persuading an efficient minority to coerce an indifferent and self-indulgent majority.
   Liberty, Equality and Fraternity (1873)

Laurence Sterne 1713-1768
Irish-born English novelist and Anglican clergyman

My brother Toby, quoth she, is going to be married to Mrs Wadman.
Then he will never, quoth my father, lie *diagonally* in his bed again as long as he lives.
   Tristram Shandy (1759-67)

Brooks Stevens 1911-95
American industrial designer

Our whole economy is based on planned obsolescence.
   V. Packard *The Waste Makers* (1960)

Adlai Stevenson 1900-65
American Democratic Party politician

I suppose flattery hurts no one, that is, if he doesn't inhale.
   television broadcast, 30 March 1952

Let's talk sense to the American people. Let's tell them the truth, that there are no gains without pains.
accepting the Democratic nomination
   speech at the Democratic National Convention, Chicago, Illinois, 26 July 1952

If the Republicans will stop telling lies about the Democrats, we will stop telling the truth about them.
   speech during 1952 Presidential campaign; J. B. Martin *Adlai Stevenson and Illinois* (1976)

In America any boy can become President and I suppose that it's just one of the risks he takes.
   speech in Indianapolis, 26 September 1952

A funny thing happened to me on the way to the White House.
   speech in Washington, 13 December 1952, following his defeat in the Presidential election campaign
   Alden Whitman *Portrait: Adlai E. Stevenson* (1965)

Eggheads of the world unite; you have nothing to lose but your yolks.
   speech at Oakland, 1 February 1956
   attributed

The idea that you can merchandize candidates for high office like breakfast cereal – that you can gather votes like box tops – is, I think, the ultimate indignity to the democratic process.
speech at the Democratic National Convention, 18 August 1956

It is hard to make Communists out of Poles: they are too Catholic and they have a sense of humour.
Friends and Enemies (1959)

You have taught me a lesson I should have learned long ago – to take counsel always of your courage and never of your fears.
on losing the Presidential nomination in 1960
Herbert J. Muller *Adlai Stevenson* (1968)

If I had any epitaph that I would rather have more than another, it would be to say that I had disturbed the sleep of my generation.
epigraph to Jack W. Germand and Jules Witcover *Wake Us When It's Over* (1985)

Public confidence in the integrity of the Government is indispensable to faith in democracy; and when we lose faith in the system, we have lost faith in everything we fight and spend for.

It is not enough to have every intelligent person in the country voting for me – I need a majority.

A politician is a person who approaches every subject with an open mouth.

I like Republicans, and I would trust them with anything in the world except public office.

Robert Louis Stevenson 1850-94
Scottish novelist, poet, essayist and travel writer

Politics is perhaps the only profession for which no preparation is thought necessary.
Familiar Studies of Men and Books (1882)

When I am grown to man's estate
I shall be very proud and great.
And tell the other girls and boys
Not to meddle with my toys.
A Child's Garden of Verses (1885)

A child should always say what's true
And speak when he is spoken to,
And behave mannerly at table;
At least as far as he is able.
A Child's Garden of Verses, 'The Whole Duty of Children' (1885)

Once you are married, there is nothing for you, not even suicide, but to be good.
Viginibus Puerisque (1881)

Jon Stewart 1962-
American political satirist, writer, television host, actor, media critic and stand-up comedian

Democracy works. Against us.
*referring to the victory of George W. **Bush** in the 2004 election*
The Daily Show

Rod Stewart 1945-
British singer-songwriter

I don't think I'll get married again. I'll just find a woman I don't like and give her a house.

They could do with a pub here, a nice pint of lager would be nice.
at a Buckingham Palace garden party

Henry Stimson 1867-1950
Republican Party politician

The only way to make a man trustworthy is to trust him.

Lord St. John of Fawsley 1929-
British Conservative politician and author

The monarchy has become our only truly popular institution at a time when the House of Commons has declined in public esteem and the Lords is a matter of controversy. The monarchy is, in a real sense, underpinning the other two estates of the realm.
  The Times 1 February 1982

Lord Stockton 1943-
British peer, grandson of Harold Macmillan

As an old man he only had nightmares about two things: the trenches in the Great War and what would have happened if the Cuban Missile Crisis had gone wrong.
of Harold Macmillan
  in 1998; Peter Hennessey *The Prime Minister: the Office and its Holders since 1945* (2000)

Mervyn Stockwood 1913-95
English Anglican clergyman, Bishop of Southwark 1959-80

A psychiatrist is a man who goes to the Folies-Bergère and looks at the audience.
  in *Observer* 15 October 1961

Clement Stone 1902-2002
American businessman, philanthropist and self-help book author

Everyone who achieves success in a great venture, solved each problem as they came to it. They helped themselves. And they were helped through powers known and unknown to them at the time they set out on their voyage. They kept going regardless of the obstacles they met.

I. F. Stone 1907-89
American journalist

The difference between burlesque and the newspapers is that the former never pretended to be performing a public service by exposure.

Tom Stoppard 1937-
British playwright

McFee . . . whose chief delusion is that Edinburgh is the Athens of the North . . . McFee's dead . . . He took offence at my description of Edinburgh as the Reykjavik of the South.

Jumpers (1972)

The House of Lords, an illusion to which I have never been able to subscribe – responsibility without power, the prerogative of the eunuch throughout the ages.
Lord Malquist and Mr Moon (1966)

Comment is free but facts are on expenses.
Night and Day (1978)

I'm with you on the free press. It's the newspapers I can't stand.
Travesties (1975)

Eternity's a terrible thought. I mean, where's it all going to end?
Rosencrantz and Guildenstern are Dead (1967)

Life is a gamble at terrible odds – if it was a bet, you wouldn't take it.
Rosencrantz and Guildenstern are Dead (1967)

I don't think I can be expected to take seriously any game which takes less than three days to reach its conclusion.
a cricket enthusiast on baseball
The Guardian (24 December 1984)

I agree with everything you say, but I would attack to the death your right to say it.

Lord Strathclyde

Freedom does not die in one blow, it dies by inches in public legislation.

John Whitaker ('Jack') Straw 1946-
British Labour politician

There is no list, and Syria isn't on it.
on the US description of Syria as a rogue state
speech, Qatar, in *The Guardian* 15 April 2003

G. A. Studdert Kennedy 1883-1929
British poet

When Jesus came to Birmingham they simply passed Him by,
They never hurt a hair of him, they only let Him die.
'Indifference' (1921)

Simeon Strunsky 1879-1948
Russian-born Jewish-American essayist

People who want to understand democracy should spend less time in the library with Aristotle and more time on buses and in the subway.
No Mean City (1944)

Louis Sullivan 1933-
American politician, Secretary of Health and Human Services

What we would have is a combination of the compassion of the Internal Revenue Service and the efficiency of the post office.
on the probable nature of a nationalized health service
   Newsweek February 1992

Maximilien de Béthune, Duc de Sully 1559-1641
French statesman

The English take their pleasures sadly, after the fashion of their country.
attributed

Edith Summerskill 1901-80
British Labour politician

Nagging is the repetition of unpalatable truths
   speech to the Married Women's Association, 14 July 1960

Charles Sumner 1811-74
American Republican Party politician, lawyer and orator.

There is the national flag. He must be cold, indeed, who can look upon its fold rippling in the breeze without pride of country. If in a foreign land, the flag is companionship, and country itself, with all its endearments.
   Are We a Nation? 19 November 1867

From the beginning of our history the country has been afflicted with compromise. It is by compromise that human rights have been abandoned. I insist that this shall cease. The country needs repose after all its trials; it deserves repose. And repose can only be found in everlasting principles.

William Graham Sumner 1840-1910
American academic

The assertion that all men are equal is perhaps the purest falsehood in dogma that was ever put into human language; five minutes' observation of facts will show that men are unequal through a very wide range of variation.
   Earth Hunger (1913)

Hannen Swaffer 1879-1962
British journalist

Freedom of the press in Britain means freedom to print such of the proprietor's prejudices as the advertisers don't object to.
   said to Tom Driberg c. 1928 *Swaff* (1974)

Anne S. Swan 1859-1943
Scottish-born novelist

O God, give me work till the end of my life
And life till the end of my work.

We Travel Home (1935)

Jonathan Swift 1667-1745
Irish satirist, essayist, political pamphleteer (first for the Whigs, then for the Tories), poet and cleric

Last week I saw a woman flayed, and you will hardly believe, how much it altered her person for the worst.
A Tale of a Tub (1704)

Party is the madness of many for the gain of a few.
Thoughts on Various Subjects (1711)

I cannot but conclude the bulk of your natives to be the most pernicious race of little odious vermin that nature ever suffered to crawl upon the surface of the earth.
Gulliver's Travels (1726)

And he gave it for his opinion, that whoever could make two ears of corn or two blades of grass to grow upon a spot of ground where only one grew before, would deserve better of mankind, and do more essential service to his country than the whole race of politicians put together.
Gulliver's Travels (1726)

I have been assured by a very knowing American of my acquaintance in London, that a young, healthy child well nursed is at a year old a most delicious, nourishing, and wholesome food, whether stewed, roasted, baked, or boiled, and I make no doubt that it will equally serve in a fricassee, or a ragout.
A Modest Proposal for Preventing the Children of Ireland from Being a Burden to their Parents or Country (1729)

I never saw, heard, nor read, that the clergy were beloved in any nation where Christianity was the religion of the country. Nothing can render them popular, but some degree of persecution.
Thoughts on Religion (1765)

It is useless to attempt to reason a man out of a thing he was never reasoned into.

Herbert Bayard Swope 1882-1958
American journalist and editor

Swope enunciated no rules for success, but offered a sure formula for failure: *Just try to please everyone*
E. J. Kahn Jr. *World of Swope* (1965)

Thomas Szasz 1920-
Hungarian-born psychiatrist

The following quotations are from *The Second Sin* (1973):

The stupid neither forgive nor forget; the naive forgive and forget; the wise forgive but do not forget.

Happiness is an imaginary condition, formerly often attributed by the living to the dead, now usually attributed by adults to children, and by children to adults.

Formerly, when religion was strong and science weak, men mistook magic for medicine; now, when science is strong and religion weak, men mistake medicine for magic.

A child becomes an adult when he realises that he as a right not only to be right but also to be wrong.

Traditionally, sex has been a very private, secretive activity. Herein perhaps lies its powerful force for uniting people in a strong bond. As we make sex less secretive, we may rob it of its power to hold men and women together.

Two wrongs don't make a right, but they make a good excuse.

Albert von Szent-Györgyi 1893-1986
Hungarian-born American biochemist

Discovery consists of seeing what everybody has seen and thinking what nobody has thought.
    I. Good (ed.) *The Scientist Speculates* (1962)

t

Tacitus 56-117
Roman senator and historian

The more corrupt the republic, the more numerous the laws.
Annals

Sony Labou Tansi 1947-95
African writer

What good is an ounce of justice in an ocean of shit?
The Antipeople (1983)

R. H. Tawney 1880-1962
British economic historian

The characteristic virtue of Englishmen is power of sustained practical activity and their characteristic vice a reluctance to test the quality of that activity by reference to principles.
The Acquisitive Society (1921)

Freedom for the pike is death for the minnows.
Equality (ed. 3 1938)

Taxi American television sitcom 1978-83

Alex Rieger (Judd Hirsch)

I'm not really a cab driver. I'm just waiting for something better to come along. You know, like death.

A. J. P. Taylor 1906-90
British historian

Conformity may gave you a quiet life; it may even bring you a University Chair. But all change in history, all advance, comes from the nonconformist. If there had been no trouble makers, no Dissenters, we should still be living in caves.
The Troublemakers (1957)

Like Johnson's friend Edwards, I, too have tried to be a Marxist but common sense kept breaking in.
Journal of Modern History (1977)

Sir Edward ('Teddy') Taylor 1937-
British Conservative Party politician

You know you have to get out of Westminster when you start wanting to punch people.

Harold Taylor
American physicist

The roots of true achievement lie in the will to become the best that you can become.

Henry Taylor 1800-86
British writer

The following quotations are from *The Statesman* (1836):

It is very certain that there may be met with, in public life, a species of conscience which is all bridle and no spurs.

To choose that which will bring him the most credit with the least trouble, has hitherto been the sole care of the statesman in office.

Good nature and kindness towards those with whom they come in personal contact, at the expense of public interests, that is of those whom they never see, is the besetting sin of public men.

Men in high places, from having less personal interest in the character of others – being safe with them – are commonly less acute observers, and with their progressive elevation in life become, as more and more indifferent to what other men are, so more and more ignorant of them.

James Taylor 1948-
American singer-songwriter and guitarist

Yes, it's true. Joni **Mitchell** and Carole **King** were both my bitches for a time. I'm kinda proud of that.

Norman Tebbit 1931-
British Conservative politician

I hope Mrs **Thatcher** will go to the end of the century looking like Queen Victoria.

We cannot ignore the price that unemployment today is exacting from the failures of the past. I know about these things. I grew up in the Thirties with an unemployed father. He did not riot. He got on his bike and looked for work.

William Temple 1881-1944
English theologian and Archbishop

Personally, I have always looked on cricket as organised loafing.
   remark to parents when Headmaster of Repton School in about 1914

In place of the conception of the power-state we are led to that of the welfare-state.
   Citizen and Churchman (1941)

Alfred Tennyson, 1st Baron Tennyson 1809-92
British poet

Into the valley of death
Rode the six hundred.

Cannon to the right of them,
Cannon to the left of them,
Cannon in front of them
Volleyed and thundered.
Stormed at with shot and shell,
Boldly they rose and well,
Into the jaws of Death,
Into the mouth of Hell
Rode the six hundred.
   Other Poems 'The Charge of the Light Brigade' (1855)

That man's the true Conservative
Who lops the mouldered branch away.
   Hands All Round (1885)

A louse in the locks of literature.
of critics
   Life and Letters of Sir Edmund Gosse (1931)

Terence 185-159BC
Roman playwright

There is a demand in these days for men who can make wrong appear right.

William Makepeace Thackeray 1811-1863
English novelist

This I set down as a positive truth. A woman with fair opportunities and without a positive hump, may marry whom she likes.
   Vanity Fair (1847-8) ch. 4

Denis Thatcher 1915-2003
British businessman and husband of Margaret Thatcher, former British Prime Minister

REPORTER:	Who wears the pants in your house?
DENIS THATCHER:	I do, but I also wash and iron them.

Margaret Thatcher 1925-
British Conservative politician, Leader of the Conservative Party 1975-90, Prime Minister of the United Kingdom 1979-90. Finest peacetime British Prime Minister of the 20th century. No contest. Destroyer of bolshy trade unions, nemesis of Arthur **Scargill**, former president of the National Union of Mineworkers, currently the leader of the Socialist Labour Party.

No woman will in my time be Prime Minister or Chancellor or Foreign Secretary – not the top jobs. Anyway I wouldn't want to be Prime Minister. You have to give yourself 100%.
on her appointment as Shadow Education Spokesman
   in *Sunday Telegraph* 26 October 1969

I'll always be fond of dear Ted, but there's no sympathy in politics.
*of her predecessor, Edward **Heath***
   attributed, 1975

I stand before you tonight in my red chiffon evening gown, my face softly made up, my fair hair gently waved . . . the Iron Lady of the Western world! Me? A cold war warrior? Well, yes – if that is how they wish to interpret my defence of values and freedoms fundamental to our way of life.
referring to 'the iron lady' as the name given to her by the Soviet defence ministry newspaper Red Star, which accused her of trying to revive the cold war
   speech at Finchley, 31 January 1976

Pennies don't fall from heaven. They have to be earned here on earth.
   Observer, 18 November 1979

No one would remember the Good Samaritan if he'd only had good intentions. He had money as well.
   The Times, 12 January 1980

We have to get our production and earnings in balance. There's no easy popularity in what we are proposing, but it is fundamentally sound. Yet I believe people accept there is no real alternative.
   speech at Conservative Women's Conference, 21 May 1980

To those waiting with baited breath for that favourite media catch-phrase, the U-turn, I have only this to say. 'You turn if you want; the lady's not for turning.'
   speech at Conservative Party Conference in Brighton, 10 October 1980

Economics are the method; the object is to change the soul.
   Sunday Times 3 May 1981

Just rejoice at that news and congratulate our armed forces and the Marines. Rejoice!
on the recapture of South Georgia, usually quoted as, 'Rejoice, rejoice!'
   to newsmen outside 10 Downing Street, 25 April 1982

It is exciting to have a real crisis on your hands, when you have spent half your political life dealing with humdrum issues like the environment.
on the Falklands campaign, 1982
   speech to Scottish Conservative Party Conference, 14 May 1982

We have to see that the spirit of the South Atlantic – the real spirit of Britain – is kindled not only by war but can now be fired by peace. We have the first prerequisite. We know that we can do it – we haven't lost the ability. That is the Falklands Factor.
   speech in Cheltenham, 3 July 1982

I was asked whether I was trying to restore Victorian values. I said straight out I was. And I am.
*referring to an interview with Brian **Walden** on 17 January 1983*
   speech to the British Jewish Community, 21 July 1983

Now it must be business as usual.
   on the steps of Brighton police station a few hours after the bombing of the Grand Hotel, Brighton; often quoted as 'We shall carry on as usual.'
   The Times 13 October 1984

In church on Sunday morning – it was a lovely morning and we haven't had many lovely days – the sun was coming through a stained glass window and falling on some flowers, falling right across the church. It just occurred to me that this was the day I was meant not to see. Then all of a sudden I thought, 'there are some of my dearest friends who are not seeing this day.'
after the Brighton bombing
   television interview, 15 October 1984

We can do business together.
*of Mikhail **Gorbachev***
   in *The Times* 18 December 1984

We got a really good consensus during the last election. Consensus behind my convictions.
   attributed, 1984

I think we've been through a period where too many people have been given to understand that if they have a problem, it's the government's job to cope with it. 'I have a problem, I'll get a grant.' 'I'm homeless, the government must house me.' They're casting their problem on society. And, you know, there is no such thing as society. There are individual men and women, and there are families. And no government can do anything except through people, and people must look to themselves first. It's our duty to look after ourselves and then, also to look after our neighbour. People have got the entitlements too much in mind, without the obligations. There's no such thing as entitlement, unless someone has first met an obligation.
   Woman's Own, October 31 1987

No generation has a freehold on this earth. All we have is a life tenancy – with a full repairing list.
   speech to the Conservative Party Conference, 14 March 1988

We have not successfully rolled back the frontiers of the state in Britain only to see them reimposed at European level, with a European super-State exercising a new dominance from Brussels.
   speech in Bruges, 20 September 1988

I am extraordinarily patient, provided I get my own way in the end.
   Observer, April 4, 1989

You don't reach Downing Street by pretending you've travelled the road to Damascus when you haven't even left home.
*of Neil **Kinnock***
   Independent 14 October 1989

Advisers advise and ministers decide.
*on the respective roles of her personal economic adviser, Alan **Walters**, and her Chancellor, Nigel **Lawson** (who resigned the following day)*
   in the House of Commons, 26 October 1989

Others bring me problems, David brings me solutions.
*of Lord **Young***
   Observer 1 July 1990

No! No! No!
making clear her opposition to a single European currency, and more centralised controls from Brussels
   in the House of Commons, 30 October 1990

It's a funny old world.
on withdrawing from the contest for leadership of the Conservative party
   comment, 22 November 1990

I shan't be pulling the levers there but I shall be a very good back-seat driver.
*on the appointment of John **Major** as the next Prime Minister*
   Independent 27 November 1990

Given time, it would have been seen as one of the most far-reaching and beneficial reforms ever made in the working of local government.

of the poll tax
  The Downing Street Years (1993)

Treachery with a smile on its face.
on being told by a majority of her Cabinet that she could not continue as Prime Minister
  The Thatcher Years (BBC 1), 20 October 1993

I'm worried about that young man. He's getting awfully bossy.
*on Tony **Blair** in February 1999*

In my lifetime, all our problems have come from mainland Europe and all the solutions have come from the English-speaking nations of the world.
  Times 6 October 1999

That such an unnecessary and irrational project as building a European superstate was ever embarked on will seem in future years to be perhaps the biggest folly of the modern era. And that Britain, with traditional strengths and global destiny should ever have become part of it will appear a political error of the first magnitude.
  Statecraft: Strategies for a Changing World (2003)

Every prime minister needs a Willie.
*unwitting pun when referring to William **Whitelaw** at a retirement dinner in his honour*

If it is once again one against forty-eight, then I am very sorry for the forty-eight.

I don't want to get to a position when we have women (in senior roles) because they're women, we want to have women because they are able and as well equipped as men and sometimes better.

To wear your heart on your sleeve isn't a very good plan; you should wear it inside, where it functions best.

Europe will never be like America. Europe is a product of history. America is a product of philosophy.

The problem with socialism is that eventually you run out of other people's money.

You may have to fight a battle more than once to win it.

The cocks may crow, but it's the hen that lays the eggs.

I haven't got the figure for jeans.

I don't understand Cool Britannia. I believe in Rule Britannia.

I can trust my husband not to fall asleep on a public platform. And he usually claps in the right places.

Any woman who understands the problem of running a home will be nearer to understanding the problems of running a country.

In politics if you want anything said, ask a man. If you want anything done, ask a woman.

I don't mind how much ministers talk as long as they do what I say.

I think sometimes the prime minister should be intimidating. There's not much point in being a weak, floppy thing in the chair, is there?

Dylan Thomas 1914-53
Welsh poet

The land of my fathers. My fathers can have it.
of Wales
   Adam December 1953

Do not go gentle into that good night,
Old age should burn and rave at close of day;
Rage, rage against the dying of the light.
   'Do Not Go Gentle into that Good Night' (1952)

Books that told me everything about the wasp, except why.
   A Child's Christmas in Wales (1954)

Oh, isn't life a terrible thing, thank God?
   Under Milk Wood (1954)

Someone's boring me. I think it's me.
   quoted in Rayner Heppenstall, *Four Absentees* (1960)

Poetry is not the most important thing in life . . . I'd much rather lie in a hot bath reading Agatha Christie and sucking sweets.
   Joan Wyndham *Love is Blue* (1986) 6 July 1943

An alcoholic is someone you don't like who drinks as much as you do.

Edward Thomas 1878-1917
English poet

The past is the only dead thing that smells sweet.
   'Early one morning in May I set out' (1917)

Elizabeth Thomas 1675-1731
English poet

From marrying in haste, and repenting at leisure;
Not liking the person, yet liking his treasure:
Libera nos.
   'A New Litany, occasioned by an invitation to a wedding' (1722)

Gwyn Thomas 1913-81
Welsh novelist and dramatist

There are still parts of Wales where the only concession to gaiety is a striped shroud.
   in *Punch* 18 June 1958

Irene Thomas 1919-2001
British writer and broadcaster

Protestant women may take the pill.
Roman Catholic women must keep taking *The Tablet*.
   in *Guardian* 29 December 1990

R. S. Thomas 1913-2000
Welsh poet and clergyman

There is no present in Wales,
And no future;
There is only the past,
Brittle with relics . . .
And an impotent people,
Sick with inbreeding,
Worrying the carcase of an old song.
   'Welsh Landscape' (1955)

Dorothy Thompson 1894-1961
American journalist

Peace has to be created, in order to be maintained. It is the product of Faith, Strength, Energy, Will, Sympathy, Justice, Imagination, and the triumph of principle. It will never be achieved by passivity and quietism.

Emma Thompson 1959-
English actress and screenwriter

The gym is really depressing – so I just trot in an elderly fashion around the cricket pitch for 20 minutes.
   in *Daily Mail* (online edition) 2 December 2006

E. P. Thompson 1924-
British social historian

This 'going into Europe' will not turn out to be the thrilling mutual exchange supposed. It is more like nine middle-aged couples with failing marriages meeting in a darkened bedroom in a Brussels hotel for a Group Grope.
   in *Sunday Times* 27 April 1975

Hunter S. Thompson 1937-2005
American journalist and author

As your attorney I advise you to take a hit out of the small brown bottle in my shaving kit.
   Fear and Loathing in Las Vegas

Julian Thompson 1934-
British soldier, second-in-command of the land forces during the Falklands campaign

You don't mind dying for Queen and country, but you certainly don't want to die for politicians.
   The Falklands War – the Untold Story (Yorkshire Television) 1 April 1987

Robert Norman Thompson 1914-97
American-born Canadian mission worker, politician and academic

The Americans are our best friends whether we like it or not.
   Peter C. Newman *Home Country: People, Places and Power Politics* (1973)

Henry Thoreau 1817-62
American author, poet, naturalist, tax resister, development critic, surveyor, historian, philosopher, and leading transcendentalist

If a man does not keep pace with his companions, perhaps it is because he hears a different drummer. Let him step to the music which he hears, however measured or far away.
   Conclusion (1854)

I heartily accept the motto, 'That government is best which governs least' . . . Carried out, it finally amounts to this, which I also believe . . . 'That government is best which governs not at all.'
   Civil Disobedience (1849)

Do not lose hold of your dreams or aspirations. For if you do, you may still exist but you have ceased to live.

The character inherent in the American people has done all that has been accomplished; and it would have done somewhat more, if the government had not sometimes got in its way.

The only obligation which I have a right to assume, is to do at any time what I think right.

As for the pyramids, there is nothing to wonder at in them so much as the fact that so many men could be found degraded enough to spend their lives constructing a tomb for some ambitious booby, whom it would have been wiser and manlier to have drowned in the Nile, and then given his body to the dogs.

Jeremy Thorpe 1929-
British Liberal Party politician

Greater love hath no man than this, that he lay down his friends for his life.
   after Harold Macmillan's Cabinet purge, 1962

Thucydides c.455-c.400BC
Greek historian

Party associations, it should be understood, are not based on law nor do they seek the common welfare; they are lawless and seek only self-interest.
   History of the Peloponnesian War

Happiness depends on being free, and freedom depends on being courageous.

James Thurber 1894-1961
American cartoonist and author

You can fool too many of the people too much of the time.
   The Owl who was God

I suppose that the high-water mark of my youth in Columbus, Ohio, was the night the bed fell on my father.
My Life and Hard Times (1933)

Human Dignity has gleamed only now and then and here and there, in lonely splendor, throughout the ages, a hope of the better men, never an achievement of the majority.
New Yorker, 29 April 1939

All human beings should try to learn before they die what they are running from, and to, and why.

Tiberius 32 BC-AD 37
Roman emperor from AD 14

It is the part of the good shepherd to shear his flock, not skin it.
to governors who recommended burdensome taxes
Suetonius *Lives of the Caesars* 'Tiberius'

Henrik Tikkanen

Truly great madness cannot be achieved without significant intelligence.

Tipu Sultan c.1750-99
Indian ruler

In this world I would rather live two days like a tiger, than two hundred years like a sheep.
Alexander Beatson *A View of the Origin and Conduct of the War with Tippoo Sultan* (1800)

Alexis de Tocqueville 1805-59
French political thinker and historian

America is great because she is good. If America ceases to be good, America will cease to be great.

Each citizen of a democracy generally spends his time considering the interests of a very insignificant person, namely, himself.
Democracy in America (1835)

In countries where associations are free, secret societies are unknown. In America there are factions, but no conspiracies.
Democracy in America (1835)

Americans are so enamoured of equality that they would rather be equal in slavery than unequal in freedom.
Democracy in America (1835)

The surface of American society is covered with a layer of democratic paint, but from time to time one can see the old aristocratic colours breaking through.
Democracy in America (1835)

Americans rightly think their patriotism is a sort of religion strengthened by practical service.
Democracy in America (1835)

On my arrival in the United States I was struck by the degree of ability among the governed and the lack of it among the governing.

Democracy in America (1835)

The French want no-one to be their *superior*. The English want *inferiors*. The Frenchman constantly raises his eyes above him with anxiety. The Englishman lowers his beneath him with satisfaction. On either side it is pride, but understood in a different way.
Voyage en Angleterre et en Irlande de 1835 (1958)

When a nation abolishes aristocracy, centralization follows as a matter of course.
Ancien Régime (1856)

Centralization and socialism are native of the same soil: one is the wild herb, the other the garden plant.
Ancien Régime (1856)

The Americans combine the notions of Christianity and of liberty so intimately in their minds, that it is impossible to make them conceive the one without the other.

The American Republic will endure until the day Congress discovers that it can bribe the public with the public's money.

Lands produce less by reason of their fertility than by reason of the liberty of their inhabitants.
The Old Regime and the Revolution (1856)

Lily Tomlin 1939-
American actress, comedian, writer and producer

No matter how cynical you are, you can never keep up.

99% of the adults in this country are decent, honest, hard-working, honest Americans. It's the other lousy 1% that gets all the publicity and gives us a bad name. But then . . . we elected them.

F. H. Townsend 1868-1920
English cartoonist

MR BINKS: One of my ancestors fell at Waterloo.
LADY CLARE: Ah? Which platform?
   Punch, Vol 129 1 November 1905 Caption to cartoon

Arnold Toynbee 1852-83
English economic historian

America is a large friendly dog in a small room. Every time it wags its tail it knocks over a chair.

Arnold J. Toynbee 1889-1975
British historian

Civilisation is a movement and not a condition, a voyage and not a harbour.
  in *Readers Digest* October 1958

It is a paradoxical but profoundly true and important principle of life that the most likely way to reach a goal is to be aiming not at that goal itself but at some more ambitious goal beyond it.

Sir Herbert Beerbohm Tree 1853-1917
English actor-manager

Ladies, just a little more virginity, if you don't mind.
to a motley collection of females, assembled to play ladies-in-waiting to a queen
Alexander Woollcott *Shouts and Murmurs* (1923)

My poor fellow, why not carry a watch?
to a man struggling under the weight of a grandfather clock

I'll have that one, please.
pointing at stamp in middle of sheet at Post Office

Dear Sir, I have read your play. Oh, my dear Sir. Yours faithfully . . .
to a would-be dramatist

A committee should consist of three men, two of whom are absent.

Richard Chenevix Trench 1807-96
English Anglican Archbishop of Dublin

Archbishop Chenevix Trench retired from the see of Dublin and spent his last two years in London. On returning to visit his successor Lord **Plunkett**, in Dublin, his memory lapsed and he forgot that he was no longer host, remarking to his wife:

I'm afraid, my love, that we must put this cook down among our failures.

G. M. Trevelyan 1876-1962
English historian

The following quotations are from *English Social History* (1942):

If the French nobles had been capable of playing cricket with their peasants, their chateaux would never have been burnt.

Disinterested intellectual curiosity is the life-blood of real civilisation.

Education has produced a vast population able to read but unable to distinguish what is worth reading, an easy prey to sensations and cheap appeals.

Hugh Trevor-Roper 1914-2003
British historian

Those who exercise power and determine policy are generally men whose minds have been formed by events twenty or thirty years before.
From Counter-Reformation to Glorious Revolution (1992)

Calvin Trillin 1935-
American journalist, humoirst, food writer, poet, memoirist and novelist

In modern America, anyone who attempts to write satirically about the events of the day finds it difficult to concoct a situation so bizarre that it may not actually come to pass while the article is still on the presses.

Marriage is part of a sort of 50's revival package that's back in vogue along with neckties and naked ambition.

I'm in favour of liberalised immigration because of the effect it would have on restaurants. I'd let just about everybody in, except the English.

Tommy Trinder 1909-89
British comedian

Overpaid, overfed, oversexed, and over here.
of American troops in Britain during the Second World War

Anthony Trollope 1815-82
English novelist

There is no road to wealth so easy and respectable as that of matrimony.
Doctor Thorne (1858)

When taken in the refreshing waters of office any pill can be swallowed.
The Bertrams (1859)

To me it seems that no form of existing government – no form of government that ever did exist – gives or has given so large a measure of individual freedom to all who live under it as a constitutional monarchy.
North America (1862)

There is nothing more tyrannical than a strong popular feeling among a democratic people.
North America (1862)

I have sometimes thought there is no being so venomous, so bloodthirsty as a professed philanthropist.
North America (1862)

Equality is a doctrine to be forgiven when he who preaches it is . . . striving to raise others to his own level.
North America (1862)

What good government ever was not stingy?
South Africa (1878)

Men don't know women, or they would be harder to them.
Lady Ongar in *The Claverlings* (1867)

Leon Trotsky 1879-1940
Russian revolutionary

Old age is the most unexpected of all things that happen to a man.
Diary in Exile (1959) 8 May 1935

It was the supreme expression of the mediocrity of the apparatus that Stalin himself rose to his position.
My Life (1930)

Not believing in force is the same thing as not believing in gravitation.
   G. Maximov *The Guillotine at Work* (1940)

In a country where the sole employer is the State, opposition means death by slow starvation. The old principle: he who does not work shall not eat, has been replaced by a new one: who does not obey shall not eat.
   attributed

Pierre Trudeau 1919-2000
Canadian Liberal statesman, Prime Minister, 1968-79 and 1980-4

The twentieth century really belongs to those who will build it. The future can be promised to no one.
   in 1968

Living next to you is in some ways like sleeping with an elephant. No matter how friendly and even-tempered the beast, one is affected by every twitch and grunt.
on relations between Canada and the US
   speech at National Press Club, Washington DC, 25 March 1969

Harry S. Truman 1884-1972
Artillery officer in WWI, 33rd President of the United States 1945-53

He'll sit right here and he'll say do this, do that! And nothing will happen. Poor Ike – it won't be a bit like the Army
*of his successor **Eisenhower***
   Harry S. Truman (1973) vol. 2

If you can't stand the heat, get out of the kitchen.
   attributed by Truman himself to his White House aid Harry **Vaughan** (1893-1981), his 'military' jester
   in *Time* 28 April 1952

All the President is, is a glorified public relations man who spends his time flattering, kissing and kicking people to get them to do what they are supposed to do anyway.
   letter to his sister, 14 November 1947

Those who want the Government to regulate matters of the mind and spirit are like men who are so afraid of being murdered that they commit suicide to avoid assassination.
   address at the National Archives, Washington D.C., 15 December 1952

Sixteen hours ago an American airplane dropped one bomb on Hiroshima . . . The force from which the sun draws its power has been loosed against those who brought war to the Far East.
first announcement of the dropping of the atomic bomb
   on 6 August 1945

Wherever you have an efficient government you have a dictatorship.
   lecture at Colombia University, 28 April 1959

I didn't fire General **MacArthur** because he was a dumb son of a bitch, although he was, but that's not against the law for generals. If it was, half to three-quarters of them would be in jail.

Democracy is, first and foremost, a spiritual force, it is built upon a spiritual basis – and on a belief in God and an observance of moral principle. In the long run only the church can provide that basis. Our founders knew this truth – and we will neglect it at our peril.

I always remember an epitaph which is in the cemetery at Tombstone, Arizona. It says: 'Here lies Jack Williams. He done his damnedest.' I think that is the greatest epitaph a man can have – when he gives everything that is in him to do the job he has before him. That is all you can ask of him and that is what I have tried to do.

I have found the best way to give advice to your children is to find out what they want and then advise them to do it.

Sophie Tucker 1884-1966
Russian-born American vaudeville artiste

From birth to 18 a girl needs good parents. From 18 to 35, she needs good looks. From 35 to 55, good personality. From 55 on, she needs good cash.
M. Freedland *Sophie* (1978)

Desmond Tutu 1931-
South African Anglican clergyman, Archbishop of Cape Town 1986-96

We may be surprised at the people we find in heaven. God has a soft spot for sinners. His standards are quite low.
in *Sunday Times* 15 April 2001

Mark Twain 1835-1910
American author and humorist

Barring that natural expression of villainy which we all have, the man looked honest enough.
A Mysterious Visit

The following quotations are from *The Innocents Abroad* (1869):

Travel is fatal to prejudice, bigotry, and narrow-mindedness, and many of our people need it sorely on these accounts.

The Creator made Italy with designs by Michelangelo.

They spell it Vinci and pronounce it vinchy; foreigners always spell better than they pronounce.

It used to be a good hotel, but that proves nothing – I used to be a good boy.

One is apt to overestimate beauty when it is rare.

I must have a prodigious quantity of mind; it takes me as much as a week sometimes to make it up.

The following quotations are from *Roughing It* (1872):

When it comes down to pure ornamental cursing, the native American is gifted above the sons of men.

Trial by jury is the palladium of our liberties. I do not know what a palladium is, having never seen a palladium, but it is a good thing no doubt at any rate.

Nothing helps scenery like bacon and eggs.

To promise not to do a thing is the surest way in the world to make a body want to go and do that very thing.
The Adventures of Tom Sawyer (1876)

War talk by men who have been in a war is always interesting; whereas moon talk by a poet who has not been in the moon is likely to be dull.
Life on the Mississippi (1883)

The following quotations are from *Adventures of Huckleberry Finn* (1884):

Pilgrim's Progress: a book about a man that left his family, it didn't say why.

All I say is kings is kings, and you got to make allowances. Take them all around, they're a mighty ornery lot. It's the way they're raised.

The average man's a coward.

The preacher never charged nothing for his preaching, and it was worth it, too.

Persons attempting to find a motive in this narrative will be prosecuted; persons attempting to find a moral in it will be banished; persons attempting to find a plot in it will be shot.

The best coffee in Europe is Vienna coffee, compared to which all other coffee is fluid poverty.
Greatly Exaggerated (1888)

The following quotations are from *A Connecticut Yankee in King Arthur's Court* (1889)

I was gradually coming to have a mysterious and shuddery reverence for this girl; nowadays whenever she pulled out from the station and got her train fairly started on one of those horizonless transcontinental sentences of hers, it was borne in upon me that I was standing in the awful presence of the Mother of the German Language . . . She had exactly the German way; whatever was in her mind to be delivered, whether a mere remark, or a sermon, or a cyclopedia, or the history of a war, she would get it into a single sentence or die. Whenever the literary German dives into a sentence, that is the last you are going to see of him till he emerges on the other side of his Atlantic with his verb in his mouth.

You can't reason with your heart; it has its own laws and thumps about things which the intellect scorns.

I was born modest; not all over, but in spots.

No people in the world ever did achieve freedom by goody-goody talk and moral suasion: it being immutable law that all revolutions that will succeed must *begin* in blood.

There are written laws – they perish; but there are also unwritten laws – they are eternal.

My kind of loyalty was loyalty to one's country, not to its institutions or its office-holders.

We have no thoughts of our own, no opinions of our own: they are transmitted to us, trained into us.

Tyrannical, murderous, rapacious, and morally rotten as they [the nobility] were, they were deeply and enthusiastically religious.

Many a small thing has been made large by advertising.

It is the little conveniences that make the real comfort of life.

When red-headed people are above a certain social grade, their hair is auburn.

The following quotations are from *Pudd'nhead Wilson* (1894):

If you pick up a starving dog and make him prosperous, he will not bite you. This is the principal difference between a dog and a man.

Training is everything . . . cauliflower is nothing but cabbage with a college education.

Adam did not want the apple for the apple's sake, he wanted it only because it was forbidden. The mistake was in not forbidding the serpent; then he would have eaten the serpent.

Courage is resistance to fear, mastery of fear, not absence of fear.

It is not best that we should all think alike; it is difference of opinion that makes horse races.

Few things are harder to put up with than the annoyance of a good example.

When angry, count four; when very angry, swear.

Let us endeavour so to live that when we come to die even the undertaker will be sorry.

The holy passion of Friendship is of so sweet and steady and loyal and enduring a nature that it will last through a whole lifetime, if not asked to lend money.

He is useless on top of the ground; he ought to be under it, inspiring the cabbages.

Consider well the proportion of things. It is better to be a young June-bug than an old bird of paradise.

All say, 'How hard it is that we have to die' – a strange complaint to come from the mouths of people who have had to live.

One of the striking differences between a cat and a lie is that a cat has only nine lives.

Habit is habit, and not to be flung out of the window by any man, but coaxed downstairs a step at a time.

Why is it we rejoice at a birth and grieve at a funeral? It is because we are not the person involved.

July 4th. Statistics show that we lose more fools on this day than in all the other days of the year put together. This proves, by the number left in stock, that one Fourth of July per year is now inadequate, the country has grown so.

The following quotations are from *Following the Equator* (1897):

When people do not respect us we are sharply offended; yet in his private heart no man much respects himself.

A crime preserved in a thousand centuries ceases to be a crime, and becomes a virtue. This is the law of custom, and custom supersedes all other forms of law.

Man will do many things to get himself loved, he will do all things to get himself envied.

A human being has a natural desire to have more of a good thing than he needs.

The way it is now, the asylums can hold the sane people, but it we tried to shut up the insane we should run out of building materials.

The timid man yearns for full value and asks a tenth. The bold man strikes for double value and compromises on par.

Nothing is so ignorant as a man's left hand, except a lady's watch.

To be good is to be noble; but to show others how to be good is noble and no trouble.

There is a Moral Sense and there is an Immoral Sense. History shows us that the Moral Sense enables us to perceive morality and how to avoid it, and that the Immoral Sense enables us to perceive immorality and how to enjoy it.

Nothing so needs reforming as other people's habits.

Make it a point to do something every day that you don't want to do. This is the golden rule for acquiring the habit of doing your duty without pain.

There are several good protections against temptations but the surest is cowardice.

However, we must put up without clothes as they are – they have their reason for existing. They are on us to expose us – to advertise what we wear them to conceal.

We should be careful to get out of an experience only the wisdom that is in it – and stop there; lest we be like the cat that sits down on a hot stove-lid. She will never sit down on a hot stove-lid again – and that is well; but also she will never sit down on a cold one anymore.

Also, to be fair, there is another word of praise due to this ship's library: it contains no copy of Oliver **Goldsmith**'s *The Vicar of Wakefield* . . . a book which is one long waste-pipe discharge of goody-goody puerilities and dreary moralities . . .

Jane **Austen's** books, too, are absent from this library. Just that one omission alone would make a fairly good library out of a library that hadn't a book in it.

There are many humorous things in the world; among them, the white man's notion that he is less savage than the other savages.

She was not quite what you would call refined. She was not quite what you would call unrefined.

She was the kind of person that keeps a parrot.

It could probably be shown by facts and figures that there is no distinctly American criminal class except Congress.

A human being has a natural desire to have more of a good thing than he needs.

The secret source of humor itself is not a joy but sorrow. There is no humor in heaven.

We begin to swear before we can talk.

If the desire to kill and the opportunity to kill came always together, who would escape hanging?

It takes your enemy and your friend, working together, to hurt you to the heart; the one to slander you and the other to get the news to you.

Prosperity is the best protector of principle.

It is by the goodness of God that in our country we have those three unspeakably precious things: freedom of speech, freedom of conscience, and the prudence never to practice either of them.

Noise proves nothing. Often a hen who has merely laid an egg cackles as if she had laid an asteroid.

I have traveled more than anyone else, and I have noticed that even the angels speak English with an accent.

Few of us can stand prosperity – another man's I mean.

Everyone is a moon, and has a dark side which he never shows to anyone.

It could probably be shown by facts and figures that there is no distinctly native American criminal class except Congress.

If a man doesn't believe as we do, we say he is a crank, and that settles it. I mean it does nowadays, because now we can't burn him.

There are those who scoff at the schoolboy, calling him frivolous and shallow. Yet it was the schoolboy who said, 'Faith is believing what you know ain't so.'

Let me make the superstitions of a nation and I care not who makes its laws.

India has two million gods, and worships them all. In religion other countries are paupers; India is the only millionaire.

Wrinkles should merely indicate where smiles have been.

When in doubt tell the truth.

Truth is the most valuable thing we have. Let us economize it.

I never could tell a lie that anyone would doubt, nor a truth that anybody would believe.

Don't part with your illusions. When they are gone you may still exist, but you have ceased to live.

The old saw says, 'Let a sleeping dog lie.' Still, when there is much at stake it is better to get a newspaper to do it.

Perhaps no poet is a conscious plagiarist; but there seems to be warrant for suspecting that there is no poet who is not at one time or another an unconscious one.

He was as shy as a newspaper is when referring to its own merits.

In the first place God made idiots. This was for practice. Then he made school boards.

The only way to keep your health is to eat what you don't want, drink what you don't like, and do what you'd druther not.

There are two times in a man's life when he should not speculate: when he can't afford it, and when he can.

Custom makes incongruous things congruous.

Each person is born to one possession which outvalues all his others – his last breath.

The Autocrat of Russia possesses more power than any other man in the earth; but he cannot stop a sneeze.

The English are mentioned in the Bible; Blessed are the meek, for they shall inherit the earth.

Nearly all black and brown skins are beautiful, but a beautiful white skin is rare.

The man with a new idea is a crank until the idea succeeds.

The following quotations are from *The Mysterious Stranger* (1910):

Mankind is governed by minorities, seldom or never by majorities. It suppresses its feelings and its beliefs and follows the handful that makes the most noise. Sometimes the noisy handful is right, sometimes wrong, but no matter, the crowd follows it.

Of course, no man is entirely in his right mind at any time.

Man is the only animal that blushes. Or needs to.

Two or three centuries from now it will be recognized that all the competent killers are Christians; then the pagan world will go to school with the Christian – not to acquire his religion, but his guns.

Monarchies, aristocracies, and religions are all based upon that large defect in your race – the individual's distrust of his neighbour, and his desire, for safety's or comfort's sake, to stand well in his neighbor's eye.

Against the assault of laughter nothing can stand.

The following quotations are from *The Lowest Animal*:

Man is the Reasoning Animal. Such is the claim. I think it is open to dispute.

Man is the only animal that has the True Religion – several of them.

Of all the animals, man is the only one that is cruel. He is the only one that inflicts pain for the pleasure of doing it.

The following quotations are from *Mark Twain's Notebook*, ed. A. B. Paine (1935)

Man was made at the end of the week's work, when God was tired.

When we remember we are all made, the mysteries of life disappear and life stands explained.

One of the proofs of the immortality of the soul is that myriads have believed in it. They have also believed that the world was flat.

Heaven for climate, Hell for company.

The human race consists of the dangerously insane and such as are not.

Concerning the difference between man and the jackass: some observers hold that there isn't any. But this wrongs the jackass.

The more things are forbidden, the more popular they become.

Always acknowledge a fault frankly. This will throw those in authority off guard and give you an opportunity to commit more.

Familiarity breeds contempt – and children.

A man should not be without morals; it is better to have bad morals than none at all.

Each race determines for itself what indecencies are. Nature knows no indecencies; man invents them.

Irreverence is the champion of liberty and its only sure defense.

Never refuse to do a kindness unless the act would work great injury to yourself, and never refuse to take a drink – under any circumstances.

The radical of one century is the conservative of the next. The radical invents the views; when he has worn them out the conservative adopts them.

The first thing a missionary teaches a savage is indecency.

There is nothing more awe-inspiring than a miracle except the credulity that can take it at par.

True irreverence is disrespect for another man's god.

In God We Trust. I don't believe it would sound any better if it were true.

The book of nature tells us distinctly that God cares not a rap for us – nor for any living creature.

There is no sadder sight than a young pessimist.

Education consists mainly in what we have unlearned.

If I cannot swear in heaven I shall not stay there.

Temperate temperance is best.

It takes me a long time to lose my temper, but once lost I could not find it with a dog.

Whenever you find you are on the side of the majority, it is time to reform.

An uneasy conscience is a hair in the mouth.

Good breeding consists in concealing how much we think of ourselves and how little we think of the other person.

I am only human, although I regret it.

The proverb says that Providence protects children and idiots. This is really true. I know it because I have tested it.

Thanksgiving Day originated in New England when the Puritans realized they had succeeded in exterminating their neighbors, the Indians, instead of getting exterminated by their neighbors, the Indians.

We lavish gifts upon them [children]; but the most precious gift – our personal association, which means so much to them – we give grudgingly.

I looked as out of place as a Presbyterian in hell.

In certain trying circumstances, urgent circumstances, desperate circumstances, profanity furnishes a relief denied even to prayer.

Do right and you will be conspicuous.

Suppose you were an idiot. And suppose you were a member of Congress. But I repeat myself.

The Church has opposed every innovation and discovery from the day of Galileo down to our own time, when the use of Anaesthetics in childbirth was regarded as a sin because it avoided the biblical curse pronounced against Eve.

I haven't a particle of confidence in a man who has no redeeming petty vices whatever.

The man who is a pessimist before 48 knows too much; if he is an optimist after it, he knows too little.

It isn't so astonishing, the number of things that I can remember, as the number of things I can remember that aren't so.

The following are from *More Maxims of Mark*, Merle Johnson, ed.

'The noblest work of God.' Man. 'Who found it out?' Man.

Clothes makes the man. Naked people have little or no influence in society.

Some of us cannot be optimists, but all of us can be bigamists.

Heroine: girl who is perfectly charming to live with, in a book.

Morals consist of political morals, commercial morals, ecclesiastical morals, and morals.

Do good when you can, and charge when you think they will stand it.

We all live in the protection of certain cowardices which we call our principles.

You can straighten a worm, but the crook is in him and only waiting.

Do not put off till tomorrow what can be put off till day-after-tomorrow just as well.

No man has a wholly undiseased mind . . . in one way or another all men are mad.

One ought never to do wrong when people are looking.
A Double-Barreled Detective Story

To believe yourself brave is to be brave.
Joan of Arc

That's the difference between governments and individuals. Governments don't care, individuals do.
A Tramp Abroad (1880)

The church is always trying to get other people to reform; it might not be a bad idea to reform itself a little by way of example.
A Tramp Abroad (1880)

An honest man in politics shines more than he would elsewhere.
A Tramp Abroad (1880)

A nation is only an individual multiplied.
The Turning-Point of My Life

Such is the human race. Often it does seem such a pity that Noah didn't miss the boat.
Christian Science

Principles have no real force except when one is well fed.
Adam's Diary

Religion had its share in the changes of civilization and national character, of course. What share? The lion's.
Bible Teaching and Religious Practice

Eternal Rest sounds comforting in the pulpit ... Well, you try it once, and see how heavy time will hang on your hands.
'Captain Stormfield's Visit to Heaven' (essay, 1909)

Whatever a man's age, he can reduce it several years by putting a bright-colored flower in his button hole.

The American Claimant (1892)

Everything has its limit - iron ore cannot be educated into gold.
What Is Man?

I always take Scotch whisky at night as a preventative of toothache. I have never had the toothache; and what is more, I never intend to have it.
Europe and Elsewhere

He is now rising fast from affluence to poverty.
Henry Ward Beecher's Farm

I have found out that there ain't no surer way to find out whether you like people or hate them than to travel with them.
Tom Sawyer Abroad

There are several 'sights' in the Bermudas, of course, but they are easily avoided. This is a great advantage - one cannot have it in Europe.
Notes of an Idle Excursion

To me Edgar Allen **Poe**'s prose is unreadable - like Jane **Austen**'s. No, there is a difference. I could read his prose on a salary, but not Jane's.
Mark Twain's Letters

If the statistics are right, the Jews constitute but 1% of the human race. It suggests a nebulous dim puff of star dust lost in the blaze of the Milky Way. Properly the Jew ought hardly to be heard of; but he is heard of, has always been heard of. He is as prominent on the planet as any other people, and his commercial importance is extravagantly out of proportion to the smallness of his bulk. His contributions to the world's list of great names in literature, science, art, music, finance, medicine, and abstruse learning are also way out of proportion to the weakness of his numbers. He has made a marvelous fight in this world, in all the ages; and has done it with his hands tied behind him. He could be vain of himself and be excused for it. The Egyptian, the Babylonian, and the Persian rose, filled the planet with sound and splendor, then faded to dream-stuff and passed away; the Greek and Roman followed, and made a vast noise, and they are gone; other peoples have sprung up and held their torch high for a time, but it burned out, and they sit in twilight now, or have vanished. The Jew saw them all, beat them all, and is now what he always was, exhibiting no decadence, no infirmity of age, no weakening of his parts, no slowing of his energies, no dulling of his alert and aggressive mind.
Harper's Magazine (1899) 'Concerning the Jews'

Compliments always embarrass a man. You do not know anything to say. It does not inspire you with words . . . I have been complimented myself a great many times, and they always embarrass me - I always feel that they have not said enough.
speech on Fulton Day, at Jamestown, 23 September 1907

From Twain's speech at his birthday dinner, New York City, 5 December 1905:

I have never taken any exercise, except for sleeping and resting, and I never intend to take any. Exercise is loathsome.

Morals are an acquirement - like music, like a foreign language, like piety, poker, paralysis - no man is born with them.

And I urge upon you this – which I think is wisdom – if you find you can't make seventy by any but an uncomfortable road, don't you go.

I have achieved my seventy years in the usual way; by sticking strictly to a scheme of life which would kill anybody else.

I have made it a rule never to smoke more than one cigar at a time.

I have never taken any exercise, except sleeping and resting, and I never intend to take any. Exercise is loathsome. And it cannot be any benefit when you are tired; and I was always tired.

As a sweetheart, she has few equals and no superiors; as a cousin, she is convenient; as a wealthy grandmother with an incurable distemper, she is previous; as a wet-nurse, she has no equal among men.
speech, 'Woman – An Opinion'

What, sir, would the people of the earth be without woman? They would be scarce, sir, almighty scarce.'
speech 'Woman – An Opinion'

Some civilised women would lose half their charm without dress; and some would lose all of it.
speech 'Woman, God Bless Her!'

Demagogue – a vessel containing beer and other liquids.
speech 'Girls'

If a person offends you and you are in doubt as to whether it was intentional or not, do not resort to extreme measures. Simply watch your chance and hit him with a brick.
speech 'Advice to Youth'

Yes, always avoid violence. In this age of charity and kindliness, the time has gone by for such things. Leave dynamite to the low and unrefined.
speech 'Advice to Youth'

You want to be very careful about lying; otherwise you are nearly sure to get caught.
speech 'Advice to Youth'

A truth is not hard to kill . . . a lie told well is immortal.
speech 'Advice to Youth'

Diligence is a good thing, but taking things easy is much more – restful.
speech 'Business'

Honesty is the best policy – when there is money in it.
speech 'Business'

My axiom is, to succeed in business: avoid my example.
speech, 'Business'

To lead a life of undiscovered sin! That is true joy.
speech 'My Real Self'

If any man has just merciful and kindly instincts he would be a gentleman, for he would need nothing else in the world.

speech 'Layman's Sermon'

Citizenship is what makes a republic; monarchies can get along without it. What keeps a republic on its legs is good citizenship.
speech 'Layman's Sermon'

We are called the nation of inventors. And we are. We could still claim that title and wear its loftiest honors if we had stopped with the first thing we ever invented – which was human liberty.
speech 'On Foreign Critics'

We have a criminal jury system which is superior to any in the world; and its efficiency is only marred by the difficulty of finding twelve men every day who don't know anything and can't read.
speech 'Americans and the English'

Loyalty to petrified opinions never yet broke a chain or freed a human soul.
speech 'Consistency'

'This atrocious doctrine of allegiance to party plays directly into the hands of politicians of the baser sort – and doubtless for that it was borrowed – or stolen – from the monarchical system.'
speech 'Consistency'

What then is the true gospel of consistency? Change.
speech 'Consistency'

There are two kinds of Christian morals, one private and the other public. These two are so distinct, so unrelated, that they are no more akin to each other than are archangels and politicians.
speech 'Taxes and Morals'

The idea that no gentleman ever swears is all wrong; he can swear and still be a gentleman if he does it in a nice and benevolent and affectionate way.
speech 'Taxes and Morals'

Why, Sarah **Bernhardt** is the youngest person I ever saw, except myself – for I always feel young when I come in the presence of young people.
speech 'Russian sufferers'

I don't mind what the opposition say of me so long as they don't tell the truth about me.
speech, Republican Rally

A classic – something that everybody wants to have read and nobody wants to read.
speech 'The Disappearance of Literature'

I am not one of those who in expressing opinions confine themselves to facts. I don't know anything that mars good literature so completely as too much truth.
speech 'The Savage Club Dinner'

It seems to me that just in the ratio that our newspapers increase, our morals decay.
speech 'License of the Press'

That awful power, the public opinion of a nation, is created in America by a horde of ignorant, self-complacent simpletons who failed at ditching and shoemaking and fetched up in journalism on their way to the poorhouse.
speech 'License of the Press'

It is noble to teach oneself, but still nobler to teach others – and less trouble.
speech 'Doctor Van Dyke'

I do not make any pretense that I dislike compliments. The stronger the better and I can manage to digest them.
speech, The Last Lotos Club

These natives are strange people – they can die whenever they want to – don't mind dying anymore than a jilted Frenchman.
speech, 'The Sandwich Islands'

There is nothing more beneficent than accident insurance. I have seen an entire family lifted out of poverty and into affluence by the simple boon of a broken leg.
speech, 'Accident Insurance'

I cannot keep from talking, even at the risk of being instructive.
speech, London

I don't believe any of you have ever read *Paradise Lost*, and you don't want to. That's something that you just want to take on trust. It's a classic ... something that everybody wants to have read and nobody wants to read.
at dinner of the Nineteenth Century Club, New York, 20 November 1900

Marriage – yes, it is the supreme felicity of life. I concede it. And it is also the supreme tragedy of life. The deeper the love, the surer the tragedy.
letter

Always do right. This will gratify some people, and astonish the rest.
note to Young People's Society

Some people lie when they tell the truth. I tell the truth lying.
Interview

I can't stand George **Eliot** and **Hawthorne** and those people. I see what they are at a hundred years before they get to it and they just tire me to death.
letter

As for *The Bostonians* [by Henry **James**], I would rather be damned to John **Bunyan's** heaven than read that.
letter

They [the Concord, Mass. Library] have expelled Huck from their library as 'trash and only suitable for the slums.' That will sell 25,000 copies for us sure.
letter

The reports of my death are greatly exaggerated.
Cablegram

Unexpected money is a delight. The same sum is a bitterness when you expect more.
letter

Thunder is good, thunder is impressive; but it is the lightning that does the work.
letter

Twenty-four years ago, Madam, I was incredibly handsome. The remains of it are still visible through the rift of time. I was so handsome that women became spellbound when I came in view. In San Francisco, in rainy seasons, I was frequently mistaken for a cloudless day.
from a letter written towards the end of his life

A tortoise-shell cat having a fit in a platter of tomatoes.
of Turner's The Slave Ship

They are a London specialty. God has not permitted them to exist elsewhere . . . All the modern inconveniences are furnished, and some that have been obsolete for a century. The bedrooms are hospitals for incurable furniture.
on London family hotels

Keep away from people who try to belittle your ambitions. Small people always do that, but the really great make you feel that you, too, can become great.

A banker is a fellow who lends you his umbrella when the sun is shining and wants it back the minute it begins to rain.

Giving up smoking is easy. I've done it hundreds of times.

As to the Adjective: when in doubt strike it out.

I take my only exercise acting as pallbearer at the funerals of my friends who exercise regularly.

I am pushing sixty. That is enough exercise for me.

The lack of money is the root of all evil.

What is the difference between a taxidermist and a tax collector? The taxidermist takes only your skin.

You can't reason someone out of something they weren't reasoned into.

All you need is ignorance and confidence; then success is assured.

In religion and politics, people's beliefs and convictions are in almost every case gotten at second hand, and without examination.

Fleas can be taught nearly everything a congressman can.

The man who doesn't read good books has no advantage over the man who can't read them.

When a man can prove that he is not a jackass, I think he is in the way to prove that he is no legitimate member of the race.

Damn these human beings; if I had invented them I would go hide my head in a bag.

Both marriage and death ought to be welcome: the one promises happiness, doubtless the other assures it.

A baby is an inestimable blessing and bother.

This nation is like all the others that have been spewed upon the earth – ready to shout for any cause that will tickle its vanity or fill its pocket. What a hell of a heaven it will be when they get all these hypocrites assembled there!

Life should begin with age and its privileges and accumulations, and end with youth and its capacity to splendidly enjoy such advantage . . . It's an epitome of life. The first half of it consists of the capacity to enjoy without the chance. The last half consists of the chance without the capacity.

Yet, even I am dishonest. Not in many ways, but in some. Forty-one, I think.

When I was a boy of fourteen, my father was so ignorant I could hardly stand to have the old man around. But when I got to be twenty-one, I was astonished how much he had learned in seven years.
    attributed

A lie can travel halfway round the world while the truth is putting on its shoes.
    attributed

He was good natured, obliging and immensely ignorant, and was endowed with a stupidity which by the least little stretch would go around the globe four times and tie.
    Autobiography (1924)

All you need in this life is ignorance and confidence; then success is sure.
    quoted in *When Huck Went Highbrow*, ed. Benjamin de Carseres (1934)

Sane and intelligent human beings are like all other human beings, and carefully and cautiously and diligently conceal their private real opinions from the world and give out fictitious ones in their stead for general consumption.
    Mark Twain In Eruption (1940)

Jill Tweedie 1936-93
British journalist

I blame the women's movement for ten years in a boiler suit.
    attributed, 1989

The Two Ronnies British television comedy series 1971-87

A cement mixer today collided with a prison van on the Kingston bypass. Motorists are asked to look out for sixteen hardened criminals.

A lorry with a cargo of cheese has today collided with another lorry in South Wales. Motorists are asked to drive Caerphilly.

Alexander Tyler 1747-1813
Scottish-born British lawyer and writer

A democracy will continue to exist up until the time that voters discover that they can vote themselves generous gifts from the public treasury. From that moment on, the majority always votes for the candidates who promise the most benefits from the public treasury, with the result that every democracy will finally collapse due to loose fiscal policy, which is always followed by a dictatorship.

Kenneth Tynan 1927-80
English theatre critic

Oh, I think so, certainly. I doubt if there are very many rational people in this world to whom the word 'fuck' is particularly diabolical or revolting or totally forbidden.
   on 14 November 1965 on a late-night programme called BBC-3; the comment caused considerable outrage
   Kathleen Tynan (ed.) *Kenneth Tynan: Letter* (1994)

U

Tracey Ullman 1959-
British actress

The most remarkable thing about my mother is that for 30 years she served nothing but leftovers. The original meal was never found.
   in *Observer* 23 May 1999

Kay Ullrich 1943-
Scottish Nationalist politician

As a lady of a certain age, I am willing to let the photographers and their zoom lenses stay, but only if they use their Joan Collins lens on me for close-ups.
on the decision to ban photographers from the debating chamber of the Scottish Parliament
   Scotsman 18 March 2000

Miguel de Unamuno 1864-1937
Spanish philosopher and short-story writer

Life is doubt,
And faith without doubt is nothing but death.
   'Salmo II' (1907)

John Updike 1932-2009
American novelist, poet, short story writer, art critic and literary critic

I've never much enjoyed going to plays . . . The unreality of painted people standing on a platform saying things they've said to each other for months is more than I can overlook.
   George Plimpton (ed.) *Writers at Work* (1977)

America is a vast conspiracy to make you happy.
   Problems and Other Stories (1985)

Any activity becomes creative when the doer cares about doing it right, or better.
   Problems and Other Stories (1985)

A mistress knows the man to be a liar, where the wife only guesses.
   Terrorist (2006)

You shouldn't sit in judgment of your parents. We did the best we could while being people too.
   Rabbit at Rest (1990)

A healthy male adult bore consumes *each year* one and a half times his own weight in other people's patience.
   Assorted Prose (1956) 'Confessions of a Wild Bore'

A soggy little island huffing and puffing to keep up with Western Europe.
of England
  Picked Up Pieces (1976) 'London Life' (written 1969)

I sometimes think I shall never view
A French film lacking Gérard Depardieu.

Peter Ustinov 1921-2004
British actor, writer, dramatist, filmmaker, theatre and opera director, stage designer, screenwriter, comedian, humorist, newspaper and magazine columnist, radio broadcaster, television presenter, wit, raconteur, intellectual and diplomat

I believe that the Jews have made a contribution to the human condition out of all proportion to their numbers: I believe them to be an immense people. Not only have they supplied the world with two leaders of the stature of Jesus Christ and Karl Marx, but they have even indulged in the luxury of following neither one nor the other.
Dear Me (1977)

At the age of four with paper hats and wooden swords we're all Generals. Only some of us never grow out of it.
Romanoff and Juliet (1956)

Laughter would be bereaved if snobbery died.
  in *Observer* 13 March 1955

Toronto is a kind of New York operated by the Swiss.
  in *Globe & Mail* 1 August 1987; attributed

The only reason I made a commercial for American Express was to pay for my American Express bill.

The difference between Maggie **Thatcher** and **Joan of Arc** is that Thatcher only hears her own voice.

V

Marcus Valerius Martialis 40-103
Roman poet

Why do strong arms fatigue themselves with frivolous dumbbells? To dig a vineyard is worthier exercise for men.

Paul Valéry 1871-1945
French poet, essayist and philosopher

The following quotations are from *Tel Quel* (1941):

Politics is the art of preventing people from sticking their noses into things that are properly their business.

An attitude of permanent indignation signifies great mental poverty. Politics compels its votaries to take that line and you can see their minds growing more and more impoverished every day, from one burst of righteous anger to the next.

God created man and, finding him not sufficiently alone, gave him a companion to make him feel his solitude more keenly.

Sir John Vanbrugh 1664-1726
English architect and dramatist

No man worth having is true to his wife or can be true to his wife, or ever was, or ever will be so.
The Relapse (1696)

Two years' marriage has debauched my five senses. Everything I see, everything I hear, everything I feel, everything I smell, and everything I taste, methinks has wife in't.
The Provok'd Wife (1697)

Ernest Van Den Haag 1914-2002
Dutch-American sociologist and social critic

The less we are sustained by faith in a world beyond, the more reluctant we are to give up the hope of paradise this side of eternity.
Punishing Criminals (1975)

Laurens Van der Post 1906-96
Afrikaner author, farmer, war hero, political adviser to British heads of government, close friend of **Prince Charles**, godfather of **Prince William**, educator, journalist, humanitarian, philosopher, explorer and conservationist

Human beings are perhaps never more frightening than when they are convinced beyond doubt that they are right.
The Lost World of the Kalahari (1958)

Henry Van Dyke 1852-1933
American author, educator, and clergyman

Use what talent you possess: the woods would be very silent if no birds sang except those that sang best.

William E ('Bill') Vaughan 1915-77
American author and columnist

Money won't buy you happiness, but it will pay the salaries of a large research staff to study the problem.

Ralph Vaughan Williams 1872-1958
English composer

I don't know whether I like it, but it's what I meant.
on his 4th symphony
   Christopher Headington *Bodley Head History of Western Music* (1974)

Marquis de Vauvenargues 1715-47
French moralist, essayist and author

It is not true that equality is a law of nature. Nature has no equality. Its sovereign law is subordination and dependence.

To achieve great things we must live as though we were never going to die.

The greatest achievement of the human spirit is to live up to one's opportunities and make the most of one's resources.

Robert Veninga

Human pain does not let go of its grip at one point in time. Rather, it works its way out of our consciousness over time. There is a season of sadness. A season of anger. A season of tranquility. A season of hope.

Robert Venturi 1925-
American architect, pioneer of postmodernist architecture

Less is a bore.
   Complexity and Contradiction in Architecture (1966)

Gianni Versace 1949-97
Italian designer, known for his extravagant designs for both men and women

I like to dress egos. If you haven't got an ego today, you can forget it.
   in *Guardian* 16 July 1997 'Obituary'

A. Lou Vickery

Nothing average ever stood as a monument to progress. When progress is looking for a partner it doesn't turn to those who believe they are only average. It turns instead to those who are forever searching and striving to become the best they possibly can. If we seek the average level we cannot hope to achieve a high level of success. Our only hope is to avoid being a failure.

Queen Victoria 1819-1901
Queen of the United Kingdom of Great Britain and Ireland 1837-1901

He speaks to me as if I was a public meeting.
of Gladstone
G. W. E. Russell *Collections and Recollections* (1898)

The danger to the country, to Europe, to her vast Empire, which is involved in having all these great interests entrusted to the shaking hand of an old, wild, and incomprehensible man of 82, is very great!
on Gladstone's last appointment as Prime Minister
letter to Lord Lansdowne, 12 August 1892

The Queen is most anxious to enlist every one who can speak or write to join in checking this mad, wicked folly of 'Woman's Rights', with all its attendant horrors, on which her poor feeble sex is bent, forgetting every sense of womanly feeling and propriety.
letter to Theodore Martin, 29 May 1870

Gore Vidal 1925-
American author, playwright, essayist, screenwriter and political activist

It is not enough to succeed. Others must fail.
G. Irvine *Antipanegyric for Tom Driberg* 8 December 1976

I'm all for bringing back the birch, but only between consenting adults.
in *Sunday Times Magazine* 16 September 1973

Whenever a friend succeeds, a little something in me dies.
in *Sunday Times Magazine* 16 September 1973

A triumph of the embalmer's art.
of Ronald Reagan
in *Observer* 26 April 1981

A genius with the IQ of a moron.
of Andy Warhol
in *Observer* 18 June 1989

A narcissist is someone better looking than you are.
in *New York Times* 12 March 1981

Good career move.
of Truman Capote's death
attributed

Any American who is prepared to run for President should automatically, by definition, be disqualified from ever doing so.

He will lie even when it is inconvenient: the sign of the true artist.
attributed

Half of the American people never read a newspaper. Half never voted for President. One hopes it is the same half.

Stephen Vincent Benet 1898-1943
American author, poet, short story writer and novelist

We thought, because we had power, we had wisdom.
Litany for Dictatorships (1935)

Virgil 70-19BC
Roman poet

I sing of arms and of the man, fated to be an exile.
The Aeneid (29-19BC)

John Viscount Morley 1838-1923
British Liberal statesman, writer and newspaper editor

You have not converted a man because you have silenced him.

It is not enough to do good; one must do it the right way.

Viz British adult comic magazine 1979-

I have never been attracted to another man, but I like to touch myself around my penis when I masturbate. As a result, I am worried that I might be homosexual. What do readers thing?
fake reader's letter, signed 'Big Straight Jock, Glasgow' May 2003

Philanderers: Avoid the embarrassment of shouting out the wrong name in bed by only having flings with girls who have the same name as your wife.
'Top Tips' August 2003

Stephen Vizinczey 1933-
Hungarian author

Modesty is an excuse for sloppiness, laziness, self- indulgence; small ambitions evoke small efforts.
Truth and Lies in Literature

Voltaire, pseudonym of François-Marie Arouet 1694-1778
Writer, essayist.

The art of government consists in taking as much money as possible from one class of citizens to give to the other.
Dictionnaire philosophique (1764)

This agglomeration which was called and which still calls itself the Holy Roman Empire was neither holy, nor Roman, nor an Empire.
Essai sur l'histoire générale et sur les moeurs at l'esprit des nations (1756)

One day Cunegonde was walking near the castle, in the little copse which was known as 'the park', when through the bushes he saw Dr Pangloss giving a lesson in applied physics to her mother's maid, a pretty and obliging little brunette.
Candide (1759)

Governments need both shepherds and butchers.
   'The Piccini Notebooks' (c.1735-50)

If one must serve, I hold it better to serve a well-bred lion, who is naturally stronger than I am, than two hundred rats of my own breed.
   letter to a friend; Alexis de Tocqueville *Ancien Régime (1856)*

I disapprove of what you say, but I will defend to the death your right to say it.

It is dangerous to be right when the government is wrong.

Every man is guilty of all the good he didn't do.

To succeed in the world it is not enough to be stupid, you must also be well-mannered.

You despise books; you whose lives are absorbed in the vanities of ambition, the pursuit of pleasure or indolence; but remember that all the known world, excepting only savage nations, is governed by books.

Marriage is the only adventure open to the cowardly.

To succeed in chaining the crowd you must seem to wear the same fetters.
   attributed

Kurt Vonnegut 1922-2007
American novelist, satirist, humanist and honorary president of the American Humanist Association

Thanks to TV and for the convenience of TV, you can only be one of two kinds of human beings, either a liberal or a conservative.
   In These Times, May 10 2004

Bernard de Voto 1897-1955
American historian and writer

You can no more keep a martini in the refrigerator than you can keep a kiss there. The proper union of gin and vermouth . . . is one of the happiest marriages on earth and one of the shortest lived.
   Harper's Magazine December 1949

W

Charles Wadsworth
American classical pianist and musical promoter

By the time a man realizes that maybe his father was right, he usually has a son who thinks he's wrong.

Loudon Wainwright III 1946-
American songwriter, folk singer, humorist and actor

No, I'm *not* going to sing that song. I'm going to sing a song *I* want to sing. My therapist has told me to be *particularly* assertive towards women.
   to a female fan in the audience, who had just shouted out a song request

Tom Waits 1949-
American singer-songwriter, composer and actor

You have to keep busy. After all, no dog's ever pissed on a moving car.

I don't have a drink problem, except when I can't get one.

Lord Waldegrave 1946-
British Conservative politician

In exceptional circumstances it is necessary to say something that is untrue in the House of Commons.
   to a House of Commons Select Committee
   Guardian 9 March 1994

It was much more what cabinet government is supposed to be like ... the problem was that when people began to be disloyal later on, they were not very frightened of him.
   *of John **Major** as Prime Minister*

Labour are pushing lies through our doorstep.

George Walden 1939-
Conservative Party politician and author, father of Celia **Walden**, the beautiful and talented *Daily Telegraph* columnist

Why has there been a sharp rise in emigration to a million people, particularly amongst the young? Why is no one talking about what's happening in our country? Why do we all have to watch our tongues, and think the same? If an Englishman is no longer at liberty to say out loud and in all honesty what he sees before him, what's the point of remaining English?
   Time to Emigrate? (2006)

Jimmy Wales 1966-
American Internet entrepreneur, co-founder and promoter of Wikipedia

Wikipedia is a non-profit. It was either the dumbest thing I ever did or the smartest thing I ever did. Communities can build amazing things, but you have to be part of that community and you can't abuse them. You have to be very respectful of what their needs are.
   keynote speech, SXSW (2006)

Walter Walker 1883-1956
Democratic Party politician

Britain has invented a new missile. It's called the civil servant – it doesn't work and it can't be fired.

George Wallace 1919-98
Democratic Party politician

I've seen many politicians paralyzed in the legs as myself, but I've seen more of them who were paralyzed in the head.

Edmund Waller 1606-87
English poet

Others may use the ocean as their road,
Only the English make it their abode.
   'Of a War with Spain' (1658)

Wall Street 1987 film

Gordon Gekko (Michael Douglas)
Greed – for lack of a better word – is good. Greed is right. Greed works.

Horace Walpole (4th Earl of Orford) 1717-97
English art historian, man of letters, antiquarian and politician

They seem to know no medium between a mitre and a crown of martyrdom. If the clergy are not called to the latter, they never deviate from the pursuit of the former. One would think their motto was, *Canterbury or Smithfield*.
   in 1758; *Memoirs of the Reign of King George II* (1946) vol. 2

By the waters of Babylon we sit down and weep, when we think of thee, O America!
   letter to Revd William Mason, 12 June 1775

A philosophising serpent . . . that hyena in petticoats.
of feminist Mary Wollstonecraft

Robert Walpole 1676-1745
English Whig statesman; first British Prime Minister, 1721-42; father of Horace Walpole

All those men have their price.
of fellow parliamentarians
   W. Coxe *Memoirs of Sir Robert Walpole* (1798)

No man is fit for business with a ruffled temper.
>the normally imperturbable Walpole having lost his temper at a Council, broke up the meeting
Edmund Fitzmaurice *Life of Shelburne* (1875)

There is enough pasture for all the sheep.
on his ability to spread round patronage satisfactorily
attributed

Julie Walters 1950-
British actress

I have a rare intolerance to herbs which means I can only drink fermented liquids, such as gin.
in *Observer* 14 March 1999

Clare Ward 1972-
British Labour politician

I don't always admit to being an MP. If I'm in a bar with people I don't know, to say you're a Labour MP isn't always a good move. I have said I'm a solicitor.
Independent on Sunday 14 March 1999

Charles Dudley Warner 1829-1900
American writer and editor

Politics makes strange bedfellows.
My Summer in a Garden (1871)

Sylvia Townsend Warner 1893-1978
English writer

One cannot overestimate the power of a good rancorous hatred on the part of the *stupid*. The stupid have so much more industry and energy to expend on hating. They build it up like coral insects.
diary, 26 September 1954

George Washington 1732-99
American statesman; 1st President of the United States

The time is now near at hand which must probably determine whether Americans are to be freemen or slaves; whether they are to have any property they can call their own . . . The fate of unborn millions will now depend, under God, on the courage and conduct of this army. Our cruel and unrelenting enemy leaves us only the choice of brave resistance, or the most abject submission. We have, therefore, to resolve to conquer or die.
General orders, 2 July 1776, in J. C. Fitzpatrick (ed.) *Writings of George Washington* (1932)

Keith Waterhouse 1929 - 2009
English novelist, newspaper columnist, television series writer

Jeffrey Bernard is unwell.
the Spectator's habitual explanation for the non-appearance of Jeffrey Bernard's column
title of play (1989)

Brighton has the perennial air of being in a position to help the police with their inquiries.

It is a town that looks as if it has been out on the tiles all night.
on Brighton

Maxine Waters 1938-
Democratic Party politician

I have a right to my anger, and I don't want anybody telling me I shouldn't be, that it's not nice to be, and that something's wrong with me because I get angry.'

Denis Watley

The reason most people never reach their goals is that they don't define them, or ever seriously consider them as believable or achievable. Winners can tell you where they are going, what they plan to do along the way, and who will be sharing the adventure with them.

Bill Watterson 1958-
American cartoonist, *Calvin and Hobbes*

I'm right and everybody else is wrong! See, now everyone's happy!

God put me on this earth to accomplish a certain number of things. Right now I am so far behind that I will never die.

Ethel Watts Mumford 1876-1940
American authoress

Knowledge is power, if you know it about the right person.

Auberon Waugh 1939-2001
British author and journalist

No man is so boring, or so unpleasant or unattractive that he cannot find an equally boring, unpleasant or unattractive woman to be his life's companion if he sets his mind to it, and I have no doubt that the same must be true in the homosexual world.
Another Voice The Nilsen Millennium (1986)

Few even pretend to enjoy the job, they make no secret of despising their customers and being in it only for the money . . . If a job is worth doing at all, it is worth doing well, and these women are a disgrace.
of prostitutes
Spectator 25 May 1985

Evelyn Waugh 1903-66
English novelist

I expect you'll be becoming a schoolmaster, sir. That's what most of the gentlemen does, sir, that gets sent down for indecent behaviour.
Decline and Fall (1928)

The sound of English county families baying for broken glass.
Decline and Fall (1928)

Anyone who has been to an English public school will always feel comparatively at home in prison. It is the people brought up in the gay intimacy of the slums, Paul learned, who find prison so soul-destroying.
Decline and Fall (1928)

All this fuss about sleeping together. For physical pleasure I'd sooner go to my dentist any day.
Vile Bodies (1930)

You might think about me a bit and whether ... you could bear the idea of marrying me . . . I can't advise you in my favour because I think it would be beastly for you, but think how nice it would be for me.
letter to Laura **Herbert** of spring 1936

Feather-footed through the plashy fen passes the questing vole.
Scoop (1938)

Other nations use 'force'; we Britons alone use 'Might'.
Scoop (1938)

I believe that inequalities of wealth and position are inevitable and that it is therefore meaningless to discuss the advantages of their elimination.
Mexico: An Object Lesson (1939)

To see him fumbling with our rich and delicate language is to experience all the horror of seeing a Sèvres vase in the hands of a chimpanzee.
*of Stephen **Spender***
  in *Tablet* 5 May 1951

Army always queer in best regiments, hence decent appearance.
postcard to Penelope **Betjeman** of 3 July 1956, collected in *The Letters of Evelyn Waugh* ed. Mary Amory (1980)

'In a democracy,' said Mr Pinfold, with more weight than originality, 'Men do not seek authority so that they may impose a policy. They seek a policy so that they may achieve authority.'
The Ordeal of Gilbert Pinfold (1957)

He abhorred plastics, Picasso, sunbathing and jazz – everything in fact that had happened in his own lifetime.
The Ordeal of Gilbert Pinfold (1957)

It was a typical triumph of modern science to find the only part of Randolph that was not malignant and remove it.
it had been announced after an operation on Randolph Churchill that a tumour was 'not malignant'
Michael Davie (ed.) *Diaries of Evelyn Waugh* (1976)

You would have no idea how much nastier I would be if I was not a Catholic. Without supernatural aid I would hardly be a human being.
Noel Annan *Our Age* (1990)

Richard M. Weaver 1910-1963
American scholar

Hysterical optimism is a sin against knowledge.
Ideas Have Consequences (1948)

No thoughtful person can feel that we have found means of getting our political authority regularly into the hands of the wise.
Ideas Have Consequences (1948)

The idea of virtue is assimilated and grows into character through exercise, which means freedom of action in a world in which not all things are good.
The Intercollegiate Review, September 1965

Beatrice Webb 1858-1943
English socialist

Restless, almost intolerably so, without capacity for sustained and unexcited labour, egotistical, bumptious, shallow-minded and reactionary, but with a personal magnetism, great pluck and some originality, not of intellect but of character.
*in 1903, of Winston **Churchill***
Martin Gilbert *In Search of Churchill* (1994)

If I ever felt inclined to be timid as I was going into a room full of people, I would say to myself, 'You're the cleverest member of one of the cleverest families in the cleverest class of the cleverest nation in the world, why should you be frightened?'
Bertrand Russell *Autobiography* (1967)

Sidney Webb 1859-1947
English socialist

Once we face the necessity of putting our principles first into Bills, to be fought through committee clause by clause; and then into the appropriate machinery for carrying them into execution from one end of the kingdom to the other . . . the inevitability of gradualness cannot fail to be appreciated.
presidential address to the annual conference of the Labour Party, 26 June 1923

Marriage is the waste-paper basket of the emotions.
Bertrand Russell *Autobiography* (1967)

Max Weber 1864-1920
German sociologist

The Protestant ethic and the spirit of capitalism.
Archiv für Sozialwissenschaft Sozialpolitik

The State is a relation of men dominating men, a relation supported by means of legitimate (i.e. considered to be legitimate) violence.
'Politik als Beruf' (1919)

Simon Weil 1909-43
French essayist and philosopher

I would suggest that barbarism be considered as a permanent and universal human characteristic which becomes more or less pronounced according to the play of circumstances.
Écrits historiques et politiques (1960)

All sins are attempts to fill voids.
La pesanteur et la grâce (1948)

Max Weinreich 1894-1969
Russian-born linguist

A language is a dialect with an army and a navy.

Chaim Weizmann 1874-1952
Russian-born Israeli statesman; President 1949-52

Something had been done for us which, after two thousand years of hope and yearning, would at last give us a resting-place in this terrible world.
of the Balfour declaration
speech in Jerusalem, 25 November 1936

Thomas Earle Welby 1881-1933
English writer

'Turbot, Sir,' said the waiter, placing before me two fishbones, two eyeballs, and a bit of black mackintosh.
The Dinner Knell (1932)

Fay Weldon 1931-
British novelist and scriptwriter

Natalie had left the wives and joined the women.
Heart of the Country (1987)

What makes women happy? Nothing, for more than ten minutes at a time, so stop worrying.
What Makes Women Happy (2006)

Orson Welles 1915-85
American film director, writer, actor and producer

In Italy for thirty years under the Borgias they had warfare, terror, murder and bloodshed but they produced Michelangelo, Leonardo da Vinci and the Renaissance. In Switzerland, they had brotherly love; they had five hundred years of democracy and peace and what did that produce? The cuckoo clock.
The Third Man (1949)

I hate television. I hate it as much as I hate peanuts. But I can't stop eating peanuts.
in *New York Herald Tribune* 12 October 1956

There are only two emotions in a plane: boredom and terror.
interview to celebrate his 70th birthday, in *Times* 6 May 1985

1st Duke of Wellington (Arthur Wellesley) 1769-1852
Anglo-Irish soldier and statesman

Hard pounding this, gentlemen; let's see who will pound the longest.
at the Battle of Waterloo
Sir Walter Scott *Paul's Letters* (1816)

Publish and be damned.
replying to Harriet Wilson's blackmail threat, c.1825
attributed; Elizabeth Longford *Wellington: The Years of the Sword* (1969)

An extraordinary affair. I gave them their orders and they wanted to stay and discuss them.
of his first Cabinet meeting as Prime Minister
   Peter Hennessy *Whitehall* (1990)

I used to say of him [**Napoléon**] that his presence on the field made the difference of forty thousand men.
   Philip Henry Stanhope *Notes of Conversations with the Duke of Wellington* (1888)

I never saw so many shocking bad hats in my life.
on seeing the first Reformed Parliament
   William Fraser *Words on Wellington* (1889)

You must build your House of Parliament upon the river . . . the populace cannot exact their demands by sitting down round you.
   William Fraser *Words on Wellington* (1889)

Nothing the people of this country like so much as to see their great men take part in their amusements. The aristocracy will commit a great error if they ever fail to mix freely with their neighbours.
on foxhunting
   Philip Henry Stanhope *Notes of Conversations with the Duke of Wellington* (1888)

All the business of war, and indeed all the business of life, is to endeavour to find out what you don't know by what you do; that's what I called 'guessing what was at the other side of the hill.'
   in *The Croker Papers* (1885)

The battle of Waterloo was won on the playing fields of Eton.
   oral tradition, but not found in this form of words; C. F. R. Montalembert *De l'avenir politique de l'Angleterre* (1856)

I have no small talk and **Peel** has no manners.
   G. W. E. Russell *Collections and Recollections* (1898)

Next to a battle lost, the greatest misery is a battle gained.
   in *Diary of Frances, Lady Shelley 1787-1817*

Try sparrow-hawks, Ma'am.
*on being asked by **Queen Victoria** how hundreds of sparrows could be removed from the Glass Palace of the Great Exhibition (1851)*

I have seen their backs before.
when French marshals turned their backs on him at a reception

As Lord Chesterfield said of the generals of his day, 'I only hope that when the enemy reads the list of their names, he trembles as I do.'
   usually quoted as 'I don't know what effect these men will have upon the enemy, but, by God, they frighten me'
   letter, 29 August 1810

Trust nothing to the enthusiasm of the people. Given them a strong and a just, and, if possible, a good, government; but, above all, a strong one.
   letter to Lord William **Bentinck**, 24 December 1811

H. G. Wells 1866-1946
English author

The Social Contract is nothing more or less than a vast conspiracy of human beings to lie to an humbug themselves and one another for the general Good. Lies are the mortar that bind the savage individual man into the social masonry.
Love and Mr Lewisham (1900)

Human history becomes more and more a race between education and catastrophe.
Outline of History (1920)

In England we have come to rely upon a comfortable time-lag of fifty years or a century intervening between the perception that something ought to be done and a serious attempt to do it.
The Work, Wealth and Happiness of Mankind (1931)

Man is born a predestined idealist, for he is born to act. To act is to affirm the worth of an end, and to persist in affirming the worth of an end is to make an ideal.

Man's mind, once stretched by a new idea, never regains its original dimensions.

Non-violence is the policy of the vegetable kingdom.

Go away. I'm all right.
Last words

Irvine Welsh 1957-
Scottish novelist

It's nae good blamin' it oan the English fir colonising us. Ah don't hate the English. They're just wankers. We can't even pick a decent vibrant, healthy culture to be colonised by.
Trainspotting (1994)

Eudora Welty 1909-2001
American novelist, short-story writer, and critic

I am a writer who came of a sheltered life.
A sheltered life can be a daring life as well.
For all serious daring starts from within.
One Writer's Beginnings (1984)

Oliver Wendell Holmes Jr. 1841-1935
American lawyer

The utterly distinguished Justice Wendell Holmes once boarded a train in Washington D.C. but soon found out that he had lost his ticket. The conductor recognized him and said, 'Don't worry about it, sir. I'm sure when you find it, you'll send it in.' Justice Holmes replied: 'Young man, the question is not, Where is my ticket?, but rather, without it, how am I supposed to know where I am going?'
source untraced

Oliver Wendell Holmes Sr. 1809-94
American physician, medical reformer, professor, lecturer and author

Man has his will – but woman has her way.

Nature, when she invented, manufactured and patented her authors, contrived to make critics out of the chips that were left.

Arnold Wesker 1932-
English dramatist

The Khomeini cry for the execution of Rushdie is an infantile cry. From the beginning of time we have seen that. To murder the thinker does not murder the thought.
   in *Weekend Guardian* 3 June 1989

Mae West 1892-1980
American actress, playwright, screenwriter and sex symbol

Between two evils, I always pick the one I never tried before.
   Klondike Annie (1936 film)

Give a man a free hand and he'll try to put it all over you.
   Klondike Annie (1936 film)

It's better to be looked over than overlooked.
   Belle of the Nineties (1934 film)

It's not the men in my life that counts – it's the life in my men.
   I'm No Angel (1933 film)

Beulah, peel me a grape.
   I'm No Angel (1933 film)

When I'm good, I'm very, very good, but when I'm bad, I'm better.
   I'm No Angel (1933 film)

'Goodness, what beautiful diamonds!'
'Goodness had nothing to do with it.'
   Night After Night (1932 film)

I used to be Snow White . . . but I drifted.
   J. Weintraub *Peel Me a Grape* (1975)

I've been in *Who's Who*, and I know what's what, but it'll be the first time I ever made the dictionary.
   letter to the RAF, early 1940s, on having an inflatable life jacket named after her
   Fergus Cash *Mae West* (1981)

A curved line is the loveliest distance between two points.

A hard man is good to find.
   attributed

You only live once, but if you do it right, once is enough.

MAE: How tall are you, son?
MAN: Ma-am, I'm six feet seven inches.
MAE: Let's forget about the six feet and talk about the seven inches.

Is that a gun in your pocket or are you just pleased to see me?

Rebecca West 1892-1983
English novelist and journalist

The point is that nobody likes having salt rubbed into their wounds, even if it is the salt of the earth.
The Salt of the Earth (1935)

There is, of course, no reason for the existence of the male sex except that sometimes one needs help with moving the piano.
in *Sunday Telegraph* 28 June 1970

There is no such thing as conversation. It is an illusion. There are intersecting monologues, that is all.
'The Harsh Voice' (1935)

Life ought to be a struggle of desire toward adventures whose nobility will fertilise the soul.

Loelia, Duchess of Westminster 1902-93
English aristocrat

Anybody seen in a bus over the age of thirty has been a failure in life.
Cocktails and Laughter (1983); habitual remark

William C. Westmoreland 1914-2005
American general

Vietnam was the first war ever fought without censorship. Without censorship, things can get terribly confused in the public mind.
attributed, 1982

John Fane, Lord Westmorland 1759-1841
English peer

Merit, indeed . . . We are come to a pretty pass if they talk of *merit* for a bishopric.
noted in Lady Salisbury's diary, 9 December 1835

R. P. Weston 1878-1936 and Bert Lee 1880-1947
British songwriters

Good-bye-ee! – Good-bye-ee!
Wipe the tear, baby dear, from your eye-ee!
Tho' it's hard to part, I know,
I'll be tickled to death to go.
Don't cry-ee – don't sigh'ee!
Bonsoir, old thing! cheerio! chin-chin!
Nahpoo! Toodle-oo! Good-bye-ee!
'Good-bye-ee!' (c.1915 song)

Edith Wharton 1862-1937
American novelist, short story writer and designer

Mrs Ballinger is one of the ladies who pursue Culture in bands, as though it were dangerous to meet it alone.
Xingu and Other Stories (1916) 'Xingu'

There are lots of ways of being miserable, but there's only one way of being comfortable, and that's to stop running round after happiness. If you make up your mind not to be happy there's no reason why you shouldn't have a fairly good time.
The Last Asset (1904)

To your generation, I must represent the literary equivalent of tufted furniture and gas chandeliers.
letter to F. Scott Fitzgerald, 8 June 1925

Ella Wheeler Wilcox 1850-1919
American author and poet

Laugh, and the world laughs with you;
Weep, and you weep alone.
Solitude (1883)

No question is ever settled until it is settled right.

Alan Whicker 1925-
British journalist and broadcaster

It's annoying when you land in Scandinavia and they speak better English than you do.

James McNeill Whistler 1834-1903
American painter

Why drag in Velasquez?
to enthusiast who said she knew of only two painters in the world, himself and Velasquez
quoted in D. C. Seitz, *Whistler Stories* (1913)

E. B. White 1899-1985
American writer

Democracy is the recurrent suspicion that more than half of the people are right more than half the time.
New Yorker, July 3, 1944

Hugh White 1773-1840
American politician

When you make a mistake, don't look back at it long. Take the reason of the thing and then look forward. Mistakes are lessons of wisdom. The past cannot be changed. The future is yet in your power.

Theodore H. White 1915-86
American writer and journalist

Johnson's instinct for power is as primordial as a salmon's going upstream to spawn.
of Lyndon Johnson
   The Making of the President (1964)

The flood of money that gushes into politics today is a pollution of democracy.
   in *Time* 19 November 1984

Alfred North Whitehead 1861-1947
English philosopher and mathematician

Art is the imposing of a pattern on experience, and our aesthetic enjoyment is recognition of the pattern.
   Dialogues (1954) 10 June 1943

Intelligence is quickness to apprehend as distinct from ability, which is capacity to act wisely on the thing apprehended.
   Dialogues (1954) 15 December 1939

What is morality in any given time or place? It is what the majority then and there happen to like, and immorality is what they dislike.
   Dialogues (1954) 30 August 1941

Wisdom alone is true ambitions aim,
Wisdom the source of virtue, and of fame,
Obtained with labor, for mankind employed,
And then, when most you share it, best enjoyed.

The vitality of thought is in adventure. Ideas won't keep. Something must be done about them.

The total absence of humour from the Bible is one of the most singular things in all literature.

Katharine Whitehorn 1928-
British photographic model for advertisement for the energy drink Lucozade, writer, journalist, editor and broadcaster

Being young is not having any money; being young is not minding not having any money.
   Observations (1970)

The easiest way for your children to learn about money is for you not to have any.
   How to Survive Children (1975)

An office party is not, as is sometimes supposed, the Managing Director's chance to kiss the tea-girl. It is the tea-girl's chance to kiss the Managing Director, however bizarre an ambition this may seem to anyone who has seen the Managing Director face on.
   Roundabout (1962) 'The Office Party'

I wouldn't say when you've seen one Western you've seen the lot; but when you've seen the lot you get the feeling you've seen one.
   Sunday Best (1976) 'Decoding the West'

Outside every thin girl is a fat man, trying to get in.

The trouble with so many born-again people is that you wish they hadn't been born the first time.

I am all for people having their heart in the right place; but the right place for a heart is not inside the head.

I am firm. You are obstinate. He is a pig-headed fool.

Americans, indeed, often seem to be so overwhelmed by their children that they'll do anything for them except stay married to the co-producer.

William Whitelaw 1918-99
British Conservative politician

Those who say I am not in agreement with the policy are, rightly or wrongly, quite wrong.
on immigration

I have the thermometer in my mouth and I am listening to it all the time.
using an unfortunate choice of words in October 1974 during an election campaign

Harold **Wilson** is going around the country stirring up apathy.
of the British Prime Minister during the 1970 General Election

We mustn't pre-judge the past.

I don't blame anyone except perhaps all of us.

It is never wise to appear to be more clever than you are. It is sometimes wise to appear slightly less so.
attributed, 1975

Walt Whitman 1819-1892
American poet, essayist, journalist and humanist

Where the populace rise at once against the never-ending audacity of elected persons.
Song of the Broad Axe (1881)

The United States themselves are essentially the greatest poem.
Leaves of Grass (1855) preface

Strange, (is it not?) that battles, martyrs, blood, even assassination, should so condense – perhaps only really, lastingly condense – a Nationality.
of the American Civil War
Geoffrey C. Ward *The Civil War* (1991)

The genius of the United States is not best or most in its executives or legislatures, nor in its ambassadors or authors or colleges, or churches, or parlors, nor even in its newspapers or inventors, but always most in the common people.

Robert Whittington 1480-1553
English grammarian

As time requireth, a man of marvellous mirth and pastimes, and sometimes of sad gravity, as who say: a man for all seasons.
of Thomas More
   Vulgaria (1521)

Ann Widdecombe 1947-
British Conservative Party politician, television presenter and novelist

He has something of the night about him.
on Michael Howard

How dare he tell me what to do when he has a circumference to rival the equator.
after Frank Dobson, then Health Minister, advised her to take more fibre to reduce her weight in 1998

I think you have to be very careful when you say, 'God is on my side'. I much prefer to say, 'I am on God's side.'

Elie Wiesel 1928-
Romanian-born American writer and Nobel prize winner; Auschwitz survivor

God of forgiveness, do not forgive those murderers of Jewish children here.
of Auschwitz
   in *The Times* 27 January 1995

The opposite of love is not hate, it's indifference. The opposite of art is not ugliness, it's indifference. The opposite of faith is not heresy, it's indifference. And the opposite of life is not death, it's indifference.
   in *U. S. News and World Report* 27 October 1986

Ultimately, the only power to which man should aspire is that which he exercises over himself.

William Wilberforce 1759-1833
British politician, philanthropist, and abolitionist

As soon as ever I had arrived thus far in my investigation of the slave trade, I confess to you, so enormous, so dreadful, so irremediable did its wickedness appear that my own mind was completely made up for the abolition.
   speech, 12 May 1789; in W. Cobbett et al. (eds.) *The Parliamentary History of England* (1806-20)

Richard Wilbur 1921-
American poet

Mind in its purest play is like some bat
That beats about in caverns all alone,
Contriving by a kind of senseless wit
Not to conclude against a wall of stone.
   'Mind' (1956)

Oscar Wilde 1854-1900
Irish playwright, aesthete, poet, author of numerous short stories and one novel. In 1884 he married Constance Lloyd, who later bore their two sons

Democracy means simply the bludgeoning of the people by the people for the people.
The Soul of Man Under Socialism (1881)

Disobedience, in the eyes of anyone who has read history, is man's original virtue. It is through disobedience and rebellion that progress has been made.
The Soul of Man Under Socialism (1881)

The following quotations are from *The Picture of Dorian Gray* (1891):

Anybody can be good in the country. There are no temptations there.

Faithfulness is to the emotional life what consistency is to the life of the intellect, simply a confession of failure.

Young men want to be faithful and are not; old men what to be faithless and are not.

A dowdy dull girl, with one of those characteristic British faces that, once seen, are never remembered.

You seem to forget that I am married, and that the one charm of marriage is that it makes a life of deception absolutely essential for both parties.

It is only shallow people who do not judge by appearances.

It is better to be beautiful than to be good. But . . . it is better to be good than to be ugly.

I can believe in anything, provided that it is quite incredible.

A bishop keeps on saying at the age of eighty what he was told to say when he was a boy of eighteen, and as a natural consequence he always looks absolutely delightful.

With an evening coat and a white tie, anybody, even a stockbroker, can gain a reputation for being civilised.

The following quotations are from *A Woman of No Importance* (1893):

Moderation is a fatal thing, Lady Hunstanton. Nothing succeeds like excess.

One must have some sort of occupation nowadays. If I hadn't my debts I shouldn't have anything to think about.

Talk to every woman as if you loved her, and to every man as if he bored you, and at the end of your first season you will have the reputation of possessing the most perfect social tact.

The English country gentleman galloping after a fox – the unspeakable in full pursuit of the uneatable.

One should never trust a woman who tells one her real age. A woman who would tell one that, would tell one anything.

MRS ALLONBY: They say, Lady Hunstanton, that when good Americans die they go to Paris.
LADY HUNSTANTON: Indeed? And when bad Americans die, where do they go to?
LORD ILLINGWORTH: Oh, they go to America.

One should never take sides in anything . . . Taking sides is the beginning of sincerity, and earnestness follows shortly afterward, and the human being becomes a bore.

After a good dinner, one can forgive anybody, even one's own relations.

She was a curious woman, whose dresses always looked as though they had been designed in a rage and put on in a tempest.

The following quotations are from *An Ideal Husband* (1895)

One should always play fairly . . . when one has the winning cards.

Fashion is what one wears oneself. What is unfashionable is that other people wear.

Fathers should neither be seen nor heard. That is the only proper basis for family life.

Women have a wonderful instinct about things. They can discover everything except the obvious.

I always pass on good advice. It is the only thing to do with it. It is never of any use to oneself.

In England people actually try to be brilliant at breakfast. That is so dreadful of them! Only dull people are brilliant at breakfast.

The following quotations are from *The Importance of Being Earnest* (1895)

No gentleman ever takes exercise.

To speak frankly, I am not in favour of long engagements. They give people the opportunity of finding out each other's characters before marriage, which I think is never advisable.

Divorces are made in heaven.

I never travel without my diary. One should always have something sensational to read on the train.

I love hearing my relations abused. It is the only thing that makes me put up with them at all.

No woman should ever be quite accurate about her age. It looks so calculating.

Thirty-five is a very attractive age. London society is full of women who have, of their own free choice, remained thirty-five for years.

The General was essentially a man of peace, except in his domestic life.'

Really, if the lower orders don't set us a good example, what on earth is the use of them?

It is always a silly thing to give advice, but to give good advice is absolutely fatal.
The Portrait of Mr W. H. (1889)

All charming people, I fancy, are spoiled. It is the secret of their attraction.
The Portrait of Mr W. H. (1889)

The growth of common sense in the English Church is a thing very much to be regretted.
Nineteenth Century (January 1889)

The man who sees both sides of the question is a man who sees absolutely nothing at all.
The Critic as Artist (1890)

Ah, don't say that you agree with me. When people agree with me I always feel that I must be wrong.
The Critic as Artist (1890) and also in *Lady Windermere's Fan* (1892)

Every great man nowadays has his disciples, and it is always Judas who writes the biography.
The Critic as Artist (1890)

To be born, or at any rate bred, in a hand-bag, whether it had handles or not, seems to me to display a contempt for the ordinary decencies of family life that reminds one of the worst excesses of the French Revolution.
Lady Windermere's Fan (1892)

We are all in the gutter, but some of us are looking at the stars.
Lady Windermere's Fan (1892)

It's most dangerous nowadays for a husband to pay any attention to his wife in public. It always makes people think that he beats her when they are alone.
Lady Windermere's Fan (1892)

Many a woman has a past, but I am told that she has at least a dozen, and they all fit.
Lady Windermere's Fan (1892)

A man who knows the price of everything and the value of nothing.
Lord Darlington's definition of a cynic, *Lady Windermere's Fan* (1892)

It was a great success but the audience was a total failure.
on being asked by a friend how his latest play – Lady Windermere's Fan – *had gone*

Cynicism is merely the art of seeing things as they are instead of as they ought to be.
Oscariana (1910)

The old believe in everything: the middle-aged suspect everything; the young know everything.
The Chameleon (December 1894)

Ambition is the last refuge of the failure.
The Chameleon (December 1894) 'Phrases and Philosophies for the Use of the Young'

I care only to see doctors when I am in perfect health; then they comfort one, but when one is ill they are most depressing.
The Letters of Oscar Wilde

This wallpaper will be the death of me – one of us'll have to go.
about the furnishings in his room

To disagree with three-fourths of the British public on all points is one of the first elements of sanity, one of the deeper consolations in all moments of spiritual doubt.

He hasn't a single redeeming vice.

WILDE:	I shall always regard you as the best critic of my plays.
BEERBOHM TREE:	I have never criticised your plays.
WILDE:	That's why.

Consistency is the last refuge of the unimaginative.

Anybody can sympathise with the sufferings of a friend, but it requires a very fine nature to sympathise with a friend's success.

One is tempted to define man as a rational animal who always loses his temper when he is called upon to act in accordance with the dictates of reason.

America has been discovered before, but it has always been hushed up.

Rich bachelors should be heavily taxed. It is not fair that some men should be happier than others.

Anyone who lives within their means suffers from a lack of imagination.

Work is the curse of the drinking classes.

After the first glass of absinthe you see things as you wish they were. After the second you see them as they are not. Finally you see things as they really are, and that is the most horrible thing in the world.

He never touches water: it goes to his head at once.

All Americans lecture, I believe. I suppose it is something in their climate.

As long as a woman can look ten years younger than her own daughter, she is perfectly satisfied.

Arguments are to be avoided: they are always vulgar, and often convincing.

The English public, as a mass, takes no interest in a work of art until it is told that the work in question is immoral.

It is only an auctioneer who should admire all schools of art.

Where will it all end? Half the world does not believe in God, the other half does not believe in me.

When I think of all the harm that the Bible has done, I despair of ever writing anything to equal it.

Bigamy is having one wife too many. Monogamy is the same.

Little boys should be obscene and not heard.

Somehow or other, I'll be famous, and if not famous, I'll be notorious.

The Catholic Church is for saints and sinners alone. For respectable people the Anglican Church will do.

We have really everything in common with America nowadays except, of course, language.

Women's styles may change but their designs remain the same.

When I ask for a watercress sandwich, I do not mean a loaf with a field in the middle of it.

Billy Wilder 1906-2002
American film director and writer

It used to be that we in films were the lowest form of art. Now we have something to look down on.
of television
   A. Madesen *Billy Wilder* (1968)

I'm very uncomfortable living in a world where the Pope is twenty-five years younger than I am.
   The Independent, 17 July 1993

Unable obtain bidet. Suggest handstand in shower.
   Cabled response to his wife's cabled complaint from Paris just after the Second World War, that her accommodation did not have a bidet, and could he arrange to have one sent to her?

Thornton Wilder 1897-1975
American playwright and novelist

My advice to you is not to inquire why or whither, but just enjoy your ice cream while it's on your plate.

George Will 1941-
Newspaper columnist, journalist, author and political philosopher

The nice part about being a pessimist is that you are constantly being either proven right or pleasantly surprised.
   Newsweek, February 22 1993

With so many perfectionist dreams, from Rousseau's to Marx's, thoroughly discredited, it is late in the day for serious people to believe that something straight can be made form the crooked timber of humanity.
   syndicated column, 20 January 1994

The Berlin Wall is the defining achievement of socialism.

In the lexicon of the political class, the word 'sacrifice' means that the citizens are supposed to mail even more of their income to Washington so that the political class will not have to sacrifice the pleasure of spending it.

Will and Grace American television sitcom 1998-2006

Jack McFarland (Sean Hayes) to Karen Walker (Megan Mulally)

Women: you can't live with them . . . end of sentence.

Unlike your thighs, your argument does not retain water.

William III 1650-1702
British monarch, King of Great Britain and Ireland from 1688

'Do you not see your country is lost?' asked the Duke of Buckingham. 'There is one way never to see it lost,' replied William, 'and that is to die in the last ditch.'
  Bishop Gilbert Burnet *History of My Own Time* (1838)

Robin Williams 1951-
American comic and actor

Cocaine is God's way of saying you're making too much money.
  Screen International (15 December 1990)

There were rather a lot of doctors in rehab. It's rather like being in a fat farm with nutritionists.
  quoted in www.metro.co.uk 29 December 2006 'Quotes of the Year'

A woman wouldn't make a bomb that kills you. A woman would make a bomb that makes you feel bad for a while. That's why there should be a woman President. There'd never be any wars, just every twenty-eight days there'd be very intense negotiations.
  Robin Williams: Live at the Met (1987)

Bruce Willis 1955-
American actor

Balding is God's way of showing you are only human . . . he takes the hair off your head and sticks it in your ears.
  The Observer 3 March 1996

Tennessee Williams 1911-83
American dramatist

I'm not living with you. We occupy the same cage.
  Cat on a Hot Tin Roof (1955)

We're all of us sentenced to solitary confinement inside our own skins, for life!
  Orpheus Descending

William Carlos Williams 1883-1963
American poet

Is it any better in Heaven, my friend Ford,
Than you found it in Provence?
  'To Ford Madox Ford in Heaven' (1944)

Marianne Williamson 1953-
American writer and philanthropist

Our deepest fear is not that we are inadequate. Our deepest fear is that we are powerful beyond measure. It is our light, not our darkness, that most frightens us.
  A Return to Love (1992)

A. N. Wilson 1950-
British novelist

I should prefer to have a politician who regularly went to a massage parlour than one who promised a laptop computer for every teacher.
Observer 21 March 1999

Angus Wilson 1913-91
English novelist and short-story writer

Once a Catholic always a Catholic.
The Wrong Set (1949)

Earl Wilson 1907-87
American journalist

Women's liberation will not be achieved until a woman can become paunchy and bald and still think that she's attractive to the opposite sex.

If you think nobody cares if you're alive, try missing a couple of car payments.
attributed

Edward O. Wilson 1929-
American sociobiologist, expert on ants

Marxism is sociobiology without biology . . . Although Marxism was formulated as the enemy of ignorance and superstition, to the extent that it has become dogmatic it has faltered in that commitment and is now mortally threatened by the discoveries of human sociobiology.
On Human Nature (1978)

Wonderful theory, wrong species.
on Marxism
   in *Los Angeles Times* 21 October 1994

Every human brain is born not as a blank tablet (*a tabula rasa*) waiting to be filled in by experience but as an 'exposed negative' waiting to be slipped into 'developer fluid'.
on the nature v. nurture debate

Gahan Wilson 1930-
American author, cartoonist and illustrator

When I was young, I used to think that wealth and power would bring me happiness. I was right.

Harold Wilson, Baron Wilson of Rievaulx 1916-95
British Labour Party politician, Prime Minister of the United Kingdom, 1964-70, 1974-76

This party is a bit like an old stagecoach. If you drive along at a rapid rate, everyone aboard is either so exhilarated or so seasick that you don't have a lot of difficulty.
of the Labour Party, c.1974
   Anthony Sampson *The Changing Anatomy of Britain*

The trouble is when the old problems reappear I reach for the old solutions.
to his Press Secretary Joe Haines, July 1975

Peter Hennessy *The Prime Minister: the Office and its Holders since 1945* (2000)

The one thing we need to nationalise in this country is the Treasury, but no one has ever succeeded.
   in 1984; Peter Hennessy *Whitehall* (1990)

From now the pound abroad is worth 14 per cent less in terms of other currencies. It does not mean, of course, that the pound here in Britain, in your pocket or purse or in your bank, has been devalued.
   often quoted as 'the pound in your pocket'
   ministerial broadcast, 19 November 1967

He immatures with age.
*on Tony **Benn**, a prominent left-wing politician*

If I had the choice between smoked salmon and tinned salmon, I'd have it tinned. With vinegar.

She missed the last lobby briefing, I hear. At the vet's with hardpad, no doubt.
of a woman journalist he disliked

All these financiers, all the little gnomes in Zurich and the other financial centres about whom we keep on hearing.
   in the House of Commons, 12 November 1956

I think it's a trap, but I suppose you can always walk into a trap provided you are packing a Luger.
   in 1961 when pressed by Hugh **Gaitskell** to exchange his successful shadow Treasury portfolio for Foreign Affairs

I myself have always deprecated . . . in crisis after crisis, appeals to the Dunkirk spirit as an answer to our problems.
   in the House of Commons, 16 July 1961

I believe that the spirit of Dunkirk will carry us through . . . to success.
   speech to the Labour Party Conference, 12 December 1964

This party is a moral crusade or it is nothing.
   speech at the Labour Party Conference, 1 October 1962

We are restating our socialism in terms of the scientific revolution ... the Britain that is going to be forged in the white heat of this revolution will be no place for restrictive practices or outdated methods on either side of industry.
   speech at the Labour Party Conference, 1 October 1963

A week is a long time in politics.
   probably first said at a lobby briefing at the time of the 1964 sterling crisis

Get your tanks off my lawn, Hughie.
   to the trade union leader Hugh **Scanlon**, at Chequers in June 1969

One man's wage increase is another man's price increase.
   speech at Blackburn, 8 January 1970

Whichever party is in office, the Treasury is in power.
   while in Opposition, c. 1974

I've buried all the hatchets. But I know where I've buried them and I can dig them up if necessary.
of the Cabinet in 1974

Labour is the natural party of government.
in 1965

Richard Wilson 1942-
British civil servant and Cabinet Secretary

There are occasions on which you have to say 'bollocks' to Ministers.
Times 10 February 2000

Woodrow Wilson 1856-1924
American Democratic statesman; 28th President of the United States 1912-21

If I am to speak for ten minutes, I need a week for preparation; if fifteen minutes, three days; if half an hour, two days; if an hour, I am ready now.
Josephus Daniels *The Wilson Era* (1946)

Liberty has never come from the government. Liberty has always come from the subjects of government. The history of liberty is the history of resistance. The history of liberty is a history of the limitation of governmental power, not the increase of it.
speech to the New York Press Club, 9 September 1912

The day has come when America is privileged to send her blood and her might for the principles that gave her birth and happiness and the peace which she has treasured.
speech to Congress, 2 April 1917

The world must be made safe for democracy.
speech to Congress, 2 April 1917

America is the only idealistic nation in the world.
speech at Sioux Falls, South Dakota, 8 September 1919

When men take up arms to set other men free, there is something sacred and holy in the warfare.

A conservative is a man who just sits and thinks, mostly sits.

The man who is swimming against the stream knows the strength of it.

America lives in the heart of every man everywhere who wishes to find a region where he will be free to work out his destiny as he chooses.

Just what is it that America stands for? If she stands for one thing more than another it is for the sovereignty of self-governing people.

The way to stop financial joy-riding is to arrest the chauffeur, not the automobile.

Duchess of Windsor (Wallis Simpson) 1896-1986

You can never be too rich or too thin.
attributed

Oprah Winfrey 1954-
American television host, producer and philanthropist

Luck is preparation meeting opportunity.
>interview, Academy of Achievement, 21 February 1991

The biggest adventure you can ever take is to live the life of your dreams.
>*O: the Oprah Magazine*

There's no easy way out. If there were, I would have bought it. And believe me, it would be one of my favourite things!
of exercise
>in *O: the Oprah Magazine* February 2005

Understand that the right to choose your own path is a sacred privilege. Use it. Dwell in possibility.
>interview for O magazine

Real integrity is doing the right thing, knowing that nobody's going to know whether you did it or not.
>interview for *Good Housekeeping*

Everyone in the world is constantly fighting an internal battle. A battle between what the brain knows is right and what the heart knows it wants.

Shelley Winters 1920-2006
American actress

In Hollywood, all the marriages are happy. It's trying to live together afterwards that causes all the problems.

I did a picture in England one winter and it was so cold I almost got married.

Sir Nicholas Winterton 1938-
British Conservative politician, Member of Parliament for Macclesfield since 1971

People who travel standard class are a totally different type of person. First class train travel enables you to have peace and quiet in which to work.
>BBC Radio 5 Live interview, 18 February 2010, in which he defended the right of MPs to travel first-class on trains at the taxpayer's expense. A Conservative party spokesmen shortly afterwards said Sir Nicholas held 'out of touch views which . . . do not in any way represent the views of the Conservative party'.
>[Editor's note: Give me strength. Sir Nicholas was making a perfectly valid point.]

Ludwig Wittgenstein 1889-1951
Austrian-born British philosopher

Philosophy is a battle against the bewitchment of our intelligence by means of language.
>*Philosophische Untersuchungen* (1953)

The limits of my language mean the limits of my world.
>*Tractatus Logico-Philosophicus* (1922)

Sir Pelham Grenville ('P. G.') Wodehouse KBE 1881-1975
English writer whose body of work included novels, collections of short stories, and musical theatre

James's uncle had just about enough brain to make a jay-bird fly crooked.
   The Man Upstairs (1914)

It is a good rule in life never to apologise. The right sort of people do not want apologies, and the wrong sort take a mean advantage of them.
   The Man Upstairs (1914)

Jeeves lugged my purple socks out of the drawer as if he were a vegetarian fishing a caterpillar out of his salad.
   My Man Jeeves (1919)

She fitted into my biggest armchair as if it had been built around her by someone who knew they were wearing armchairs tight about the hips that season.
   My Man Jeeves (1919) 'Jeeves and the Unbidden Guest'

Chumps always make the best husbands . . . All the unhappy marriages come from the husbands having brains.
   The Adventures of Sally (1920)

I turned to Aunt Agatha, whose demeanour was now rather like that of one who, picking daisies on the railway, has just caught the down express in the small of the back.
   The Inimitable Jeeves (1923)

It was my Uncle George who discovered that alcohol was a food well in advance of medical thought.
   The Inimitable Jeeves (1923)

When Aunt is calling to Aunt like mastodons bellowing across primeval swamps.
   The Inimitable Jeeves (1923)

'What ho!' I said.
'What ho!' said Motty.
'What ho! What ho!'
'What ho! What ho! What ho!'
After that it seemed difficult to go on with the conversation.
   Carry on Jeeves (1925)

I'm not absolutely certain of my facts, but I rather fancy it's Shakespeare – or, if not, it's some equally brainy bird – who says that it's always just when a fellow is feeling particularly braced with things in general that Fate sneaks up behind him with the bit of lead piping. And what I'm driving at is that the man is perfectly right.
   Carry On, Jeeves! (1925)

To my daughter Leonora, without whose never-failing sympathy and encouragement this book would have been finished in half the time.
   Dedication in *The Heart of a Goof* (1926)

'You're too young to marry,' said Mr McKinnon, a stout bachelor.
'So was Methuselah,' said James, a stouter.
   Meet Mr Mulliner (1927)

Unseen in the background, Fate was quietly slipping the lead into the boxing-glove.
Very Good, Jeeves (1930)

For the first time since sudden love had thrown them into each other's arms, she had found herself beginning to wonder if her Blair was quite the godlike superman she had supposed. There even flashed through her mind a sinister speculation as to whether, when you came right down to it, he wasn't something of a pill.
Hot Water (1932)

I can honestly say that I always look on Pauline as one of the nicest girls I was engaged to.
Thank You, Jeeves (1934)

It is never difficult to distinguish between a Scotsman with a grievance and a ray of sunshine.
Blandings Castle and Elsewhere (1935) 'The Custody of the Pumpkin'

He spoke with a certain what-is-it in his voice, and I could see that, if not actually disgruntled, he was far from being gruntled.
The Code of the Woosters (1938)

It's no use telling me that there are bad aunts and good aunts. At the core, they are all alike. Sooner or later, out pops the cloven hoof.
The Code of the Woosters (1938)

Roderick Spode? Big chap with a small moustache and the sort of eye that can open an oyster at sixty paces?
The Code of the Woosters (1938)

As a rule, when he fell in love at first sight, his primary impulse was a desire to reach out for the adored object and start handling her like a sack of coals, but the love which this girl inspired in him was a tender, chivalrous love.
Uncle Fred in the Springtime (1939)

Ice formed on the butler's upper slopes.
Pigs Have Wings (1952)

I was in rare fettle and the heart had touched a new high. I don't know anything that braces one up like finding you haven't got to get married after all.
Jeeves in the Offing (1960)

Rose was the sweetest girl in a world where sweet girls are rather rare, but experience had taught him that, given the right conditions, she was capable of making her presence felt as perceptibly as one of those hurricanes which become so emotional on reach Cape Hatteras.
Plum Pie (1966) 'Bingo Bans the Bomb'

'Alf Todd,' said Ukridge, soaring to an impressive burst of imagery, 'has about as much chance as a one-armed blind man in a dark room trying to shove a pound of melted butter into a wild cat's left ear with a red-hot needle.'

The door behind Lord Emsworth opened, and Beach the butler entered, a solemn procession of one.

The fascination of shooting as a sport depends almost wholly on whether you are at the right or wrong end of the gun.

Sir Terry Wogan 1938-
Irish broadcaster

Television contracts the imagination and radio expands it.
: in *Observer* 30 December 1984

James Wolfe 1727-59
British general; captor of Quebec

The General . . . repeated nearly the whole of Gray's Elegy . . . adding, as he concluded, that he would prefer being the author of that poem to the glory of beating the French tomorrow.
: J. Playfair *Biographical Account of J. Robinson* in *Transactions of the Royal Society of Edinburgh* (1815)

Thomas Wolfe 1900-38
American novelist

'Where they got you stationed now, Luke?' said Harry Tugman peering up snoutily from a mug of coffee. 'At the p-p-p-present time in Norfolk at the Navy base,' Luke answered, 'm-m-making the world safe for hypocrisy.'
: *Look Homeward, Angel* (1929)

Tom Wolfe 1931-
American writer

A liberal is a conservative who's been arrested.
: *The Bonfire of the Vanities* (1987)

The idea was to prove at every foot of the way up that you were one of the elected and anointed ones who had *the right stuff* and could move higher and higher and even – ultimately, God willing, one day – that you might be able to join that special few at the very top, that elite who had the capacity to bring tears to men's eyes, the very Brotherhood of the Right Stuff itself.
referring to pilots and astronauts training in the NASA space program
: *The Right Stuff* (1979)

Victoria Wood 1953-
British writer and comedienne

JACKIE: (*very slowly*) Take Tube A and apply to Bracket D.
VICTORIA: Reading it slower does not make it any easier to do.
: *Mens Sana in Thingummy Doodah* (1990)

CONNIE: Our neighbours had sex again last night.
BEATTIE: Not again!
CONNIE: I mean, I like a joke, but that's twice this month. I could not think what the noise was. I thought our central heating had come on a month early.
: *Victoria Wood as Seen on TV* (1985)

It will be a very traditional Christmas, with presents, crackers, doors slamming and people bursting into tears, but without the big dead thing in the middle.
of a vegetarian Christmas
: in *Sunday Times* 24 December 2000

A man is designed to walk three miles in the rain to phone for help when the car breaks down – and a women is designed to say 'you took your time' when he comes back dripping wet.
 Up to You, Porky – The Victoria Wood Sketch Book (1985)

George Woodcock 1912-95
Canadian writer and essayist

Canadians do not like heroes, and so they do not have them.
 Canada and the Canadians (1970)

John Wooden

Consider the rights of others before your own feelings, and the feelings of others before your own rights.

Joseph Wood Krutch 1893-1970
American author

Cats seem to go on the principle that it never does any harm to ask for what you want.
 Twelve Seasons (1949)

Joanne Woodward 1930-
American actress, television and theatrical producer

Acting is like sex. You should do it, not talk about it.

Lord Woolf 1933-
British judge, Lord Chief Justice

What is the difference between a Lord Chancellor and a Secretary of State, the man on Clapham Omnibus could, with reason, ask. After all, that engagingly friendly and cheerful chappie, Lord Falconer, seems to be quite happy playing both roles.
 quote from Lord Woolf's Squire Centenary Lecture 'The Rule of Law and a Change in the Constitution'
 Guardian Unlimited 4 March 2004

Virginia Woolf 1882-1941
English novelist, essayist, and critic

So that is marriage, Lily thought, a man and a woman looking at a girl throwing a ball.
 To The Lighthouse (1927)

And now with some pleasure I find that it's seven; and must cook dinner. Haddock and sausage meat. I think it is true that one gains a certain hold on sausage and haddock by writing them down.
 diary, 8 March 1941

As an experience, madness is terrific . . . and in its lava I still find most of the things I write about
 letter to Ethel Smyth, 22 June 1930

Alexander Woollcott 1887-1943
American writer and critic

She was like a sinking ship firing on the rescuers.
 of Mrs Patrick **Campbell**

While Rome Burns (1944) 'The First Mrs Tanqueray'

She is so odd a blend of Little Nell and Lady Macbeth. It is not so much the familiar phenomenon of a hand of steel in a velvet glove as a lacy sleeve with a bottle of vitriol concealed in its folds.
*of Dorothy **Parker***
 While Rome Burns (1944) 'Our Mrs Parker'

To all things clergic
I am allergic.

William Wordsworth 1770-1850
English poet

Getting and spending, we lay waste our powers.

Steven Wright 1955-
American comedian, actor and writer

I drive way too fast to worry about cholesterol.

It's a small world, but I wouldn't want to paint it.

I saw a subliminal advertising executive, but only for a second.

Tony Wright 1948-
British Labour politician

Don't you think it's bizarre at all that the House of Commons can have endless votes on whether it wants to kill foxes, but not on whether it wants to kill people?
 to the Prime Minister
 at a hearing of the House of Commons Liaison Committee, 21 January 2003

Harry Wu 1937-
Chinese-born American political activist

I want to see the word *laogai* in every dictionary in every language in the world. I want to see the laogai ended. Before 1974, the word 'gulag' did not appear in any dictionary. Today, this single word conveys the meaning of Soviet political violence and its labour camp system. 'Laogai' also deserve a place in our dictionaries.
the laogai *are Chinese labour camps*
 in *Washington Post* 26 May 1996

Y

Minoru Yamasaki 1912-88
American architect, designer of the World Trade Center

The World Trade Center should, because of its importance, become a living representation of man's belief in humanity, his need for individual dignity, his belief in the cooperation of men, and through this cooperation his ability to find greatness.
   Paul Heyer *Architects on Architecture* (1967)

W. B. Yeats 1865-1939
Irish poet and dramatist

I have certainly seen more men destroyed by the desire to have a wife and child and to keep them in comfort than I have seen destroyed by drink or harlots.

David Yelland 1963-
British journalist, Editor of the *Sun*

I don't think the **Blairs** are *Sun* readers.
   News from Number Ten (BBC2 documentary), 15 July 2000

Yes, Minister British sitcom 1980-1984

Well Minister, if you ask me for a straight answer, then I shall say that, as far as we can see, looking at it by and large, taking one thing with another in terms of the average of departments, the in the final analysis it is probably true to say that at the end of the day, in general terms, you would probably find that, not to put too fine a point on it, there probably wasn't very much in it one way or the other, as far as one can see, at this stage.

He's suffering from Politicians' Logic. Something must be done, this is something, therefore we must do it.
Sir Humphrey Appleby (Nigel **Hawthorne**)

I don't want the truth. I want something I can tell Parliament.
Jim Hacker (Paul **Eddington**)

A cynic is what an idealist calls a realist.
   Sir Humphrey **Appleby**

'Opposition's about asking awkward questions.' 'Yes . . . and government's about not answering them.'

The PM - whose motto is . . . 'In Defeat, Malice - in Victory, Revenge!'

If you wish to ascribe a proposal in a way that guarantees that a Minister will reject it, describe it as *courageous*.

The Official Secrets Act is not to protect secrets but to protect officials.

Yes, Prime Minister British sitcom 1986-1988
I think it will be a clash between the political will and the administrative won't.

Yorkshireman's advice to his son

Hear all, see all, say nowt.
Eat all, sup all, pay nowt.
And if ever tha does owt for nowt,
Allus do it for thi'sen.

G. M. Young 1882-1959
English historian

Being published by the Oxford University Press is rather like being married to a duchess: the honour is almost greater than the pleasure.
   Rupert Hart-Davis, letter to George Lyttleton, 29 April 1956

Neil Young 1945-
Canadian singer

'Heart of Gold' put me in the middle of the road. Travelling there soon became a bore so I headed for the ditch. A rougher ride but I saw more interesting people there.
of the success of this song from his 1972 album 'Harvest'
   liner notes to Decade (1977)

The Young Ones BBC television sitcom 1982-4

Of course I'm a feminist. You have to be these days – it's the only way to pull the chicks.

Henny Youngman 1906-98
British-born comedian and violinist

Do you know what it means to come home at night to a woman who'll give you a little love, a little affection, a little tenderness? It means you're in the wrong house, that's what it means.

My wife lost all her credit cards, but I'm not going to report it. Whoever found them is spending less than she did.

Take my wife – please!

When I read about the evils of drinking, I gave up reading.

My Grandmother is over eighty and still doesn't need glasses. Drinks right out of the bottle.

A car hit a Jewish man. The paramedic said, 'Are you comfortable?' The man said, 'I make a good living.'

I've been in love with the same woman for forty-one years. If my wife finds out, she'll kill me.

Z

Israel Zangwill 1864-1926
Jewish spokesman and writer

America is God's Crucible, the great Melting-Pot where all the races of Europe are melting and re-forming!
The Melting Pot (1908)

Frank Zappa 1940-93
American composer, electric guitarist, record producer and film director

Rock journalism is people who can't write interviewing people who can't talk for people who can't read.
L. Botts *Loose Talk* (1980)

I'm interested in the capitalistic way of life, and the reason I like it better than anything else I've seen so far is because competition produces results. Every socialistic type of government where the State theoretically owns everything, and everybody does their little part to help the State, inevitably produces bad art, it produces social inertia, it produces really unhappy people, and it is more repressive than any other kind of government.

Communism doesn't work because people like to own stuff.

Grigori Zinoviev 1883-1936
Soviet politician

Armed warfare must be preceded by a struggle against the inclinations to compromise which are embedded among the majority of British workmen, against the ideas of evolution and peaceful extermination of capitalism. Only then will it be possible to count upon complete success of an armed insurrection.
letter to the British Communist Party, 15 September 1924

Hiller B. Zobel 1932-
American judge

Asking the ignorant to use the incomprehensible to decide the unknowable.
'The Jury on Trial', *American Heritage* July-August 1995

David Zucker 1947-

Quit now, you'll never make it. If you disregard this advice, you'll be halfway there.

appendix 1

political correctness

I suppose true sexual equality will come when a general called Anthea is found having an unwise lunch with a young, unreliable model from Spain.

John Mortimer, *The Spectator*, 26 March 1994

This appendix covers:

- Why political correctness particularly antagonises those of a right-of-centre political persuasion
- The antipathy of political correctness towards Western values
- Political correctness is cultural Marxism
- Political correctness as the solution to patriarchal hegemony
- The 'unacceptable' gender pay differential
- The 'acceptable' differential between the retirement ages of men and women
- Discrimination, now one of the most unforgivable sins
- How political correctness undermines marriage
- A triumph of British common sense – how to reduce the number of divorces
- Harriet Harman's suspicion of ageism on *Strictly Come Dancing*

Political correctness antagonises those of a right-of-centre political persuasion (such as myself) more than it does those of a left-of-centre persuasion. I can thank the author of one splendid book for helping me understand why this is the case. The author is Anthony Browne, the book the snappily-titled *The Retreat of Reason: Political Correctness and the Corruption of Public Debate in Modern Britain* (2006). It was published by Civitas, The Institute for the Study of Civil Society. From chapter one, 'What is Political Correctness?':

> The phrase 'political correctness' conjures up images of left-wing councils banning black bin-bags, nativity scenes being banned by the Red Cross and handicapped people being called 'otherwise-abled'. Some of these cases, such as renaming firemen as firefighters, merely reflect a changing reality. Others are just the most overt symptoms of political correctness, and easily ridiculed: he's not dead, he's metabolically challenged.
>
> But political correctness is more than a joke or updating of historic language usage. It is a system of beliefs and pattern of thoughts that permeates many aspects of modern life, holding a vice-like grip over public debate, deciding what can be debated and what the terms of debate are, and which government policies are acceptable and which aren't. It has grown in influence over the last few decades to the extent that it has now become one of the most dominant features of public discourse, not just in Britain, but across the Western – and particularly the Anglophone – world.
>
> PC is also surprisingly unexamined as a phenomenon, the subject of few academic treatises and few books, at least outside the US. Criticism of it has rarely graduated from ridicule to analysis. Part of the problem is that there is no standard definition of political correctness. Peter Coleman, a former Australian government minister from the Liberal Party, wrote:

> Political Correctness is a heresy of liberalism. It emerges where liberalism and leftism intersect. What began as a liberal assault on injustice has come to denote, not for the first time, a new form of injustice.

He said that it was liberalism that has been taken over by dogmatism, that it is 'intolerant', 'self-righteous' and 'quasi-religious'. The Politically Correct are more intolerant of dissent than traditional liberals or even conservatives. Liberals of earlier generations accepted unorthodoxy as normal. Indeed the right to differ was a datum of classical liberalism. The Politically Correct do not give that right a high priority. It distresses their programmed minds. Those who do not conform should be ignored, silenced or vilified. There is a kind of soft totalitarianism about Political Correctness.

The US conservative commentator Paul Weyrich, the President of the Free Congress Foundation, is also exercised by the intolerance of political correctness, although his main concern is its antipathy to Western values:

> The United States is very close to becoming a state totally dominated by an alien ideology, an ideology bitterly hostile to Western culture. Even now, for the first time in their lives, people have to be afraid of what they say. This has never been true in the history of our country. Yet today, if you say the 'wrong thing', you suddenly have legal problems, political problems, you might even lose your job or be expelled from college. Certain topics are forbidden. You can't approach the truth about a lot of different subjects. If you do, you are immediately branded as 'racist', 'sexist', 'homophobic', 'insensitive', or 'judgmental.'

The US commentator William Lind, director of the Center for Cultural Conservatism, is among those who have described PC as 'cultural Marxism', declaring that it is 'Marxism translated from economic into cultural terms'. [Author's note: Marxism. Does this explain why political correctness makes us see red?] He wrote:

> The cultural Marxism of Political Correctness, like economic Marxism, has a single factor explanation of history. Economic Marxism says that all of history is determined by ownership of means of production. Cultural Marxism, or Political Correctness, says that all history is determined by power, by which groups defined in terms of race, sex, etc, have power over which other groups. Nothing else matters.

The *New York Times'* culture correspondent, Richard Bernstein, who came out against multiculturalism in his book *The Dictatorship of Virtue*, was also concerned about how PC tried to overturn the dominant culture and power structures. In a landmark 1990 article which sparked debate about PC in the US, he wrote:

> Central to pc-ness, which has its roots in 1960s radicalism, is the view that Western society has for centuries been dominated by what is often called 'the white male power structure' or 'Patriarchal hegemony.' A related belief is that everybody but white heterosexual males has suffered some form of repression and been denied a cultural voice.

Across much of Britain's public discourse, a reliance on reason has been replaced with a reliance on the emotional appeal of an argument. Parallel to the once-trusted world of empiricism and deductive reasoning, an often overwhelmingly powerful emotional landscape has been created, rewarding people with feelings of virtue for some beliefs, punishing with feelings of guilt for others. It is a belief system that echoes religion in providing ready, emotionally satisfying answers for a world too complex to understand fully, and providing a gratifying sense of righteousness absent in our otherwise secular society...

Because the politically correct believe they are not just on the side of right, but of virtue, it follows that those they are opposed to are not just wrong, but malign. In the PC mind, the pursuit of virtue entitles them to curtail the malign views of those they disagree with. Rather than say, 'I would like to hear your side', the politically correct insist: 'you can't say that'.

Believing that their opponents are not just wrong but bad, the politically correct feel free to resort to personal attacks on them. If there is no explicit bad motive, then the PC can accuse their opponents of a sinister ulterior motive – the unanswerable accusations of 'isms'. It is this self-righteous sense of virtue that makes the PC believe they are justified in suppressing freedom of speech. Political correctness is the dictatorship of virtue...

But what is the point of political correctness? Why are some things politically correct, and others not? At its most fundamental, political correctness seeks to redistribute power from the powerful to the powerless. At its most crude, it opposes power for the sake of opposing power, making no moral distinction between whether the power is malign or benign, or whether the powerful exercise their power in a way that can be rationally and reasonably justified...

America, as the world's most powerful country, can never do any good, even though it is the world's most powerful liberal democracy, the largest donor of overseas aid, and it defeated both Nazism and Communism.

The West, as the world's most powerful cultural and economic group, can safely be blamed for all the world's ills, even though it is largely responsible for the worldwide spread of prosperity, democracy and scientific advance.

Multinational corporations are condemned as the oppressors of the world's poor, rather than seen as engines of global economic growth with vast job-creating investments in the world's poorest countries, pushing up wages and transferring knowledge.

Conversely, political correctness automatically supports the weak and vulnerable, classifying them as nearly untouchable victims, irrespective of whether they merit such support or not...

In the battle between emotion and reason, emotion wins most of the time for most people: the heart trumps the head because it is more difficult to live with bad feelings than bad logic. Few are the souls tortured by bad reasoning; many are those tortured by guilt. However overwhelming the evidence, people believe what they want to believe, and find it very difficult to believe what they don't want to.

The easiest way to overcome the dissonance between what you want to believe and the evidence is not to change what you believe, but to shut out the evidence and silence those who try to highlight it...

People tend to believe that which makes them feel virtuous, not that which makes them feel bad. Most people have a profound need to believe they are on the side of virtue, and can do that by espousing beliefs publicly acknowledged as virtuous. Nothing makes multimillionaire Hollywood actors who live in Beverly Hills feel better about themselves than campaigning against world poverty by demanding more aid from the West (rather than holding African leaders responsible for the plight of their people by demanding better governance).

From the chapter 'How Political Correctness Affects Policies':

One of the rallying cries of the politically correct is the 'unacceptable' gender pay gap between men and women: women's full-time hourly pay is on average just 80% of that of men. Unions and the Equal Opportunities Commission regularly launch campaigns on the issue, insisting it shows just how prevalent sex discrimination still is in the workplace. Few ask whether the gender pay gap may be due to other factors, because that would be to appear to justify the pay gap and thus sex discrimination.

It is clear that, other factors being the same, equal pay for equal work is not just fundamentally fair and just, but also an essential basis for an efficient economy taking optimal advantage of the skills of all workers. If women are paid less for equal work than men just because of their gender, then that is irrational, prejudicial and unjust.

But even in a workforce with a total absence of sex discrimination, there could still be a gender pay gap. The presumption that any pay gap is only explicable by sex discrimination is a presumption that men and women are identical in all their lifestyle choices and legal rights, when they are not.

Men's legal retirement age is five years later than women's, encouraging them to work longer careers, which uplifts their average earnings. Women get far more extensive parental leave than men, encouraging career breaks and limiting their lifetime work experience, thus depressing their average wages. On average, each week, men work nearly twice as many hours in paid employment as women, building up considerably more experience in their careers, which in a meritocracy would be reflected in greater pay. In addition, surveys suggest that women opt for more socially rewarding or emotionally fulfilling jobs, while men put a higher priority on high wages at whatever cost.

The danger is that if the only accepted explanation for income differentials is discrimination, then a range of policies will be adopted that may either be counterproductive, or actually introduce discrimination. Policies that specifically favour women at the expense of men are not only unfair, but by undermining meritocracy they undermine the efficiency of the labour market.

From the chapter 'The Trouble with Discrimination':

> Once upon a time, 'discrimination' - which is so central to much of political correctness it is worth special consideration - was seen as a positive attribute, which enabled people to discriminate between good and bad. People of discernment actually tried to educate themselves to become 'discriminating', a by-word for having good judgement.
>
> Now 'discrimination' - an ill-defined, catch-all term - has become one of the most unforgivable sins, something that no respectable person would seek to justify under any circumstances. Anything that is portrayed as 'discriminatory' in any way is automatically deemed intolerable.
>
> The fight against discrimination is one of the foundation stones of political correctness, underpinning and motivating much of it. Shami Chakrabarti, on becoming director of the left-wing pressure group Liberty, declared she believed in 'zero tolerance of any form of discrimination'. The European Charter of Fundamental Rights promises to outlaw all discrimination, turning politically correct sloganeering into Europe-wide law upheld by a court in Luxembourg:
>
>> Any discrimination based on any ground such as sex, race, colour, ethnic or social origin, genetic features, language, religion or belief, political or any other opinion, membership of a national minority, property, birth, disability, age or sexual orientation shall be prohibited.
>
> There are noble intentions behind these declarations that few civilised people would disagree with, and making these declarations rewards the declarers by making them feel virtuous (as one government lawyer said to me). The fight against discrimination has righted many hideous wrongs, such as denial of services to ethnic minorities and women's disenfranchisement. But having won the most obvious and justifiable battles,

the intentions are often rendered meaningless by the flawed, often hypocritical and usually intolerant thinking behind them...

There are widespread double standards on various forms of discrimination. In general, discrimination - even irrational, prejudicial discrimination - is either tolerated or promoted so long as it is against the powerful, while discrimination against those deemed vulnerable is deemed indefensible. 'Gender profiling' by police forces that targets men is perfectly acceptable, while 'racial profiling' which targets blacks is not.

Those who wage war on 'all forms of discrimination' often promote so-called 'positive discrimination', which is nonetheless discrimination which should thus supposedly be worthy of 'zero tolerance'.

The difference in retirement age between men and women is irrational prejudicial discrimination, the continuation of which (at least until 2020) is only explicable because it is men (otherwise perceived to be privileged) who are discriminated against. It is inconceivable that if it were women who were discriminated against that it would not have ended by now, even though it would be slightly more justifiable because women actually live longer.

There are no longer any male-only colleges in Oxford and Cambridge, having come under great pressure to change. But women-only colleges, which are just as blatantly sexist, continue to justify their existence on the grounds that they benefit women - despite the fact that women greatly outperform men at all levels of the education system, up to and including the attainment of first-class university degrees.

I contend that men are become increasingly frustrated by the yawning gap between how some women in the developed world continue to portray themselves - as *still* disadvantaged - and the reality they see all around them in their working and personal lives. And I suggest that this frustration leads to increasing animosity among men towards women, which manifests itself in two ways: firstly, in men's increasing reluctance to enter the institution of marriage while it remains so disadvantageous to them, particularly in financial terms upon divorce; and secondly, as another contributor to gender rancour, which helps drive up the divorce rate.

Steve Moxon's insightful 2008 book *The Woman Racket* is 'a serious scientific investigation into one of the key myths of our age - that women are oppressed by the patriarchal traditions of Western societies'. Drawing on the latest developments in evolutionary psychology, Moxon convincingly demonstrates that the opposite is true. He shows how men - or at least the majority of low-status males - have always been the victims of deep-rooted prejudice, and have been manipulated by women, because women have always been the 'limiting factor' in reproduction. That is, they have power over men because they control which men can, and which cannot, have children. Moxon explains why the idea that men exercise 'power' over women is nonsense, biologically speaking. He shows that domestic violence - even of the most violent nature - is more often committed by women against men than vice versa. And he overturns numerous other gender-related myths. It hardly needs saying, but Harriet Harman makes a number of appearances in the book.

From *The Daily Telegraph* of 13 February 2009, an article by Nick Allen entitled 'Marriage at lowest rate ever recorded':

> The number of marriages is at its lowest level since records began nearly 150 years ago, as an increasing number of people choose to live out of wedlock. High-profile divorce cases, the rising cost of weddings, and the failure of the Government to support the institution of marriage are among the factors blamed. It is now likely that official figures will show married couples to be in a minority by next year.
>
> Latest figures from the Office for National Statistics for the year 2007 in England and Wales showed that 21.6 out of every 1,000 men got married, down from 23 the previous year. The rate for women was 19.7 per 1,000, down from 20.7 in 2006.
>
> The levels were the lowest since records began in 1862. There were 231,450 marriages in 2007, a fall of 3.3% in a year, and the lowest total since 1885, when the population was little more than half its present level.

The figures predate the current financial crisis, which is likely to have exacerbated the downward trend as couples put off their weddings because of the cost. Average costs have more than doubled over the past decade to more than £21,000.

The Government has been accused of reinforcing the breakdown of marriage by introducing changes to the tax and benefits system that left married couples up to £5,000 a year worse off than people who stay single. The Conservative Party has promised to provide incentives for married couples and shift the tax burden away from families. Publicity surrounding divorce cases and large payments for wives are also thought to have encouraged people to avoid the altar.

Civil ceremonies accounted for 67% of all marriages, while religious ceremonies fell 4.5% to 77,490. The average age of people getting married for the first time was 31.9 for men and 29.8 for women, a slight increase on the previous year. In 1862, when marriage rates were first calculated, 58.7 men per 1,000 and 50 women got married. Even during the Second World War, the marriage rate for women never dropped below 40 per 1,000.

A triumph of British common sense. How do you reduce the number of divorces? By reducing the number of marriages. Marvellous.

I couldn't resist ending this appendix with another newspaper article involving the indefatigable Harriet Harman. The article was written by Anita Singh for *The Daily Telegraph* of 17 July 2009 and entitled ' "Ageist" BBC must reinstate Arlene, says Harman':

Arlene Phillips, the *Strictly Come Dancing* judge who was dropped from the show in favour of a younger star, was the victim of age discrimination, according to Harriet Harman. In a surprising government intervention [Author's note: Hardly 'surprising' given that the intervention involves Harriet Harman; the woman has the stamina of ten ordinary mortals] Labour's deputy leader and the Equalities Minister described the BBC's decision to replace Phillips as 'absolutely shocking' and called for her to be reinstated.

The veteran choreographer, 66, has been replaced by Alesha Dixon, 30, a pop star who won the ballroom competition in 2007. The male judges, who range in age from 44 to 65, and the show's 81-year-old host, Bruce Forsyth, have been retained, while the ballet dancer, Darcey Bussell, 40, will also join the show.

Miss Harman told the Commons yesterday, 'It's shocking that Arlene Phillips is not going to be a judge on *Strictly Come Dancing*. As Equalities Minister I am suspicious that there is age discrimination there. So I'd like to take the opportunity of saying to the BBC: if it is not too late, we want Arlene Phillips in the next edition of *Strictly Come Dancing*.'

Harriet Harman. The gift that just keeps on giving.

appendix 2

the different natures of men and women

> Hogamus, Higamous,
> Man is polygamous.
> Higamus, Hogamous,
> Woman monogamous.
>
> William James, *Oxford Book of Marriage*

This chapter covers:

- *'What does a woman want?'*
- *God and the big question*
- *Why women are always right in debates about relationships*
- The modern denial of human nature
- Why men and women are so frequently at odds with each other
- The different attitudes of the sexes to sex
- Fairytale weddings and honeymoons
- 1:20,000 plus (ratio of wedding day to the number of days of marriage that might follow)
- *Women as emotional managers in marriage*
- *Women and men's physiological responses to stress in marriage*
- *Gender bias among people working in the 'relationship industry'*
- *Relate, a highly 'feminised' organisation*
- The 'battle of the sexes'
- Why is there no *Men's* Institute?
- Men-only members clubs
- *Woman's Hour* and the 'gender pay imbalance' debate
- 'Why can't a man be more like a woman?'
- *Surrendered wives*
- Women's search for 'Mr Right'

[Editor's note: this appendix contains extracts from a chapter in my fourth book, *The Marriage Delusion: the fraud of the rings?* It's a hardback, and was recently published as a paperback under the title *The Fraud of the Rings*. In the contents list above, content summaries in italics have been omitted from this appendix, for lack of relevance to this book.]

The eminent Canadian-American psychologist Steven Pinker is the author of a number of remarkable books including *The Blank Slate: The Modern Denial of Human Nature* (2002). He starts the book with the following passage on 'The Blank Slate, the Noble Savage, and the Ghost in the Machine':

> Everyone has a theory of human nature. Everyone has to anticipate the behavior of others, and that means we all need theories about what makes people tick. A tacit theory of human nature – that behavior is caused by thoughts and feelings – is embedded in the very way we think about people.
>
> We fill out this theory by introspecting on our own minds and assuming that our fellows are like ourselves, and by watching people's behavior and filing away

generalizations. We absorb still other ideas from our intellectual climate: from the expertise of authorities and the conventional wisdom of the day.

Our theory of human nature is the wellspring of much in our lives. We consult it when we want to persuade or threaten, inform or deceive. It advises us on how to nurture our marriages, bring up our children, and control our own behavior. Its assumptions about learning drive our educational policy; its assumptions about motivation drive our policies on economics, law, and crime. And because it delineates what people can achieve easily, what they can achieve only with sacrifice or pain, and what they cannot achieve at all, it affects our values: what we believe we can reasonably strive for as individuals and as a society. Rival theories of human nature are entwined in different ways of life and different political systems, and have been a source of much conflict over the course of history. . .

Every society must operate with a theory of human nature, and our intellectual mainstream is committed to one. The theory is seldom articulated or overtly embraced, but it lies at the heart of a vast number of beliefs and policies. Bertrand Russell wrote, 'Every man, wherever he goes, is encompassed by a cloud of comforting convictions, which move with him like flies on a summer day.'

For intellectuals today, many of those convictions are about psychology and social relations. I will refer to those convictions as the Blank Slate: the idea that the human mind has no inherent structure and can be inscribed at will by society or ourselves.

That theory of human nature – namely, that it barely exists – is the topic of this book . . . the Blank Slate has become the secular religion of modern intellectual life. It is seen as a source of values . . .

The Blank Slate theory of human nature has been described as the intellectual foundation of feminism. Pinker convincingly explains that it is deeply flawed. From the same book:

Contrary to popular belief, parents in contemporary America do not treat their sons and daughters very differently. A recent assessment of 172 studies involving 28,000 children found that boys and girls are given similar amounts of encouragement, warmth, nurturance, restrictiveness, discipline, and clarity of communication. The only substantial difference was that about two-thirds of the boys were discouraged from playing with dolls, especially by their fathers, out of a fear that they would become gay. (Boys who prefer girls' toys often do turn out gay, but forbidding them the toys does not change the outcome.)

Nor do differences between boys and girls depend on their observing masculine behavior in their fathers and feminine behavior in their mothers. When Hunter has two mommies, he acts just as much like a boy as if he had a mommy and a daddy.

Things are not looking good for the theory that boys and girls are born identical except for their genitalia, with all other differences coming from the way society treats them. If that were true, it would be an amazing coincidence that in every society the coin flip that assigns each sex to one set of roles would land the same way (or that one fateful flip at the dawn of the species should have been maintained without interruption across all the upheavals of the past 100,000 years).

It would be just as amazing that, time and again, society's arbitrary assignments matched the predictions that a Martian biologist would make for our species based on our anatomy and the distribution of our genes. It would seem odd that the hormones that make us male and female in the first place also modulate the characteristically male and female mental traits, both decisively in early brain development and in smaller degrees throughout our lives.

It would be all the more odd that a second genetic mechanism differentiating the sexes (genomic imprinting) also installs characteristic male and female talents. Finally, two key predictions of the social construction theory – that boys treated as girls will grow up with girls' minds, and that differences between boys and girls can be traced to differences in how their parents treat them – have gone down in flames.

Of course, just because many sex differences are rooted in biology does not mean that one sex is superior, that the differences will emerge for all people in all circumstances, that discrimination against a person based on sex is justified, or that people should be coerced into doing things typical of their sex. But neither are the differences without consequences.

By now many people are happy to say what was unsayable in polite company a few years ago: that males and females do not have interchangeable minds . . . But among many professional women the existence of sex differences is still a source of discomfort. As one colleague said to me, 'Look, I know that males and females are not identical. I see it in my kids, I see it in myself, I know about the research. I can't explain it, but when I read claims about sex differences, *steam comes out of my ears.*'

In his 1993 bestseller *Men Are from Mars, Women Are from Venus*, John Gray wrote tellingly about the differences between men and women:

> Without the awareness that we are supposed to be different, men and woman are at odds with each other. We usually become angry or frustrated with the opposite sex because we have forgotten this important truth. We expect the opposite sex to be more like ourselves. We desire them to 'want what we want' and 'feel the way we feel'.
>
> We mistakenly assume that if our partners love us they will react and behave in certain ways – the ways we react and behave when we love someone. This attitude set us up to be disappointed again and again and prevents us from taking the necessary time to communicate lovingly about our differences.
>
> Men mistakenly expect women to think, communicate, and react the way men do; women mistakenly expect men to feel, communicate, and respond the way women do. We have forgotten that men and women are supposed to be different. As a result our relationships are filled with unnecessary friction and conflict. Clearly recognising and respecting these differences dramatically reduce confusion when dealing with the opposite sex.

The end of the first chapter concludes with:

> Falling in love is always magical. It feels eternal, as if love will last forever. We naively believe that somehow we are exempt from the problems our parents had, free from the odds that love will die, assured that it is meant to be and that we are destined to live happily ever after.
>
> But as the magic recedes and daily life takes over, it emerges that men continue to expect women to think and react like men, and women continue to expect men to feel and behave like women. Without a clear awareness of our differences, we do not take the time to understand and respect each other. We become demanding, resentful, judgmental and intolerant.
>
> With the best and most loving intentions love continues to die. Somehow the problems creep in. The resentments build. Communication breaks down. Mistrust increases. Rejection and repression result. The magic of love is lost. We ask ourselves:

How does it happen? Why does it happen? Why does it happen to us?

To answer these questions our greatest minds have developed brilliant and complex philosophical and psychological models. Yet still the old patterns return. Love dies. It happens to almost everyone.

Each day millions of individuals are searching for a partner to experience that special loving feeling. Each year, millions of couples join together in love and then painfully separate because they have lost that loving feeling. For those that are able to sustain love long enough to get married, only 50% stay married. Out of those who stay married, possibly another 50% are not fulfilled. They stay together out of loyalty and obligation or from the fear of starting over again.

Very few people, indeed, are able to grow in love. Yet, it does happen. When men and women are able to respect and accept their differences then love has a chance to blossom.

Through understanding the hidden differences of the opposite sex we can more successfully give and receive the love that is in our hearts. By validating and accepting our differences, creative solutions can be discovered whereby we can succeed in getting what we want. And, more importantly, we can learn how to best love and support the people we care about.

Love is magical, and it can last, if we remember our differences.

Gray really hits the nail on the head with his descriptions of men and women in the second chapter of the book, 'Mr. Fix-It and the Home-Improvement Committee':

The most frequently expressed complaint women have about men is that men don't listen. Either a man completely ignores her when she speaks to him, or he listens for a few beats, assesses what is bothering her, and then proudly puts on his Mr Fix-It cap and offers her a solution to make her feel better. He is confused when she doesn't appreciate this gesture of love. No matter how many times she tells him that he's not listening, he doesn't get it and keeps doing the same thing. She wants empathy, but he thinks she wants solutions.

The most frequently expressed complaint men have about women is that women are always trying to change them. When a woman loves a man she feels responsible to assist him in growing and tries to help him improve the way he does things. She forms a home-improvement committee, and he becomes her primary focus. No matter how much he resists her help, she persists – waiting for any opportunity to help him or tell him what to do. She thinks she's nurturing him, while he feels he's being controlled. Instead, he wants her acceptance.

These two problems can finally be solved by first understanding why men offer solutions, and why women seek to improve. Let's pretend to go back in time, where by observing life on Mars and Venus – before the planets discovered one another – we can gain some insights into men and women.

LIFE ON MARS
Martians value power, competency, efficiency, and achievement. They are always doing things to prove themselves and develop their power and skills. Their sense of self is defined through their ability to achieve results. They experience fulfilment primarily through success and accomplishment. A man's sense of self is defined through his ability to achieve results.

Everything on Mars is a reflection of these values. Even their dress is designed to reflect their skills and competence. Police officers, soldiers, businessmen, scientists, cab drivers, technicians, and chefs all wear uniforms or at least hats to reflect their competence and power.

They don't read magazines like *Psychology Today*, *Self*, or *People*. They are more concerned with outdoor activities, like hunting, fishing, and racing cars. They are interested in the news, weather, and sports and couldn't care less about romance novels and self-help books.

They are more interested in 'objects' and 'things' rather than people and feelings. Even today on Earth, while women fantasise about romance, men fantasise about powerful cars, faster computers, gadgets, gizmos, and new more powerful technology.

Men are preoccupied with the 'things' that can help them express power by creating results and achieving their goals.

Achieving goals is very important to a Martian because it is a way for him to prove his competence and thus feel good about himself. And for him to feel good about himself he must achieve these goals by himself. Someone else can't achieve them for him.

Martians pride themselves in doing things all by themselves. Autonomy is a symbol of efficiency, power, and competence. Understanding this Martian characteristic can help women understand why men resist so much being corrected or being told what to do. To offer a man unsolicited advice is to presume that he doesn't know what to do or that he can't do it on his own. Men are very touchy about this, because the issue of competence is so very important to them. To offer a man unsolicited advice is to presume that he doesn't know what to do or that he can't do it on his own.

Because he is handling his problems on his own, a Martian rarely talks about his problems unless he needs expert advice. He reasons: 'Why involve someone else when I can do it by myself?' He keeps his problems to himself unless he requires help from another to find a solution. Asking for help when you can do it yourself is perceived as a sign of weakness.

However, if he truly does need help, then it is a sign of wisdom to get it. In this case, he will find someone he respects and then talk about his problem. Talking about a problem on Mars is an invitation for advice. Another Martian feels honored by the opportunity. Automatically he puts on his Mr. Fix-It hat, listens for a while, and then offers some jewels of advice.

This Martian custom is one of the reasons men instinctively offer solutions when women talk about problems. When a woman innocently shares upset feelings or explores out loud the problems of her day, a man mistakenly assumes she is looking for some expert advice. He puts on his Mr. Fix-It hat and begins giving advice; this is his way of showing love and of trying to help. He wants to help her feel better by solving her problems. He wants to be useful to her. He feels he can be valued and thus worthy of her love when his abilities are used to solve her problems.

Once he has offered a solution, however, and she continues to be upset, it becomes increasingly difficult for him to listen because his solution is being rejected and he feels increasingly useless. He has no idea that by just listening with empathy and interest he can be supportive. He does not know that on Venus talking about problems is not an invitation to offer a solution.

LIFE ON VENUS
Venusians have different values. They value love, communication, beauty, and relationships. They spend a lot of time supporting, helping, and nurturing one another. Their sense of self is defined through their feelings and the quality of their relationships. They experience fulfilment through sharing and relating.

A woman's sense of self is defined through her feelings and the quality of her relationships. Everything on Venus reflects these values. Rather than building highways and tall buildings, the Venusians are more concerned with living together in harmony, community, and loving cooperation. Relationships are more important than work and technology. In most ways their world is the opposite of Mars.

They do not wear uniforms like the Martians (to reveal their competence). On the contrary, they enjoy wearing a different outfit every day, according to how they are feeling. Personal expression, especially of their feelings, is very important. They may even change outfits several times a day as their mood changes.

Communication is of primary importance. To share their personal feelings is much more important than achieving goals and success. Talking and relating to one another is a source of tremendous fulfilment.

This is hard for a man to comprehend. He can come close to understanding a woman's experience of sharing and relating by comparing it to the satisfaction he feels when he wins a race, achieves a goal, or solves a problem.

Instead of being goal oriented, women are relationship oriented; they are more concerned with expressing their goodness, love, and caring. Two Martians go to lunch to discuss a project or business goal; they have a problem to solve. In addition, Martians view going to a restaurant as an efficient way to approach food: no shopping, no cooking, and no washing dishes. For Venusians, going to lunch is an opportunity to nurture a relationship, for both giving support to and receiving support from a friend. Women's restaurant talk can be very open and intimate, almost like the dialogue that occurs between therapist and patient.

On Venus, everyone studies psychology and has at least a master's degree in counselling. They are very involved in personal growth, spirituality, and everything that can nurture life, healing, and growth. Venus is covered with parks, organic gardens, shopping centres, and restaurants.

Venusians are very intuitive. They have developed this ability through centuries of anticipating the needs of others. They pride themselves in being considerate of the needs and feelings of others. A sign of great love is to offer help and assistance to another Venusian without being asked.

Because proving one's competence is not as important to a Venusian, offering help is not offensive, and needing help is not a sign of weakness. A man, however, may feel offended because when a woman offers advice he doesn't feel she trusts his ability to do it himself.

A woman has no conception of this male sensitivity because for her it is another feather in her hat if someone offers to help her. It makes her feel loved and cherished. But offering help to a man can make him feel incompetent, weak, and even unloved.

On Venus it is a sign of caring to give advice and suggestions. Venusians firmly believe that when something is working it can always work better. Their nature is to want to improve things.

When they care about someone, they freely point out what can be improved and suggest how to do it. Offering advice and constructive criticism is an act of love.

Mars is very different. Martians are more solution oriented. If something is working, their motto is don't change it. Their instinct is to leave it alone if it is working. 'Don't fix it unless it is broken' is a common expression.

When a woman tries to improve a man, he feels she is trying to fix him. He receives the message that he is broken. She doesn't realise her caring attempts to help him may humiliate him. She mistakenly thinks she is just helping him to grow.

Gray's book then provides sections giving advice to men ('Learning to Listen') and women ('Give Up Giving Advice').

From an evolutionary and genetic perspective, men should want to scatter their genes as widely as possible, i.e. have unprotected sex with as many women as possible. And of course in certain periods of history powerful men have been able to satisfy this want, with harems. Some cultures and religions, even those that are very strict morally and have harsh penalties for moral transgression, still permit individual men to have a number of wives.

Of course there are numerous restraints on the number of women that individual men are likely to have unprotected sex with over the course of their lives. They include:

- The scarcity of women prepared to allow them to exercise their desires
- The improved life chances of their progeny if they 'stay around' to support the mother and child
- The institution of marriage

When men are unfaithful to their partners, visit a prostitute, or watch pornography, they are guilty of nothing more than failing to suppress their natural urges, whatever anyone might think of them *morally*. And what are many sexual morals other than a set of rules designed to stop men acting on their natural urges?

It is only natural that men should become bored with having sex with just one woman for years, even decades. And vice versa, to be fair. In which other area of life are modern humans expected to display such a lack of interest in variety? We wouldn't expect a person to eat the same dinner every day for half a century, no matter how well-prepared and well-balanced the meal might be nutritionally...

The shelves of the women's magazine section of my local newsagent's are groaning under the weight of numerous glossy magazines about weddings and honeymoons, containing articles with titles such as 'Be a princess for a day!', and 'Book that fairytale honeymoon in the Caribbean now!'

What are we to make of this? Belief in fairytales surely belongs to childhood, and it's unfortunate that women are being encouraged to marry through the use of images and articles appealing to that side of their natures. A wedding day takes up just one day of a person's life, while a 54-year-long marriage will take up about 20,000 days, and some last even longer. Given that 1:20,000 plus ratio, shouldn't we be spending a lot more time preparing for our marriages than we spend preparing for our wedding days?

Men have become accustomed to women aiming criticisms – witty and otherwise – at them. One of my favourites is the saying attributed to Gloria Steinem, 'A woman without a man is like a fish without a bicycle.' But the reality of many women's desperate search for a life partner, obsession with relationships in general and marriage in particular, surely gives the lie to a lot of the jibes.

Women aren't too happy when even the mildest of criticisms come in their direction. A personal example: I had barely started to explain the content of this chapter to a lady acquaintance when she sneered, 'Oh right – so all men are perfect!' And so any debate is quashed at the outset.

On to the 'battle of the sexes', where women in the developed world fought to win equal rights with men. Women conclusively won the battle many years ago, and yet they keep fighting it. Or at least some of them do. Some women deem themselves qualified to speak for women in general – their elections to these positions are held in secret, one imagines – as if women were a feeble-minded lot who needed such representation. But these stalwart ladies keep fighting the good fight, even though their targets become ever fewer in number as the years roll by.

The combined membership of Women's Institutes in the United Kingdom is around 205,000. They 'play a unique role in providing women with educational opportunities and the chance to build new skills, to take part in a wide variety of activities and to campaign on issues that matter to them and their communities'. Membership is, not unnaturally, restricted to women.

If men had an equivalent body to the Women's Institute – the Men's Institute, say – and excluded women from its membership, doubtless the body would face demands to admit women, and change its name to the People's Institute. But I've never met a man even slightly bothered by the fact that he can't join the Women's Institute. Indeed, I can't recall any man even mentioning the matter.

Men happily recognise that while men and women enjoy the company of the opposite sex, at times they welcome just the company of their own sex, which is why they have no problem with bodies such as the Women's Institute. Or with phenomena such as women-only book competitions, or women-only competitions in sports even when men do not have an advantage on physical strength grounds (snooker, darts . . .).

But do women accord men the same courtesy? Of course not. Readers of *The Independent* might have become a little agitated by the following articles in December 1999. The first is by Paul Waugh and Gary Finn, entitled 'Men-only clubs will not be outlawed', published 7 December 1999:

> The Government last night denied reports that it has secret plans to ban men-only members clubs following admissions from ministers that clubs that barred women from membership were 'anachronisms'.
>
> The moves were said to be being discussed by at least four ministers, including the Cabinet Office Minister, Mo Mowlam. They would lead to the end of membership

restrictions from every body ranging from the 17th century St James's Club in London to golf clubs and the traditional Labour bastion, the working men's club.

It was claimed that private clubs, exempted by the Sex Discrimination Act, would be modernised under an amendment to the Equal Opportunities Bill in the next session of parliament. Senior Labour figures are said to be heartened by recent about-turns by men-only stalwarts such as the MCC which last year voted to admit women after 211 years.

A Government spokesman rejected reports of new laws in the pipeline. Many topics were covered in ministerial discussions on equality but Government plans for anti-discrimination legislation did not extend beyond public bodies.

Last night Nicholas Soames MP, the former Tory defence minister, who is a member of White's, Pratt's and the Turf, said: 'This is another sign that living under New Labour is like living in Soviet Russia. What sensible woman wants to be a member of a men's club?'

A good point Mr Soames, and well made. Now there's a man you can imagine tucking enthusiastically into his rhubarb crumble and custard at his club. The following was written by Joan Smith for the paper the next day, entitled 'The Irritations of Modern Life: Men-only Clubs':

I have often wondered what men do in all-male clubs. Million-pound deals? Homosexual rituals? Men, especially if they belong to the Garrick Club, are reticent, giving the impression that it involves little more than long lunches, at which they get slightly squiffy and eat nursery food. Yet, as soon as someone proposes changing the law to force such clubs to admit women, it is as if the very foundations of civilisation had begun to shudder.

'A grotesque curtailment of freedom of association – an almost totalitarian assertion that the state should be able to decide with whom you can spend your own free time on property private to you . . .' is how *The Daily Telegraph* greeted the news that the Government is thinking of banning men-only establishments. Yikes! Next thing you know, Tony Blair will be personally knocking on *Telegraph* readers' doors, pushing a female across the threshold and instructing them to talk to her.

Of course, there are few subjects so likely to fire up a right-wing leader-writer. The age-old right of the British upper classes to exclude outsiders is slowly being whittled away. The Reform Club has admitted women for years; even Lord's is not the bastion it was. What's left for the man who sometimes feels the need to be with people who, not to put too fine a point on it, aren't going to go all funny and exhibit symptoms of pre-menstrual tension?

Men's clubs are an anachronism. Their very existence institutionalises discrimination, draping it with a veil of respectability. When I witnessed the reaction to this mild move towards equality, I felt as if I'd been transported back to a time when misogyny was so firmly taken for granted that most people didn't even have a name for it. Now we do, and it's not acceptable. The bad news for club bores, tucking into bread-and-butter pudding in Covent Garden – or, indeed, a working men's club in Halifax – is that the time has come to grow up.

Ah yes. 'An anachronism.' 'The time has come to grow up.' I don't suppose Ms Smith is quite so agitated by the Women's Institute, even ten years on. And with such reasoning women seek to hide the real reasons why they don't want men to associate freely with one another. Whatever they are. Maybe they've learned about the campaign to withdraw voting rights from them. Damn. We've managed to keep that under wraps for *years*.

On to BBC Radio's *Woman's Hour*, a staple of BBC Radio since shortly after the Second World War. From their website: 'October 7 1946 was the start of something big – it was the first broadcast of a programme designed to celebrate, entertain and inform women.' I have never heard a man say that there should be a programme for men, *Man's Hour*, never mind that it should be 'a programme designed to celebrate, entertain and inform men'.

I often hear *Woman's Hour* when driving around the country on business, and did so on 27 April 2009. It's often an interesting programme but some topics do come up with monotonous regularity, one being the so-called 'gender pay imbalance', annoyingly – to some – still a reality nearly 40 years after the 1970 Equal Pay Act. Today's report concerned The Rt Hon Harriet Harman MP QC who is putting forward the 2009 Equality Bill, which will include provisions to require organisations to publicise wage rates etc.

But the gender pay imbalance *probably doesn't exist* once a number of factors are taken into account, such as choice of profession, career breaks for having children, and many women preferring part-time work. Not that you'll ever hear this mentioned on *Woman's Hour*. Or at least I haven't heard it in the past 30 years of listening occasionally to the programme.

A later discussion in the same episode concerned women giving up highly paid stressful jobs to enable them to work for themselves, often on low incomes, or to do jobs they found more fulfilling. One of the women had been a 'high-flying lawyer'. The general tone of the discussion was a celebration of women who decided to forsake lucrative but demanding jobs in favour of more job satisfaction. One woman made the following observation:

> So many women I know are crying themselves to sleep on a Sunday night, because they really can't bear the thought of going to work the next day.

Needless to say, no connection was made between the 'gender pay imbalance' and women voluntarily opting out of highly paid, stressful, unfulfilling jobs. Nor was it even considered worth raising that even if a gender pay balance does still exist, it might be attributable to men being more willing than women to continue with such jobs. And so the myths of the 'gender pay imbalance' and the 'glass ceiling' roll on year after year.

The enthusiasm with which politicians – both female and male – keep perpetuating the myth of the gender pay imbalance is surely a testimony to their enduring vote-delivering powers among female voters. Anyone who believes that the gender pay imbalance is still attributable to male discrimination against women should read a remarkable book written by a Canadian-American psychologist, Susan Pinker. The book is *The Sexual Paradox: Men, Women, and the Real Gender Gap* (2008)...

Why do some women remain convinced (at least in their public utterances) that female 'under-representation' is attributable to discrimination on the part of men in positions of authority, regardless of all the evidence to the contrary? Maybe it's because feminism has become a religion of an increasingly secular age, with women as its gods. All women. And just as religions over the ages have persecuted people for defying their authority, so feminists try to persecute non-believers – mainly but not exclusively men – whenever and wherever they can. They have become very ingenious at the game, and few men appear to be conscious of the persecution. Maybe it's because men don't want to be accused of that most heinous crime of the modern era, sexism.

When you look for it, it's not difficult to find examples of women working together to advance their interests at the expense of men. Let's start with The Rt Hon Harriet Harman QC, Member of Parliament for Camberwell and Peckham, Deputy Leader of the Labour Party, Labour Party Chair, Minister for Women and Equality, Leader of the House of Commons, and The Lord Privy Seal. She must have the largest business card on the planet.

In the foreword of the paper *Women's Changing Lives: Priorities for the Ministers for Women – One Year On Progress Report*, presented to Parliament in July 2008, Harriet Harman wrote the following:

> A modern democracy must be fair and equal. The government has fought for equal representation and it's because of this that we have record levels of women MPs, as well as more black and Asian MPs and councillors than ever before. But we need more women and more black, Asian and minority ethnic MPs and councillors to make our democracy truly representative.

> That's why in March I announced that political parties will be able to use all-women shortlists for the next five elections . . .

Wow. So through government diktat, for the next 22 years or so I – and every other man in the United Kingdom – could be stopped from becoming a prospective MP *solely on the ground of our gender*, regardless of our fitness for the office. And the least competent female candidate will *automatically* be deemed more worthy of public office than the most competent otherwise electable male candidate.

To ban *either* of the sexes merely on the grounds of gender would surely and inevitably reduce the pool of competent people willing to stand for public office. Which can only lead over time to Parliament being filled with even fewer competent MPs and ministers. Still, in Hattieworld that's a small price to pay for equal representation. Equality is clearly now far more important than quality.

The possible prospect of women-only MP candidate shortlists is so extraordinary that even the Labour Party must surely have mentioned the matter in its 2005 General Election manifesto. Sorry, I couldn't resist that little joke. Of course it didn't. But it did contain the following gem (one of many):

> The EU now has 25 members and will continue to expand. The new Constitutional Treaty ensures the new Europe can work effectively, and that Britain keeps control of key national interests like foreign policy, taxation, social security and defence. The Treaty sets out what the EU can do and what it cannot. It strengthens the voice of national parliaments and governments in EU affairs. It is a good treaty for Britain and the new Europe. We will put it to the British people in a referendum and campaign whole-heartedly for a 'Yes' vote to keep Britain a leading nation in Europe.

British readers will need no reminding that we're still waiting for that referendum. For £0.01 plus postage and packaging you can order the 2005 Labour Party General Election manifesto from Amazon resellers. I can't wait for the 2010 manifesto. It should be a real hoot.

From *The Daily Telegraph* of 13 July 2009:

> Discrimination against northerners by public bodies could be banned under plans being considered by Harriet Harman, the Equalities Minister. Her office is looking at how it can ensure that the boards of national organisations are not dominated by Londoners and other southerners, her deputy disclosed. The remarks were made by Michael Foster, an equalities minister, in a parliamentary debate on 'diversity in public appointments' when replying to Meg Munn, a Labour MP.

Marvellous. That's yet another clipping for my file *Harriet Harman MP (stuff you couldn't make up)*. It's nearly full. I've noticed myself that short fat people with beards – both men and women, I'm not making a sexist point here – are under-represented as bar staff in upmarket wine bars. I must alert Ms Harman to this shocking reality.

Am I becoming a little obsessed with Harriet Harman? Possibly. But I'm not alone. A friend told me he once had a dream in which he was a Cabinet minister, and Harriet Harman was chairing a Cabinet meeting, the first in her new role as Prime Minister. The meeting took place in the context of a national emergency. As the meeting was about to begin, in an effort to lighten the mood my friend remarked out loud to Miss Harman, 'Harriet, may I kick off proceedings by remarking on how very *pretty* you're looking this morning?' Whereupon she frowned and drew a .44 Magnum revolver [Author: The gun used by Clint Eastwood in *Dirty Harry*] from her handbag, slowly took aim, and shot his right arm clean off his shoulder. She then glared at the other ministers and growled, 'Does anyone *else* think I'm looking pretty this morning?' They all stared glumly at their papers and mumbled, 'No, Prime Minister.'

I wrote a letter to Harriet Harman in the hope of securing a meeting, but unfortunately she was too busy to meet with me. It was only later that it came to my attention that she had written a book published in 1993, *The Century Gap (20th Century Man, 21st Century Woman)*. I looked for the book on Amazon and found 22 used copies available for £0.01 (plus postage and packaging). At that price, I couldn't resist ordering a copy. From the back cover:

> Women have arrived ahead of time in the 21st century – then, as now, they will have an important role in the workforce as well as at home. But this revolution in women's lives has not yet been matched by men, who remain firmly stuck in the 20th century. That is the Century Gap.

The book contains two chapters on marriage. The following extract is taken from just three successive paragraphs in a section titled 'Men Contributing More':

> What must men do . . . They will have to . . . They will have to . . . Then they will feel able to . . . They must begin to . . . They must dramatically increase . . . They must . . . Men must . . . They must . . . They must . . . they must . . .

On behalf of men everywhere, might I respond feebly with, '*Why* must we, Mistress Harriet?'

While I'm writing this – early August 2009 – numerous high-profile women are whingeing about the supposed 'shortage' of women in Gordon Brown's cabinet. Which brings me neatly to a remark made a few weeks ago on BBC Radio by Diane Abbott, a Labour MP. It followed the 'resignation' of her fellow Labour MP Hazel Blears, widely regarded as an incompetent minister:

> Some weeks ago, before Hazel Blears resigned, a number of us went to a minister very close to Gordon Brown and told him Hazel just *had* to be fired. The minister responded with, 'But who could we replace her with?' I laughed and told him, 'Just about anyone with a pulse, to be honest!'

Daniel Goleman had some interesting points to make about the sexes' different perspectives in his 1995 bestseller *Emotional Intelligence*. After outlining how the sexes develop differing perspectives over the course of their school lives, he continues:

> These differing perspectives mean that men and woman want and expect very different things from a conversation, with men content to talk about 'things', while women seek emotional connection.
> In short, these contrasts in schooling in the emotions foster very different skills, with girls becoming 'adept at reading both verbal and nonverbal emotional signals, at expressing and communicating their feelings,' and boys becoming adept at 'minimising emotions having to do with vulnerability, guilt, fear and hurt' . . . women, on average, experience the entire range of emotions with greater intensity and more volatility than men – in this sense, women *are* more emotional than men. . .
> All of this means that, in general, women come into a marriage groomed for the role of emotional manager, while men arrive with much less appreciation of the importance of this task for helping a relationship survive. Indeed, the most important element for women – but not for men – in satisfaction with their relationship reported in a study of 264 couples was the sense that the couple had 'good communication.' Ted Huston, a psychologist at the University of Texas who has studied couples in depth, observes, 'For the wives, intimacy means talking things over, especially talking about the relationship itself. The men, by and large, don't understand what the wives want from them. They say, 'I want to do things with her, and all she wants to do is talk.'

Notice here an unwritten but clear value judgement, one that is repeated in much of the literature on the subject of relationships. The judgement is that men *should* become more communicative about their emotions, and women *shouldn't* need to recognise that their (male) partners are different and act accordingly; for example, not expect them to talk to them (or indeed listen to them) at great length about emotions.

How exactly has this value judgement come to be so universally accepted in the developed world in the modern era? My hunch is that it results from the very high proportion of the following groups of people, who are women:

- Writers of books and articles about relationships
- Readers of material about relationships, in books, women's magazines etc
- Psychologists
- Relationship counsellors
- Literary agents

A relation is a psychologist, and he graduated from Leeds University in 2007. Over 90% of his fellow psychology students were female. I mention literary agents because they are the 'gatekeepers' between writers and publishers, which might help explain the paucity of books about relationships with any sympathy towards masculine perspectives.

In her book *The Relate Guide to Better Relationships* (2001), the author – Sarah Litvinoff – takes up about a quarter of the book's length with a chapter on communication. The chapter includes the following advice:

> Make a date to talk to your partner for one hour specifically about yourselves and your feelings. Toss a coin to see who begins. Take half an hour each to talk about how you feel and what you want in life – as if you are explaining yourself to a stranger. While each person talks, the other must be silent and listen with full attention. On the half-hour you switch roles. During this time you must not talk about your partner or your relationship, though you can talk about your past. . .

Now I know a number of women who could talk for half an hour without interruption about themselves and their feelings, but not one man who could. Most men would, I'm sure, prefer to remove their own teeth with a pair of old rusty pliers, without the benefit of anaesthetic.

A thought prompted by a line from George Bernard Shaw's *My Fair Lady*. The line is Professor Higgins's, 'Why can't a woman be more like a man?' Today we would all think the remark chauvinistic and old-fashioned. But what is the implied question underlying much of the criticism so often aimed by women at men? Nothing less than 'Why can't a man be more like a woman?'. Surely the question that defines female chauvinism in the modern age.

I emailed a copy of the last few pages to a male friend, a fellow businessman and writer, and asked for his comments. He replied:

> If asked about my emotions I don't need half an hour to explain them. Half a minute would do. I'm either happy, relaxed, stressed, tired, pissed off or bored. Very occasionally anxious, but usually only when tired or stressed. Covers everything. Nothing else to say. It's not a big deal. When I'm fed up, I wait until I'm not fed up. I don't want to bloody talk about it. I want a beer.
>
> You have uncovered an interesting broader point. When my wife and I go to our place in Brighton, she and I often walk on the beach for half an hour. She wants to *talk*, I want to look at things – the sea, clouds, pebbles etc – and *think*. I always thought it was me who was weird. Maybe it's simply because I'm a man.

In his 1998 book *The Secrets of Love and Lust*, Simon Andreae had some interesting things to say about women's search for 'Mr Right':

> Handsome men will pass their physical advantages down to the children of whoever they mate with, giving those children a head-start in the race for reproductive success. The indices of conventional male good looks – a rugged jaw, broad shoulders, a full

head of hair and a healthy physique – are also indications of genetic health and strength. Yet looks in the opposite sex seem to be less important to women than they are to men, and less important than other factors.

In Douglas Kenrick's study of the percentages required of potential partners before women would consent to dating, having sex, steady dating or marrying them, 'good looks' was the only criterion where women, across the board, were ready to accept a lower percentage value than men. They were even prepared to consider men of below-average physical attractiveness . . . as long as they had other things to offer.

Legend has it that, some years ago, the actor Dustin Hoffman was sitting in a restaurant quietly enjoying dinner when he began to notice the attentions of a number of female diners. They were looking at him, whispering, giggling. Hoffman began to feel a little uncomfortable. Eventually, they approached him and asked for his autograph. One even asked him out on a date. At this point, Hoffman began to grow exasperated and, turning to his audience, uttered in mock dismay: 'Girls, please, where were you when I needed you?'

Hoffman is, by most standards, not conventionally handsome. As a male model, stripped to the waist and lined up next to the Diet Coke hunk, he probably wouldn't have made the grade. But Hoffman, like most famous men, has other attributes. In Glenn Wilson's study of British sexual fantasies, men were found to fantasise more frequently about group sex than any of the other scenarios he presented to them.

But women had a very different fantasy life. For them, by far the most characteristic fantasy was straight, monogamous sex with a famous personality. The argument runs that famous men today, like village headmen in the past, and successful hunters during the early period in which we evolved, would have acquired the status and resources to furnish a woman and her children with more food and protection than the next man.

Over the incremental advances of time, evolution would therefore have favoured women who developed mental programmes which allowed them to judge the signs of status within their particular environment and culture, and calibrate their desire accordingly.

Fame is not the only indicator of a man who is high in status and rich in resources. In 1986 the American psychologist Elizabeth Hill published the results of an experiment in which she asked her students to describe what sort of clothes they considered high-status men to wear, and what sort of clothes they considered low-status men to wear. Among the former were smart suits, polo shirts, designer jeans and expensive watches; among the latter were nondescript jeans, tank tops and T-shirts.

She then photographed a number of different men in variations of both styles of dress and showed the photographs to a different group of female students, asking them to rate each one for attractiveness. Overall, the same models were found more attractive when wearing the high-status costumes than when wearing the low-status ones.

It's important to note, though, that it's not just status symbols, and resources they indicate, that women find attractive. It's also those personality characteristics which indicate the capacity to acquire such symbols in the future. In most cultures, women rarely have the luxury of being able to wait for a man to achieve all that he sets out to do before pairing up with him; as a result they have to calibrate his desirability partly on unrealised potential.

To find out what these characteristics of future success might be, and to see how they correlated with female desire, psychologist Michael Wiederman examined more than a thousand personal ads placed in various American periodicals between January and June 1992. He speculated that, in an arena where men and women were paying to attract potential mates, they would be more than usually forthright in specifying the attributes they sought, and more than usually direct in how they expressed their priorities.

Taking the various descriptions of what people wanted, and arranging them into categories, Wiederman noticed that terms denoting high status and plentiful resources (terms such as 'business owner', 'enjoys the finer things', 'successful', 'wealthy', 'well-to-do', and 'financially affluent') cropped up ten times as often in the women's wish lists as in the men's.

But there was also a considerable female preference for terms like 'ambitious', 'industrious', 'career-oriented', and 'college-educated'; in other words, for terms which clearly indicated the potential to acquire status and amass resources in the future.

Wiederman's results have been backed up by numerous other studies covering different decades and geographical areas. The American periodical *The Journal of Home Economics* took the sexual temperature of the nation's youth in the 1940s, '50s and '60s and found in each decade that young women rated financial prospects as highly desirable (though not absolutely essential) in men they were considering dating.

Douglas Kenrick, in his study of how intelligent, attractive and so on men and women had to be before they were considered sexually attractive by the opposite sex, found that earning capacity was much more important to women than to men; and David Buss, in a massive study of mating habits which covered 10,000 people in 37 cultures around the world, found that women rated financial resources on average at least twice as highly as men did.

Some researchers argue that an evolutionary explanation is not justified here. Women only desire wealthy men, they say, because most cultures don't allow women to make much money for themselves. But the female preference for wealth seems to exist regardless of the financial status of the women in question.

There is an unprecedented number of independent, self-supporting women with resources of their own in the world today, yet their mate preferences still seem to be following the age-old, evolved pattern of looking for men who can offer more.

One study of American newly-wed couples in 1993 found that financially successful brides placed an even greater importance on their husbands' earning capacities than those who were less well-off. And another, conducted among female college students, reported that those who were likely to earn more in respected professions placed greater importance on the financial prospects of their potential husbands than those who were likely to earn less. Buss's fellow psychologist Bruce Ellis summed up the prospect for future mate choice by saying, 'Women's sexual tastes become more, rather than less, discriminatory as their wealth, power, and social status increase.'

So there you have it. Women are keen that resources such as money flow in one direction only, *to* them *from* men. And what better mechanism to ensure this happens, than marriage?

appendix 3

the letter to the rt. hon. david miliband m.p.

Rt. Hon. David Miliband M.P.
Secretary of State, Department for Environment, Food and Rural Affairs
Nobel House
17 Smith Square
London SW1P 3JR

16 May 2007

Dear Secretary of State,

My friend, who is in farming at the moment, recently received a cheque for £3,000 from the Rural Payments Agency, for not rearing pigs. I would now like to join the 'not rearing pigs' business.

In your opinion, what is the best kind of farm not to rear pigs on, and which is the best breed of pigs not to rear? I want to be sure I approach this endeavour in keeping with all government policies, as dictated by the EU under the Common Agricultural Policy.

I would prefer not to rear bacon pigs, but if this is not the type you want not rearing, I will just as gladly not rear porkers. Are there any advantages in not rearing rare breeds such as Saddlebacks or Gloucester Old Spots, or are there too many people already not rearing these?

As I see it, the hardest part of this programme will be keeping an accurate record of how many pigs I haven't reared. Are there any Government or Local Authority courses on this? My friend is very satisfied with this business. He has been rearing pigs for forty years or so, and the best he ever made on them was £1,422, in 1968. That is - until this year, when he received a cheque for not rearing any. If I get £3,000 for not rearing 50 pigs, will I get £6,000 for not rearing 100?

I plan to operate on a small scale at first, holding myself down to about 4,000 pigs not raised, which will mean about £240,000 for the first year. As I become more expert in not rearing pigs, I plan to be more ambitious, perhaps increasing to, say, 40,000 pigs not reared in my second year, for which I should expect about £2.4 million from your department.

Incidentally, I wonder if I would be eligible to receive tradable carbon credits for all these pigs not producing harmful and polluting methane gases? Another point: these pigs that I plan not to rear will not eat 2,000 tonnes of cereals. I understand that you also pay farmers for not growing crops. Will I qualify for payments for not growing cereals to not feed the pigs I don't rear?

I am also considering the 'not milking cows' business, so please send any information you have on that too. Please could you also include the current DEFRA advice on set-aside fields? Can this be done on an e-commerce basis with virtual fields (of which I seem to have several thousand hectares)?

In view of the above, you will realise that I will be totally unemployed, and will therefore qualify for unemployment benefits. I shall of course be voting for your party at the next general election.

Yours faithfully,

Nigel Johnson-Hill

appendix 4

if the battle of trafalgar had been fought in a politically correct age . . .

The death of Nelson was felt in England as something more than a public calamity; men started at the intelligence, and turned pale, as if they had heard of the loss of a dear friend.

Richard Southey (1774 - 1843), *The Life of Nelson* (1813)

From Wikipedia:

> The Battle of Trafalgar (21 October 1805) was a sea battle fought between the British Royal Navy and the combined fleets of the French Navy and Spanish Navy, in the War of the Third Coalition . . . of the Napoleonic Wars (1803-1815). It was the most decisive British naval victory of the war. 27 British ships of the line led by Admiral Lord Nelson aboard HMS Victory defeated 33 French and Spanish ships of the line under French Admiral Pierre Villeneuve off the south-west coast of Spain, just west of Cape Trafalgar. The Franco-Spanish fleet lost 22 ships, no British vessels being lost.

On the *Mail Online* internet site on 29 April 2007, English author, broadcaster and journalist Richard Littlejohn (1954 -) speculated on how Admiral Nelson might have fared at Trafalgar if he had been subject to modern health and safety regulations. The scene is set on the deck of the recently renamed British flagship, HMS Appeasement, shortly before the battle.

Order the signal, Hardy.
Aye, aye, Sir.
Hold on, that's not what I dictated to the signal officer. What's the meaning of this?
Sorry Sir?
England expects every person to do his or her duty, regardless of race, gender, sexual orientation, religious persuasion or disability. What gobbledegook is this?
Admiralty policy, I'm afraid, Sir. We're an equal opportunities employer now. We had the devil's own job getting 'England' past the censors, lest it be considered racist.
Gadzooks, Hardy. Hand me my pipe and tobacco.
Sorry sir. All naval vessels have now been designated smoke-free working environments.
In that case, break open the rum ration. Let us splice the mainbrace to steel the men before battle.
The rum ration has been abolished, Admiral. It's part of the Government's policy on binge drinking.
Good heavens, Hardy. I suppose we'd better get on with it. Full speed ahead.
I think you'll find that there's a four knot speed limit in this stretch of water, Sir.
Damn it man! We are on the eve of the greatest sea battle in history. We must advance with all dispatch. Report from the crow's nest, please.
That won't be possible, sir.
What?

Health and Safety have closed the crow's nest, Sir. No harness. And they said that the rope ladders don't meet regulations. They won't let anyone up there until proper scaffolding can be erected.

Then get me the ship's carpenter without delay, Hardy.

He's busy knocking up a wheelchair access to the fo'c'sle, Admiral.

Wheelchair access? I've never heard anything so absurd.

Health and Safety again, sir. We have to provide a barrier-free environment for the differently abled.

Differently abled? I've only one arm and one eye and I refuse even to hear mention of the term. I didn't rise to the rank of Admiral because of the disability card.

Actually, sir, you did. The Royal Navy is under-represented in the areas of visual impairment and limb deficiency.

Whatever next! Give me full sail. The salt spray beckons.

A couple of problems there too, sir. Health and Safety won't let the crew up the rigging without hard hats. And they don't want anyone breathing in too much salt – haven't you seen the latest adverts?

I've never heard such infamy. Break out the cannon and tell the men to stand by to engage the enemy.

The men are a bit worried about shooting at anyone, Admiral.

What? This is mutiny.

It's not that, sir. It's just that they're afraid of being charged with murder if they actually kill anyone. There's a couple of legal aid lawyers on board, watching everyone like hawks.

Then how are we to sink the Frenchies and the Spanish?

Actually, sir, we're not.

We're not?

No, sir. The French and the Spanish are our European partners now. According to the Common Fisheries Policy, we shouldn't even be in this stretch of water. We could get hit with a claim for compensation.

But you must hate a Frenchman as you hate the devil.

I wouldn't let the ship's diversity co-ordinator hear you saying that sir. You'll be up on a disciplinary.

You must consider every man an enemy who speaks ill of your King.

Not any more, sir. We must be inclusive in this multicultural age. Now put on your Kevlar vest; it's the rules.

Don't tell me – Health and Safety. Whatever happened to rum, sodomy and the lash?

As I explained, sir, rum is off the menu. And there's a ban on corporal punishment.

What about sodomy?

I believe it's to be encouraged, sir.

In that case . . . kiss me, Hardy.

Supplementary notes from Richard Littlejohn:

Shortly after I wrote this, the organisers of the official Trafalgar bicentenary celebrations decided that rather than reconstruct the battle in which the British fleet defeated a much larger Franco-Spanish fleet, they would simply stage a simulated confrontation between a Red Fleet and a Blue Fleet, so as not to upset the sensibilities of French and Spanish visitors.

In Devon, Totnes council announced that it was refusing to mark the anniversary of the battle in case it upset their twin town in Normandy, France.

If Nelson were alive today, he'd wonder why he ever bothered.

books referenced in the appendices

Andreae, Simon (2000), *The Secrets of Love and Lust* (London: Abacus).

Browne, Anthony (2006), *The Retreat of Reason: Political Correctness and the Corruption of Public Debate in Modern Britain* (London: The Institute for the Study of Civil Society [Civitas]).

Gray, John (1993), *Men Are From Mars, Women Are From Venus* (New York: HarperCollins).

Harman, Harriet (1993) *20th Century Man, 21st Century Woman: How Both Sexes Can Bridge The Century Gap* (London: Vermillion)

Litvinoff, Sarah (2001), *Better Relationships: Practical Ways to Make Your Love Last (Relate Guides)* (London: Vermillion).

Moxon, Steve (2008), *The Woman Racket* (Exeter: Imprint Academic).

Pinker, Steven (2003), *The Blank Slate: The Modern Denial of Human Nature* (London: Penguin).

Pinker, Susan (2008), *The Sexual Paradox: Men, Women, and the Real Gender Gap* (New York: Scribner).

index

Abbey, Edward, 1
Abbott, Diane, 1
Abbott, Tony, 1
Absolutely Fabulous, 1
Abzug, Bella, 1
Acheson, Dean, 2
Acton, Lord, 2
Adams, Abigail, 2, 4
Adams, Ansel, 2
Adams, Douglas, 2
Adams, Franklin P., 3
Adams, Henry, 3
Adams, John, 2, 3, 4, 193
Adams, John Quincy, 2, 4, 286
Adams, Samuel, 4
Adams, Scott, 4
Adler, Mortimer J., 4
Agar, Herbert, 5
Agate, James, 5
Agnew, Spiro T., 5
Aitken, Jonathan, 5
Albran, Kehlog, 5
Alcuin, 5
Aldington, Richard, 6
Aldrich, Henry, 6
Aldrin, Buzz, 6
Alejandro King, John, 6
Alexander, Cecil Frances, 6
Algren, Nelson, 6
Allen, Fred, 7
Allen, Tim, 7
Allen, Woody, 7
Ally McBeal, 9
Alvarez, Luis Walter, 9
The American Declaration of Independence, 9
Ameringer, Oscar, 9
Amery, Julian, 10
Amery, Leo, 10, 109
Amiel, Henri-Frédéric, 10
Amies, Hardy, 10
Amis, Sir Kingsley, 10, 11
Amis, Martin, 11
Amory, Cleveland, 11
Amsterdam, Morey, 11
Anarcharsis, 11
Anderson, Clive, 11
Anderson, Pamela, 11
Andrássy, (Count) Julian, 11
Angelou, Mary, 12
Angus, Robin, 12
Annan, Kofi, 12

Anne, British Princess Royal, 12
Appleby, Sir Humphrey (Nigel Hawthorne), 405
Arafat, Yasser, 15
Arbuthnot, Geoff, 15
Arc, Joan of, 359, 368
Archer, Jeffrey, 11, 15, 16, 185, 260
Archer, Mary, 16, 87
Ardrey, Robert, 16
Arendt, Hannah, 16
Aristophanes, 17
Aristotle, 17
Armey, Dick, 17
Armstrong, Louis, 18
Armstrong, Robert, 18
Armstrong, William, 18
Arnold, Matthew, 18
Arnold, Thomas, 18
Aron, Raymond, 18
Arthur (film, 1981), 18
Asaf, George, 18
Ashcroft, John, 19
Ashdown, Paddy, 19
Asquith, Herbert Henry, 10, 19, 62, 92, 175
Asquith, Lady (Margot), 19
Asquith, Raymond, 20
Astor, Lady, 95
At Last The 1948 Show, 20
Atatürk, Kemel, 20
Atkinson, Brooks, 20
Attie, Eli, 20
Attlee, Clement, 13, 21, 45, 95, 113, 175, 259
Attlee, Tom, 21
Auden, W. H., 22
Augustine, Norman, 22
Aung San Suu Kyi, 22
Aurelius, Marcus, 22
Austen, Jane, 23, 229, 354, 360
Ayckbourn, Alan, 23
Ayer, Sir Alfred J., 24
Ayesha, 24

Babel, Isaac, 25
Bach, Arthur (Dudley Moore), 18
Bach, Johann Sebastian, 25
Bacon, Sir Francis, 25
Baer, Arthur, 26
Baez, Joan, 26
Bagehot, Walter, 26
Bailey Aldrich, Thomas, 29
Bailey Hutchison, Kay, 29

Bailey, David, 29
Bailey, Pearl, 29
Bain, Ewen, 30
Bainville, Jacques, 30
Baker, James, 30
Baker, Kenneth, 30
Bakewell, Joan, 253
Bakunin, Michael, 30
Baldwin, James, 30
Baldwin, Stanley, 31, 94, 95
Balfour, A. J., 31
Balfour, Arthur, 92, 166, 305, 381
Baltzell, E. Digby, 32
Balzac, Honoré de, 32
Bancroft, Lord, 32
The Band Wagon, (film, 1953), 33
Bankhead, Tallulah, 33
Barbellion, W. N. P., 33
Barker, Pat, 33
Barkley, Alben W., 33
Barnes, Clive, 33, 41
Barnett, Lord, 33
Barnier, Michael, 34
Barnum, P. T., 34, 219
Barr, Roseanne, 34
Barrie, Sir James M., 34
Barry, Dave, 34
Barry, Gerald, 34
Barrymore, John, 35
Bartol, C. A., 35
Barton, Bruce, 35
Baruch, Bermard, 35
Bastiat, Claude-Frédéric, 35
Baudelaire, Claude, 36
Bauer, Lord, 36
Bauer, Yehuda, 36
Baum, Vicki, 36
Baxter, Beverley, 36
Beard, Charles Austin, 36
Beard, Mary Ritter, 36
Beatty, Warren, 36
Beaverbrook, Lord, 36, 37, 221
Beazley Snr., Kim, 37
Beazley, Kim, 37
Becket, Thomas, 175
Beckham, David, 37
Becque, Henry, 37
Bedingfield, Natasha, 37
Beecham, Sir Thomas, 38
Beerbohm, Sir Max, 38
Behan, Brendan, 38
Bell, Gertrude, 39
Bellamy, Francis, 39
Belloc, Hilaire, 39
Benchley, Robert, 39
Benedict, Ruth Fulton, 40

Benenson, Pat, 40
Benn, Ernest, 40
Benn, Tony, 21, 40, 217, 397
Bennett, Alan, 41
Bennett, Arnold, 41
Benny, Jack, 41
Benson, A. C., 42
Bentham, Jeremy, 42
Bentinck, Lord William, 382
Bentley, E. C., 42
Bentsen, Lloyd, 42
Beresford, Lord (Charles), 92
Berger, Peter, 43
Berlin, Irving, 43
Berlin, Isaiah, 43
Berlusconi, Silvio, 43
Bernard, Jeffrey, 44, 377
Berners, Lord, 38
Bernhardt, Sarah, 362
Berrigan, Daniel, 44
Berryman, John, 44
Besant, Annie, 44
Betjeman, Sir John, 44
Betjeman, Penelope, 379
Bevan, Aneurin, 45, 94, 95, 229
Beveridge, Albert Jeremiah, 46
Beveridge, William Henry, 46
Bevin, Ernest, 21, 46, 138
Bhutto, Benazir, 47
Bialystock, Max (Zero Mostel), 281
Bible, The, 38, 47, 313
Bidault, Georges, 48
Bidder, Revd H. J., 48
Bierce, Ambrose, 48
Biffen, John, 55
Biko, Steve, 55
Bilko, Master Sgt. Ernest G. (Steve Martin), 309
Billings, Josh, 55
Bin Laden, Osama, 297
Binyon, Laurence, 56
Birch, Nigel, 56
Birch, Stanley F. Jr, 56
Birkenhead, Lord, 19, 56, 62
Bismarck, Otto von, 57
Bjelke-Petersen, Johannes ('Joh'), 57
Black, Conrad, 58
Black, Hugo La Fayette, 58
Blackadder, 58
Blackadder, Edmund (Rowan Atkinson), 58
Blair, Cherie, 59, 405
Blair, Tony, 58, 70, 82, 91, 165, 172, 183, 191, 196, 221, 253, 269, 278, 315, 320, 342, 405
Blake, William, 60
Blears, Hazel, 1

Blix, Hans, 60
Bloomfield, Bishop, 321
Blunkett, David, 60
Blunt, Crispin, 208
Bly, Robert, 60
Blythe, Ronald, 61
Boabdil (Muhammad XI), 24
Boaz, David, 61
Bobeck, Mimi (Kathy Kinney), 120
Boesky, Ivan, 61
Boetcker, William J. H., 61
Bogan, Louise, 61
Bogart, Humphrey, 89
Bold, Alan, 62
Bolingbroke, Lord (Henry St. John), 62
Bonaparte, Napoléon, 62, 84, 99, 113, 174, 251, 382
Bonar Law, Andrew, 19, 62, 102
Bonham Carter, Violet, 62
Bono, 63
Bono, Sonny, 90
Booker, Christopher, 63
Boorstin, Daniel J., 63
Booth Luce, Clare, 268
Boothroyd, Betty, 63
Boren, James H., 63
Borges, Jorge Luis, 63
Boswell, James, 64
Boult, Sir Adrian, 38
Bow, Clara, 64
Bowden, Reggie, 64
Bowen, Lord, 64
Bradbury, Sir Malcolm, 64
Braddock, Ben (Dustin Hoffman), 160
Bradshaw, John, 65
Bragg, Melvyn, 276
Bramah, Ernest, 65
Brand, Jo, 65
Brandeis, Louis D., 65
Brandreth, Louis D., 65
Branson, Sir Richard, 65
Brant, Joseph, 66
Braque, Georges, 66
Braymance, Martha, 66
Brebner, J. Bartlett, 66
Brecht, Bertolt, 66
Brennan, William Joseph Jr., 66
Brenner, Norman, 67
Brenner, Richard, 67
Brezhnev, Leonid, 67
Bridges, Edward, 67
Bridson, D. G., 67
Bright, John, 67
Brinsley Sheridan, Richard (1751-1816), 67
Brinsley Sheridan, Richard (1806-88), 68
Brittain, Vera, 68

Brockway, Fenner, 68
Brodie, Sor Benjamin Collins, 68
Brogan, D. W., 68
Bronowski, Jacob, 68
Bronson, Charles, 69
Brontë, Charlotte, 69
Brooke, Rupert, 69
Brooks, Martha, 69
Brougham, Lord, 69
Brown, Anne, 277
Brown, Charlie, 69
Brown, Gordon, 1, 12, 14, 69, 71, 98, 101, 183, 276
Brown, H. Rap, 70
Browning, Robert, 70
Bruce, Lenny, 70
Buchan, John (Lord Tweedsmuir), 70
Buchanan, Kerry Portia, 71
Buchanan, Malcolm, 71
Buchanan, Marie, 71
Buchanan, Mike, 71
Buchanan, Pat, 71
Buchanan, Sarah Mercedes, 71
Buchman, Frank, 72
Buck, Pearl S., 72
Buckley, William F. Jr., 72
Buffett, Warren, 73
Bukowski, Charles, 74
Buñuel, Luis, 74
Bunyan, John, 363
Burchill, Julie, 75
Burke, Edmund, 74
Burns, Dr. David M., 76
Burns, George, 76
Burns, John, 76
Burns, Robert, 76
Burroughs, William S., 76
Burton, Richrad, 76
Burton, Robert, 77
Bush, George W., 77, 231, 281, 330
Bush, George Sr., 77
Butler, David, 78
Butler, Nicholas Murray, 78
Butler, R. A. ('Rab'), 78, 115
Butler, Samuel, 78
Byers, Stephen, 279
Byrnes, James F., 78
Byron, Lord, 78
Bywater, Michael, 79

Cabot Lodge, Henry, 243
Cady Stanton, Elizabeth, 81
Caesar, Julius, 81, 184
Caldwell Calhoun, Joseph, 81
Caligula, 249, 286
Callaghan, James, 78, 81

Callahan, Harry (Clint Eastwood), 116
Camden, Lord, 82
Cameron, David, 59, 82
Cameron, Simon, 82
Campbell of Eskan, Lord, 83
Campbell, Alastair, 14, 82, 270
Campbell, Sir George, 82
Camus, Albert, 83
Capone, Al, 83
Capote, Truman, 83, 371
Cardinal Gibbons, James, 83
Carey, Drew, 83
Carey, George, 84
Carey, James B., 84
Carlyle, Thomas, 84
Carnegie, Andrew, 84
Carnegie, Dale, 84
Carrington, Colonel Edward, 193
Carrington, Lord, 85
Carrington, Paul, 84
Carroll, Lewis (Charles Dodgson), 85
Carson, Frank, 86
Carson, Johnny, 86
Carter, Angela, 86
Cartland, Dame Barbara, 86
Cartmill, M., 86
Carville, James, 87
Cary, Lucius, Lord Falkland, 131
Casanova, Giovanni Jacopo, 87
Cassandra (Sir William Connor), 87
Castle, Barbara, 87, 279
Castro, Fidel, 87, 88
Catherine the Great, 21, 172
Catlin, Wyn, 87
Caulfield, Mr Justice, 87
Cavell, Edith, 88
Ceausescu, Nicolae, 88
Cecil, Lady Gwendolen, 117
Cervantes, Miguel de, 88
Chamberlain, Joseph, 88
Chamberlain, Neville, 45, 88, 109, 180, 221, 292
Chambers, Whittaker, 88
Chandler, Raymond, 88
Channon, Henry ('Chips'), 36, 89
Chapin, Edward, 89
Charles I, King, 272
Charles, British Prince of Wales, 89, 369
Charles, Ray, 89
Chasen, Dave, 89
Cheek, Mavis, 89
Cheney, Dick, 90, 231
Cher, 90
Chernenko, Konstantin, 90
Chesterfield, Lord, 90, 382
Chesterton, G. K., 90

Chirac, Jacques, 91, 165
Chodorov, Frank, 91
Chrétien, Jean, 91
Christie, Agatha, 92, 343
Churchill, Clementine, 92
Churchill, Lady Randolph (Jennie Jerome), 92
Churchill, Randolph, 92, 379
Churchill, Sir Winston, 15, 19, 21, 31, 32, 45, 56, 92, 95, 175, 222, 254, 259, 380
Ciano, Count Galeazzo, 97
Ciardi, John, 97
Clark Ridpath, John, 99
Clark, Alan, 82, 97, 269
Clark, Blake, 98
Clark, Kenneth, 97
Clarke, Kenneth, 98
Clarke, Sir Arthur C., 98
Clavin, Cliff (John Ratzenberger), 89
Clay, Henry, 99, 156
Clayton Powell, Adam Jr., 99
Cleese, John, 99
Clemenceau, Georges, 99
Cleveland, Grover, 100
Cleves, Anne of, 176
Clinton, Bill, 13, 100, 215
Clinton, Hilary, 215
Clive, Lord, 100
Close, Glenn, 320
Clough, Arthur Hugh, 101
Cochran, Jacqueline, 101
Cockburn, Claud, 218
Cocks, Sir Barnett, 101
Cohen, Leonard, 101
Cohn, Al, 101
Cohn, Harry, 317
Colbert, Jean-Baptiste, 101
Coleman, Vernon, 101, 102
Coleridge, Samuel Taylor, 102
Colette, 102
Collins, Joan, 102, 289, 367
Collins, Mortimer, 102
Colombo, John Robert, 102
Colton, Charles Caleb, 103
Confucius, 103
Congreve, William, 103
Connery, Sean, 327
Connolly, Billy, 104
Connolly, Cyril, 104
Conran, Shirley, 104
Conybeare, Rev. Charles, 305
Cook, Peter, 104
Cook, Robin, 104, 165, 232
Cooke, Alistair, 105
Coolidge, Calvin, 33, 105, 220, 223, 243, 268
Cooper, Alice, 105
Cooper, Gary, 64

Cooper, Jilly, 106
Cooper, Thomas, 194
Cooper, Tommy, 106, 172
Corenk, Alan, 106
Cosby, Bill, 106
Cotter, Simon, 106
Cousin, Victor, 109
Coward, Sir Noël, 106
Coxe, Trench, 193
Crane, Frasier (Kelsey Grammar), 89
Crane, Niles (David Hyde Pierce), 142
Creighton, (Bishop) Mandell, 2
Crèvecoeur, Michel Guillaume Jean de, 108
Crewe, Ivor, 108
Cripps, Sir Stafford, 20, 92, 94
Crisp, Quentin, 108
Critchley, Julian, 108
Crompton, Colin, 108
Cromwell, Oliver, 109
Crosland, Anthony, 109
Crum, Paul (Roger Pettiward), 109
Cummings, E. E., 110
Cunard, Lady, 38
Currie, Edwina, 16, 110, 118
Curzon, Lord, 13

d'Orsay, Comte, 117
Dale Davidson, James, 111
Dalton, Hugh, 78
Daniels, Paul, 253
Darre, Walther, 111
Darrow, Clarence, 111
Davenport, Rita, 111
Davies, Robertson, 111
Davis, Bette, 112
Dawson, Les, 112
Day, Doris, 227, 236
Day-Lewis, Cecil, 213
de Beauvoir, Simone, 112
de Gaulle, Charles, 94, 113
de Vauvenargues, Marquis, 370
Debs, Eugene Victor, 112
DeCaprio, Leonardo (Jack Dawson), 112
Deedes, W. F., 112
Defoe, Daniel, 113
DeGeneres, Ellen, 114
Delaney, Shelagh, 114
Dell, Floyd, 114
Dembina, Ivor, 114
Derby, 17th Earl of, 166
Devonshire, 10th Duke of, 114
Diana, Princess of Wales, 59, 75, 325
Dicey, A. V., 115
Dick, Philip K., 115
Dickens, Charles., 115
Dickinson, John, 115

Dickson Wright, Clarissa, 115
Diller, Phyllis, 115
Dillon, John, 116
Dillow, Chris, 116
Dinesen Isak (Karen Blixen), 116
Dirksen, Everett, 116
Dirty Harry (film, 1971), 116
Disraeli, Benjamin, 15, 116
Dobbs, Michael, 118
Dobson, Frank, 118, 232, 389
Dodd, Ken, 118
Dole, Bob, 118
Donnelly, Michael, 118
Donoso Cortés, Don Juan, 118
Dos Passos, John, 119
Dostoevsky, Fyodor, 119
Douglas, Justice William O., 119
Douglas, Mack R., 119
Douglas, Stephen, 220
Downey Jr, Robert, 119
Doyle, Sir Arthur Conan, 119
Dr. Strangelove (film 1964), 120
Drabble, Margaret, 119
Drake, Francis, 120
The Drew Carey Show, 120
Driberg, Tom, 37
Drucker, Peter, 120
Drummond, Hugh, 120
Dryden, John, 120
Duck Soup (film 1933), 121
Dukakis, Michael, 30, 77
Duncan, Alan, 121
Duncan, Isadora, 121
Dunne, Finley Peter, 121
Durant, Will, 121
Durocher, Leo, 121
Durst, Will, 122
Dworkin, Andrea, 122
Dylan, Bob, 26, 122

Earhart, Amelia, 123
Eastwood, Clint, 288
Eden, Anthony, 47, 78, 95, 123, 152, 253, 292
Edison, Thomas A., 123
Edward VII, King, 28
Edward VIII, King, 13, 123
Edwards, Bob, 123
Edwards, Eugene, 123
Edwards, Patrick H., 123
Egleton, Clive, 124
Einstein, Albert, 124, 143
Eisenhower, Dwight D., 125, 139
Eliot, George (Mary Anne Evans), 125, 363
Eliot, T. S., 125
Elizabeth I, 126
Elizabeth II, 126, 229, 273

Elizabeth, Queen, the Queen Mother, 126
Elizabeth, Princess Bibesco, 47
Ellery Channing, William, 125
Elliott, Ebenezer, 126
Ellis, Havelock, 126
Elton, Ben, 126
Emerson Fosdick, Harry, 128
Emerson, Ralph Waldo, 127
Emmett Tyrrell Jr, R., 128
Engels, Friedrich, 128, 205, 236
Ennius, 128
Epictetus, 128
Erasmus, 128
Erhard, Ludwig, 129
Ertz, Susan, 129
Esar, Evan, 129, 196
Everett, Edward, 129
Ewing, Sam, 129

Faguet, Émile, 131
Fairchild, Henry P., 131
Falwell, Jerry, 132
Family Guy, 131
Faraday, Michael, 132
Farquhar, George, 132
Faulkner, William, 132
Fawkes, Guy, 133
Fawlty Towers, 133
Fawlty, Basil (John Cleese), 133
Fawlty, Sybil (Prunella Scales), 133
Feiffer, Jules, 133
Feldman, Marty, 133
Femina, Jerry Della, 134
Fenimore Cooper, James, 134
Ferguson, Adam, 134
Fermi, Enrico, 9
Ferrara, Adam, 134
Feyerabend, Paul, 134
Fielding, Helen, 134
Fielding, Henry, 134
Fields, Suzanne, 135
Fields, W. C., 135, 296
Fischer, John, 135
Fish, Michael, 136
Fisher, Carrie, 136
Fisher, Eddie, 136
Fisher, H. A. L., 136
Fisher, John Arbuthnot, 136
Fisher, Marve, 136
Fitzgerald, F. Scott, 137, 386
Fleming, Peter, 137
Flynn, Errol, 137, 259
Foch, Ferdinand, 137
Foot, Michael, 138, 270
Forbes, Barry, 138
Forbes, C. F. (Miss), 138

Ford, Gerald, 1, 138, 197
Ford, Harrison, 138
Ford, Henry, 138
Forgy, Howell, 138
Forster, E. M., 139
Forsyth, Frederick, 139
Fortescue, William, 275
Foster Dulles, John, 139
Foster, Jodie, 139
Fowler, H. W., 139
Fowler, Norman, 139
Fox, Charles James, 139
Foxworthy, Jeff, 140
Frame, Janet, 140
France, Anatole, 140
Francis, Dick, 140
Franju, Georges, 157
Frank, Anne, 140
Frank, Lawrence K., 140
Frank, Tellis, 140
Franken, Al, 141
Frankfurter, Felix, 141
Frankl, Viktor, 141
Franklin, Benjamin, 141
Fraser Tytler, Alexander , Lord Woodhouselee, 141
Fraser, Malcolm, 142, 170, 202
Frazer, Sir James, 142
Frederick the Great, 142
French, Dawn, 142
French, Marilyn, 142
Freud, Sigmund, 118, 143
Freud, Sir Clement, 143
Friedman, Kinky, 143
Friedman, Milton, 143, 147
Frisch, Max, 144
Fromm, Erich, 144
Frost, Sir David, 145, 260
Frost, Robert, 145
Froude, James A., 145
Fry, Stephen, 145
Fuentes, Carlos, 146
Fukuyama, Francis, 146
Fuller, Dr. Thomas, 146
Fuller, Thomas, 146

Gabor, Zsa Zsa, 147
Gaitskell, Hugh, 147, 397
Galbraith, John Kenneth, 14, 147, 197
Galloway, George, 148
Galsworthy, John, 148
Gandhi, Mahatma, 148
García Márquez, Gabriel, 149
Gardner, Ava, 132
Garfield, James A., 149
Garner, John Nance, 149

Garofalo, Janeane, 149
Garrick, David, 149
Gaskell, Elizabeth, 149
Gates, Bill, 150
Gates, Horatio, 3
Gay, John, 150
Geddes, Eric, 150
Geldof, Bob, 150
Gellhorn, Martha, 150
Genet, Jean, 150
Geoffrey Crump, Geoffrey, 109
George III, King, 66, 151
George V, King, 151
George VI, King, 126, 152
George, Daniel (Daniel George Bunting), 151
George, Henry, 151
George, W. L., 151
George-Brown, Lord, 151
Gervais, Ricky, 152
Getty, J. Paul, 152
Ghostbusters, 153
Gibbon, Edward, 153
Gibbon, Lewis Grassic, 153
Gibran, Kahlil, 153
Gide, André, 153
Gielgud, Sir John, 154
Gilbert, Gustave, 157
Gilbert, Sir W. S., 154
Gilder, George, 155
Gingold, Hermione, 155
Gingrich, Newton, 155
Giovanni, Nikki, 155
Giuliani, Rudi, 156
Gladney, Edna, 156
Gladstone, Catherine, 156
Gladstone, William, 27, 93, 117, 132, 156, 172, 175, 305, 371
Gladstone, William E., 15
Glascock, Thomas, 156
Glendinning, Victoria, 156
Glyn, Elinor, 156
Godard, Jean-Luc, 157
Godfrey, Arthur, 157
Goebbels, Joseph, 157
Goebbels, Joseph, 265
Göering, Hermann, 157
Goethe, Johann Wolfgang von, 157
Goldberger, Ludwig Max, 158
Golding, William, 158
Goldman, Emma, 158
Goldman, William, 158
Goldsmith, Oliver, 158, 354
Goldwater, Barry, 158
Gompers, Samuel, 105
Goncourt, Edmond de, 159
Goodwin, Richard, 159

Gorbachev, Mikhail, 159, 341
Gordon, Giles, 159
Gore, Al, 159
Gorman, Teresa, 159
Goschen, Lord, 168
Gould, Philip, 159, 279
Gould, Stephen Jay, 160
Gowers, Ernest, 160
Grade, Lord (Lew), 160
Grade, Michael, 160
The Graduate (film, 1967), 160
Graham, D. M., 160
Graham, Katherine, 248
Gramm, Phil, 160
Gramsci, Antonio, 161
Granby, Lord, 305
Grange, Marquis de la, 161
Granger, Gideon, 194
Granholm, Jennifer, 161
Grant, Bernie, 161
Grant, Hugh, 161
Grant, Ulysses S., 161
Grass, Günther, 161
Gray, Muriel, 161
Green, Jeff, 162
Green, Pauline, 162
Greene, Graham, 162
Greenspan, Alan, 162
Greer, Germaine, 162
Greeves, Arthur, 217
Gregory, Dick, 163
Grenfell, Julian, 163
Grenville, George, 151
Grey of Falladon, Lord, 163
Grubb, Norman, 163
Grymeston, Elizabeth, 163
Guevara, Che, 163
Guggenheimer, Richard, 164
Guinness, Sir Alec, 163
Guinon, Albert, 164
Gulbenkian, Nubar, 164
Gunther, John, 164
Guthrie, Woody, 164

Hacker, Jim (Paul Eddington), 405
Haddon Spurgeon, Charles, 165
Hagman, Larry, 165
Hague, Ffion, 165
Hague, William, 165, 206
Haig, Lady, 166
Haig, Lord, 56, 165, 222
Hailsham, Lord (Quintin Hogg), 166
Haines, Joe, 396
Haldane, Richard Burdon, 166
Half, Robert, 166
Halifax, Lord (1633-95), 166

Halifax, Lord (1881-1959), 167
Hall, Jerry, 167
Hall, Rich, 167
Halsey, Margaret, 167
Hamilton, Alexander, 167
Hampton, Christopher, 167
Hancock, Tony, 168
Hanks, Tom, 168
Harcourt, Miss G., 321
Harcourt, William, 168
Hardie, Kier, 168
Hardiman, Larry, 168
Harding, Warren, 316
Hardy, G. H., 168
Hardy, Jeremy, 168
Hardy, Thomas, 168
Hargreaves, W. F., 169
Harkness, Richard, 169
Harlow, Jean, 20
Harman, Harriet, 32, 71, 169, 170, 278
Harris, Chris, 169
Harris, Frank, 31
Harris, Sidney J., 169
Harrison, Clyde, 169
Harrison, Thomas (Major General), 272
Harrod, Dominic, 181
Harrod, Sir Roy, 181
Hart-Davis, Rupert, 225, 406
Hartington, Lord, 172
Hartley, Hal, 170
Hastings, Sir Max, 170
Hattersley, Roy, 170
Hawke, Bob, 170
Hawke, Ethan, 170
Hayek, Friedrich August von, 171
Hayes, Helen, 171
Hazlitt, William, 171
Headlam, Cuthbert Morley, 172
Healey, Denis, 166, 172
Heath, Edward, 12, 173, 175, 199, 339
Hegel, Georg, 173
Heine, Heinrich, 173
Heinlein, Robert A., 174
Heller, Joseph, 174
Helpmann, Sir Robert, 174
Hemingway, Ernest, 137, 150, 174
Hendra, Tony, 175
Hennessey, Peter, 175
Henry Cate VII, 87
Henry II, King, 175
Henry IV (of Navarre), King, 176
Henry VIII, King, 176
Henry, William A. III, 175
Henry, Patrick, 176
Henson, Jim, 176
Hepburn, Katharine, 176

Herbert, A. P., 176
Herbert, Frank, 177
Herbert, George, 177
Herbert, Laura, 379
Herford, Oliver, 177
Herzen, Alexander Ivanovich, 177
Heseltine, Michael, 108, 178
Heslop, Andrew, 177, 178
Heslop, Holly, 178
Heston, Charlton, 178
Hibberd, Jack, 178
Hicks, Bill, 178
Hightower, Cullen, 179
Hightower, Jim, 179
Hill, Benny, 179
Hill, Joe, 179
Hindenburg, Paul von, 179
Hitchcock, Sir Alfred, 179
Hitler, Adolf, 72, 88, 93, 94, 111, 157, 174, 179, 221, 292
Hobbes, Thomas, 180
Hobson (John Gielgud), 18
Hodnett, Edward, 180
Hoffer, Eric, 180
Hoffman, Abbie, 181
Hoffman, Dustin, 262
Hoggart, Simon, 181, 279
Hölderlin, Friedrich, 181
Hollis, Roger, 175
Home, Caroline Douglas, 119, 181
Home, Lord (Sir Alec Douglas), 15, 119, 181, 272
Hoover, Herbert, 181
Hoover, J. Edgar, 197
Hope, Bob, 182
Hoppus, Mark, 182
Horace, 151, 182
Hornby, Nick, 182
Horsman, Edward, 67
Hosaka, Arisa, 187
Hoskyns, John, 182
Houdini, Harry, 196
Houston, Sam, 182
Howard, John, 202
Howard, Michael, 183, 270, 389
Howe, Edgar W., 183
Howe, Geoffrey, Lord Howe, 172, 183
Howe, Louis McHenry, 183
Howell, James, 183
Hubbard, Elbert, 183
Hubbard, Kim, 184
Hubbard, L. Ron, 184
Hughes, Howard, 184, 251
Hughes, Robert, 184
Hugo, Victor, 184
Hume, David, 184

Humphrey, Hubert, 184
Humphreys, John, 280
Humphries, Dame Edna Everage, 185
Humphrys, John, 82
Hunt of Tanworth, Lord, 185
Hunter, William, 194
Hurd, Douglas, 98, 185
Hurrell Mallock, William, 185
Hussein, Saddam, 12, 148
Hutchins, Robert M., 185
Hutchinson, Sir Robert, 185
Hutton, Sir Len, 185
Huxley, Aldous, 186
Huxley, Thomas H., 186

Iannone, Carol, 187
Ibsen, Henrik, 187
Ickes, Harold L., 187
Ikkaku, Takayuki, 187
Illich, Ivan, 187
Inge, William Ralph, 188
Ingersoll, Robert, 188
Ingham, Bernard, 188
Isherwood, Christopher, 188
Ismay, Hastings Lionel ('Pug'), 189
Issigonis, Alec, 189
Izzard, Eddie, 189

Jackson, Andrew, 191
Jackson, Glenda, 191, 233
Jackson, Robert H., 191
James, Clive, 191
James, Henry, 191, 363
James, P. D., 191
James, William, 192
Jameson, Anna, 192
Jameson, Storm, 192
Jarrell, Randall, 192
Jarvis, William Charles, 194
Jay, Antony, 188, 192
Jay, Lord (Douglas Jay), 192
Jefferson, Thomas, 182, 192
Jellinek, George, 195
Jenkins, Roy, 19, 195
Jennings Bryan, William, 195
Jerome, Jerome K., 195
Jerrold, Douglas, 196
Jevons, W. Stanley, 196
Jilted John, 196
John Paul II, 196
Johnson, Boris, 196
Johnson, Lyndon B., 196
Johnson, Paul, 197, 246
Johnson, Samuel, 64, 197
Johnston, Tom, 199
Jones, Barry Owen, 199

Jones, Robert, 199
Jones, Steve, 199
Jong, Erica, 199
Jopling, Michael, 97
Joseph, Sir Keith, 172, 199
Judt, Tony, 200
Jung, Carl, 200
Junius, 200
Junor, John, 200

Kant, Immanuel, 201
Kaufman, Beatrice, 201
Kaufman, George S., 201
Kaufman, Gerald, 201
Kaufman, Margo, 201
Kawabata, Toshihiro, 187
Kay, Peter, 201
Keating, Paul, 201
Keaton, Diane, 8
Keillor, Garrison, 202
Keller, Helen, 202
Kennan, George F., 202
Kennedy, John F., 42, 182, 203
Kennedy, Joseph P., 203
Kennedy, Ludovic, 203
Kennedy, Robert F., 203
Kenyatta, Jomo, 204
Kerouac, Jack, 204
Kerr, Jean, 204
Kerry, John, 215
Keynes, John Maynard, 204
Khan, Genghis (Temujin), 150
Khayyam, Omar, 204
Khrushchev, Nikita, 205
Kierkegaard, Søren, 205
Kiley, Brian, 205
Kilmuir, Lord, 13, 205
King, Carole, 338
King, Daren, 205
Kinnock, Neil, 178, 206, 213, 232, 341
Kinsley, Michael, 206
Kipling, Rudyard, 206
Kirk, Russell, 207
Kirkpatrick, Jeane J., 207
Kissinger, Henry, 207
Kitchener, Lord, 19, 208
Knox, John, 208
Koestler, Arthur, 208
Kohl, Helmut, 208
Korda, Michael, 208
Krakel, Dean, 209
Krishnamurti, Jiddu, 209
Kristol, Irving, 209
Kupcinet, Irv, 209
Kuyper, Abraham, 209

La Rochefoucauld, François de, 212
Labour Party, 211
Laing, R. D., 211
Lamont, Norman, 211
Lampedusa, Giuseppe de, 211
Landers, Ann, 211
Lao-tzu, 211
Lardner, Ring, 212
Larkin, Philip, 212
Larson, Doug, 212
Laski, Harold, 21, 213
Lauder, Harry, 213
Law, Richard (Lord Coleraine), 102
Lawrence, D. H., 213
Lawrence, T. E., 213
Lawson, Dominic, 291
Lawson, Mark, 213
Lawson, Nigel, 213, 341
Lazarus, Emma, 214
Le Roy, Jean Baptiste, 141
Leach, Edmund, 214
Lear, Edward, 214
Lebowitz, Fran, 214
Lec, Stanislaw, 214
Lee, Bert, 385
Lee, Harper, 214
Lee, Robert E., 215
Lehrer, Tom, 215
Lenin, Vladimir, 200, 205, 215, 275, 288
Lennon, John, 215
Leno, Jay, 215
Leonard, Elmore, 216
Lerner, Alan Jay, 216
Lessing, Doris, 216
Letterman, David, 216
Letts, Winifred Mary, 216
Levant, Oscar, 216, 236
Levenson, Sam, 216
Lever, Leslie, 217
Leverhulme, Lord, 217
Leverson, Ada, 217
Levin, Bernard, 217
Lewin, Kurt, 217
Lewinsky, Monica, 100
Lewis, C. S., 217
Lewis, Joe E., 218
Lewis, Sinclair, 218
Lewis, Willmott, 218
Lewis-Smith, Victor, 218
Liberace, 218
Life of Brian (film, 1979), 218
Limbaugh, Rush, 219
Lincoln, Abraham, 61, 77, 219
Lindh, John Walter, 19
Lindquist, Raymond, 220
Lippmann, Walter, 220

Livingston, Edward, 286
Livingstone, Ken, 15, 118, 220, 306
Lloyd George, David, 19, 37, 99, 175, 204, 221
Lloyd Wright, Frank, 222
Lloyd, Selwyn, 56
Locke, John, 222
Loelia, Duchess of Westminster, 385
Lombardi, Vince, 222
London, Jack, 222
The Lone Ranger, 222
Long, Huey, 187
Long, Russell, 222
Longfellow, Henry Wadsworth, 223
Longford, Lord, 223
Longworth, Alice Roosevelt, 223
Louis XIV, King, 101, 223
Louis XVI, King, 223
Louis XVIII, King, 223
Lowe, Robert, 67, 224
Lurie, Alison, 224
Luther King, Martin, 224
Luther, Martin, 224
Lyons, Lord, 304
Lyttleton, George, 225, 406
Lytton, Lord, 304

MacArthur, Douglas (General), 227, 350
Macaulay, Lord, 227
MacDonald, Dwight, 227
Macdonald, Jeanette, 135
Macdonald, John A., 227
MacDonald, Ramsay, 93, 228
MacFarlane, Seth, 131
Machiavelli, Niccolò, 228
Mackenzie, Compton, 228
Mackintosh, James, 229
MacLeod, Iain, 229
Macmillan, Harold, 45, 46, 104, 175, 217, 229, 253, 331, 345
MacNeice, Louis, 230
Maddox, Lester, 230
Madison, James, 230
Madonna, 230
Mae Brown, Rita, 231
Maher, Bill, 231
Mahon, Derek, 231
Mahoney, David, 231
Mailer, Norman, 231
Maistre, Joseph de, 231
Major, Sir John, 13, 16, 110, 231, 277, 314, 341, 375
Mallory, George Leigh, 232
Maltz, Maxwell, 232
Mancroft, Lord, 232
Mandela, Nelson, 215, 233
Mandela, Winnie, 215

Mandelson, Peter, 181, 269
Manio, Jack de, 233
Mankiewicz, Herman J., 233
Mankiewicz, Joseph L., 233
Manners, Lady Janetta, 305
Mansfield, Jayne, 173
Mansfield, Stephen, 233
Mao, Zedong, 217, 233
Marley, Bob, 234
Marquis, Don, 234
Marsh, Lord (Richard Marsh), 234
Marshall, George C., 234
Marshall, John, 235
Marshall, Peter (Reverend), 235
Marshall, S. L. A., 235
Martin, Dean, 235
Martin, Steve, 235
Martin, Theodore, 371
Martz, H. E., 235
Marx Brothers, 121
Marx, Chico, 236
Marx, Groucho, 235
Marx, Karl, 21, 40, 73, 205, 236, 288, 307, 368, 394
Mary, Queen, 152
Mason, Jackie, 237
Mason, Revd. William, 376
Matthau, Walter, 237
Maudling, Reginald, 56
Maugham, Robin, 237
Maugham, W. Somerset, 237
Mawrey, Richard, 238
May Alcott, Louisa, 238
Maynard Hutchins, Robert, 238
Mayo, Charles H., 238
McAdoo, William G., 238
McBeal, Ally (Calista Flockhart), 9
McCarthy, Charlie (dummy of Edgar Bergen), 238
McCarthy, Eugene, 239
McCarthy, Joseph, 239, 255
McCarthy, Mary, 239
McChord Crothers, Samuel, 239
McClellan, Foster C., 239
McCormack, Eric, 239
McCoughey, J. D., 239
McEwan, Ian, 228, 239
McFarland, Jack (Sean Hayes), 394
McFote, Alfred, 240
McGee, Debbie, 253
McGough, Roger, 240
McGregor, Ewan, 240
McGuinty, Dalton, 13
McKain, Robert J., 240
McMaster Bujold, Lois, 240
McVeigh, Timothy, 178

Meacher, Michael, 241
Medawar, Peter, 241
Megarry, Robert, 241
Meir, Golda, 241
Melbourne, Lord, 241
Mellor, David, 241
Mencken, H. L., 241
Menninger, Dr. Karl, 244
Mercer, Rick, 244
Meredith, George, 244
Merton, Mrs (Caroline Aherne), 253
Merton, Thomas, 245
Metternich, Klemens von, 245
Michelet, Jules, 245
Midler, Bette, 245
Mikes, George, 245
Mill, John Stuart, 207, 245
Miller, Alice Duer, 246
Miller, Dennis, 246
Miller, Henry, 246
Miller, Max, 246
Miller, Sir Jonathan, 246
Miller, Zell, 247
Milligan, Spike, 247
Millikan, Robert, 247
Milner, Lord, 248
Milton, John, 248
Misez, Ludwig von, 248
Mitchell, Austin, 248
Mitchell, George, 248
Mitchell, John, 248
Mitchell, Joni, 338
Mitchell, Margaret, 248
Mitchell, Warren, 249
Mitchum, Robert, 184
Mitford, Nancy, 249
Mitterrand, François, 249
Mizner, Wilson, 249
Molière (Jean-Baptiste Poquelin), 249
Monkhouse, Bob, 249
Monroe, Marilyn, 249
Monsoon, Edina (Jennifer Saunders), 1
Montagu, Lady Mary Wortley, 249
Montaigne, Michel de, 250
Montesquieu, Charles de, 250
Montgomery, Robert, 250
Montgomery., Lord, 95
Monty Python, 250
Monty Python and the Holy Grail (film, 1975), 250
Moore, George, 251
Moore, Jo, 251
Moore, Sir Roger, 251
Moran, Ed, 251
More, Thomas, 389
Morecambe, Eric, 251

Morgan, Ted, 251
Morley, Christopher, 251
Morley, John, 252
Morley, Robert, 252
Morrissey, 252
Mortimer, Sir John, 252
Morton, J. B., 252
Mosley, Oswald, 21, 253
Moss, Kate, 142
Mowlem, Mo, 98
The Mrs Merton Show, 253
Mugabe, Robert, 253
Muggeridge, Malcolm, 253
Muir, Frank, 15, 253
Mull, Martin, 254
Müller, Adam, 254
The Muppets, 176
Murakami, Haruki, 254
Murdoch, Iris, 254
Murphy, Christy, 254
Murphy, Maureen, 254
Murrow, Edward R., 254
Mussolini, Benito, 97, 179, 255
Myers, Mike, 255

Nader, Ralph, 257
Naidu, Sarojini, 257
Nash, Ogden, 257
Nathan, George Jean, 258
Nehru, Jawaharlal, 258
Neil, Andrew, 14
Nelson, Horatio, (Vice-Admiral), 258
Nemerov, Howard, 258
Neumann, Johann von, 258
Newman, Alfred E., 258
Newman, Paul, 259
Newman, Randy, 259
Nicklaus, Jack, 259
Nicolson, Harold, 21, 31, 99, 259
Nietzsche, Friedrich, 259
Niven, David, 259
Nixon, Richard, 1, 197, 259
Norden, Denis, 260
Norquist, Grover, 260
Norris, Steven, 260
North, Lord, 274
Northcliffe, Lord, 221
Not Only . . . But Also, 260
Nugent, Ted, 260
Nyad, Diana, 260

O'Brien, Conan, 261
O'Brien, Edna, 261
O'Brien, Pat, 132
O'Farrell, John, 261
O'Neal, Shaquille, 263

O'Rourke, P. J., 263
O'Sullivan, John, 81
O'Sullivan, John L, 266
Oakeshott, Michael, 261
Obama, Barack, 261
The Office, 262
Ogilvy, David, 262
Olasky, Marvin, 262
Oliver, Vic, 262
Olivier, Sir Lawrence, 262
Onassis, Jackie, 178
Onslow, Lord, 263
Oppenheim, James, 263
Orben, Robert, 263
Orton, Joe, 264
Orwell, George, 232, 264
Osborne, George, 265
Osborne, John, 265
Osgood, Charles, 265
Osler, Sir William, 265
Otis, James, 266
Owen, Dr. David (Lord Owen), 30, 266
Owen, Robert, 266
Oxenstierna, Count, 266

Page, Walter, 267
Paine, Thomas, 267
Palin, Sarah, 267
Paltrow, Gwyneth, 267
Parker, Dorothy, 267, 404
Parkinson, C. Northcote, 268
Parks, Rosa, 161
Parr, Jack, 13
Parris, Matthew, 269, 278
Parsons, Geoffrey, 269
Parton, Dolly, 98
Pascal, Blaise, 269
Pasternak, Boris, 270
Patrick, John, 270
Patten, Chris, 270
Paulsen, Pat, 270
Paxman, Jeremy, 270, 289
Pearsall Smith, Logan, 271
Peel, Sir Robert, 117, 175, 271, 382
Pell, Claiborne, 271
Pepper, Claude D., 271
Pepys, Samuel, 271
Peres, Shimon, 272
Peric, Marko, 272
Perot, H. Ross, 272
Peter, Laurence J., 264, 272
Peters, Mike, 272
Peyton, Lord, 272
Phelps, Arthur, 273
Philip, Prince, 273
Philips, Emo, 273

Pienaar, John, 273
Pike, Albert, 273
Pinero, Sir Arthur Wing, 274
Pinter, Harold, 274
Pitt, William, 274
Pius XII, 274
Plato, 274
Plutarch, 274
Poe, Edgar Allan, 275
Polanski, Roman, 275
Pollock, Channing, 275
Pomeroy, Jack, 275
Pompidou, Georges, 275
Pope, Alexander, 275
Popper, Sir Karl, 275
Portillo, Michael, 276
Potter, Dennis, 276
Potter, Stephen, 276
Pound, Ezra, 276
Pournelle, Jerry, 276
Powell, Anthony, 276
Powell, Enoch, 277
Preece, Sir William, 277
Prescott, John, 65, 165, 172, 241, 277, 279
Presley, Elvis, 280
Price, Bill, 280
Price, Richard, 280
Priestley, J. B., 281
Prodi, Romano, 281
The Producers (film, 1968), 281
Profumo, John, 166, 229
Proops, Greg, 281
Pryor, Richard, 281
Pulitzer, Joseph, 281
Pullman, Philip, 281
Putnam, George, 123
Pym, Barbara, 212

Quayle, Dan, 42, 71, 99, 283
Quintilian, 283

Rabbi, The Belzer, 285
Rabelais, François, 285
Radcliffe, Lord, 285
Raleigh, Walter, 285
Rand, Ayn, 285
Randolph, John, 286
Rappaport, Herbert, 287
Raspberry, William, 287
Rasputin, Grigori, 172
Rawhide, 287
Raymond, F. J., 287
Reagan, Nancy, 287
Reagan, Ronald, 77, 287, 371
Rees, Nigel, 288
Reeve, Christopher, 288

Reger, Max, 289
Reid, John, 270, 289
Reisman, George, 289
Retz, Cardinal de, Jean-François Paul de Gondi, 289
Reuther, Walter, 289
Reynolds, Burt, 289
Reynolds, Debbie, 136
Rhodes, Cecil, 290
Rhys, John, 290
Rice, Grantland, 290
Rich, Adrienne, 290
Richter, Jean Paul, 290
Rickover, Hyman G., 290
Ridley, Adam, 291
Ridley, Nicholas, 291
Rieger, Alex (Judd Hirsch), 337
Riesman, David, 291
Ritz, César, 291
Rivers, Joan, 291
Robbins, Tom, 291
Robert, Véronique, 280, 291
Roberts, Andrew, 11, 292
Roberts, Frank, 292
Robertson, Frederick William, 292
Robespierre, Maximilien, 292
Robinson, Edward G., 292
Robinson, Mrs. (Anne Bancroft), 160
Robinson, Nick, 278
Rocherolle, Narenda, 292
Rockefeller, David, 293
Rodriguez, Sue, 293
Roeben, Scott, 293
Rogers, Roy, 293
Rogers, Will, 293
Rook, Jean, 294
Roosevelt, Eleanor, 294
Roosevelt, Franklin D., 94, 294
Roosevelt, Theodore, 77, 223, 295
Rosebery, 5th Earl of (Archibald Philip Primrose), 295
Ross, Dick, 295
Rossiter, Clinton, 296
Rosten, Leo, 236, 296
Rothschild, Lord, 31
Rousseau, Jean-Jacques, 14, 43, 131, 296, 394
Rowland, Helen, 296
Rowling, J. K., 296
Royden, Maude, 297
Royko, Mike, 297
Rudner, Rita, 297
Rumsfeld, Donald, 297
Rush, Richard, 286
Ruskin, John, 297
Russell of Killowen, Lord, 300
Russell, Lord Bertrand, 298

Russell, Lord John, 117, 300

Safire, William, 301
Sagan, Carl, 301
Sahl, Mort, 301
Saint-Exupéry, Antoine de, 301
Saint-Gaudens, Augustus Homer, 301
Saki (Hector Hugo Munro), 302
Salinger, J. D., 302
Salisbury, Lord, 11, 57, 117, 175, 302
Salmond, Alex, 305, 327
Salzberg, Sharon, 305
Samuel, Herbert, 222, 305
Samuels, Jim, 305
Sandford, G. M., 304
Santayana, George, 305
Sarraute, Nathalie, 306
Sartre, Jean-Paul, 6, 14, 113, 306
Satie, Erik, 306
Sayers, Dorothy L., 306
Sayle, Alexei, 306
Scanlon Hugh, 306, 397
Scargill, Arthur, 306, 339
Scarman, Lord, 307
Schiller, Friedrich von, 307
Schlessinger, Dr. Laura, 307
Schnabel, Artur, 307
Schopenhauer, Arthur, 307
Schulz, Charles M., 307
Schulz, Martin, 43
Schumpeter, J. L., 307
Schurz, Carl, 308
Schwartzkopf, H. Norman III, 308
Schwarzenegger, Arnold, 308
Schweitzer, Albert, 308
Scott, C. P., 308
Scott, Robert Falcon, 308
Scott, Sir Walter, 84, 308, 381
Scott, William, 158
Sedgewick, John, 309
Seinfeld, Jerry, 309
Seldon, Arthur, 220, 309
Seneca, 309
Sex and the City, 309
Sexwale, Tokyo, 309
Sgt Bilko (film, 1996), 309
Shakespeare, William, 15, 265, 309
Shatner, William, 312
Shaw, George Bernard, 312
Shawcross, Hartley, 314
Sheehy Skeffington, Hanna, 116
Shelburne, Lord, 314
Shelley, Percy Bysshe, 314
Shepherd, Gillian, 314
Sherman, William Tecumseh, 314
Shinwell, Emanuel, 315

Shipley, Jonathan, 315
Short, Clare, 273, 315
Sibelius, Jean, 315
Silber, John, 315
Silone, Ignazio (Secondo Tranquilli), 315
Simon, John, 316
Simpson, Bart, 316
Simpson, Homer, 316
Simpson, Kirke, 316
Simpson, Wallis, Duchess of Windsor, 13, 398
The Simpsons, 182, 316
Sinatra, Frank, 14, 132
Sinclair, Upton, 317
Singleton, G., 317
Sisson, C. H., 317
Sitwell, Dame Edith, 317
Skelton, 'Red', 317
Skelton, Noel, 317
Skinner, B. F., 317
Sloan, Joan, 318
Smiles, Samuel, 318
Smirnoff, Yakov, 318
Smith, Adam, 73, 318
Smith, Alfred E., 319
Smith, Arthur, 319
Smith, Cyril, 64
Smith, Dame Maggie, 320
Smith, Dodie, 319, 322
Smith, Godfrey, 319
Smith, Iain Duncan, 170, 241, 279, 320
Smith, Ian, 320
Smith, John Alexander, 320
Smith, Linda, 320
Smith, Marion, 320
Smith, Sir Cyril, 319
Smith, Stevie, 320
Smith, Sydney, 321
Smith, W. S., 193
Smollett, Tobias, 321
Smyth, Ethel, 403
Snagge, John, 321
Snow, C. P., 322
Snowden, Philip, 322
Soaper, Senator, 322
Socrates, 322
Solow, Robert, 322
Solzhenitsyn, Aleksandr, 322
Somers, Lord, 126
Sondheim, Stephen, 323
Soper, Lord, 323
Sorenson, Charles, 324
Southey, Robert, 324
Sowell, Thomas, 324
Soyinka, Wole, 324
Span, Samuel, 74
Spander, Art, 324

Spark, Muriel, 325
Sparrow, John, 325
Speare, Grace, 325
Spencer, Herbert, 325
Spencer, Lord, 325
Spender, Stephen, 325, 379
Spengler, Oswald, 325
Spielberg, Stephen, 326
Spring-Rice, Cecil, 326
Squire, J. C., 326
St. John of Fawsley, Lord, 331
Stalin, Josef, 25, 159, 326, 349
Stanley, Bessie A., 326
Stanley, Edward 14th Earl of Derby, 114
Stanley, Venetia, 19
Stanshall, Vivian, 327
Stanwyck, Barbara, 327
Stark, Freya, 327
Stark, Jim, 327
Starkie, Enid, 327
Starr, Roger, 327
Stassinopoulos, Arianna, 41
Steel, David, 138, 185, 319, 327
Steel, Judy, 185
Steele Commager, Henry, 328
Steele, Richard, 327
Steele, Shelby, 328
Steffens, Lincoln, 328
Stein, Gertrude, 328
Steinbeck, John, 328
Steinem, Gloria, 329
Stephen, James Fitzjames, 329
Sterne, Laurence, 329
Stevens, Brooks, 329
Stevenson, Adlai, 329
Stevenson, Robert Louis, 330
Stewart, Jon, 330
Stewart, Rod, 331
Stimson, Henry, 331
Stockton, Lord, 331
Stockwood, Mervyn, 331
Stone, Clement, 331
Stone, I. F., 331
Stoppard, Tom, 331
Stourton, Edward, 279
Strang, Lord, 46
Strathclyde, Lord, 332
Straw, John Whitaker ('Jack'), 332
Streep, Meryl, 83
Stronach, Belinda, 1
Strunsky, Simeon, 332
Studdert Kennedy, G. A., 332
Sullivan, Louis, 333
Sully, Duc de, Maximilien de Béthune, 333
Summerskill, Edith, 333
Sumner, Charles, 333

Sumner, William Graham, 333
Swaffer, Hannen, 333
Swan, Anne S., 333
Swift, Jonathan, 334
Swope, Herbert Bayard, 334
Szasz, Thomas, 334
Szent-Györgyi, Albert von, 335

Tacitus, 337
Tansi, Sony Labou, 337
Tawney, R. H., 337
Taxi, 337
Taylor, A. J. P., 37, 57, 337
Taylor, Harold, 338
Taylor, Henry, 338
Taylor, James, 338
Taylor, John, 3
Taylor, Sir Edward ('Teddy'), 337
Tebbit, Norman, 138, 338
Temple, Shirley, 176
Temple, William, 338
Tennyson, Alfred 1st Baron Tennyson, 338
Terence, 339
Thackery, William Makepeace, 339
Thatcher, Denis, 339
Thatcher, Margaret, Baroness Thatcher of
    Kesteven, 5, 55, 70, 81, 85, 87, 108, 172,
    173, 175, 183, 188, 191, 199, 206, 221,
    231, 249, 269, 338, 339, 368
Thomas, Dylan, 343
Thomas, Edward, 343
Thomas, Elizabeth, 343
Thomas, Gwyn, 343
Thomas, Irene, 344
Thomas, J. H., 56
Thomas, R. S., 344
Thompson, Dorothy, 344
Thompson, E. P., 344
Thompson, Emma, 344
Thompson, Hunter S., 344
Thompson, Julian, 344
Thompson, Robert Norman, 345
Thoreau, Henry, 345
Thorpe, Jeremy, 345
Thucydides, 345
Thurber, James, 345
Tiberius, 346
Tikkanen, Henrik, 346
Tipu Sultan, 346
Titanic (film, 1997), 112
Tocqueville, Alexis de, 180, 346, 373
Tomlin, Lily, 347
Townsend, F. H., 347
Toynbee, Arnold, 347
Toynbee, Arnold J., 347
Tree, Sir Herbert Beerbohm, 348

Trench, Richard Chenevix, 348
Trevelyan, G. M., 348
Trevor-Roper, Hugh, 348
Trillin, Calvin, 348
Trinder, Tommy, 349
Trollope, Anthony, 349
Trotsky, Leon, 349
Trudeau, Pierre, 350
Truman, Harry, 77, 152, 242, 350
Tucker, Sophie, 201, 351
Tutu, Desmond, 351
Twain, Mark, 117, 351, 357
Tweedie, Jill, 365
Tyler, Alexander, 365
Tyler, John, 295
Tynan, Kenneth, 366

Ullman, Tracey, 367
Ullrich, Kay, 367
Unamuno, Miguel de, 367
Updike, John, 367
Ustinov, Peter, 368

Valera, Eamonn de, 222
Valerius Martialis, Marcus, 369
Valéry, Paul, 369
Van Den Haag, Ernest, 369
Van der Post, Laurens, 369
Van Dyke, Henry, 370
Vanbrugh, Sir John, 369
Vaughan Williams, Ralph, 370
Vaughan, Harry, 350
Vaughan, William E ('Bill'), 370
Veninga, Robert, 370
Venkman, Dr Peter (Bill Murray), 153
Venturi, Robert, 370
Versace, Gianni, 370
Vickery, A. Lou, 370
Victoria, Queen, 28, 241, 338, 371, 382
Vidal, Gore, 371
Vincent Benet, Stephen, 372
Virgil, 372
Viscount Morley, John, 372
Viz, 372
Vizinczey, Stephen, 372
Voltaire (François-Marie Arouet), 372
Vonnegut, Kurt, 373
Vosburgh, Dick, 233
Voto, Bernard de, 373

Wadsworth, Charles, 375
Wainwright III, Loudon, 375
Waits, Tom, 375
Waldeck, Meyer von, 57
Waldegrave, Lord, 375
Walden, Brian, 340

Walden, George, 375
Wales, Jimmy, 376
Walker, Walter, 376
Walker, Karen (Megan Mulally), 394
Wall Street (film, 1987), 376
Wallace, George, 376
Waller, Edmund, 376
Walpole, Horace, 376
Walpole, Robert, 376
Walters, Julie, 377
Ward, Clare, 377
Warhol, Andy, 16, 371
Waring, Eddie, 64
Warner, Charles Dudley, 377
Warner, Sylvia Townsend, 377
Washington, George, 377
Waterhouse, Keith, 377
Waters, Alan, 213
Waters, Maxine, 378
Watley, Denis, 378
Watterson, Bill, 378
Watts Mumford, Ethel, 378
Waugh, Auberon, 378
Waugh, Evelyn, 92, 378
Weaver, Richard M., 379
Webb, Beatrice, 380
Webb, Sidney, 380
Weber, Max, 380
Weeks, Edward, 89
Weil, Simon, 380
Weinreich, Max, 381
Weizmann, Chaim, 381
Welby, Thomas Earle, 381
Weldon, Fay, 381
Welles, Orson, 381
Wellington, 1st Duke of (Arthur Wellesley), 381
Wellington, Duke of, 174
Wells, H. G., 34, 152, 383
Welsh, Irvine, 383
Welty, Eudora, 383
Wendell Holmes Jr., Oliver, 99, 213, 383
Wendell Holmes Sr., Oliver, 384
Wesker, Arnold, 384
West, Mae, 384
West, Rebecca, 269, 385
Westmoreland, William C., 385
Westmorland, Lord (John Fane), 385
Weston, R. P., 385
Weydemeyer, Georg, 236
Wharton, Edith, 386
Wheeler Wilcox, Ella, 386
Whicker, Alan, 386
Whistler, James McNeill, 386
White, E. B., 386
White, Hugh, 386

White, Theodore H., 387
Whitehead, Alfred North, 387
Whitehorn, Katharine, 387
Whitelaw, William, 342, 388
Whitman, Walt, 388
Whittington, Robert, 389
Widdecombe, Ann, 389
Wiesel, Elie, 389
Wilberforce, William, 389
Wilbur, Richard, 389
Wilde, Oscar, 390
Wilder, Billy, 394
Wilder, Thornton, 394
Will and Grace, 239, 394
Will, George, 394
William III, King, 395
William, Prince, 369
Williams, Robin, 395
Williams, Tennessee, 395
Williams, William Carlos, 395
Williamson, Marianne, 395
Willis, Bruce, 395
Wilson, A. N., 396
Wilson, Angus, 396
Wilson, Earl, 396
Wilson, Edward O., 396
Wilson, Francis, 294
Wilson, Gahan, 396
Wilson, Harold, 12, 40, 56, 77, 109, 173, 200, 388, 396
Wilson, Harriet, 381
Wilson, Richard, 398
Wilson, Woodrow, 99, 195, 267, 398
Winfrey, Oprah, 399
Winters, Shelley, 399
Winterton, Sir Nicholas, 399
Wise, Ernie, 251
Wittgenstein, Ludwig, 399
Wodehouse, Sir Pelham Grenville ('P.G.'), 400

Wogan, Sir Terry, 402
Wolfe, James, 402
Wolfe, Thomas, 402
Wolfe, Tom, 402
Wollstonecraft, Mary, 376
Wood Krutch, Joseph, 403
Wood, Victoria, 402
Woodard, Rev. Nathaniel, 303
Woodcock, George, 403
Wooden, John, 403
Woodward, Joanne, 403
Woolf, Lord, 403
Woolf, Virginia, 317, 403
Woollcott, Alexander, 348, 403
Wordsworth, William, 404
Wright, Steven, 404
Wright, Tony, 404
Wu, Harry, 404

Yamasaki, Minoru, 405
Yeats, W. B., 405
Yelland, David, 405
Yes, Minister, 405
Yes, Prime Minister, 406
The Young Ones, 406
Young, G. M., 406
Young, Lord, 341
Young, Neil, 406
Youngman, Henny, 406

Zangwill, Israel, 407
Zappa, Frank, 407
Zedong, Mao, 217, 233
Zeta-Jones, Catherine, 165
Zinoviev, Grigori, 407
Zobel, Hiller B., 407
Zucker, David, 407